FIELD WORK IN SOCIAL WORK EDUCATION

By the same author

- Social Work Perspectives on Poverty.
- Integration of National Service Scheme with the Curriculum Vols. I & II (co-author).

About the Editor

RISHI RAM SINGH was born in 1939 in village Rampur (U.P.), graduated from the Banaras Hindu University in 1958 and obtained his Master's degree in Social Work from the Institute of Social Sciences, Kashi Vidyapeeth, Varanasi in 1960. He visited the United States under the Gleveland International Programme for Social Workers and Youth Leaders in 1964 and also completed a certificate course in social work from the School of Social Service Administration, University of Chicago. He obtained his doctoral degree from the University of Udaipur in 1974 for his research on social planning and welfare services in India.

Dr. Singh has taught at the Udaipur and Indore Schools of Social Work, and is currently on the teaching Staff of the Delhi School of Social Work, University of Delhi. His articles on Social Work, Social Welfare, and Youth have appeared in various professional journals in India. His book on *Social Work Perspectives on Poverty* was published in 1980 (Concept).

FIELD WORK IN SOCIAL WORK EDUCATION

A Perspective for Human Service Professions

Edited by

R.R. SINGH

CONCEPT PUBLISHING COMPANY PVT. LTD.
NEW DELHI-110059

ISBN: 978-81-7022-108-1

Edition 2025

Published and Printed by

Concept
Since 1974

Concept Publishing Company Pvt. Ltd.
A/15-16, Commercial Block, Mohan Garden,
New Delhi-110059 (India)
T: 91-11-41101460
E: publishing@conceptpub.com, *W*: www.conceptpub.com

Dedicated to

Students
who are a source of my
continuing education in
social work practice

PREFACE

THE Department of Social Work, University of Delhi, organised a Faculty Development Workshop on Field Work from March 16, 1981 to March 29, 1981. The Workshop was financed by the University Grants Commission. Thirty-five participants from 27 schools of social work attended the Workshop. The profile of all the participants is given in the Appendix at the end. Apart from several informal meetings, the participants held fourteen plenary and twenty group sessions altogether.

The present volume contains papers presented or circulated by the resource persons, individuals, and a few of the participants ; reports of the plenary and group sessions ; and relevant appendices. Since a majority of the participants came from institutions which offer post-graduate programmes in social work, this aspect was stressed upon more in the formal sessions than the undergraduate programme. A sub-committee therefore was constituted by the workshop consisting of interested members which did a good job of preparing guidelines on field work at the undergraduate level by devoting extra time.

The Report gives at the end the list of only participants and resource persons and has omitted the names of chairpersons, rapporteurs, and sessional resource persons because plenary and group sessions were many, and mention of all the names, when the entire participant group was involved as resource, would have taken more space without at the same time serving any useful purpose.

As Director of the Workshop I received assistance from several quarters and therefore it is my duty to express my gratitude to all concerned. The proposal to hold a faculty development workshop was forwarded by the then Acting Head of the Department Dr. K.D. Gangrade who had also offered comments and suggestions on the proposal. But for his temporary physical disability, I am sure, he would have closely associated himself with the Workshop. I wish to express my gratitude to him. But for the financial assistance from the University Grants Commission, the Workshop could never have been held. The interest shown by the UGC and the Panel on Social Work in our proposal has been a great source of inspiration to us. The co-operation received from the schools of social work has been most encouraging, and creative participation of their representatives in different capacities beggars description. Although the participant group was the greatest resource, formally invited resource persons took keen interest, and worked towards the success of our endeavour. I sincerely thank all of them. The Management and the Principal of the Rajdhani College, University of Delhi came to our rescue when we faced difficulty in accommodating participants. The role of Mr. Sudheer Upadhyaya, Programme Officer, National Sevice Scheme and his volunteers was pivotal in this aspect. In fact Mr. Upadhyaya's arrangements enabled me to attend all the formal sessions of the Workshop. I therefore express my gratitude to him and to my friends at the Rajdhani College. Thanks are also due to : the UNICEF for supplying film ; T.B. Hospital for permission to visit their innovative project ; students of the Department of Social Work, University of Delhi for their case records, and notes on supervision and evaluation ; College of Social Work, Nirmala Niketan, Bombay for sending material ; School of Social Service Administration, University of Chicago for granting permission to publish their extract ; the Ministry of Social Welfare for giving publication grant ; Mrs. Sushma Batra and other colleagues in the NSS Unit for assistance in the preparation of participants' profile ; NSS Unit, University of Delhi for providing transport ; Mr. P.C. Mahapatra, NSS Regional Centre, Government of India for supplying blankets ; library staff of the Department of Social Work, and the Department of Field Work for their support ; Mr. Krishan Kumar, Director of Field Work for his interest, assistance and contribution ; the concerned office staff of the Department, especially the two Section Officers Mr. B.C. Jain and Mr. K.C. Ahuja for help at all stages ; local agency supervisors, colleagues from the National Institute of Public Co-operation and Child Development, and the Department of Social Work and Applied Social Sciences, Jamia Millia for their interest and encouragement ; Fr. Irduraj (participant) and Mr. Surender Kumar for their voluntary typing work, and Mr. Purshotam Lal Sehgal for major secretarial assistance.

Professor S.N. Ranade took keen interest in the progress of the Workshop at different stages and also spent time in some of the group sessions. I wish to express my deep sense of gratitude to him for his generosity and kind consideration. Mr. Shankar Pathak's name has neither been included among the participants (because he was not formally nominated), nor among the resource persons (because he had declined to play any such role although he did contribute an excellent background paper for circulation among the participants). When all of us were in doubt about his status (because he was not even an observer !) he helped us with the term "intruder." I cannot forget this intruder's formal and informal help *before*, *during* and even *after* the Workshop. I shall remain beholden to him for his kindness.

The Workshop, on the whole, was a rewarding educational experience for me, and its deliberations were helpful. It is hoped that the present report shall serve as a guideline for such ventures in general, and for the proper organisation of field work programmes in the schools of social work in particular.

The approach outlined in the present report could also be adopted by educators, students and functionaries—both lay and professional—who are engaged particularly in the fields of community health and nutrition, community nursing, mental health, legal aid ; pre-school, elementary, non-formal and adult education; family planning, social planning, social forestry and extension ; community development and social activism.

Department of Social Work
University of Delhi

R. R. SINGH

INTRODUCTION

NEED FOR THE WORKSHOP

The pattern of field work in the schools of social work which offer post-graduate generic and specialization courses in the first and second years varies greatly from one institution to another. Field work programme particularly at the undergraduate level has not been discussed at any national seminar or workshop, and the schools of social work offering graduate and undergraduate programmes have made different field work arrangements. Surprisingly, when field work is regarded to be the core programme in social work education, none of the prospectuses of the schools of social work in the country or even the second UGC Report on Social Work Education have given the content of field work as it has evolved in different institutions. Except for a few publications on field work or on supervision, notably by the Delhi School of Social Work, Faculty of Social Work, M.S. University of Baroda, College of Social Work, Nirmala Niketan, the Tata Institute of Social Sciences and the two seminars on Field Work organised by the Association of Schools of Social Work in India (1964, and 1978) concerted effort has not yet been made by most of the schools to develop the content of field work and to define its various elements, beginning from the placement of students through supervision and guidance to evaluation.

The second UGC Review Committee Report has observed that field work consists of concurrent work for five hours a week to eighteen hours a week at the post-graduate level in the Indian schools of social work and it also includes study tours, camps and institutional visits. Some of the schools of social work have made block placement compulsory ; others have made it voluntary, and still others do not have any such programme. The heads of field work agencies also have their own conception of field work in the schools of social work, and they give guidance on that bases.

Quite a few schools have started field projects to train students. The effectiveness of these projects in training social work students however has not yet been examined. In view of the above mentioned developments and varied patterns, the need for a workshop on field work programme in social work at the undergraduate and post-graduate levels has been felt for quite some time.

It has also been thought necessary to examine the organisation of the Department/Unit of Field Work at different schools of social work with regard to its effectiveness or otherwise because field work constitutes a core programme of social work education.

Some of the schools of social work have been placing students under trained supervisors who have been working as agency supervisors. The agency supervisors have either been trained under the generic or specialization programmes. Some have worked for a number of years without any inservice training, whereas others have been exposed to new developments in the field. Many of them, who have been trained by the schools of social work (and also those who are untrained) need to be asked whether they visualize any new area or goal for field work practice. The schools of social work follow different practices on field work recording, supervision and evaluation and these practices not only vary from school to school but even from supervisor to supervisor in the same school. Some emphasize summary recording, others process-recording, and still others a combination of process and role records. Similarly, emphasis varies on individual and group conferences, their periodicity and duration. Questions on evaluation relate to whether it should be mid-term or annual, and how it should be conducted : whether by the supervisor, by the staff group, by the external examiner, or by a combination of these, and which method is more effective and why ?

Some of the schools of social work place students both in the first and the second years in the structured settings. The first year placements are generally made in the field of general social welfare, and second year placements in the field of specialization. Those schools which offer generic programmes place students in the first year in the communities which are rather unstructured, and in social welfare settings in the second year. One school is trying a combination of the two settings in the first and second years. There is, therefore, a need to review the effectiveness of the existing programme from the supervisors' point of view and also from the students' point of view in respect of field work content, goals, and learning through practice. Similarly the utility or otherwise of block placement, its duration, nature of supervisory control, its compulsory or optional character etc. needs to be examined.

Objectives

The primary aim of the workshop therefore was staff development. It sought to spell out the content and practice of field work, to initiate exchange of views, on the field work, phases of recording, supervision and evaluation, and to develop criteria for the placement of students in different agencies for concurrent and for block field work. Briefly stated, the objectives of the workshop in terms of staff development were as follows :

1. Development of field work content in social work.
2. Organization of field work unit as part of the school/department for effective implementation of field work programme.
3. Criteria for selection of agencies—structured and non-structured the for concurrent and block field work.
4. Criteria for placement of students.
5. Nature of supervision at the schools and the agencies of placement.
6. Evaluation of field work.
7. Development of a format for report writing by students and recording of students' progress by the supervisors.
8. Identification of gaps in the field work programme in terms of content, learning goals, supervisory practices, and evaluation.
9. Examination of a common base of field work practice with a developmental perspective.

The process and the outcome

Within the limited time, the workshop dealt with all the above objectives. In fact, the proposal which was first submitted to the

University Grants Commission for financial support was for a 5-week workshop. The Panel on Social Work considered this proposal but it suggested that a revised proposal for a 2-week workshop should be submitted which was done. As the workshop progressed, participants began to experience acutely the limitation of time. The perception of the Panel on Social Work on the duration of the workshop however is significant in that it thought the duration of two weeks adequate to achieve the above stated objectives. The idea in conducting a 5-week workshop was to engage participants for two weeks in the field to explore its different aspects on the basis of discussions of the first two weeks, and then reassemble in the last week to reflect upon their experiences ; to document them ; and to see how these experiences could be linked with theory courses. In other words, the participants would have examined as to which theory courses contained more field work component, and how those components could be taught in practical work. Selected students would also have been involved at this stage so that their perceptions could be shared with those of the educators. For example, in a school of social work where the students decide upon the sequence of papers for theory examinations, an analysis of examination schedules of the past three years gives an idea as to which papers are considered easy or difficult by students. Easy papers are scheduled first, and difficult ones later. In the M.A. previous class, the paper on *Man and Society* is generally kept for the first day and, either *Individual Development and Social Psychology*, or *Methods of Working with People* are scheduled for the last day. In the final year, a paper on *Areas of Social Work Practice* used to be placed for the first day for a number of years because it was thought most easy, but with the change of examiner and trend of this paper, it secured a third place for itself in subsequent years. Papers on *Social Policy* and *Social Research* are given the fifth or sixth (last) place in the examination schedule. With changes in the trend of question papers as perceived by students (in terms of more or less demanding course, method of teaching, trend of questions etc.) schedules are modified year after year. Continuation of a paper as number one for long however is a clear indication for the school concerned to make the course more demanding. Such perceptions on field work, especially agencies, could have provided adequate feed-back to the workshop by involving student participants, and would have also helped in examining the linkage between theory and practice.

The teachers deputed for the workshop were generally of the younger age group. In fact one school had asked whether the workshop was meant for the senior or junior faculty members. In some quarters there is still a feeling that senior faculty members know field work well and that they could contribute to such workshops only as resource persons. Since these notions are held widely, a few participants had even been asked by the heads of their institutions as to what they would do on a subject like field work for two weeks. They should come back soon. A couple of others had come with the impression that the demand of work would remain light and therefore they would adequately combine it with their personal and other formal obligations. The workshop experience however belied their hopes, and very soon they began to play the role of active contributors. An observer commented after the workshop that it had a depth, a purpose, and a direction. The following is taken from the letter of a participant: "...And the evenings invariably rolled into nights, one, two, three, or even later into the mornings. . . . (Although) it was a Faculty Development Workshop, I never found anyone with a feeling of being taught, and yet everyone felt that he/she had learnt a lot. This was the best thing about the workshop. There was high morale. Each one felt he was participating in a very important endeavour, something which had not been done ; something which would be a landmark in social work education. The perceived exalted goals coupled with exacting purposiveness... unleashed energies of the participants, but not without safeguards."

There is a tradition that every seminar or workshop should invite a few resource persons. But the selection of resource persons posed problems for the organisers in this case because only four social work educators had done some work on field work. The focus of the workshop being developmental, even this choice was limited. For a 2-week workshop however more resource persons were needed lest the participants who were used to such arrangements could have formed the wrong impression of the workshop being inadequately planned and organized.

Therefore resource persons were invited to represent many schools although the participant group itself was to act as a major resource. This plan used to be communicated to the concerned resource persons before their sessions.

All the resource persons had been invited for at least 5-7 days, but barring two, none could find it possible to spend so much time. Secondly, all of them considered the guidelines and the objectives as separate topics and not as interrelated phases of a core programme. They therefore showed preferences for one 'topic' or the other of the programme. Local participants likewise chose 'topics' of their preference. Very soon however they realized that missing a few sessions or confining themselves to the sessions of preference or assignment created problems, and this made participants to comment later that some resource persons had wasted the time of the workshop.

As the workshop progressed, it gathered momentum, and generated its own resource dynamics by the third day. This report does not capture all the qualitative dimensions. More was experienced and shared than what could be brought into the Report. Process reporting of the dynamics was thought of in the beginning and a participant had been requested to try it ; he however could not catch up with this work for want of time, and abandoned the idea on the third day. Most participants were finding it difficult to appreciate developmental perspective, and there was a conflict between the old and the new at all levels and in all the sessions. In spite of the heavy input all along, the group could secure notionally 55 per cent on the developmental ladder as the graph prepared by a participant shows at the end of the Report. Agencies were also seen as moving from one to the other perspective, and again regressing back to the earlier one. Dynamism and re-education pervaded all the workshop sessions, and a definite change in the perception of participants was noticeable. The following descriptions on the roll-up board in a way catch the mood of the workshop :

(i) **Dynamic property of the field**

(a) The field is like an avalanche which gathers snow in motion ; (b) time, person and space are indivisible and always interacting.

(ii) Discovery of field

Paths are made by walking.

(iii) Level of involvement

One learns to swim only in deep waters.

(iv) Resource development

Purposive interaction with time in space generates resource and acts like a breeder reactor once it picks up motion. These, and the two charts supplied by the Department of Social Work on school social work, and non-formal education, among others, created a conducive environment for the workshop.

For a couple of days in the beginning the senior social work educators felt uncomfortable in the company of less experienced colleagues. Some of them had expected to act as resource persons. There were also informal queries about persons who were (or were not) invited as resource persons. The matter was explained at length in one session which laid the doubts of the participants at rest.

One of the implicit objectives of the workshop was to transcend the futile generic-specialization controversy, and adopt a rational-holistic approach to examine different aspects of field work. This however was not easy. Even though participants appreciated the new approach, the 'ghost' used to occasionally 'haunt' them, and waylay their deliberations for a while before the group was reminded of its surreptitious arrival. Such reminders in course of time were sufficient to 'exorcise the ghost'.

The difficulty in the pursuit of rational approach of the kind mentioned above became clear on the third day when the group was not able to come to a definite conclusion regarding the approach to the workshop. The group was at this stage informed that a learner in field work passed through several interrelated phases ; he concentrated upon certain aspects more than others; his focus varied with the level of training (undergraduate or graduate) ; and the learning phases were marked by changes in supervisory inputs and ways of evaluation. After some discussion, and also because there was no other way out, the group adopted this approach and divided itself into three groups. The "going" in all the groups was equally difficult when it came to operationalize the above format. On account of this difficulty, the groups were running behind the schedule, and at one stage it was feared that the format would prove unworkable by the end of the day. A day's wasted effort on the third day itself would have proved a turning point for the workshop in that it would have disillusioned and demoralized the participants, and would also have reflected upon the poor ability of the organisers. In fact two senior colleagues had even advised that if the groups could not accomplish the task, it should not be pursued ! All the participants had also realized that the assignment was difficult but since they were in deep waters they continued their struggles meaningfully. The 'delivery' at the end of the day was quite joyful. The hurdle had been crossed ; a sense of achievement had been generated ; and the groups were determined to pursue the format even on the following day. After this experience the groups became self-confident and tackled other difficult issues with relative ease. Certain aspects demanded more time than others, and this led to the revision of the workshop schedule. An analysis of time-budget of the earlier and the revised schedule (see appendix) gives an idea of change, and priorities as these were perceived by the group. Attempts were made to synthesize a few of the sub-group reports, and recommendations were drafted by a sub-Committee. Supervision, evaluation, recording, content, organisation and administration thus emerged as priorities in that order.

The bibliography on field work covered the period 1971-1980, and it was subsequently revised to include more material on developmental aspects of social work. In fact the entire experience, and the approach to the workshop was 'developmental', as one participant put it.

A significant development which is worthy of note was the formation of three sub-groups to discuss evaluation of field work. Fifty per cent participants chose the sub-group on Integrated Methods of Social Work ; and the remaining divided themselves into two groups : (a) evaluation by fields of specialization, and (b) evaluation by methods of social work, namely, community organisation. After having worked for one-and-a-half days all the groups arrived at similar conclusions ; and the group on evaluation by fields of specialization pointedly mentioned that they had chosen a hospital, and a factory as their points of reference but they had to abandon the same in favour of a rational and holistic approach. By experience therefore the group proved the futility of the generic-specific controversy. Out of eight members of this sub-group, six came from institutions which offered specialization courses, and two from a school which had a generic programme.

The three groups on supervision after the plenary session worked on the guidelines evolved by them. Only one group was helped by the resource person invited for the purpose. The other two set down their own priorities which guided their deliberations. The respective group reports reflect this difference.

The two review sessions during the workshop helped the participants to take stock of their work and to assign responsibilities to informal groups. This proved helpful in the completion of work at hand. Not only the review sessions, but even sessions on supervision and evaluation enabled participants to establish a link between what they were considering and what they had done before. The groups used to be reminded that criteria of evaluation were linked with content of field work at different phases, and so was the case with supervisory input. The groups therefore did not consider them as isolated topics, and an effort was made to relate one with the other.

It is customary in a seminar or a workshop to ask the participants to evaluate their work. Here too the participants were given sufficient time for evaluation but they were not given any proforma. The participants divided themselves into three groups, evolved their own guidelines on which they held discussions, and came out with their reports. The three evaluation reports incorporated in this monograph have not left any aspect of the workshop uncovered. One wonders whether similar results would have been achieved through the use of a proforma. If so, the rich educational experience through interaction would indeed have been lost. (A need was also felt by the group at this stage to conduct an empirical study on the nature of linkage between theoritical and field instruction at the schools of social work.) The workshop was thus not only a rewarding experience in the exchange of views on different aspects of field work, but more importantly, it was an exercise in thematic exploration, re-education, and perspective development which, at times even transcended the objectives set for the workshop.

CONTENTS

APPENDICES

PART ONE

PROCEEDINGS OF THE WORKSHOPS

1

FIELD WORK PROGRAMME IN THE SCHOOLS OF SOCIAL WORK IN INDIA
A Review*

R.R. Singh

OBJECTIVES OF FIELD WORK AND ITS PATTERN

FIELD WORK is considered to be an integral part of social work education by all the schools of social work in India. The Review Committee on Social Work Education (1978) has mentioned the following objectives of field work :

1. Development of professional skills through learning to use knowledge for the study and analysis of problems and selection of appropriate means to solve them;
2. Development of skills in problem-solving at the macro and micro levels;
3. Integration of class-room learning with field practice;
4. Development of skills required for professional practice

*This review has been prepared on the basis of the following :

(a) *Review of Social Work Education in India : Prospect and Retrospect.* (New Delhi, University Grants Commission, 1978).

(b) T. Krishnan Nair, *Field Instruction in Schools of Social Work : A Survey* (Association of Schools of Social Work in India, 1978).

(c) *Status Report on Social Work Education and Profiles of Institutions,* (University Grants Commission, 1979). The report makes only a brief mention of field work.

(d) Information supplied by the institutions for the Faculty Development Workshop on Field Work, 1981.

at the particular level of training;
5. Development of professional attitudes, values and commitment; and
6. Development of self-awareness and professional ideal.

The Committee has listed eight objectives of field work which have been regrouped in this Review.[1] The Committee has further noted that the schools of social work have developed evaluation criteria before specifying field work content, and that there is lack of linkage between the class-room theory and the realities of the field.[2] While the Committee has stressed the need for including programme and skills of communication, community and group process, programme development, record maintenance, and use of data in the first year of instruction, it has altogether left un-specified the second year programme of field work.[3]

The committee has recommended development of specific programme skills, organisation of community programmes, and understanding of cause-effect relationship as desirable objectives of field work sequence at the BSW level in the first, second and third years in that order.[4] The pattern suggested at this level is 8-10 hours of work per week in the first year, and 12 hours per week in the second and third years.[5] It has also been suggested that field work at the BSW level should be assigned one-third of the total marks in a three-year degree course.

For the M.A. Degree programme, the Committee has listed specific objectives of field work, which have been further spelled out for the 1st and 2nd years.[6] The specific objectives of field work are : application and selective use of knowledge; development of skill at the level of professional job expectation; ability to manage and utilise professional relationships; and development of appropriate and expected attitudes.

In the first year, the Committee has stressed upon learning skills which revolve around specific tasks where cause and effect relationships are understood; where persons are victims of their life circumstances than showing pathology; and where a lower order of skill in intervention is required.

In the second year-field work the emphasis has been placed on complex social and psychological processes, less obvious cause-effect relationships, advanced knowledge and skills for developmental and remedial work in dealing with people and institutional process, and use of inter-disciplinary knowledge.

It has been stated that students with BSW degree should be helped to deepen their knowledge and skills in the functions they are likely to perform in administration, policy, planning, research, supervision, teaching and specific service delivery.*

The survey conducted by Nair, based on the information supplied by 28 schools, reports that only five schools have formulated field work objectives. Seventeen have specified separate objectives for the first and second years of field work; one school prefers to use the term 'expectations' to 'objectives' ; two schools have general objectives for field work and also specific objectives for the first and second years; and one school has formulated specialization-wise objectives for the second year in addition to that of the first year. Some schools have stated field work as 'core' programme or an 'integral part' of social work education, and have prescribed field experience in basic method(s) of social work in the first year, and in the field of specialization in the second year.

The above data show marked variation in the existing pattern among the schools. These are evident from the following statements of expectations from or importance of field work : broad objectives only; specific objectives (?) for first and second years; broad objectives along with specific objectives for first and second years; and broad objectives with separate objectives for the first year as well as for the area of specialization. With such variations in objectives or approaches the position taken by the schools on field work as 'core' or 'integral part' of the professional education rests rather on shaky foundations. The survey also gives the following pattern of field work prevailing in the schools :

*It may be added in this connection that schools of social work rarely make a distinction between a BSW and a non-BSW student after admission in terms of course teaching, and provision of field experience. One is also tempted to ask whether, given the present level of training generally, should such a distinction be made at all ?

Distribution of schools by the type of field work programme

	Field Work Programme	*Number of Schools*
1.	Observational visit, and concurrent field work	1
2.	Observational visit+concurrent field work+camp	4
3.	Observational visit+concurrent field work+block placement	7
4.	Observational visit+concurrent field work+camp+block placement	7
5.	Observational visit+concurrent field work+camp+study tour	2
6.	Observational visit+concurrent field work+block field work+study tour	1
7.	Observational visit+concurrent field work+camp+block placement+study tour	4
8.	Observational visit+concurrent field work+camp+block field work+practicals on the campus	1
9.	Observational visit+concurrent field work+block field work+study tour+internship	1
		28

The variation in pattern has been attributed by Nair to location, financial resources of the school, availability of agencies, strength of staff, stage of a school's development, differential thrust of an institution and so on. According to another study* variation is also reflected on the assignment of marks for field work ranging

*The study classifies schools into categories and grades them. There are schools with social work orientation; with mixed orientation; and with minimum orientation to social work. . . . Out of thirteen schools, three fall under Grade-I on the basis of the qualification of staff and its likely influence on field work; two fall in Grade-II, five in Grade-III, and four in Grade-IV. See Philomena D' Souza ; *Field Instruction in Social Work Education* (Ph. D. Dissertation, Tata Institute of Social Sciences, 1978, unpublished).

from 200 to 800.[7] The objectives and the universe of the two studies mentioned above, however, are different, otherwise it would have been interesting to compare the pattern of field work with the grade (class) of institutions. It would also have been of interest to know about the effectiveness of different types of field work programme, reasons for addition or deletion of its different components over the years in a school; the impressionistic or empirical bases of such exercises; and whether a school with a large variety of field work components could be deemed to offer the best programme of professional education.

For the purpose of the present workshop, letters of invitation were sent to 43 schools of social work including an institution which runs training programmes only for para-professionals. The participants were requested to send a note on field work programme at their respective schools in not more than 500 words. The objectives of the workshop had been communicated to the schools and it was hoped that the participants would particularly pay attention to those aspects in their write-ups, or will at least report those features of the programme which they consider most important. Information was received from 31 institutions, and its content ranged from 100 words to 1500 words including proformas and appendices.

As far as the concept of field work is concerned, perhaps, all the schools presume it to be well understood. The manuals, guidelines and the prospectuses begin with descriptive statements about the importance of field work without defining it. Only 10 schools have stated the objectives of field work in some form or the other, and out of these, objectives of field work in two institutions are identical. The form of instruction generally does not conform to its substance.[8] As it has turned out, field work, rather than being an integral part of social work education, has, by and large, remained only its peripheral activity.* One school in this case appears to have adopted the objectives of another in toto. These are : work and experience in real life situations requiring social intervention or assistance by individuals, groups or communities from a professional social worker; the acquisition of

*It is common knowledge that some teachers regard field work days as 'unofficial holidays'.

skills in social work methods through practice of theory; inculcation of appropriate attitudes; and development of capacity for conceptualization from practice. Further, the schools' attempts to make field work look more respectable and rational in the decade of seventies have led to the emergence of a plethora of cards, proformas and sheets which have cost the substance of field work a great deal. One wonders whether these do not characterize the intrinsic authoritarian response of a traditional society and of social work education as its sub-system. In the first year field work, the specific objectives of one of these schools are : understanding of a particular community : its needs, resources and problems by the student and involving the community in problem-solving; and guidance to student to initiate and carry on tasks in the area of social action, social change and development as a preparation for performing preventive-developmental functions in the field of social welfare.

The second year field work in this school is supposed to complement the experience of the first year by providing opportunities to carry out developmental social welfare tasks in the existing welfare organizations. The emphasis is not only on the rendering of services but also on the preventive-developmental aspect of welfare work.[9]

While comparing the broad and the specific objectives, one however gets an impression that 'tasks in the areas of social action, change and development' should have rather formed a part of the broad objectives. (It may be noted in this connection that one of the members of the staff of a school was of the view that this component of field work should be introduced only in the second year, whereas others favoured its inclusion in the first year. After the experimentation of the new scheme for four years, half of the M.A. previous and final students now have been placed in the community and the agency settings together as far as possible.)

One school has mentioned field work programme as 'generic', 'method and field-oriented' ; two others have mentioned it as 'training in application of professional skills', or 'development of skills, attitudes and testing of theory' ; one school stresses upon 'exposure of students to field situations, learning about human behaviour in different situations, methods of working with people, and learning to function as agency personnel' ; three others refer either to sensitization of students to the reality situation, skill in helping process, application and deeper understanding of theory, or 'equipping one-self with skills and attitudes, and developing professional self and social competence'. Or still, developing a scientific and questioning mind, acquisition of skills through the application of theory, experience of the dynamics of actual life, attempt at solution of problems, and implementation of developmental programmes are the objective of another school.

One school which offers both under-graduate and post-graduate programmes has worked out the objectives of field work separately for them and also for each year of these programmes. It is interesting to note that a BSW student in the third year is required, among others, to gain learning experience in 'supervision of para-professionals and volunteers; analysis of lags in agency administration with suggestions for alternatives, and also analysis of lags in the existing community resources with suggestions for or initiation of new services'. A similar experiene is also required, among others, of a second year student at the post-graduate level. Since the factual information on this aspect is not available, one can only surmise that these experiences are being provided at a more intensive level to post-graduate students !

Those schools which have not formulated field work objectives explicitly, an idea could be obtained from the guidelines developed by them either on the content of field work supervision, or evaluation.

STRUCTURE AND ORGANISATION OF FIELD WORK

Most schools appoint a Co-ordinator/Director for field work programme. In one school, however, the Co-ordinator of field work looks after the field work programme of only the first year students whereas the Heads of the Departments look after the field work arrangements in the area of their respective specialization. In the survey conducted by Nair, in eleven schools, the Head of the Institution was the Co-ordinator of field work; whereas in twelve schools, this responsibility was shouldered by a member of the teaching staff. The Co-ordinator or Director of field work is responsible for correspondence, liaison, distribution of students under different supervisors on the basis of their work-load, and their placements in agencies after making an assessment of the available opportunities in consultation with the school and/or agency supervisor. Change of placement of students, convening of school and agency supervisors' meetings, workshops, seminars, initiation of studies on field work etc., are his other functions. In view of these responsibilities, the Co-ordinator is assigned less number of students for field work supervision in some schools. In others, the distribution of students among school supervisors is done almost on an equal basis. It all depends upon the strength of the staff and students. Thus the number of students placed under a supervisor may vary from 2 to 14.* The Heads of institutions are normally not assigned field work supervision which incidently reflects upon the importance attached to field work as a 'core' programme.

In one school the responsibility of co-ordinating field work rotates every two years among the senior members of the staff with teaching experience of ten years or more.

Most of the schools conform to a semester pattern of field work; others go by annual pattern. Each term's field work task in case of the former is graded in some schools; in others an evaluation is done but without grades; in still others which follow annual pattern, field work done during the year as a whole is taken into account for evaluation. The time allotted for field work varies from 10 to 15 hours per week at the post-graduate level.

As far as the structure of field work at the BSW level is concerned, first year is generally devoted to the exposure of student to the field, and observation; second year for community placement, and the third year in the agencies. One school, however, places first year BSW students in the agencies, and in the second and third years to practise case work, group work and community organisation in welfare centres and other agencies.

Another school requires of students to plan and organise

*For BSW level this number is more. In the post-graduate programmes, sometimes lack of concern shown to this aspect makes field work appear almost farcical.

simple specific tasks and involve individuals and groups in them. It also requires students to solve simple problems at the individual and family levels. This school is the only one which has worked out a sequence which links the BSW programme of field work with that of the post-graduate level.

At the post-graduate and para-professional levels, the following structure of field work emerges in the schools of social work. The field work pattern of the BSW level falls in the second and the fourth categories generally.*

Concurrent field work

	First Year Placement	*Second Year Placement*
1.	Placement in welfare agency	Placement in the area of specialisation
2.	Placement in the community setting (urban and rural)	Placement in the welfare agency
3.	Placement in the community setting	Placement in the area of specialisation (social welfare field only)
4.	Placement in community and agency settings (mixed)	Placement in community and agency settings (mixed)
5.	Placement in the community setting	Continuation of placement in the community setting to finish the remaining task and to provide support to new students at least for 2-3 months and then change to another agency
6.	Multiple agency placement, for (i) variety of experience, or (ii) multiple agency placement to effectively utilise the resource for	

*Two schools with BSW programmes do not offer field work at all to students. One school suspended the programme because it was not found workable; the other faces the problem of overwhelming number of students.

First Year Placement	*Second Year Placement*
the solution of community problem	
7. Specific agency placement for the training of para-professionals in a particular scheme or project	

It may be noted that the first pattern is most common among the schools of social work whereas the fifth and (ii) of the sixth obtain only in a couple of schools which give importance to innovations and experimentation in field work.

Normally with the change of a placement, the school supervisor also changes. However if the placement is changed for providing a variety of experience during a particular year, the same supervisor may continue with the student. The common practice is to provide a student experience of having worked under two supervisors atleast. In extra-ordinary circumstances however—vacancies, illness, strained supervisor-supervisee or school-agency supervisor relationships, a student during his two years of stay may get the experience of having received guidance from more than two school/agency supervisors. Another feature which is noticeable is that over the years supervisor's association with an agency, area or block of the community (or even the method of social work practice) becomes so close to heart that these begin almost to be treated as one's private preverse. Supervisors with single track minds are known to have shown reluctance to supervise students in new agencies/situations on the ground of familiarity, expertise or specialization, notwithstanding the need to explore a new field which can be developed better by an experienced supervisor. In some cases there arises a need to accommodate a new colleague. While students are expected to learn and grow through confrontation with reality, the supervisors hesitate to meet this expectation in their work and practices. (The idea of specialisation thus sounds almost ridiculous when one looks at the undefined, vague and varying objectives of field work, and of social work education for that matter, in the schools where 'basics' are yet to be defined.)

CONTENT OF FIELD WORK

'The difficulty in organizing field work in teaching units', arises, because 'it deals with problems which defy orderly progression'.[10] Nevertheless the development of field work content by the schools should be considered as a continuing and meaningful exercise. Most of the schools have not worked out contents of field work. Those which have done so, have followed different approaches. One approach favours the 'content of social work' in four learning areas : skill in the helping process, adjustment within the agency, capacity to use supervision, and development of professional qualities and attitudes, and adds that these are dependent upon the type of placements i.e. health, correction, labour welfare, family and ehild welfare, etc. (One is really at a loss to make out what is meant to be conveyed). The other approach regards field instruction as consisting of (a) assignment of learning experience, (b) integration of theory and practices, and (c) evaluation of field learning.[11] Under this arrangement, the student is helped to formulate his goals in 3-4 areas every six months. This school holds the view, and perhaps rightly so, that products of the institution will not come out as 'trained' but that they would be ready to start educating themselves in the vast field of social action and service development, and thereby change their outlook and ways. The third approach is to work out semester-wise goals of field work and their corresponding tasks assuming that it would be a community placement in the second year or vice-versa. (The schools which offer specialization necessarily provide for either social welfare agency or community placement or both only in the first year). Those schools which have tried to work out content of field work according to the third approach, also show a wide variation, although their number is small.

Some schools have stated 'expectations' in field work without giving its contents. One school has particularly spelled out these expectations as *general* (regularity, punctuality), *professional* (relationship, adjustment), and *programme* (problems of clients, organisation or programmes). Other schools have listed agencies, projects or activities to illustrate the nature of field work. One school has mentioned the practice of social case work in the forenoon and social group work in the afternoon as field work programme in the first year ! Quite a few schools have worked out contents semester-wise, method-wise and agency or field-wise. Wherever method-wise contents have been outlined under the headings—knowledge, skills and attitudes—separate evaluation guidelines have been prepared. It is worthy to note that one school under the content of community organisation (under the sub-heading attitudes) has included 'willingness to involve people in developmental movements'. This dimension particularly has serious implications and it would be useful to know about the experiences of this school. Another school which offers both under-graduate and post-graduate programme of social work education has worked out semester-wise contents and has also tried to link the same with skill, theory, and task. Further, it has attempted an exercise according to the three primary methods, and in the process has evolved a pattern which is rather confusing. It has at no stage given any indication as to how this pattern is applied both to the BSW and the MSW programmes.

The content of field work therefore is characterized by variations and ambiguities. No school seems to have tried to explicitly develop content of field work in relation to the goals of social work education, and practice. Developed outlines of one school have been used by the other generally in order to make field work programme of the institution concerned appear more impressive. Determination of goals of social work education and practice in the context of developmental needs of an area, region or population group; identification of human and environmental situations which would provide field learning experiences at different levels; identification of corresponding placements, (existing or emerging) as far as possible; and the development of content of practice at the generic and differential levels have therefore remained hitherto unattempted tasks which must engage the attention of social work educators on a continuing basis, and should give direction to a profession which has remained adrift throughout its 48 years of history, with an average of one school being added to its fold every year. Marriages of convenience reflected in contrived field or method-oriented approaches, new brands of specialisations to attract students and to fool the society, or adoption of another school's pattern are bound to prove counter-productive for the profession in the long run.

There is a need to spell out the kind of educational and service experiences that the schools would like to offer at different levels and their design of the projects, activities or programmes so that one component does not suffer at the cost of the other. It is commonly seen that if a programme is not educationally meaningful, achievements or results come as ready defences; or these are stressed more than the educational process, and vice-versa. Students generally ask whether they are learners, achievers or both; and the supervisors project an ambivalent attitude in dealing with these questions. Vague instructions on do's and don'ts should not be regarded as contents of field work. One school, for example, says that the very problems or limitations of the agency provide rich learning experience. Such exhortations are made because the 'field' of field work is not yet clear; agencies are conceived of as four walls mostly located in metropolises and in developed regions or countries; and visits or study tours are found to be the only ways by which these 'temples of God' could be visited because schools themselves are not in a position to establish them. There is a need to discover or identify local human-environmental situations and strive to work *through*, *with* and *upon* them, and to organise educational and service (action-reflection) experiences accordingly. Over-reliance on agencies, and waiting for the day of deliverance through them are attitudes which are positively anti-developmental. In fact, the very concept of agency has been the bane of social work education and practice in developing countries.

If one makes an analysis of contents of field work in the area of specialization worked out by some schools, personnel management and labour welfare occupies almost eight pages and all that is included in theory has been listed for field work. One needs to ask therefore as to what is *specific* in social work to this field and how this could be applied ? And in so applying, how the educational (learning process) and service goals would be achieved in a balanced manner ?

SELECTION AND TYPES OF FIELD WORK OPPORTUNITIES

Selection of an agency, area, or field opportunity is largely dependent not only upon the orientation of a school but also upon the orientation of its individual field instructors. An agency or a situation can be looked at from the point of view of a problem requiring solution, methods of social work practice, field of social work, job training, or part of a larger system requiring inter-disciplinary effort. It can be seen both from traditional-remedial, and preventive-developmental perspectives. For example, viewing a delinquent either as a 'case' or a 'class' (a client or neighbourhood system) makes all the difference in the approach to the problem, levels of training, type of guidance, goals of education, and definition of tasks. Briefly stated, a 'case approach' is traditional, whereas the 'class approach' is preventive and developmental. Further, a school may formally profess a generic and developmental orientation but the same may not be reflected in its teaching and practice. There may be teachers in such a school who only appreciate the new orientation but do not practise it; there may be others who not only appreciate, but are committed to the new orientation and therefore they take pains to practise it; there is a third group which neither appreciates nor practises it on account of the hang-over of old learning, and resistance for accepting anything new; and lastly, there is a category which is either cynical or totally indifferent to the new approach.

The problem therefore is more with the lenses that one wears. It may be further clarified that the developmental approach is not anti-traditional; on the contrary, it is bi-focal; is both restrospective and prospective; and is a creative advance over and subsumption of the traditional. It calls for not only the selection of 'field' but also for its seizure,* providing adequately in the process for its development through calculated risks.

The problem in field work thus arises not only due to the surfeit or deficit of agencies, or situations, but how one views them; how learning opportunities are identified, and learning goals are defined; how educational guidance is given to students to achieve those goals; how both the supervisor and the

*There is a saying that learning is *caught*, it is not *taught*.

supervisee experience growth as part of the *field* (measured against the 'core-periphery' scale of participation), and how the same agency, problem, or the human situation is 'reviewed' for testing or shaping future intervention strategies and formulation or modification of theory. This is a creative, continuing and challenging exercise where specialists or experts are few and learners are many. If this yardstick is applied to agency or community-based field work, the combined score of the schools of social work would be rather disheartening because this yardstick implies a perspectival growth in the teacher, student, and also in the active participants of the agency or 'field'. If such a growth has not occurred, it only implies more pains-taking study, planning, and action on the part of educators. The definition and the selection of 'field' for work through this approach need to be done differently, and this in itself is a serious academic exercise pregnant with implications for learning goals, tasks, and the type of guidance. The approach does not accept the field as given but as one which is evolving, and also a part of the larger whole. (A school of social work reported that it has not been able to develop its own agencies and it may be able to do so once it becomes an autonomous institution. One can only wish that this school shall take into account the above considerations before launching its own agency developmental project.)

Moreover, information on this important aspect has been received only from two schools of social work. This shows that agencies are taken for granted, and that the attachment of student to a four-walled structure in the field of social welfare does not pose any problem. Selection of agencies/need situations or areas was done through an evolutionary process in the beginning years of the Tata Institute of Social Sciences.[12] Other schools which came into existence between the forties and early fifties also struggled to identify and develop emerging fields. But schools of the later years generally prepared the lists of agencies because older schools were placing students in those settings. In the recent past, a school of social work appointed a staff sub-committee to report on the placement in community settings. The report of the sub-committee was discussed by the staff council and only then the new placements were accepted for the purpose of field work. Upon the recommendations of the school supervisors, certain agencies have of course been added or deleted but the Director of Field Work has to make a report on them in the staff council. (In fact such an exercise should be undertaken every two years, if not every year).[13]

Field work in some cases is used more as a means of controlling students than an educational experience for them. A field work supervisor who also had some administrative responsibilities succeeded in getting allotted some students for supervision by the Co-ordinator who were identified as possible leaders in the institution/hostel, and who could possibly remain under control through field work, though not necessarily in all cases. The Co-ordinators are known to allot students with destructive leadership potential and immature personalities to such supervisors, agencies or communities who could set limits on them so that they could be relieved of their administrative concerns. The existing university rules permit a student to complete an M.A. course within a span period of four years or so. Therefore even if a student acts unprofessionally, and either fails in field work or discontinues it for a while (because under the rules his name cannot be struck off, and the procedure for such an action is too cumbersome to be enforceable), he may rejoin or repeat the course. In the case of such students while agency placement may help them to regulate their work and habits, it may also spoil school-agency relations. In a school of social work located in a cosmopolitan city where hostel accommodation is scarce, some students join social work because (a) they meet the minimum eligibility requirements, and (b) hostel accommodation is mostly guaranteed to those who are not local residents. Some of these students, who already hold a post-graduate or a professional degree, after enrolment begin to prepare for civil services examinations. They absent from classes, and invest minimum required time for field work. Such unmotivated students generally do not meet their professional obligations in field work and thus create problems for the school and the agency. The community placement also in such cases results in far less regulation of students' behaviour; leads to the continuance of their old ways of 'acting out', and dealing with people; and, at times jeopardises school-community relations because such students do not work responsibly, and their actions prove detrimental to future batches of students.* In either case therefore placement is done with a 'calculated risk' because such students, once registered, use union pressures to neutralise any action against them by the school or the university unless they themselves choose to withdraw voluntarily. Only a 'strict' supervisor therefore is considered a remedy for them with field work being more of a tight-rope walking for both the supervisor and the supervisee, than its being an educationally meaningful encounter between them.

Some schools place both M.A. previous and final students both in the agencies and the communities. It is necessary for them that expectations from 1st and 2nd year students are spelt out through a structured programme; supervisory inputs are determined on the basis of known learning principles, and standards of reports and evaluation are clearly laid down in a guideline allowing for variations in the level of learning.

Educational programme in field work starts with placement and therefore decisions on the latter should be governed more by educational considerations than administrative, including provisions for contingency arrangements. Frequent changes of agencies or supervisors, allotment of the number of students per supervisor, distribution of difficult or poor students (known on the basis of past experience) among several supervisors rather than 'clustering' them under one only, allotment of field work responsibilities to supervisors both in the communities as well as in the agencies, allotment of number of agencies to be supervised by a teacher including new agencies assigned, if any, avoidance of splitting an agency between several supervisors as far as possible (this does not apply to unstructured community placements), adequate justification for including new agencies and excluding old ones in a particular academic session after proper assessment of work opportunities, and regular visits to agencies by supervisors for on-the-spot guidance—though apparently administrative—are primarily educational concerns in a professional programme. Over-emphasis on administrative aspects either in placement or in supervisory guidance reflects a perspective and an orientation which places a premium on hierachy and direction

*In such cases 'time-keeping' becomes a major pre-occupation in supervision.

more than on a democratic participatory process of educational programming which is necessary in social work education. To illustrate : in a school of social work during (1983-84), the distribution of work load between field work supervisors varied from 4 to 13 students; number of agencies per supervisor varied from 1 to 7; some supervisors were given exclusively communities and some agencies with only one-third of the staff put in charge of both types of settings; the number of split agencies (agencies with more than one supervisor) was six; placement of M.A. previous and final students in the agencies and in the communities did not correspond at all to 50 : 50 criteria determined by the school; and quite a few new agencies—some without adequate work to keep a student engaged for 15 hours a week—had been included, when vacancies in old placements were available. This only shows the need how field work as a structured programme should be methodically evolved, developed and strengthened to serve as an effective medium of education in professional skills and attitudes; and how it should not be subjected to random administrative treatment as is evident from the above illustration. Placement in a structured setting does not necessarily ensure that the programme of field work is 'structured'. Similarly, a placement in a community or resettlement area should neither be mistaken for community, work practice, nor for unstructured field work, because it may be well structured without any semblance of community work at all.

The information available from different sources indicates (apart from agencies run by the schools themselves) that agencies are selected on the following bases : (i) provision of experience in the practice of social work methods; (ii) availability of records for the use of student; (iii) availability of a trained social worker on the staff; (iv) adequate work load for student; (v) field instructor's willingness to assign responsibilities to student; (vi) agency as a training as well as experimental centre for the development of new programmes, and (vii) distance from the institution.*

*Normally the agencies selected are located at a short distance from the school. Agency placement at a longer distance is done only if the student is willing to commute, and also because agencies are not available in the vicinity. In the case of a new school however, the agency which was

There are field work agencies with trained social workers who appreciate the value of training; there are others who do not. In some agencies the staff is untrained but they give freedom to social work students in their practice. Other agencies use students as part-time support staff and pay less attention to their learning needs. One school has reported that sometimes agencies are identified on a 'contingency' basis. This school receives request from agencies for recognising them as training centres. Sometimes students request for a particular placement and in the process the agency gets recognition. This school also accepts agencies because either a new programme is going to be developed; or there is likelihood of graduates getting employment; or the agency will serve the purpose of demonstration to be undertaken by the school.

As far as the schools' own field work agencies are concerned, Nair reported that sixteen schools run them, and their projects are child care, child guidance, foster care, family service, and rural development. There is also a bureau of psycho-social therapy which has been recently started by a school. The Second Review Committee has mentioned about the wide gap in the resources of 34 such institutions[14] ranging from Rs. 5,000 to Rs. 1,80,000 per year. One can therefore imagine the variety of experiences that these placements would be offering to students. Effectiveness of these projects as models however is yet to be evaluated. For instance, one would like to know the difference between a child guidance centre, or a Mahila Kendra, run by a school of social work, and the one run by a voluntary or public sector organisation. It is also necessary to know as to how these centres strike a balance between the training and service needs ? What programmes have been formulated for this purpose and how ? What methods of social work have been practised and with what results ? What has been the input of

located at a distance of 32 miles from the town and was connected with only one bus service daily, was a boon to it. All the five trouble-making students were placed there for labour welfare work. They went for field work on Fridays and Saturdays and returned by Sunday noon. For the administration, these students were practically 'out of sight and out of mind'. One can only wonder about the usefulness of such placement from the point of view of field work.

school's staff in the development of projects ? What has been the feed-back provided by these projects which have implications for either testing, rejecting or building theory ? Some of these projects have been functioning for more than a decade. It is high time that they prepare a bench mark covering the questions raised earlier, and bring out a longitudinal profile for teaching, and also for the promotion of practice and action-research.

In the selection of community, 'open' or 'multiple agency' placements, the schools of social work need to do a great deal of preparatory work for making them meaningful learning experiences. Existence or otherwise of an agency alone should not be a guide for the selection of an area or community for field work practice.

One school of social work has reported that the three villages adopted by it have reached the follow-up phase and the school was going to select new villages for the action phase. After the self-sustaining stage is reached, the school proposes to withdraw from the scene.[15] The school considers the role of the Department as that of a 'catalyst'. Another school proposes to harness Lok Shakti and launch 'service posts' to serve the disadvantaged[16] in a metropolitan area.

At the end of this section, one aspect which should engage the attention of social work educators is that of continuity of field work in the community or 'open' settings without any full-time workers. It may be noted in this connection that a new student being placed in a community in the begining of a term, if expected to expand the work of his predecessor, will experience acute anxiety. His predicament will be that of a child who is being pushed too early to play adult roles. This pre-occupation will also conflict with the principles of learning. The exploration of a field is an experience in itself and it provides opportunity to the new student to select an area of his choice to work. The concern with the continuity of a programme may stifle the freedom and the creativity of the student. Moreover, there are both the advantages and disadvantages of a known placement. One social work educator deliberately chose a new block in the community to provide learning opportunity to students in *exploring the area and finding their moorings* which would otherwise not have been possible in a block with known contact persons.

Some schools are debating presently whether students should gain experience in two, four or more agencies during the two years of their education. If the choice of the number of agencies is guided by sound learning principles (both known and yet to be known through experience), the problem of placement in a variety of settings is not of consequence. If however the only consideration for varied agency placements is to acquaint the student with the work as many of them as possible (a 'tourist approach' to social work of education) to enhance their employment prospects (?), then the schools of social work should convert themselves into polytechnics for offering *training* in various *trades* without delay.

PLACEMENT OF STUDENTS

The placement of students for field work is linked with the process of admission. The schools of social work ask for bio-data, and also conduct individual and group tests, and panel interviews on the basis of which such students are selected who are 'socially educable'.[17] (The Tata Institute of Social Sciences is conducting a study in this area on the basis of 'entry-exit' data). Some schools however have experienced that in spite of their efforts, socially uneducable students do succeed in getting admission to schools of social work. The courts in the recent past have increasingly questioned the validity of panel interviews in the selection of students to medical and engineering colleges, as they have found them discriminatory. The discretionary powers of the Admission Committees have also come in for adverse comments. Guided by this consideration and also those of social justice a school of social work[18] changed its admission policy offered admission strictly on merit in 1981. Subsequently minimum qualifying marks were prescribed for language proficiency and panel interview to select better candidates. Most of the schools of social work seem to regard placement of students as an administrative matter. This may be the reason why placement as a process has brought forth comments only from four schools. All the schools mention about the first and second year placements. One school provides for 'matching placement' which corresponds with the choice of students. In another school 'better students are placed in better agencies, and poor students in others'.[19] The agencies are supplied with a list of students and they make the selection. The study conducted by Nair reports that out of twenty-six, eighteen schools ascertain the wishes of students but these are not always considered. In other cases students have either no say in their placements, or that this matter is decided in the staff meeting. In some schools the matter is left entirely to the discretion of the incharge of field work. In others, while there is no choice for students in the first year, their views are ascertained in the second year. One school has laid down the following criteria for the placement of M.A. previous student* : (i) professional characteristics and background of students, (ii) learning needs and level of functioning judged during the workshop conducted by the Faculty, (iii) agency needs and policies, and (iv) placement mostly in structured settings. In the case of the second year students, the criteria are : (a) preference for fields but placement according to merit for fields most in demand, (b) needs and potentials of students, and (c) agency needs and policies.

Another[20] school has mentioned a 10-point 'placement expectations' in its field work guide which includes learning about agency functions, development of skill in communication, problem identification and so on.

Still another school which has not formally prepared any criteria for placement is guided by some of the following considerations : (i) distance of the agency from the school as well as the student's place of residence[21]; (ii) agency's request for a male or female student, or specific number of students; (iii) supervisor's report on the number of students to be placed in a particular agency and quality of learning experience; (iv) proficiency of the student in local language; (v) pairing of students in case of language difficulty; (vi) personal characteristics of students and the supervisor ('serious or non-serious' student and 'lax-strict' supervisor); (vii) distribution of students in most or all the field work agencies ; (viii) preference of students in selected cases; (ix) report from the former supervisor before the second year

*Faculty of Social Work, M.S. University of Baroda.

placement in selected cases; (x) relations between individual students and the manner in which these will affect field work performance; (xi) distribution of good and poor students among all the supervisors as far as possible; (xii) consultation with the prospective supervisor on difficult students; and (xiii) change of supervisor in the case of second year students.

Placement of students are changed on the following grounds : (a) illness of student (a nearby placement is offered); (b) lack of adjustment either between the school and/or agency supervisor and the student; (c) want of work on account of staff changes in the agency; (d) students' extra-ordinary performance and the need for new experience; and (e) poor performance of a student either in an agency or under a supervisor and the change made at the suggestion of the latter.

From the above account it can be seen that placement for field work is a serious exercise and it should not be treated only as a routine administrative work. It is almost impossible for any school to follow all the above criteria in practice. It will nevertheless be useful to be guided by as many of them as possible in finalising placements, and later, in providing orientation to students so that they are neither left to fend for themselves, nor left at 'loose ends'.

SUPERVISION

If field work is considered to be an integral part of social work education, supervision should be regarded as the core of field work. The process of supervision operates at three interconnected levels of relationships*; relationship between the supervisee and the school supervisor : relationship between the supervisor and the field with trained or untrained resource persons and groups; and the relationship between the student and the 'field'. The supervisory process is both creative and dynamic, and it calls for investment by the supervisor in terms of knowledge, attitudes, skills and perspective in guiding a student to meet the

*A supervisee remarked in an individual conference that he has two 'wives' to relate to : one is the school supervisor and the other is that of the agency.

demands of learning as well as of the field. While supervision fosters growth and awareness in the student, it also engenders a similar process in the supervisor. The later is constantly at pains to strike a balance between the educational and service (or action) components of a field. Since field work demands do not run parallel to that of the class, a supervisor has also to play the role of a teacher. He has to further ensure that the student complies with the formalities of field work and in this sense he plays the role of an administrator and an authority figure. He is however expected to exercise the psychological form of authority more than the legal (or direct form) in order to help the student effectively.

The schools of social work have designated either a teacher, a field worker, or an agency personnel as field work supervisors. The supervision by teachers is generally favoured by the schools with agency supervisors playing a complementary role wherever possible. A teacher-supervisor in the schools however enjoys higher status than the one who *only* supervises students' field work without any teaching responsibility.

The school supervisor holds weekly conferences to discuss various aspects of field work and also the student's learning therefrom. In some schools these conferences are held in the first and third semesters every week, whereas in the second and fourth semesters they are held every fortnight in order to reduce the dependence of students on the supervisor, and also to enable them to do work with more freedom, responsibility, and initiative. The merit of this arrangement may however be questioned by some in that whether it should be applied even for students of the second term in the first year ?

The seriousness or the casualness that a supervisor brings to bear on the individual conferences largely determines the attitude of students towards the use they make of supervision. Each new batch of students is generally oriented (or disoriented) about a particular supervisor and also agencies by the senior students within a week of its arrival at the school. It is therefore necessary that this formal relationship is established and maintained with care; is reviewed and renewed; tasted and tested so that the supervisee is neither loosely shunted, nor excessively threatened, for, such negative relationships prove damaging for the learner in terms of his motivation, capacity and opportunity. The practice of en bloc 'casual', 'roadside', or 'occasional' supervision, adopted by some supervisors therefore is a matter of grave professional concern. A supervisor needs to adequately prepare himself for conferences so that these are, and as far as possible, remain refreshing and creative.

Some schools have introduced the system of group supervision to guide students. Group supervision can take two forms; one is that it may be treated as a substitute or supplement to individual supervision to effect economy in time, and extend benefits to students for a longer duration; the other is that it uses the group as a means for individual and collective awareness, growth and action, and also a source of mutual support for the members of the group. This also helps, in a way, to dilute the authority of the school or the agency supervisor, and the student gets a feeling of being an equal partner in a formal programme. It is this aspect of group supervision which does not obtain in the schools of social work. The responses received from the schools do mention about supervisory practices i.e. weekly conferences, fortnightly reports, agency visits etc., but they do not mention at all about the qualitative input that goes into the process of supervision.

The schools of social work also appear to hold different views on supervision. One school considers this as a means to 'help the student acquire proper attitudes and skills, understanding of self, develop a sense of objectivity, and accept constructive criticism'. Another school considers this as one of the ten stages in the field work programme of the school. The third lays emphasis on innovativeness of the process and organizes 'consultative group sessions and six monthly formulation of field work objectives for students ; provides time to the supervisor to reflect upon his own performance; and opportunity for the supervisee to evaluate supervisor's work'. Such innovations as team supervision of individual or groups of students, or per group supervision have also been tried.

A supervisor is required to help students through inputs, through-puts, and out-puts at different stages which could be identified as follows : orientation; induction; selection of problem, area or need; definition of problem, area or need; identification of resources to tackle the problem or meet the need; determination of goals; priorities and methods of intervention; assessment of impact; change of strategy; review of experiences in relation to practice-theory; assignment of reading; supportive relationship to help students accept criticism and comments positively; and enrichment of conferences through innovative and reflection sessions. The interplay of these components can be seen in each of the conferences held on a case or situation, and also longitudinally over a period of time through a series of conferences on the basis of which growth profiles of students could be prepared. One of the yardsticks of effective supervision is the learning of supervisor himself from students. If this has not occurred, the supervisor has failed both in his teaching and guiding functions. Supervision in this sense therefore is a learning and growth-producing experience both for the student as well as the supervisor in a field situation.

As part of field instruction, quite a few schools have introduced the system of group conferences* which has got three different meanings. The first type of group conference is the one which is held by the supervisor on matters pertaining to field work with a group of students under his supervision in addition to individual meetings. The second type of group conference is like a seminar where students of different groups under different supervisors or from different agencies under the same supervisor report on their experiences so that others who are not working in those agencies derive benefit from these presentations. The third type of group conference is meant to encourage a group of students under different supervisors to exchange views on any aspect of their work experience with others and invite their suggestions on own approach. Supervisors act as resource persons in these group conferences and students play the roles of chairpersons, paper presenters, and rapporteurs. It is this type of group conference which is most important (although some question its value) from the point of view of field work learning, organization of experiences, theorising, and presentation. These conferences also show the group dynamics between students and

*Group conferences have also been used as a device for '*en bloc* disposal' of students under one's charge.

teachers, students and students, teachers and teachers. To illustrate : in one of the group conferences a presenter was heckled by her adversaries through a volley of questions directed against her to prove that she was not a good worker. This situation required effective intervention by the resource persons present but they could not adequately deal with it and the student came out of the conference badly mauled.

In the case of some students the very selection of a topic to prepare the group conference paper proves difficult because their field work continues to be of a rambling type and therefore they do not find anything worth presenting on the basis of their work. This discovery by the student makes him extremely fearful of a possible negative evaluation by the supervisor later. Such students need kind support. There are still others who are sincere workers and who can organise their field experience in a paper with difficulty but find the presentation most challenging and difficult. Further, it takes a real courage for a student to volunteer as the first presenter. Alliances between chairpersons and presenters, or between presenters and supervisors at times are not uncommon in the group conferences. New supervisors particularly find the role of the resource person uncomfortable in the presence of their senior colleagues, or when they are not well prepared for the conference. The effective role played by the supervisor as a resource person builds confidence of the supervisee in the ability of the supervisor to deal with his problems in field work. Poor role performance equally shakes his confidence. These conferences also provide occasions to find out the preparedness of the supervisees to contribute to discussions of the group conference, and also their interest, indifference, dominance, passivity and so on.

In some cases, perspectival differences between supervisors come into bold relief at the time of a case discussion, and this situation poses problems in management by the group. Instances have been known to the directors of field work who have been informally approached by field work supervisors with requests for not being clubbed with colleague A or B. One can therefore look at the group conferences either as a ritual not worthy of attention and time, or as rich forums for healthy group interaction around a theme.

Another important aspect of supervision is the careful reading of students' reports and offer of helpful comments. Supervisors who keep their records properly and maintain fortnightly progress reports of students are quite aware of the importance of different types of comments. If the progress of a student is seen in retrospect during a year one can quickly notice the frequency of supportive and appreciative comments in the first quarter; appreciative comments interspersed with mildly critical comments in the second quarter; and appreciative comments, probe questions and critical comments in the last quarter. These are linked with the learning and growth cycle of the student in field work. If the student has been told on a regular basis as to where he stands in relation to his supervisor and his field work, he develops more confidence in work. The ambivalent attitude of the supervisor creates ambivalence in the mind of the student. Further, supervisors who are irregular in their practices take resort to 'positive strokes' and 'flattering phrases' in the fornightly reports in order to save themselves from troubles of various kinds. In the process, they create problems for their conscientious colleagues, including threats of assault by students.

In some schools fortnightly reports and evaluation papers are signed by students and they have a right to express dissent. However, inspite of the assurance that they would not be victimized, written expression of one's dissent is generally feared by students. They prefer to either strike a compromise or unwillingly accept the supervisor's stand. The author knows of only two cases out of about 48 under him in the last six years, who recorded their dissent—one in the fortnightly, and the other in the first-term evaluation which was graded then. Both were anxious personalities, and one of them had openly expressed a desire to form a more personal than a formal relationship.

Depending upon one's orientation a supervisor may emphasise programme achievement, or task-centred traditional approach in preference to the developmental approach which embraces all these, and also provide a wider perspective in terms of policy, change, and social justice. Supervisory conferences may thus act as a means to impart such perspectives which could be seen in a student's field work reports. The range of supervisory practices may vary from that of a routine meeting to the one which is creative, reflective and perspectival. Much depends upon the preparedness of the staff of an institution as to which end of the continuum is preferred by an individual supervisor or a group of supervisors.

EVALUATION

Most of the schools which supplied information have mentioned about the evaluation of field work. This only confirms the observation made by the Second Review Committee on Social Work Education that the schools of social work seem to have developed evaluation criteria without having done their proper home work in other important areas of field work. For the evaluation of field work again the schools have developed criteria which show wide variation. These criteria have been developed on annual and semester basis, agency or placement basis, project or task basis and also on the basis of social work methods. Factors like identification and understanding of the situation, establishment of rapport, development of skills, experience in helping and action process, and professional growth are considered important in evaluation by some schools. Understanding of the situation—individual, group or area—and development of skills relating to that of study, assessment and action are given weightage by a few others. In addition, self-discipline, adjustment to agency, community or co-worker, quality of recording and use of supervision are other aspects which are also taken into account. One school has devoted almost five pages of its field work guideline in spelling out the various components of field work evaluation. Some schools have allotted marks for each item included under the field work tasks for different semesters. These items range from 8 to 12 for each semester, and these are : ability to observe and report, sense of responsibility, resource utilization etc. The numerical value of these items ranges from 2 to 10 marks. The total score of a student thus becomes his evaluation. This approach, though apparently rational, is far too mechnical. The evaluation of a student's work is not the summation of itemised grades or fortnightly reports; on the contrary, it is qualitative, longitudinal, global and 'objectively subjective'.

Some schools have listed evaluation criteria according to the practice of one or all the primary methods of social work. Schools offering under-graduate programmes have assigned marks for agency visits, casework, group work, camp, seminar, and report-writting. In addition, professional growth also constitutes one of the important criteria. Those schools which offer specialization in social welfare and/or industrial settings have developed field-wise criteria for student evaluation. Schools have also developed criteria for the evaluation of block field work but this evaluation is different from that of the concurrent field work. In some cases the reports of the agency heads are considered adequate whereas in other cases students assemble after the block placement and they discuss their experiences with the supervisor concerned. The pattern of evaluation as it obtains in the schools of social work is as follows :

Pattern of evaluation

1. By supervisor only
2. By supervisor and faculty (sixty marks and 40 marks between them)
3. By supervisor only with the proviso for moderation by the staff and/or the Head of the Department
4. By the supervisor mainly but followed by viva-voce examination
5. By the supervisor and external examiner(s) with or without viva-voce.

Even under a pattern of evaluation where an average of grade given by two examiners (internal and external) is the final award, and in case of a difference of more than ten marks, a third examiner (external) is appointed, and an average of scores given by all the three is worked out, students have shown dissatisfaction with field work marks. This arises when serious students compare their grades with those who were easy-going, and worked under 'mild' and 'friend-supervisors' who were not quite regular in checking weekly reports, writing periodic assessments, holding individual and group conferences, and visiting the field. Field work co-ordinators are known to have occasionally confided to one colleague or the other about a student who showed his preference to a "good supervisor" by name (or mentioned some reason for not being placed under another), so that he could do his field work 'effectively'. When such students are not obliged they commence their field work on a note of disappointment. This only shows that unless there is a minimum level of agreement among supervisors on field work norms and supervisory practices, the cause of students' dissatisfaction shall persist in view of wide variation between supervisors' expectations and practices, and also differences in field work awards. In one case a senior educator is reported to have delegated the responsibility of field visits to his junior colleague or project staff. It is on account of this kind of laxity and variation that a conscientious supervisor reportedly awarded a 'protest grade' to a really deserving student with a note specifying the reason for it! The reason given was that when underdeserving students secured more than what they should normally be given, why a conscientious student should be 'victimised' by giving him only what was his due. In the former case while field work process is used as a method of 'appeasing' students for own lapses, in the latter, it amounts to 'punishing' them for exacting work done by them. The system of 'average award', possibly the best of all other systems in vogue from the point of view of its credibility is thus put under strain. The professional conduct of supervisors therefore will determine a great deal as to what can be made out of one or the other approach to evaluation. The system of average award can be further improved upon as follows.

After the supervisors have awarded grades/marks, a random sample of field reports and records from each supervisor should be drawn on the basis of high, average, and low grades. These should be passed on to another supervisor who should carefully go through the papers and present his views on different aspects before the Departmental Council for discussion. In the light of this discussion, the supervisor concerned should be asked to moderate grades/awards given by him. This procedure should be followed in the case of all supervisors. But the system can work only when the supervisors concerned do not take criticism amiss, and it is used as a regular staff development programme on field work evaluation.

Whatever pattern is followed by a school, the evaluation of field work is always a source of dissatisfaction for quite a few students each year and although some of the schools have tried to rationalise the procedure over the years, problems of variation and subjectivity in evaluation have not been completely overcome. External examiners are appointed in order to perhaps minimize the excesses committed by the supervisors in evaluation. This system has been introduced by some schools because quite a few students question the integrity of supervisors. On this aspect Frances Manis* commented thus : "I have given nine seminars on field work in both the developed and developing countries, but I am struck to find that the question of *integrity* in evaluation was raised nowhere except in India". A more rational approach to follow in evaluation would be to look at different phases of field work—from orientation to evaluation—as a continuum, work out the tasks, goals and strategies for each phase in relation to subsequent phases; and then see how a student has done in these areas. A student's evaluation indirectly is the evaluation of a supervisor's performance as well. Like supervison, evaluation could also be treated either as a routine work or as a creative and growth-promoting endeavour.

FIELD WORK RECORDS

Schools of social work lay great emphasis on the recording of field work experience. In fact these are the bases for any evaluation. Students are required to submit weekly reports; record individual and group conferences, and contacts with other agencies. Process recording is stressed by all the schools. This form of recording is the product of the practice of social case work in the beginning years of professional social work, and with minor adaptations has been followed in group work and community organisation also. Comments have already been made in the earlier section on the content and pattern of field work which show marked variation from BSW to MSW programmes. In spite of these variations, process recording appears to be a common denominator for showing the performance of student in field work. It has been the experience of a many social work educators that

*Seminar on Field Work held at the Delhi School of Social Work, July 20-29, 1977.

while a good field worker finds it difficult to record all his transactions with the client system, the poor performer finds this style a convenient opportunity to include irrelevant details. In order to rationalise the recording procedure some schools have developed formats or guidelines for interviewing and report-writing. One school has developed a format which requires students to include the following in the reports : identification of information, observation and interpretation, formulation of objectives, plan to achieve the formulated objectives, intervening activity—study, diagnosis and treatment, evaluation and plan. Another school has mentioned about survey recording, the details of which have not been supplied. In view of variations in the content of reports within and between the schools it is necessary that the content of process recording is specified along with the contents of records for integrated social work practice. (It may be noted in this connection that integrated social work practice, though an advance over the trichotomous practice of basic methods of social work, may remain traditional, and should not be regarded as synonymous with developmental social work). Thus while the content of field work, approaches to intervention in a field situation, and orientations to define a field situation vary, the records of field work do not truely reflect the differences.

In the area of recording some work has been done by Frances Manis.[21] Manis mentions about content, stance and form in field work, and has identified six stages in the field teacher-student relationships. These are contract, determination of task, role recording, analysis of student's work, preparation for evaluation, and final evaluation. He has favoured role to process recording, the former including the description of field situation, role of key participants in that situation, and the role played by the student.

The approach to recording thus deserves careful consideration by the schools of social work so that flexible guidelines are developed to record and document practice experience. Students should also be given experience in preparing project proposals, abstracts, summaries, case studies etc. in the process of doing field work.

BLOCK PLACEMENT

Like the concurrent field work, the pattern of block placement also varies from school to school. In one school field work in the fourth semester is organized after the examinations and it is called block placement.*

In other cases the block placement is either compulsory or voluntary but this experience is generally organized at the end of two years. Nair reports that 21 out of 28 schools offer block placement after the completion of concurrent field work the duration of which varies from 4 weeks to 3 months. Twelve schools have worked out criteria for evaluation of block field work whereas six rely only upon the report of the agency. As it obtains, block field work is the weakest link in the entire field work programme. Supervision is not possible from the school, and much depends upon the agency, its relationship with the school, and the immediate supervisor who is expected to provide meaningful experience during this period. Cases are well-known where students use block placement to pass time. Students generally give their options for placement agencies. Some times these options are guided by considerations of variety of experiences, deepening of concurrent field work experiences, likely opportunities for employment in the agency and own convenience or relation with an employee or resource person. The block placement by and large is practised in the traditional context. On the basis of experience of block placement in a school with a generic programme of post-graduate education, one can say that over a period of 3 to 4 years, hardly five students have opted for placements which can be called developmental, and these students had asked for these placements more for their educational value than for anything else. This area needs to be explored and developed further by the schools of social work because social action groups, people's organisations, human rights activists, and regional movements may provide rich experiences to students, and may even offer opportunities for employment.

*Institute of Social Sciences, Agra University, Agra.

DEVELOPMENTAL PERSPECTIVE IN FIELD WORK

The field work programme of schools of social work is part of a larger establishment. It is therefore difficult for the schools to associate themselves formally and directly with such efforts which intend to bring about change and social justice by challenging the establishment. Although one school of social work has reported about participation of students in 'developmental movements'* the practice of this idea is indeed difficult through the University or college auspices which enjoy autonomy only in name. The schools therefore might consider the desirability of exploring opportunities for oppositional practice which could be tried during vacations when the willing students and the faculty could participate in such programmes as *individual citizens*. In fact a senior social work educator** holds the view and rightly so, that if the schools of social work are looking for developmental orientation in social work education, and wish to provide the same to their students in field work, supervision by agency-based trained social workers then will not deliver the goods. In this area therefore what social work educator will need is to rely more on professionally 'untrained' leaders, and activists for the training of students, the school supervisor playing a complementary or auxiliary role. Field work-based research projects may also be initiated to develop theory and practice model in this area. Although community work is considered to be one of the primary methods of social work it has been practised rather softly. One can hardly conceive of community work without oppositional practice which requires confrontation with the establishment in certain cases. This is an emerging field for interdisciplinary practice. Human service professions, which are elitist both in orientation and practice, are likely to experience severe pressure from the clientele (target or beneficiary) systems and demands will be increasingly made upon them to establish experimental or counter-systems to deliver the goods. These in their turns will again be replaced by new modes. These developments are bound to shape the new 'field'

*M.S.S. Institute of Social Work, Nagpur.

**Reference is to Shankar Pathak, Delhi School of Social Work.

for social work practice and education in future.

REFERENCES

1 *The University Grants Commission Report, 1978*, p. 80 ff (mimeographed).
2 *Ibid.*, p. 91
3 *Ibid.*, p. 127.
4 *Ibid.*, p. 140
5 *Ibid.*, p. 144
6 *Ibid.*, pp. 164-66.
The specific objectives have been further edited for the purpose of this Review.
7 *Ibid.*, p. 139
8 Some of the schools have been riding on two or more horses, in that they have borrowed the goals from one school and the pattern or content from another. In the process they are involved in a serious 'accident' of 'schizophrenic orientation' without being aware of its consequences.
9 Delhi School of Social Work, *Field Work Manual* (mimeographed), p. 3.
10 Philomena D' Souza, (1978), p. 25.
11 Philomena D' Souza, p. 205
12 Clifford Manshardt, *Pioneering on Social Frontiers in India* (Bombay, Lalwani Publishing House, 1967), p. 40 ff.
13 Since information on this aspect is lacking, the following sources have been used in this section : (i) K.D. Gangrade, "Field Work in Schools of Social Work", a paper prepared for a workshop on Field Work at the Tata Institute of Social Sciences, Bombay (1979) ; (ii) Association of Schools of Social Work in India, *Report of the Seminar on Field Work in Social Work Education.* (Waltaire, ASSW, 1964), pp. 6-7 mimeographed ; (iii) Philomena D' Souza, *Field Instruction in Social Work Education* (1978) ; (iv) Reports of the Delhi School of Social Work, and the Faculty of Social Work, M.S. University Baroda.
14 *The Second Review Committee*, p. 40.
15 Ramakrishna Mission Vidyalaya Arts College, Department of Social Work, Coimbatore.
16 Institute of Social Welfare and Business Management, Post-graduate Department of General Social Welfare, Calcutta.
17 Charlottee Towle, *Learner in Education for the Profession* (Chicago, University of Chicago, 1954), p. 70-75, 175 80, 200-204 and 209-30.
18 As an experimental measures the Delhi School of Social Work has listed five eligibility requirements in an order of priority beginning with B.A. (Hons.) Social Work or B.S.W. and ending with B.Sc.

(Pass or Hons.) for admission to the School in 1981. Implicit in these requirements is perhaps the assumption that social science graduates will make better social workers. If this is so, over a period of time, this assumption would need to be substantiated by empirical evidence.

19 Philomena D' Souza, p. 196.

20 Department of Social Work, Loyola College of Social Sciences, Trivandrum, *Field Work Guide*, pp. 2-3.

21 See Philomena D' Souza, p. 142.

22 Frances Manis, *Stance and Form in Field Work Education : Guidelines for Field Teachers and Students*, Department of Social Work, University of Sidney, (Mimeographed), p. 26.

2

PROCEEDINGS OF THE WORKSHOP

R.R. Singh

INAUGURAL AND CONCLUDING SESSIONS

Professor S.N. Ranade, Head, Department of Social Work, University of Delhi, delivered both the inaugural and concluding addresses. While welcoming the participants, Professor Ranade said that there was a sense of growing cynicism among students and teachers about field work and therefore there was a need to organise field work in a better manner. He added that in matters pertaining to field work senior social work educators might not necessarily be more enlightened than their younger colleagues. The schools should therefore need to examine the nature of field work programme, its rationale, and methods.

In his concluding remarks, Professor Ranade said that since situation differed from school to school and so was the case with communities, a practice or a programme which was good at one place might not be good at another. Within a broad contour therefore variations should be possible. One should also be wary of uniformity which might lead to stagnation. The common practice particularly among the new schools was to ask for the prospectuses of other schools and dish them out. This was indeed very unfortunate because the school should formulate a programme first and then should consult others. Even though the present workshop has been richer in perspective and knowledge, its recommendations should be examined in the light of individual situations without accepting them as mandatory. The recommendations should however be used to strengthen one's hand and to give due importance to field work in an academic context in which the schools were functioning. Even in the Departments of Social Medicine, there was resistance to going out in the community. The schools of social work would also need to overcome this problem. The present workshop therefore should be regarded only a beginning, and the participants should share its experiences with their colleagues, and endeavour to give a fresh look to the field work programme in their institutions. The inaugural session was followed by a Review Paper, and the concluding session was preceded by a Perspective Paper presented by the Director of the workshop.

NATURE AND OBJECTIVES OF FIELD WORK (PLENARY SESSIONS I & II)

At the outset, the Director of the workshop, while presenting a Note on the Need for Faculty Development Workshop on Field Work, observed that patterns of field work in the schools of social work in India varied a great deal. The workshop therefore proposed to consider various components of field work and describe them so that they could be operationalised educationally at graduate (BSW) and post-graduate levels. It was pointed out that while undertaking such an exercise, the goals of social work education should also be clarified. Since the goals of social work education themselves constituted a subject matter for a separate workshop, it was decided that these should be referred only to the extent they guided the deliberations of the group.

The workshop thus could dwell upon the need and scope for developing a common core of field work practice in order to provide a meaningful link between the BSW and MSW levels of social work education offered at the schools of social work.

The workshop could also consider whether there should be a continuum in field work between BSW and MSW courses offered in different institutions. It was recognised that since students who joined social work came from different backgrounds that is BSWs with or without field work, or with a Bachelor's/ Master's degree without any course or field experience in social work, the workshop should make a note of the extent of variation in the levels of field work on account of these differences.

Keeping the above in view, the group decided that the workshop should spell out as to what constituted field work in social work education ? What were its objectives, nature and content ? and how these could be imparted to students ? The group broadly defined the objectives of field work as follows :

1. To offer learning opportunities through guided practical experience for enabling students to know and understand social phenomena;
2. To help students develop an ability to perceive and appreciate social situations (needs and problems) requiring professional intervention;
3. To help the client-system of the defined field as far as possible through the application of knowledge derived from practice and theory; and
4. To foster personal and professional growth.

It was decided that the workshop should especially consider the interlinkage between traditional and developmental approaches to social work practice, and the need for a common core of field work practicum for different levels of education. The tasks of field work were conceived of by the group as educational and developmental.

It was suggested that the following three areas should, in particular, be spelt out :

1. Concept of field work,
2. Objectives of field work, and
3. Type of learning that could be acquired only through field work.

FIELD INSTRUCTION IN SOCIAL WORK EDUCATION

Mr. Krishan Kumar highlighted the following points from his paper on field instruction. He said that field instruction ought to be independently identified. According to him while field work meant 'doing'; instruction, implied 'education'. Field work in social work was an equivalent of a laboratory for natural sciences. It was an essential component of social work education.

Three principal constituents of field work learning, according to Mr. Kumar, were : (1) teacher-supervisor, (2) student-learner, and (3) the field situation. Field work was a process of inter-action of a student with the life situation. But only selective life situations should be considered in field work where social work as a profession had a sense of concern. He added that field work must consider changing situations and priorities from developmental perspective which subsumed traditional-remedial approach. Guidance was implicit in field work.

The following questions were posed for consideration : 1. Did field work really form a part of educational programme ? 2. Had schools evolved a structure of field work which could accomplish the objects of interaction between the learner and the situation that experience offered ? 3. Was instructional process rationally planned and pursued ?

The group framed the following issues for discussion :

1. Definition of field work,
2. Attributes of the situation in field work,
3. The objectives of field work, and
4. Learning in field work which was exclusive to it.

Definition of field work

According to the Group field work in social work education was a guided interaction process between a student and the actual life situation in which social work as a profession had an abiding and deep concern, and which needed to be remedied, improved or changed for a fuller development of human-environmental potential.

Attributes of the situation

The group noted that the life situation must be such which had a potential for learning and teaching. It must offer necessary experience through supervised teaching of a non-directive nature. The students' experience might range from a stance of neutrality to that of involvement. The elements of the field might include need, problem, resource, requisite action, and even action-potential. The profession concerned should be able to broadly identify its role in, and contribution to the field. It was the situation which would provide opportunity for participation and action.

One of the members mentioned that field work began as field instruction with apprenticeship in agencies. The tasks given then were similar to the craftsman's task and there was a dichotomy between administrative and non-administrative skills.

According to one view the schools of social work owed a responsibility for strengthening professional application which implied skills, exercises, observance of practices, role play, laboratory experience, simulation games, and other similar activities. The entire application process could consist of (1) field work, (2) field instruction, and (3) professional application. It was pointed out that a situation might be identified as an event or a series of events where a student interacted with other persons—not necessarily with clients only, but also with colleagues, administrative heads and others, when he was involved either in giving or receiving help. It was a guided learning experience—programmed, self-sought, or provided.*

CONCEPT OF FIELD WORK

Field work implied both training and education. The distinction between the two was that while training was repetitive and skill oriented, education was more broad-based, and it was imparted with a perspective. It consisted of knowledge of different situations and was a creative, innovative and a dynamic process. It fostered development of intellectual and emotional processess, and attitudes.

Training might be conducted in polytechnics independently of universities. Whereas training was a mechanical repetition, education might be conceived of, to an extent, a creative repetition with the former, being viewed as one of its methods. Guidance and supervision in education were necessary to reduce chances of error and to protect both the student and the client-system from unintended harm as far as possible.

Objectives of field work

The group worked out the following objectives :

* Shankar Pathak's intervention during group discussion.

(1) To offer purposeful learning experience to student through interaction with life situations under supervisory guidance for professional growth in terms of knowledge, skills and attitudes;

(2) To foster attitudes in the student towards professional self-development, increasing self-awareness, appreciation of both capacities and limitations;

(3) To develop in the student the required skills in helping the needy through organisational work, use of social work methods, that is, listening, participation, communication and so on; and

(4) To enable the student to develop and deepen capacity to relate theory to practice, and also to relate experience to theory.

Learning exclusive to field work

Field work experience could distinctly provide learning in the following areas :

1. Participation in the process of help and change.
2. Development of positive attitudes towards self and others.
3. Acquisition and development of skills in collaboration, team work, planning and organization and so on.
4. Experience of taking responsibility to deal with critical situations.
5. Experience of confrontation with oneself as a means to self-growth and its use in action.

ORGANIZATION AND ADMINISTRATION OF FIELD WORK

The session started with the presentation of report of the plenary session I. On the word 'strategy' used in the report in relation to the role of social worker, there was some discussion on whether the word professional intervention should not be preferred.

Following this, one of the members highlighted certain aspects of his paper on the organisation of field work. Two important points were subsequently raised :

1. What was the status of the field work co-ordinator in the department or school, and especially vis-a-vis his other functions ?
2. What was the status of the field work supervisor, and by implication, field work in relation to class-room instruction ?

There was a general discussion on the role and functions of the co-ordinator. Participants from different schools spoke about practices, experiments and difficulties.

As regards fieldwork, opinions were expressed about whether field work supervision was viewed as less important than class-room instruction. Relevant to this was a point raised in an earlier session, whether field work and theory were equally important.

It was suggested that the participants be divided into two groups in order to discuss the two areas in detail. *Group I* was to discuss the type of structure that might be desirable for the organization and administration of field work; and *Group II* was to address itself to the following :

(a) How could the status of field work supervisors (where persons were appointed only for this work) be raised keeping in view the point that field work was as important as class instruction ?
(b) How could equal weightage, if possible, be given, to class-room instruction and field work ?
(c) How could theory be integrated with practice ?

The deliberations of *Group-I* were directed to answer the following questions :

1. What was the need, if any, for special structure or organization for field work within the overall education and administrative set-up of an institution ?

2. What should be the proposed structure for social work institutions, against which individual institutions could identify the adequacies or inadequacies of their own structures and try to suitably modify them ?

3. Whether and how this structure could be conducive to the integration of theory with practice ?

The need for special unit was collectively recognised by the group and the reasons advanced were as follows :

1. It would strengthen social work education;
2. More specially, this would lead to a streamlining of administrative functions;
3. It would promote public relations with agencies; and
4. It would help in maintaining continuity with agencies or client systems especially during vacations when students and the school supervisors were not in touch with them.

In order to arrive at a "proposed structure", the group first examined existing arrangements and variations. It was noted that in some cases the co-ordination work was done by the head of the institution; in others by a senior staff, and in yet others, by a junior staff. In some schools the head of the institution was assisted by field work incharges for respective classes. In some instances the responsibility of co-ordination was 'rotating' ; in others it rested with one person for a long time. (In one instance it was for about fifteen years). There were schools where there was a clear demarcation between social work teachers and field work supervisors. In one school there was a provision for a field work organiser who is accountable to the head of the institution, along with field work supervisors. In another, attempts were being made to reduce the social distance between field work supervisors and social work educators by allowing some teaching work to be done by those supervisors who had got at least three years' experience. Further, in some instances, where specialisations or separate departments existed, the heads of respective departments co-ordinated field work of their students.

The following therefore was proposed as structure which emerged out of deliberations :

1. A staff member must be assigned the responsibility of co-ordinating field work.
2. He must be a full-time member of the staff.
3. He must be a relatively senior staff member and must have received sufficient exposure to the field situation.
4. The head of the institution should not assume the

responsibility of the co-ordinator of field work as he had got various administrative responsibilities to carry out; and also, because in this arrangement field work was treated more as an administrative matter than educational.

5. The status of field work co-ordinator should be at par with other members of the staff.
6. The responsibility of co-ordination of field work must rotate.
7. The roatation must be effected, preferably, every two years. This would help staff members to remain in touch with the entire field, and would take care of situations (where others resignedly absolved themselves of field work responsibilities) by giving others an opportunity to do things for themselves and 'face the music', rather than having 'digs' at one who was at the helm of affairs. Also, this would prevent inefficiency from being prolonged and perpetuated in case a co-ordinator was not efficient and in extreme cases even his tenure might be prematurely terminated.
8. Where there were specializations or a number of departments within an institution and where the heads of these departments were co-ordinating field work of their respective departments, such a 'headship' could also be rotated intra and inter-departmentally on an experimental basis.
9. The prospective co-ordinator must be informed nearly three months in advance to prepare himself for this work. This would take care of the apprehensions and discontinuity arising out of rotation.
10. The work of co-ordination should be a delegated responsibility and the person doing the job of co-ordination should be accountable to the head of the institution. However all the crucial and sensitive decisions must be conveyed to and approved by a larger body. In such a case either the whole staff, or an academic committee/sub-committee should be taken into confidence.
11. On account of his additional responsibilities, the co-ordinator might be given some 'concessions', (not

honorarium) in the form of lesser number of students to supervise, and compensatory leave for the work done during vacations.

The proposed structure was visualised by the group as a functionally viable and a distinct one within the larger set-up of the school.

The work of co-ordination was seen to consist of distinct but inter-related phases on a pre-admission to post-evaluation continuum. A co-ordinator was excepted to be in touch with the field and identify its changing needs, and new learning situations. He must know about the opportunities offered by agencies in terms of the number of students, and must make contacts and correspondence with them before sending students in agencies under different supervisors.

Making announcements of placements and subsequent announcements formed part of his work. Mid-session reviews, discussions among supervisors, development of records for teaching purposes and so on were other aspects of his work which should be undertaken essentially to promote general standards of supervision, including moderation of biases in the system.

The group rejected the invidious distinction between social work teachers and social work supervisors and felt that all the teachers should supervise students for field work. The head of the institution should also supervise at least one student in order to symbolically enhance the importance of field work.

While attempting to answer the third question on how the proposed structure could be conducive to the integration of theory with practice, the following sugestions were made :

1. Periodic discussions could be arranged amongst supervisors to share the nature of knowledge imparted to the student so that they could assess and guide the student.
2. Lesson plans or teaching plans could be developed by teachers regarding what was planned to be taught in a particular span period and also its emphasis and sequence, especially of the methods' course. This information could be made available to the agencies, on demand or otherwise, to enable the agency supervisor to

have realistic expectations from the student, and to assign appropriate responsibilities accordingly.

3. Case presentation sessions, case conferences, and group conferences could be arranged with resource person and a group of students.
4. Periodic orientation sessions could be tried, or one orientation session followed by, say, two review sessions, could be arranged during an academic session to assess application of theory into practice through field experience.
5. The co-ordinator could request agencies to provide interesting case materials which could be suitably modified or developed into records for teaching.
6. Field work-based reading assignments could be given to students depending upon their capability to work and absorb, and with the precaution that field work supervision did not become a class teaching session.

The following issues were taken up for discussion in Group II :

1. Recognition of role of a field work supervisor in an institution.
2. Non-monetary ways of enhancing the status of supervisors.
3. Integration of theory and field work practice in the curricula.

Discussion on (1) and (2) was overlapping as the two were closely linked. In the beginning, participants reported about arrangements in their institutions for class-room teaching and field work. Three distinct patterns were reported :

(i) Institutions where there were separate posts of field work supervisors. The designation of field-work supervisors varied in different institutions; that is, faculty assistants, part-time lecturers, and teaching assistants. Lecturers did not supervise students and did teaching only,

(ii) Institutions where lecturers undertook both teaching and field work supervision. But a few ad-hoc appointments were made of supervisors to ease the workload of teaching staff, and

(iii) Institutions where ad-hoc appointees undertook class teaching and field work supervision to the same extent regular lecturers did.

Regarding the status of supervisors, the consensus was that the supervisors should be accorded the same or equal status as that of a lecturer. It was also considered desirable not to have separate categories of teachers and field work supervisors, since class-room instruction and field work supervision were only two different methods of teaching, and therefore there was no justification to consider one superior to the other. Practical difficulties in the implementation of this suggestion were also noted by the group.

As regards improvement in the status of field work supervisors the following suggestions were made :

(1) Field work supervisors should be enrolled as full-fledged members of the staff council and should participate in all the staff development activities;
(2) Field work supervisors should be appointed internal examiners and also serve on the panel for viva voce examination on field work in case of their students;
(3) Field work supervisors should be given opportunities to represent the institution in regional, national and international conferences, seminars symposia and so on; and
(4) Field work supervisors should get all facilities on par with the teaching staff to undertake any study or research project.

The next issue, of relative importance of theory and practice, was found to be closely linked with weightage in terms of hours of lectures or practice, and marks or grades allocated to each.

It was observed that students often faced difficulties in relating theory to practice for which the following steps should be taken :

(1) More intensive teaching of basic methods courses should proceed concurrent field work of new entrants;
(2) At the second year level advanced courses in methods should be introduced;
(3) Involvement of field practitioners in imparting knowledge should become an integral part of the total teaching programme;
(4) Students' records should be used as tools for class-room teaching. An innovative pattern of record writing wherein the content learnt from field work situations could be analysed would help students' understanding and integration of theoretical concepts in practice;
(5) Seminars on field work should be held regularly where students present situations for discussion; and
(6) The need for more indigenous teaching material for better application of theory into practice was felt. For this, staff meetings, exclusively on issues related to field work, were recommended.

CONTENT OF FIELD WORK

The area to be discussed was whether the group should formulate the syllabus on field work content for five years, or should identify levels for CSW, BSW and MSW separately. The concept of agency/constituency was also brought out in this context.

A member expressed the view that defining the field was the primary concern of the whole group and that field in social work did not refer to fields of interest or fields of social work practice, but the field of field work. Another member was of view that one could analyse the theory-content to structure field work.

The group then got together for a 'brain-storming' session on the content of field work. The areas to be covered were ;

(I) Identification of phases in field work;
(II) Content in each phase;
(III) Levels of education (BSW, MSW and CSW—certificate course in Social Work);
(IV) Supervisory input in each phase; and

(V) Evaluation.

A member asked whether the field should decide the content, or the content should determine the field. Problems like what was the field ? what was meant by agency ? what was generic content ? and what was specific content ? were also posed ? It was suggested that based on the objectives of field work, a common content must be identified for the field in general.

The Director of the workshop clarified that the concept of field in field work was different from fields of field work, or social work for that matter. One needed to identify a social field. In doing so one's approach needed to be rational. A learner entering a field passed through several distinct, through interrelated, phases which were like a common denominator for any field.

A member pointed out that the group should discuss the extent to which the field determined content or field instruction curriculum. It was pointed out in this connection that field should influence the content but it should not determine it. It was added that the time had come to transcend generic and specialization controversy.

The group then divided itself into two sub-groups to consider different phases in field work:

1. Orientation
2. Placement
3. Exploration-Assessment-Action
4. Evaluation

Having identified these, the group further proceeded to outline contents applicable to each phase as given below :

Group 'A' identified the following phases of field work :

1. Orientation
2. Placement
3. Exploration-Assessment-Action
4. Evaluation

Having identified these, the group further proceeded to outline contents applicable to each phase as given below :

Phase	Content
1. Orientation The orientation phase had two aspects : (a) Introduction (b) Visits	(i) Introduction to field; field work curriculum, and to the agency/area. (ii) General visits to social work settings—institutions and communities. (iii) Recording and report writing on field visits. (iv) A. Students taken for visits to institutions should be provided with certain guidelines in the following areas : (a) Historical background of the institution/area (b) Aims or objectives of the institution(s) (c) Organization and structure of the institution(s) (d) Financial position (e) Intake policy, procedure and service delivery (f) Programmes offered by the agency (g) Facilities provided by the agency and problems faced by it. B. In case students were taken to a community, a broad guideline as given below should be followed : (a) Community in history : A prospective-retrospective (evaluative) view (b) Composition of the community (c) Various facilities available to the people (d) Existing organizations in the community (e) Problems faced by the community in general
2. II-Placement	(a) Introduction by the school supervisor of field work requirements and procedures

(b) Introduction by the agency supervisor of the requirements of the agency/community

(c) Introduction to the client system

2. The second aspect of content under placement related to work assignment. It could be of three types :

(a) Definite work assignment

(b) Definite target group

(c) Work assignment that may evolve out of exploratory work by the student himself.

3. III-Exploration-Assessment-Action

The content under this phase was formulated as follows :

(a) Need-Resource-Identification

(b) Programme development

(c) Assumption of social work roles and professional involvement

(d) Individual conferences

(e) Group conference

(f) Field work seminars

(g) Recording

(h) On-going assessment and perspective guidance

4. IV-Evaluation

The evaluation of student could be done at four different levels.

(i) Student's self-evaluation

(ii) Agency evaluation

(iii) Evaluation by the supervisor at school

(iv) Faculty evaluation

The content of evaluation could be based on the following :

(a) Summary records and other documents

(b) Personal qualities and professional skills

(c) Capability of relating theory to practice.

The group further divided itself into two sub-groups to work out illustrations in relation to field work in community and institutional settings. These are presented below :

PHASE-WISE BREAK UP FOR AN AGENCY (GENERAL HOSPITAL)

1. Illustrative material on field work : general hospital

Sl. No.	Phase	Content	Supervisory input
1	2	3	4
1.	Orientation	Introduction : Health as an area of concern of social work Various agencies providing curative, preventive, promotive and developmental services Role of social workers in this field Introduction to the curriculum related to medical setting Agency visits Report writing	Information on 1-6.
2.	Placement	Introduction of the agency by agency supervisor Introduction of the agency by school supervisor Definite target group and work assignment	Contacting the agency Informing about the placement Informing about the student Informing the student about the agency contact person Planning work in consultation with agency supervisor Type of clientele in the agency Previous year's students' relationship with the agency Agency expectations

1	2	3	4
			Limitations of the agency Problems of the agency
3.	Exploration-Assessment-Action	Identifying various needs of the clientele Programme planning Knowing administrative procedures such as correspondence, maintenance of records, registers, referral work statistics Collecting information about the policy of the agency timing, staff, distribution of functions etc. Interpretation of health charts, medical reports, graphs, representation of reviews Understanding of own role as a link between the patient, family and doctor, and of a counsellor Co-ordinating medical and paramedical services in the interest of the patient Case conference Environmental modification, insight, development, preparation of the patient and the family for hospitalization/treatment Resource-raising Preparing for discharge from the hospital and exploring suitable accommodation Taking up programmes like adoption, day care	Inculcating among students a sense to discriminate between felt-need and identified need. Introducing them with documents and procedural records, helping interpret charts and medical documents Explaining the role of liaison Providing information regarding paramedical and medical services in the agency Guiding through case conference Critically explaining various avenues for environmental modification Developing insight in working with staff Explaining implications to the individual and family Motivating student for resource mobilization Informing about developmental services Informing about various provisions for the handicapped Providing a theoretical base for community health Informing on methods of health survey—phases of treatment Mentioning the significance of preventive and promotive programmes Informing on the system and relevance of record-

1	2	3	4
		centre, in keeping with the patients' needs Knowing the needs of handicapped persons Efforts in developing neighbourhood community health programmes Survey of the health status of the community Arranging diagnostic camps Preventive and promotive programmes on an on-going basis i.e. immunization Recording	narrative and process Helping to understand health problems as a social class phenomena Teaching techniques and approaches to deal with client system Giving field work-based reading assignments Providing appreciation and encouragement, and also necessary guidance to student to reflect upon his *self* and *actions*
4.	Evaluation	Self-evaluation report Summary report Supervisory relationship Integration of theory with practice Application of methods of social work Understanding of the agency Evaluation by the agency supervisor Evaluation by the School/Faculty supervisor	Orientation to inculcate objectivity Help in analytical observation Providing guidelines for writing report Qualitative and quantitative aspects of work Creating conditions for developing self-evaluation skills

2. Illustrative material—community placement

Phases	*Content*	*Supervisory Inputs*
1. Orientation	Orientation of students about the community (a) Introducing students to the community by the supervisor/self (b) Visiting important institutions and meeting key persons in the community (c) Guidelines regarding community in history—population—socio-economic conditions, problems, facilities, organisation	Exploratory contact with community by supervisor Background information about field and field work therein Guidelines for observation of community
2. Placement	Three approaches to the community : *(a) Task oriented—Definite task should be given to students such as conducting sports week, healthy baby clinic, etc **(b) Target-group oriented—for example women, youth, marginal farmers, small farmers, etc. ***(c) Non Directive—Stimulating process of self-determination and self-help	Supervisory contacts through visits and letters. Definite task to be given by the supervisor

Phases	*Content*		*Supervisory Inputs*
3. Exploration-Assessment-Action	*(a) Task oriented	(a) Needs and resources to be defined by the school (b) Exploring possible client system (c) Implementation and assessment	Supervisor acting as enabler and guide in need/resource identification/assumption of work roles and professional involvement Providing 'perspective' guidance, individual conference, group conference, and seminars
	**(b) Target group	(a) Criteria for selection of target group to be suggested by the school, for example, children upto 14 years (b) Exploration of resources (c) Evolving structure conducive to developmental skills leading to problem-solving and self-generating leadership in the community (d) Terminating the relationship with the target group	
	***(c) Non-Directive :	On account of emphasis on initiative and participation of community through the entire process of exploration, assessment and action, supervisor should ensure that students do not take to directing role	

4. Evaluation	For on-going assessment and perspective guidance, field work supervisor should use records, conferences and seminars, and evaluation should be done on the basis of scope for activity, learning opportunity, support available from the agency and school, and development of professional skills. Feed-back should be available to students. There should be flexibility in the evaluation approach and in giving assignment. Evaluation should be a joint venture between supervisor and student. ***For non-directive approach—evaluation should be done with the active participation of the community.	Supervisor to help student in identifying his capacities and drawbacks

* C.S.W. Level only (Certificate in Social Work)
** B.S.W. Level only
*** M.S.W. Level only

Field work process in the agency : General

Phase	*Content*	*Supervisory Input*
I. Orientation	Introduction to specific field namely medical, correctional etc.	Providing information Introduction of the field
II. Placement/ Induction	Study of structure, functions and clientele of the agency	Preparing the agency to receive the student and vice versa Selection and assignment of initial tasks Clarifying to student social worker's role
III. Exploration-Assessment-Action	Meeting the client/ client group Interpretation of client-worker transaction Identification of needs and problems of the client/client group Identifying areas of work Helping client and significant others to accept the situation Resource identification and mobilization Assessment of situation and resources of the client, worker and the community, and mutual interaction—listing priorities in treatment action Observation and recording Case conference Co-ordinating the work of professionals and para-professionals in the interest of the clientele Developing preventive and promotive programmes on an	Preparing student through discussion and guidelines regarding various approaches typical of the setting Providing theoretical framework, creating self-awareness, enabling professional growth and helping the student to comprehend and analyse the situation Consultation and guidance given with regard to methods and approaches in handling cases Providing opportunity for growth-producing introspection Accrediting and encouraging positive contribution Providing information and helping the student to build up a directory of community resources in tackling the problem Guidance in planning and organization of community programmes Introducing student to outside agency for speedy execution of tasks

Phase	*Content*	*Supervisory Input*
	ongoing basis Learning administrative work Enlisting involvement of client and significant others in dealing with situation	Encouraging active partnership between the supervisor and the student in (a) assessing the work plan, (b) modifying attitudes and approaches Taking an objective view of student's mistakes (if any) due to circumstances beyond control
IV. Evaluation	Evaluation of the field, client/client group, of the effectiveness of different modes of tackling problems Evaluation of community programmes undertaken by field/agency Self-evaluation of student—growth of student as a result of his experience in the field knowledge and skills he has developed and his ability to fulfil the demands of the agency Evaluation of supervisor by the student Supervisor's evaluation of the student	Listing different learning opportunities offered to the student Providing guidelines to the student to enable him to write an evaluation report Conducting evaluation conference Ensuring satisfaction of student in the process of evaluation through frank exchange of views even on a negative evaluation

With a brief introduction by the Director and also an explanation with the help of chart, Group B divided itself into two sub-groups.

A summary of its deliberations is given as follows :

Identification of various phases in field work

After serious deliberation, the group arrived at a general consensus on the following phases :

1. Orientation phase
2. Placement phase
3. Induction phase
4. Exploration and identification phase
5. Planning and implementation phase
6. Evaluation phase

Orientation phase

This phase consisted of two stages, namely (1) The preparatory phase, and (2) The orientation phase.

The preparatory phase referred to the preparation required of the staff to give adequate orientation to students as regards social work education/course content/field work content.

The orientation included such areas as.

(a) Social work and field work content;
(b) Policies, programmes, rules and regulation of the school;
(c) Exposure to various settings through observational visits, class-room discussions and conferences; and
(d) Imparting recreational and craft skills

Placement phase

In this phase, the allotment of field work agencies for training students was determined. It was necessary to bear in mind that an individualized approach was adopted where student's interest, aptitude, motivation, capabilities and maturity were given due consideration.

Content

The content of field work in placement phase included :

(a) Correspondence on field work;
(b) Procuring and sending bio-data of students to agencies concerned;
(c) Display on the notice board details regarding their field placement and respective supervisors; and
(d) Involvement of students in the choice of agency, if possible.

Induction phase

In this phase either the faculty supervisor or any senior student who was placed in a given agency should accompany the student to introduce him to the agency and its personnel.

Content

In this phase, the content included :

(a) Study of history and administrative structure of the agency.
(b) Introduction to the staff and the clientele.
(c) Relationship of the agency to the field.
(d) Physical amenities available in the agency.

Exploration and identification phase

(a) The student was expected in this phase to explore various programmes, policies and problems of the agency.
(b) As a result of the exposure he was expected to evolve methods, plan programmes and design workable tasks that was to be carried out by him in the agency in an area of need.

Content

(a) Sharing with supervisor what was explored.
(b) Studying client responses and reactions.
(c) Finding ways to mobile resources.
(d) Identifying and selecting different learning area.
(e) Making use of given guidelines on the curricula.

Planning and implementation phase

This phase referred to the execution of plans, methods and tasks designed by the student in the previous phase.

Content

(a) Identifying goals.
(b) Evaluating suitable methods to achieve those goals.
(c) Involving the client in achieving goals.
(d) Understanding student's limitations and identifying ways

to overcome them.

(e) Testing of methods adopted by the student in achieving goals.

(f) Defiining the roles of the client, the student and the agency.

Evaluation phase

This phase referred to the assessment of the entire process of field work evolved and undertaken by the student.

Content

(a) An objective evaluation of his self and his role, and the application of social work methods.

(b) Evaluation by the supervisor of the student's performance.

(c) Evaluation by the clients wherever possible.

(d) Evaluation by the student of agency programmes, policies, personnel, services and limitations.

(e) Evaluation of the ability of the student in record-writing.

CONTENT OF FIELD WORK IN THE COMMUNITY SETTING

After discussing the various phases and contents thereof, Group B (sub-divided into two small groups) undertook the responsibility of identifying contents of different phases in a community placement and in an agency setting. The discussion focussed mainly on the supervisory input in the following phases :

(a) The orientation phase;

(b) Placement phase;

(c) Induction phase;

(d) Exploration and identification phase;

(e) Planning and implementation phase;

(f) Evaluation phase.

Illustrative material : Supervisory input in community placement

The orientation phase

This phase required the following inputs :

(a) Giving information about the community which was brief, yet adequate.
(b) Inculcating in the students required values to work with groups.
(c) Exposing students to various experiences to develop a new outlook to community work.
(d) Providing support to the student, clarifying his doubts and encouraging him to work better which was to be done on the basis of feedback derived from him.
(e) Providing the cue or stimulus.

The content of this phase would include sharing of ideas by teachers and exchange of views on various community settings.

Placement phase

This phase referred primarily to the student being placed in the community.

The supervisory input included :

(a) Exposure of students to the positive and negative aspects of earlier experience in the area by the teacher.
(b) Finding out appropriate agencies to cater to the needs of students.
(c) Trying to convince the agency leadership of its role in helping students in the development of field work process and content. (Language, familial and cultural background of the student needed to be given due consideration during placement in a community).

Induction phase

The supervisory input in this phase included :

(a) Meeting community leaders and bringing about an interaction between them and the student, so that leaders could serve as resource persons.

(b) The nature and infrastructure of the community should be explained to the student before he was given an exposure to the existing conditions of the community.

(c) Care should be taken to inform the student regarding precautions to be taken in the community and not to get entangled with factions or groups and their differences.

The content of this phase included a brief outline of the following :

(a) History of the community
(b) Types of activities carried out in previous years
(c) Structure of community, its dynamics etc.

Exploration and identification phase

The supervisory input in this phase included :

(a) Strengthening of relationship between student and the community;
(b) Understanding of social, cultural and economic structure of the community; and
(e) Establishing priorities according to the felt needs of the community, and also pay attention to needs which are not yet felt.

Planning and implementation phase

This included :

(a) Helping the student to cope with problems encountered while operating in the community;
(b) Helping the student to ascertain needs and resources of the community and the impact of other agencies—governmental and voluntary—on the community.

Evaluation phase

In this phase a review of the entire field work performance of the student and the contribution of the supervisor were to be highlighted.

(a) The supervisory input in this phase consisted of the evaluation of the performance of the student at various levels or stages;
(b) Evaluation of the guidance given in terms of student's requirements;
(c) Discussion of evaluation criteria with the student.

General comments by the group on community placement

1. The qualifying terms "structured and unstructured" should be omitted while describing an agency, and it was suggested that the placement could refer to an agency, organization or a system, all of which had structures of some kind or the other.
2. In a community who funded the programmes of field work : student, the school or the agency ; or was the student himself involved in fund raising to finance his programme was considered important.
3. Issues like dependency, and the need for continuity of work in a community were also raised. The general consensus was that continuity of work in a community was not possible and "accountability" and "continuity" should be differentiated.

Field work process in community setting

Phase	*Content*	*Supervisory Inputs*
I. Orientation	Observation, community contacts, knowledge regarding organisations within and around the community, study with reference to use and non-use of services.	1. Providing background information about the field and field work 2. Providing guideline for observation
II. Placement Induction	1. Acquaintance with different approaches to community work (task, target group and non-directive), 2. Framing objectives of work, 3. Identification of resources, 4. Meeting lea-	1. Supervisory contacts through visits and introductory letters 2. Assignment of tasks. 3. Acquainting students to different resources

	ders and significant others, 5. Preparing plan of work, 6. Preparing community history, 7. Summarising previous professional effort.	
III. Exploration/ Assessment	(1) Conducting different types of surveys, (2) Exploring client systems, (3) Collecting information on needs, resources, power structures, (4) Recording and reporting, (5) Initiation of action, (6) Formulation of need-based programmes, (7) Listening and observation.	1. Guidance at different stages 2. Encouraging positive outlook 3. Strengthening programme planning 4. Providing perspective
IV. Planning & implementation	(1) Use of agencies, leaders, significant individuals and groups as a means to achieve stipulated objectives, (2) Provision of concrete services, (3) Activising groups for action projects, (4) Evolving a structure conducive to development of skills leading to problem-solving and generation of leadership, (5) Determining priorities in terms of problem, resources and action, (6) Participation, action and reflection.	1. Acting as enabler and guide in need/resource identification 2. Providing perspective guidance 3. Holding individual and group conferences and seminars 4. Giving direction and support
V. Evaluation	1. Review of work and summary record 2. Evaluation 3. Future plan	1. Providing support in learning situations 2. Encouraging scientific approach alongwith intuition 3, Review 4. Interpretation

It would be helpful to compare the components of this pattern with the following *Note** which was discussed and

*Edited version of Mr. K. Kumar's Note submitted to and discussed by the Staff Council, Delhi School of Social Work during October, 1983.

accepted in the staff meeting of a school of social work. The note has been considerably modified by the editor. But correspondence between the approach of the workshop, and that of the school concerned is striking.

Phases	Community-based field work—A suggestive outline
Induction and identification	1. Observation record of socio-economic characteristics of the local population based on 20 home visits 2. Report on existing civic amenities, major problems and agencies with their services
Exploration action	3. Identification of problems encountered in establishing rapport and also facilitating factors 4. (i) Identification of selected situations of individual distress, collection of facts, preparation of intervention plan, delineation of own roles, action and likely change (ii) Selection of group(s) in terms of work objectives, process of group formation and development, own role, and evidence of change through planned action
Reflection and evaluation	5. Reflection on progress and constraints (coverage, use of resource, participation, learning etc.) in assuming developmental role, and corresponding change in own attitudes/perspectives and the situation itself

SELECTION OF FIELD WORK AND PLACEMENT OF STUDENTS

The resource person started the session by raising the following issues on the selection of agencies :

(1) What type of professional help did educators seek from the agencies in the areas of administration, supervision, and experimentation ? Did it vary from agency to

2. Illustrative material : Child guidance clinic

Phase	*Contents in each phase*	*Supervisory input in each phase*
Orientation Placement Induction phase	(i) Introduction to the agency structure and function, team, history of the agency, (ii) Sources of referral, for example school, court, parents. general practitioner, (iii) Relationship between agency and the source of referral, (iv) Role in relation to agency and the supervior, (v) Exposing student to the types of problems and needs of the client, (vi) Exposing students to the tools used, (vii) Discussing problematic situation and handling day to day problems.	1. Preparing agency to receive the student, (2) Accompanying the student to the agency, (3) Selection and assignment of initial tasks, (4) Gaining feed-back from the interaction, (5) Clarifying the role of student, (6) Knowing about student's previous experiences and attitudes related to the agency and client group.
Exploration and identification	1. Preparing the student for the first meeting with client/client group, (2) Meeting the client/client group, (3) Interpretation of client/group worker transaction, (4) Reactions towards the client, agency personnel and himself, (5) Identifying areas of work : (a) Helping clients' family to accept the problem, (b) Identifying, utilizing and mobilizing agency and community resources and internal resources of the worker and the client, (6) Areas of work : (a) Observation, (b) Recording, (c) Relationship at all levels—parents, school; etc., (7) Areas of learning : (a) Stages of child development, (b) Com-	1. Preparing the student through discussion, stimulation, observation, demonstration and interview, (2) Guidelines regarding various approaches in dealing with situations typical of the setting, preparing and reading clinical notes, providing theoretical frame-work in understanding the client, (3) Supervisory conferences : (a) providing theoretical framework, (b) Creating self-awareness, (c) Helping the student to fit into the team, (4) Encouraging professional growth of the student : (a) In terms of identifying himself as a team member, and (b) In terms of awareness

	munication, (c) Therapeutic skills, (d) team work, (e) Impact on the child and family being brought to the agency, (f) Working with significant others in relation to the client.	when students action is likely to cause damage to the professional process/relationship; (5) Helping the student to comprehend and analyse the problem; (6) Consultation and guidance given with regard to methods and approaches in handling cases; (7) Providing opportunity for growth-producing introspection; (8) Accrediting and encouraging positive contribution.
Planning and implementation	1. Assessment of the problem, (2) Listing priorities in treatment, (3) Decision to tackle the problem, (4) Enlisting involvement of significant persons in dealing with the problem, (5) Learning administrative skills, (6) co-ordination with different experts for effective treatment, (7) Making use of consulation outside the agency towards the welfare of the client and one's own professional development, (8) Organising community programme in order to create awareness regarding behavioural and other problems of children.	1. Providing information and helping the student to build up a directory of community resources in tackling the problem, (2) Guidance in planning and organising community programmes, (3) Introducing student to outside agencies for speedy execution of tasks, (4) Exposing the student to reality situation by encouraging initiative in the student, (5) Encouraging active partnership between the supervisor and the student in : (a) Assessing the work plan,- and (b) Modifying attitudes and approaches, (6) Assuming responsibility for student's mistakes (if any) due to circumstances beyond control.
Evaluation	I. (1) Evaluation of clinic as : field work agency, (2) Evaluation of clinic as a treatment agency, (3) Evaluation of the different client groups and individual clients, (4) Evaluation of the effective-	1. Listing different learning opportunities given to the student. 2. Provide guidelines to the student to enable him to write an evaluation report. 3. Conducting evaluation conference.

Phase	*Contents in each phase*	*Supervisory input in each phase*
	ness of different modes of treatment (comparative evaluation wherever possible), (5) Assessment of the place of clinic in the community, and (6) Evaluation of community programmes undertaken by child guidance clinic.	4. Ensuring satisfaction and confidence of the student in the process of evaluation.
	II. Evaluation of the student : (i) Growth of student as a result of his experience in the C.G.C., (ii) his own effectiveness as part of the treatment team, (iii) knowledge and skills he has learnt and developed, (iv) Ability to explore and utilize community resources, (v) recording and (vi) ability to fulfil demands of the C.G.C. set-up.	—
	III. Evaluation of the supervisor by the student :	
	(1) Evaluation of the role of supervisor in the professional growth of the student.	—
	2. Evaluation of supervisory relationship.	—
	IV. Supervisor's evaluation of the student.	—
	V. Supervisor evaluating his own role.	—

agency ?

(2) What was the type of professional responsibility of the agency ? Who was responsible for the risk involved ?

(3) What was the type and level of participation of agencies specially in providing the student access to certain confidential reports, informations and so on of the agency ?

(4) How was the 'field' selected in the absence of agency situation ? Was any open community selected ?

(5) What was the extent of a student's say in choosing an agency for himself for field work ?

(6) In the case of primary and secondary settings, were our expectations different from agency to agency ? Did such a classification have anything to do with the selection of agencies at all ?

(7) How did teachers educationally diagnose a situation or agency to test its eligibility for field work ?

These observations were followed by those of another resource person who raised the following questions in the context of selection of structured agencies as field in field work :

1. What did one look for in an agency ?
2. What were the qualities of a "good" agency ?
3. How did an agency qualify to be selected ?
4. What was the involvement of Department/School of Social Work in the selection of agencies ?
5. What was the commitment of an agency while being selected for field ?
6. How did schools tackle the problems of faulty selection of agencies ?

The need for evolving a criteria for the selection of agencies was highlighted.

Since the term agency was being used often, the participants had doubt whether it included both structured and non-structured agencies. By way of clarification the Director brought to the notice of the participants that the term 'field' be substituted for the term 'agency'. The rationale behind this was that 'field' included a much wider sphere comprising of both structured and unstructured settings.

As a result of this conceptual clarification, the discussion shifted its focuss to the definition of the term 'field' in field work. A brain-storming session followed.

Some of the participants shared with the group the existing practices in the selection of field. Such practices included selection on the basis of fields of specialization in social work like community development, and also on the basis of scope for the practice of methods of social work.

One of the participants questioned if the term "setting" or "agency setting" could be equated with the term "field". There was disagreement on this point and it was felt that selection of field would be more comprehensive than agency setting. In support of this view another participant broadly defined the field as the "whole human society".

Once again the Director intervened to draw the attention of the participants to the issue of what the properties of the field were. He was of the view that instead of being preoccupied with "agencies", the concept of field should be extended to human groups, activist groups, organised, semi-organised or informal groups, communities or any situation of 'professional concern' as was given in the definition of field work evolved by the workshop on the first day.

This intervention provoked participants to attempt a definition of the 'field' :

(i) *Definition of field*

"Field" was a situation (which could be a welfare institution, hospital, industry, open community etc.) which offered avenues for a student's interaction with clients/client systems (individual, groups, communities) where he practised social work methods under supervisory guidance towards the achievement of learning goals of professional social work.

(ii) *Properties of field*

1. An area which offered possibility of human interaction;
2. A field offered scope for the practice of methods;
3. It exposed student to a variety of client systems;

4. It was possible to develop an educational unit;
5. It might offer a sound 'model' of professional practice;
6. It offered dependable supervision as far as possible; and
7. It offered sufficient workload to a student/unit.

After listing the criteria the group examined their applicability in practice. This question was posed by one of the resource persons. His contention was that a defined set of criteria would be applicable only if a school of social work had the choice in selecting agencies or field in general. According to him, in the absence of a choice or in the case of limited choice, the applicability of the criteria was in question. In such a case should a school evolve two sets of criteria, one for the agency situation and the other for the no agency situation ?

In this connection other issues were also raised by the participants :

(1) In field work, did the student see his role only in an agency situation ? Could his role be agency-oriented ?

(2) Was the concept of agency in traditional model different from that of the developmental model ? Opinions were divided on this issue. It was said that in the traditional model the concept of agency was remedial and in the other model preventive and more comprehensive. The very relevance of agency in developmental context was questioned by some.

Yet another view was that the whole community itself could be treated as agency.

From here the focuss of discussion shifted back to the selection of agencies. One of the resource persons posed the question : If there was a choice in selection, how should the agencies be selected ? In her view, if a school saw some link between its own ideology and that of the agency, the agency could be selected. For example, if a school was committed to the cause of the poor and if it came across an agency with the same ideology which was either directly dealing with the problem of poverty or with allied problems such as health, education etc., the school could choose this agency.

Secondly, an agency could qualify to be selected if it had a positive attitude towards social work. She also pointed out that faulty selection of agencies caused frustration among students.

This view was strongly supported by all. For example, a student going to an agency with an assigned role and thereafter discovering that the role expected of him by the agency was just the opposite was sure to feel frustrated. It was also highlighted how professional social workers in some cases themselves acted as blocks to the training of students of social work.

At this point the proceeding were summarised by one of the participants who also shared the following views :

It was a fact that students had been getting both positive and negative experience in the field. In some cases the experiences had been overwhelmingly negative. Whether an experience was positive or negative, it was a source of learning. All the same, he pointed out two general criteria for selecting the field :

1. The school must work out its objectives and test if a field could provide the required content of field work.

2. It must also be tested if on the whole an agency could provide positive experience to students in terms of learning and accomplishment.

According to him, on the basis of these criteria, a school must work out a 'composite index' to find out if a field could be selected.

The following characteristics of field were noted :

Selection of field in the context of educational opportunities and opportunities for accomplishment

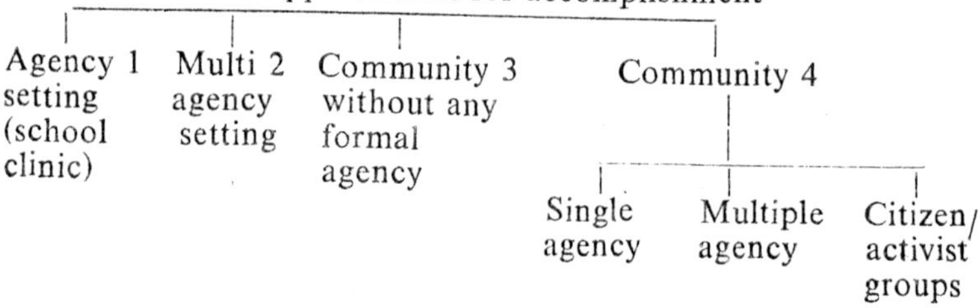

Concern was expressed on the issue of professional social workers (in the field) themselves acting as 'blocks' to the training of students of social work. One member felt that it was an area of concern and that immediate attention should be paid. The Director, while expressing equal concern on the same issue, intervened to draw the attention of the group to the origin or sources of these blocks. He attributed the same to questionable attitudes and values of staff of some of the schools, and the schools themselves from where these 'blocks' originated.

Another member brought to the notice of the group the faulty admission procedure, which often led to the entrance of 'unfit persons' into the course. He also pointed out the sad fact of double standards being practised by some leaders and educators in social work profession, and by some of the professional associations. In short, it was a question of integrity of the person.

At this point, the Director raised the question : Could anyone 'educate' a person who lacked integrity ? He also pointed out difficulties in finding a solution to this problem.

However, the group evolved consensus on the point that the educational input in the field included the interiorisation of positive attitudes and values on the part of students and the field would have to be conducive to such a process, for the 'field' moulded the attitudes of student to a large extent.

Therefore, in the selection of field for field work and placement of students, one had to assess the quality of the 'field' in terms of its capacity to provide positive experience specially in the area of inculcation of professional attitudes and values in the students. Special care had to be taken in the selection of the field where professional social workers were known to act as 'blocks'.

At this stage the workshop divided itself into two groups to consider the subject of selection of the field, and placement of students.

Group-1 sought clarification on the five issues raised in the plenary session. The members tried to share their experiences and understanding of the types of agency settings. The group discussed the following :

1. Supervisory and administrative support provided by the agency.
2. Supervision provided from the school and administrative support by the agency.
3. Supervision and administrative support, both provided by the school.
4. Experimentation, where the school took up a problem

in the community and built around it new projects where the agency structure would be flexible enough to accommodate these projects.

AGENCY SETTING

First issue

What was the extent and type of professional help sought from the field in terms of supervision, administrative support and experimentation ?

The group identified that supervision at the agency could be of two types : educational supervision and administrative supervision.

(*a*) *Administrative supervision and educational supervision*

Could be expected from the agency supervisor only, if he/she was a professionally trained person; was acquainted with current trends; and had right aptitude, calibre and professional skills.

(*b*) *Administrative support*

Could be given by the agency supervisor—trained or untrained, in terms of : (1) physical amenities, (ii) financial support, preferably when the student took up agency sponsored projects, (iii) scope for experimentation, and (iv) psychological support, warmth and understanding.

In case the agency supervisor was not a trained person, then only admininistrative supervision could be expected from the agency in terms of : (i) specifying time to be allotted, (ii) allocation of tasks, (iii) specifying accountability (i.e. to whom to report in the absence of immediate supervisor), (iv) available records and case files, (v) keeping record of the student (i.e. attendance, etc.) and (vi) involving student in administrative procedures like official correspondence, filing, agency meetings.

Second issue

How far the organisational considerations like procedures were affecting the choice of a field ?

The discussion on this issue took place on the assumption that the school had a choice of agencies. It was suggested that the organisational structure be fairly flexible in terms of policies, (ii) procedures, (iii) rules, (iv) accessibility to files, documents and budgets, and (v) programmes.

Third issue

What specific advantages and disadvantages determined the choice of agency placement as against the community placement ?

The group felt that placement both in agencies and communities had built-in advantages in terms of learning opportunities for students. However, the following advantages and disadvantages were spelt out :

Agency placement

Advantages

(i) It was a structured setting and the student felt more secure;
(ii) The student had opportunity to learn administrative and therapeutic skills in relation to agency programme;
(iii) Resistance from the clientele towards the student was less;
(iv) The student got a target in terms of what the agency wanted to achieve;
(v) The student learnt accountability and relating to the authority;
(vi) The student got timely guidance and on-the-spot supervision; and
(vii) Continuity of service.

Disadvantages

(i) The students got limited scope for work;
(ii) The students had to do more administrative and desk work and was bound by time;
(iii) Choice of clientele was limited; and
(iv) Learning experience was limited.

Community placement

Advantages :

(i) It was an open-structured setting and more scope and freedom for experimentation was possible;
(ii) The student got a variety of experience in the community setting for organising programmes, meeting people and developing communicative skills;
(iii) He got a chance to work with a variety of problems at all levels and with all age-groups; and
(iv) There was scope for learning more skills in decision-making.

Disadvantages

(i) There was insecurity felt by students when resistance from the clientele system in the community arose;
(ii) There was discontinuity in the services;
(iii) More strains and stresses were involved as the student had to fix the target himself; and
(iv) There was lack of physical amenities like place etc.

Fourth issue

How far the student's choice of a specific field and educational assessment influenced the selection of the field ?

It was felt by the group that student's choice of placement should not always guide decision as this choice would tend to be influenced by various factors. Therefore the choice of placement should be dependent upon the following :

(i) Educational objectives
(ii) Personal background and learning needs
(iii) Previous experiences
(iv) Language facility—regional or national language as one of the considerations
(v) Age
(vi) Sex
(vii) Assessment of student in relation to his health status

Fifth issue

What were the factors considered important for assessing educational needs ?

The following factors were identified :

(i) Personality traits;
(ii) Age;
(iii) Previous experience;
(iv) Socio-cultural background;
(v) Language facility; and
(vi) Level of education that is, CSW, BSW and so on.

COMMUNITY WITHOUT A FORMAL STRUCTURE

First issue

Administrative and educational supervision would be provided by the school which would otherwise have been provided by the agency.

Second issue

1. Wherever the community which had a scope for developing organised structures was generally preferred, the assumption was that the well-organised community would reduce scope for educational opportunities.
2. In a community where certain organised pressures existed which blocked the educational process of student, the student should not be placed in that setting.

For other issues, the responses of the group were the same as given earlier for the agency setting.

SELECTION OF FIELD AND PLACEMENT OF STUDENTS

Group II also discussed the following issues :

(a) Selection of field
(b) Placement of students

The following criteria for selecting the field (agency/organization/

community) were suggested :

Criteria (general)

1. The presence/absence of a trained social worker was not considered a criterion for selecting or rejecting a field.
2. Availability of administrative support.
3. Receptivity to new ideas.

Rigidity in procedures impaired field work practice, and therefore such an agency should not be selected.

Specific criteria

1. Provision of a desirable standard of service to clients and the community;
2. Receptivity to field work practice by students;
3. Programmes which lent themselves to teaching and learning of students;
4. Co-operation between the school and the agency (field);
5. Access to reports, records and other materials which were useful for field work practice of students;
6. Provision of basic facilities to students during field work; and
7. Recognition of student's work in enhancing its services.

ADVANTAGES AND DISADVANTAGES OF MULTI-AGENCY AND COMMUNITY SETTINGS

Multi-agency setting

1. *Advantages*
   (i) Definite structure for field work;
   (ii) Student exposed to the practice of methods of work; and
   (iii) Opportunity offered to understand formal procedures.

2. *Disadvantages*
   (i) Limited Scope for social work practice;

(ii) Limits to new activities on account of rules and regulations and imposition of rigid standards; and
(iii) Likely boredom and frustration.

Community

1. *Advantages*
   (i) Student's exposure to a variety of tasks;
   (ii) Scope of practice wider; and
   (iii) Leaders' and special interest groups' help likely in guiding the student.

2. *Disadvantages*
   (i) Lack of definite structure compared to agency setting; and
   (ii) Leaders, and special interest groups might misguide and create problems for students.

PLACEMENT OF STUDENTS

The group felt that the following points could be considered by the school while placing students for field work :

1. Background of students;
2. Learning needs and potentials of students;
3. Subject of interest (or specializations);
4. Agency needs and policies;
5. Distance of the agency from the school as well as the student's place of residence;
6. Agency's request for male or female student, or for specific number of students;
7. Supervisor's report on the number of students to be placed in a particular agency; and
8. Proficiency of the student in local language (pairing of students in case of language difficulty).

The group also felt that the field work infrastructure along with the needs of students might be taken into consideration while placing the students.

SUPERVISION

After going through the guidelines the workshop identified the following dimensions of supervision that could be taken up for discussion.

1. Concept;
2. Objectives;
3. Role of supervision in different areas of field work, namely, camps, observational visits, recording, concurrent and block field work;
4. Methods of supervision;
5. Problems in supervision;
6. Supervisory inputs at all phases;
7. Guidelines for effective supervision;
8. Supervision in the context of three methods of social work;
9. Elements of learning in supervision;
10. Supervision in the traditional and developmental field work; and
11. Need for supervision and orientation to new supervisors.

The resource person described supervision as an educational, administrative and a helping process. In answering a question on who was a good supervisor, the following characteristics were enumerated. He should be (1) a good teacher, (2) a good practitioner, (3) he should be good at relationship with the student so that the student's psychic energy was not dissipated.

The following two issues were raised during discussion :

(1) The validity of the previous days' work in terms of the supervisory input without having a clear idea of supervision. (It was clarified that during the first two days discussion focussed on field work with emphasis on content, selection and placement without pointedly focussing on supervision); and
(2) Field work supervision as method-oriented or field-oriented process.

The resource person in her talk highlighted the following : (1) Historical perspective of supervision; (2) Definition and objectives of supervision; (3) Need for structuring at different levels of supervision; (4) Dimensions of supervision; and (5) Methods of supervision.

This was followed by a discussion whether the supervisor should assume the role of a therapist and if so in what circumstances ? The group consensus was that barring severe pathology, other problems that impinge on learning could be tackled either by the faculty or agency supervisor. Use of authority was another area suggested for discussion.

The discussion on different aspects took place in two sub-groups.

Group A reached a consensus that deliberations should be started on the basis of problems faced by supervisors, and therefore should not straightaway start with discussion on the guidelines.

The group assumed that the students admitted to social work course were adequately responsible, honest, and carry with them the needed sense of urgency.

Problems

Background of the supervisor and the student

Members felt that the background of the supervisor and the student could have far reaching impact on the process of supervision. Therefore conscious use of information on the background of the supervisor and the student would be helpful in facilitating the process, and overcoming blocks as and when they arose.

Counselling of student by supervisor

Counselling could be undertaken by the supervisor. The problems identified in learning could be resolved either during the supervisory conference, or even outside it depending upon their nature. But major problems connected with the personality of the student might not ordinarily fall within the ambit of supervisory situation.

On-the-spot supervision

On-the-spot supervision could be done both in the agency as well as in community meetings. This consisted of supervisor himself undertaking a task and allowing students to observe and learn how the supervisor went about doing it. Such demonstration by the supervisor would facilitate participation.

The spirit behind visiting the field by the supervisor was extension of help to the student. The group strongly felt that surprise visits should be deliberately avoided because these were a reflection of an untrustworthy attitude of the supervisor towards his own self and the student.

The group made it clear that visits should normally be made with prior intimation.

Work load

Irrespective of engaging oneself in theory classes a supervisor should spend two hours a week per student for supervising. This suggestion was subject to the working pattern followed by the individual schools.

Having concluded the deliberations on the problems faced by the supervisors, the group took up the guidelines for examination.

Concept of supervision

On the basis of various elements implicit in the process of supervision, the group attempted a description of supervision as follows :

> Supervision was a two-way process between supervisor and supervisee in which the supervisor instructed, enabled, guided, supported and communicated with the student in his quest for developing professional social work skills, knowledge and attitudes.

The group then proceeded to examine the role(s) of supervisor in each of the phases in field work. It was thought that a distinction could be made between the approaches of social work education in Western society and Indian society. In Western society social work tradition focussed on ego-development whereas in India it stressed agego effacement.

The group delineated the roles of the supervisor in different phases as follows :

Orientation phase

(a) Narrating and explaining field work programme of the school to the student.
(b) Explaining the process of supervision and role and functions of the supervisor.
(c) Giving a general idea about the field of social work.
(d) Explaining general expectations from the student.

Induction phase

1. Introducing the student to the agency/field.
2. Explaining the role of the student in the client system.
3. Explaining the client system to the student.
4. Re-conditioning the student at different levels.
5. Explaining the supervisor-supervisee relationship
6. Establishing supervisor-supervisee relationship
7. Giving guidelines on work and report writing (This may be spelt out at different levels).

Implementation phase

(i) Helping the student to identify needs and resources and to evolve work assignments,
(ii) Clarifying doubts and help in problem-solving,
(iii) Sharing experiences of the supervisee,
(iv) Analysis of the feelings of the supervisee and extending support,
(v) Fostering growth and awareness in the student.

Apart from these, on-the-spot supervision, administration and developing relationship between the agency and school are the expected roles of supervisor throughout the implementation phase.

Evaluation phase

1. Formulation of a pattern of evaluation on the basis of expectation;
2. Helping the student to evaluate himself;
3. Periodic evaluation; and
4. Self evaluation by the supervisor.

The group further considered the specific educational and behavioural outcomes as regards the following three activities :

Camps

(a) Exposing student to the community;
(b) Evaluating student to adjust to new environment and difficult situations;
(c) Providing experience in group living;
(d) Developing skills in planning, organising, implementing and evaluating programmes; and
(e) Developing leadership abilities.

Field work

(a) Exposing the student to real life situations; and
(b) Developing knowledge, skills and attitudes.

Evaluation

(i) To assess one's own growth,
(ii) To assess one's own learning,
(iii) To develop in the student capacity for self-evaluation,
(iv) To help locate the strengths and weaknesses in oneself which can be termed as '*Purified Subjectivity*'.

The second main point in the guidelines, namely *objective of supervision*, was discussed by the group and following points emerged :

General objectives

General objectives could be considered as enabling the development of knowledge, skills and attitudes and fostering self-awareness and growth.

Specific objectives

1. To liaise between the agency and the school;
2. To assess whether the agency fulfilled the educational requirements;
3. To facilitate the student to make use of resources; and
4. To help the student to assess his strengths and weaknesses in a proper perspective.

As far as the third point 'areas of supervision' was concerned the group came to the conclusion that core skills themselves constituted an area of supervision. These were : observation, interviewing, relationship, recording, administrative procedures, training, fact-finding, planning, implementation, analysis and organization. Supervision was instrumental in developing these core skills in students.

Identification of needs and resources, intervention, working as pressure groups, listening and communication, programme development, resource mobilization and administrative procedures were the specific skills that could be developed through supervision.

Supervision was also instrumental in developing professional attitude. This could be achieved in the following manner :

1. Supervisor himself setting an example.
2. Appreciating and encouraging desirable attitude in the student.
3. Enabling the student to express his feelings.
4. Analysing an activity which expressed the attitude.

(When the issue of field instruction was taken up for discussion, the concept and implications were not clear to the group. For sometime the group was at a loss to proceed. There was an actual blockade in group thinking. As a reaction to this one of the group members vehemently insisted that the given guideline should be preserved as a 'specimen' guideline which hampered group thinking!)

The group then identified the following methods of supervision :

1. Individual conferences;
2. Group conferences;
3. Seminars; and
4. On-the-spot instruction.

The objectives of individual conferences identified by the group were :

1. Paying individual attention.
2. Strengthening relationship between the supervisor and supervisee and generating confidence in the latter.
3. Optimum opportunity to bring home the weak point, if any, of the student.
4. Change of student's attitude through the identification of feeling component.

The group suggested that the individual conferences should be conducted on the basis of :

(i) Adequate preparation of the supervisor,
(ii) Use of records,
(iii) Need for improvement of records, and
(iv) Action plan.

The objectives of group conferences identified by the group were :

1. Helping the student learn from one another,
2. Mutual support,
3. Developing confidence thiough group dynamics, and
4. Encouraging peer group learning.

Methods to achieve these were identified as :

1. Encouraging common issues to be discussed in the group, and
2. Encouraging students to ventilate problems connected with field work.

On the point of observation of students at work, the group was of the opinion that it could be made effective through :

1. Participant observation, and
2. Sharing the experiences, opinions and feelings.

The group accepted that role-modelling and demonstrations were also effective methods of supervision.

Field work seminars were accepted as effective tools of

supervision. The following objectives of field work seminars were identified :

1. To bring out case studies and generate literature;
2. To make participants familiar with the techniques of conducting democratic group discussions;
3. To present cases and learn to play different roles; and
4. To establish and strengthen relation with agencies where agency supervisors were invited to participate.

Supervision was also effective in developing teaching materials. These materials could be brought out in the form of :

1. Case records;
2. Case study of supervisory process from the angle of supervisor and supervisee;
3. Research reports;
4. Dissertation of students in field work areas like orientation and placement;
5. Edited records of students; and
6. Studies undertaken by the supervisor.

With regard to the use of authority by the supervisor the group ruled out the *exercise of any* authority which generated fear among students. But positive authority in the form of guidance, guidelines and intervention could be used with consideration because indiscreet use of authority hindered growth of learning.

Supervision in the context of three methods of social work was considered by the group in relation to traditional and developmental approaches to field work. In the light of increasing emphasis, of late, on developmental approach to field work the group appreciated the limitations of method-oriented supervision. On the other hand the group felt the need for emphasis on an integrated method. The main argument put forward was that since the field was indivisible, supervision should be holistic.

Group B, discussed the topic as under :

Concept of supervision

The group defined supervision as an educational, administrative and helping process which was concerned with enabling, teaching and guiding a supervisee to develop professional skills, knowledge and attitude based on the objectives of an educational programme and the needs of the supervisee.

More specifically, supervision, as an integral and essential part of social work education, was an educational process which involved more dynamic, intense and individualized educator--learner interaction and relationship, in which the educator, judiciously and creatively assumed teaching, helping and administrative roles to provide direction to learning, to promote professional growth, and to facilitate self-dependence in the learner.

Role of supervisor in relation to field

The following issues were taken up for discussion :

Implication of placing students in an agency year after year

The group felt that in cases where the supervisor-field relationship were strained change of field setting might be desirable.

Field level intervention

The supervisor should intervene in the field when it was not conducive to professional growth. In that case the supervisor should act as change agent. The school should also support the supervisor's intervention.

Objectives of supervision

These were worked out as follows :

1. To provide opportunity for learning;
2. To meet learning needs;
3. To organize and accelerate the process of learning; and
4. To facilitate the achievement of learning goals.

Areas of supervision

Apart from class room instruction the supervisor assumed responsibility to help the student in different types of recording.

Role of supervisor in individual conference

(a) The supervisor should not exercise his authority over the supervisee as far as possible;

(b) The supervisor should not use derogatory comments on the students' field work records, nor should he make demaging personal remarks;

(c) The comments of the supervisor should encourage students:

(d) The comments of the supervisor should reveal weaknesses as well as strengths of students;

(e) A student having serious difficulties with the supervisor should be provided an opportunity to convey his feelings to the appropriate authority wherever necessary;

(f) Different ways should be adopted to deal with different types of students. The supervisor should endeavour to relieve the anxiety of students;

(g) The supervisor should develop right attitudes in the student through controlled emotional involvement on his part as against negative feeling; and

(h) In case, the field/setting required a copy of the supervisee's record, the supervisor should take proper decision in that regard so that the supervisee was not harmed by it.

Group conference

The group agreed that group conference provided opportunity for the exchange of ideas, sharing of experiences, peer group learning, and that it supplemented individual conferences.

Indifferent supervision at agency level

The following suggestions were offered in this connection :

(i) Agency supervisor should be invited to the school to discuss the issue,

(ii) Seminars should be held on agency supervision, and

(iii) Contact and good liaison with agency should be established.

Different types of supervisees

The group worked out the following categories of learners :

Category I

(i) Intellectual learner,
(ii) Intuitive learner,
(iii) Experimental learner.

Category II

(i) Little Jack Horner,
(ii) Awkward learner,
(iii) Arrogant learner,
(iv) Argumentative learner,
(v) Pure intellectual.

Based on the learner characteristics, the supervisor should help students through various learning phases as follows :

(i) The supervisor should not take resort to surprise checks,
(ii) The supervisor should give consideration to students who were unable to record properly the work done in the field, and
(iii) The supervisor should not project himself as the only model.

Relationship between the supervisor and supervisee

The group identified the following four positive elements in this relationship :

(i) Demand for spending more time in conference
(ii) Meeting outside the provision of conference schedule
(iii) Emotional clinging in the learner
(iv) Attention-seeking learner

The group also identified the following negative elements in the relationship :

(i) Non-submission of records in time,
(ii) Resentment,
(iii) Hostility,
(iv) Attacking personally,
(v) Avoiding conference.

The need for proper management of positive and negative elements was stressed by the group.

The role of supervision in three phases

(i) *Initial phase* : Enabler, facilitater, guide, supporter and protector ;
(ii) *Middle phase* : Partner, sustainer, supporter, and so on ;
(iii) *Terminal phase* : Enabler, Catalyst, and Critic.
(iv) *Common role in all phases* :

(a) Spokesman,
(b) Advocate,
(c) Educator,
(d) Buffer,
(e) Shock absorber,
(f) Insulator/clutch accelerator,
(g) demonstrator,
(h) analyst, and
(i) motivator.

Role of supervisor in developmental field work

(i) Supervisor should possess knowledge of developmental field work and should know the rationale for introducing this approach,
(ii) He should introduce developmental approach even in the traditional field,
(iii) The supervisor should give opportunity to students in the use of indigenous material, creative literature and in conducting research relevant for field work.

General comments

In the plenary session, the following observations were made on the report given above:

1. The definition of supervision should include the element

of personal development of student.

2. Categories of learners were arbitrary in that a student might be arrogant in one situation but pure intellectual in another.

EVALUATION

The Director of workshop suggested the following issues for discussion :

1. Meaning of the term.
2. Rationale and method of evaluation.
3. Existing and proposed pattern of evaluation with its advantages and disadvantages.
4. Most effective method of evaluation.
5. Evolving standard proforma for evaluation.

A participant suggested that there should be method-wise and field-wise discussion on evaluation. Another stressed the need for standardization of evaluation methods in social work with other professions. After discussion, the workshop decided to discuss the following area in three sub-groups :

1. Method-wise evaluation.
2. Field-wise evaluation.
3. Global evaluation.

After general discussion on evaluation in the plenary session the group was divided into three sub-groups. Each sub-group was assigned different aspects of evaluation.

The Chairperson of sub-group A initiated discussion on the concept of evaluation. Since it was difficult to define evaluation in such a short period, effort was directed to clarify the concept.

The views offered by the participants were as follows :

(i) One member suggested that focus of evaluation should be on the effort, and achievement of the student. Achievement meant learning through efforts.

(ii) The other member was of the view that evaluation

should be made in terms of opportunities offered to the student.

(iii) It was suggested that evaluation should include such qualities as honesty and commitment.

The group described evaluation as a continuous process to help the student realise his own assets and liabilities. It was noted that :

(a) Evaluation had a growth perspective.

(b) Evaluation was the process of rating and grading student's performance.

(c) Evaluation was the total assessment of a student.

(d) Evaluation might be qualitative, quantitative, or both.

Evaluation implied rating or finding the value of student's efforts and achievement. This was done on the basis of mastery of skills, and professional growth through field learning.

Evaluation was a process to help the student realise his abilities and promote them, and also realize his limitations and to overcome them.

After discussion on the concept of evaluation the group started with the second aspect of evaluation : Why should one evaluate ?

Deliberations brought forth the following points :

(a) To know the achievement, skills and accomplishment of the student,
(b) To review work performance,
(c) To neutralise the growth arresting elements,
(d) To understand the extent to which there was development of knowledge and skill,
(e) To assess use of skills,
(f) To promote self-actualization,
(g) To foster professional growth, and to accelerate it.

The evaluation was viewed as a process designed for fostering, assessing, and accelerating professional growth; developing helping process; promoting self-actualization; assessing achievement of skills; work performance and also neutralizing growth-arresting elements.

The group then took up the third issue for discussion that is content of evaluation. The group tried to identify phases and the content of each phase of evaluation.

But there was controversy among the participants regarding the order of these phases. The group after discussion agreed upon the following order :

1. Knowledge and understanding of the field,
2. Interaction with the field,
3. Identification of specific area, needs and/or resources,
4. Planning, involvement and intervention—helping process
5. Supervisory inputs and its use,
6. Relationship of theory and practice,
7. Recording,
8. Professional development.

The content of each phase was described as under :

Knowledge and understanding of the field

Nature, purpose, function, services, recipients of services, resources, problems, limitations, socio-economic and occupational—characteristics of groups, power structure, leadership pattern, etc.

Interaction with the field

Reaction to field, agency and policy, acceptance of or adjustment with the field, understanding the potentials and drawbacks of the field, general information regarding the programme, knowledge of the field and resources, development of relationship, assessment of needs of the field.

Identification of specific area/needs/resources

Exploration of problem area and resources, identifying the core area, cause and effect relationship, analysis of situation, eliminating the peripheral areas, increasing objectivity, change of values, determining strategies, etc.

Planning, involvement and intervention

1. Development of interventional skill : (a) Interpersonal relational skill, (b) communicational skill, (c) situational analysis and

interpretation, (d) organisational skill, (e) planning skill, (f) programme development skill, (g) fund-raising, (h) training skill; (2) catalyst role; (3) adaptability; and (4) participation.

Supervisory inputs and its use

Preparation for supervisory conference, acceptance of new ideas given by the supervisor, acceptance of supervision itself, formation of professional relationship with the supervisor, response to appraisal, follow-up of decisions taken in the supervisory conference, participation in conference.

Relationship of theory and practice

Internalization of knowledge, assimilation and application of principles, methods, skills, and values of social work in practice.

Recording

Type, content, flexibility, sequence, organisation and presentation of material. (Recording includes factual data, feeling responses, assessment and action, and use of different forms of recording.)

Professional development

Inculcation of professional values, disciplined and conscious use of self, sense of responsibility, development of insight, increasing self-awareness, growing, self-independence, integrity, competence and objective self-evaluation.

The chairperson drew the attention of the group towards weightage which should be given at each phase. The group agreed to give weightage in terms of marks keeping in view 100 as maximum for field work. One participant suggested that there should be some minimum standard for pass in field work while proposing any model for evaluation. Another emphasised that minimum standard for qualifying in field work should be decided by the respective department/school of social work. But it was thought necessary to fix some minimum standard in the proposed model. So effort of the group was directed towards giving weightage to each phase of evaluation. The consensus in the group was that all the phases were equally important. One participant suggested that there should be equal weightage to each phase but it was ruled out by the group because the weightage was conditioned by the degree of professional development that was expected of a student. The weightage thus would vary from phase to phase and level to level.

The group worked out a criteria for evaluation separately for each level. The proposed model took care of all the phases of field work which the student had to undergo. It was more rational in terms of understanding the student and his field work in its totality. It also encompassed both field and method and gave an over-all view of field work activity. It was more in tune with the approach of field in field work which was the theme of the workshop.

During the course of discussion one participant suggested that each student should be provided with a copy of evaluation proforma for his self-evaluation. While framing the "evaluation format", the group thought that there should be two types of minimum standards in order to declare a student qualified in field work. There should be 40 per cent as minimum for each phase, and 50 per cent as aggregate. But one participant raised objection that there should be only one minimum standard for qualifying in field work and the group agreed upon it.

The following evaluation format was designed by the group :

The group was of the view that where only the supervisor was the evaluator there was a possibility of bias affecting evaluation. Hence it was recommended that there should be some moderation. The suggested model for the constitution of moderation committee was as under :

(i) Two external examiners
(ii) Head of the department
(iii) Field work co-ordinator
(iv) Concerned supervisor

This model was recommended because consultative supervision at the faculty level was often a failure. It was mentioned that complaints of students in relation to evaluation, if any, might also be referred to this committee. The following evaluation sheet was prepared by the group.

Evaluation format*

Criteria	CSW Part I	Level Part II	BSW Part I	Level Part II	Part III	MSW Part I	Level Part II
Knowledge and understanding of the field	20	15	20	10	10	15	10
Interaction with the field	10	10	10	10	10	10	10
Identification of specific area, needs, resources	10	10	10	10	10	10	10
Planning, involvement and intervention	10	15	10	15	15	15	15
Supervisory inputs and its use	15	15	15	15	15	15	15
Relationship of theory and practice	10	10	10	15	15	15	15
Recording	15	10	15	10	10	10	10
Professional development	10	15	10	15	15	10	15

*Also see evaluation sheet.

EVALUATION SHEET

Name of the student.............................. Year of study . ...
Name of the agency...............................
Duration of placement.......................... From.............. To ....
Agency supervisor ....
Designation.......................................
Faculty supervisor........... ....
Designation... ....
Content of field work... ....

Phases of evaluation	Marks out of	Minimum marks	Marks obtained	Total
1. Knowledge and understanding of the field				
2. Interaction with the field				
3. Identification of specific areas, need/resources.				
4. Planning, involvment and intervention.				
5. Supervisory inputs and its use				
6. Relationship of theory and practice.				
7. Recording				
8. Professional development				

Remarks of agency supervisor
Remarks of faculty supervisor

Signature
Agency supervisor

Signature
Faculty supervisor

Group II discussed evaluation with special reference to the field as follows :

1. Evaluation ? What ?

After considerable discussion, the group reached a consensus on the following definition of evaluation :

> Evaluation is a continuous process by which the professional growth of the student is critically appraised and ascertained within the broad perspectives of social work.

2. Why ?

The following objectives of evaluation were identified by the group :

(i) To assess student's knowledge and understanding of the field,

(ii) To assess the ability of the student to integrate theory and practice,

(iii) To assess the ability of the student to apply specific methods of social work,

(iv) To assess the ability of the student to write records,

(v) To assess the supervisory inputs and contribution,

(vi) To assess the student's ability to plan and act, and

(vii) To assess personal and professional growth.

3. Existing mode of evaluation—advantages and disadvantages :

Guidelines

Generally at the time of placement each student was given a set of guidelines on field work. At the end of each term/semester, the supervisor assessed the student whether he had made use of the guidelines and acquired necessary knowledge and skills.

The supervisor also assessed the student as regards his skill such as writing records, ability to make use of available resources and so on.

Evaluation forms

In some schools evaluation forms were sent to respective field work agencies where the agency supervisors were required to see the evaluation of students' performance in their respective agencies in addition to the evaluation done by the faculty supervisors. In this practice equal weightage was given to both the evaluation done by the agency and the faculty. In some schools the evaluation of the agency supervisor was not considered important and therefore no evaluation proforma was sent to the agency for assessment. Instead, based on the criteria provided by the school the student prepared his own evaluation report and the supervisor evaluated the student based on this.

Advantages

The group saw the following advantages in the existing mode of evaluation :

1. It helped both the student and the supervisor in evaluating rather objectively the performance of the student.
2. It facilitated the supervisor to assess the student periodically particularly with the help of guidelines.
3. It assisted the supervisor to quantify the quality of work performed by the student.
4. It helped the supervisor make the student aware of his achievements, and limitations during the course of field work.
5. It highlighted the limitations of the agency, and inadequacy of knowledge acquired by the student.

Disadvantages

1. In some schools the students were asked to write an evaluation of their performance based on a set of criteria given to them at the end of the term. The faculty supervisor or agency supervisor evaluated the student on the basis of final evaluation given by the student which had certain weaknesses. Those students who were able to present the final evaluation report concisely and clearly happened to score high marks/grades at the expense of hard-working and sincere students who were less articulate.
2. Exclusion of agency supervisors from the evaluation process was another aspect which affected evaluation.
3. In some schools a practice* obtained that an external examiner who was not aware of the students' performance in the field allotted marks/grades based only on the field work records.
4. The guidelines given to the students at the time of placement were often, if not always, rigid. The rigidity hampered the freedom of student to be creative in carrying out assignments for himself. Moreover, the guidelines restricted the supervisor too, from being considerate and sympathetic towards students when he

* Award of marks in field work on the basis of average worked out from marks given independently by the supervisor and the external examiner is a practice in one school which was evolved after deliberations between the staff and the students' union when the students were on strike a decade ago.

experienced difficulties in the agency.

5. The evaluation forms used for the purpose of evaluation of the student at the end of the term/semester provided scope for a great deal of subjectivity.

Model proforma of evaluation (with reference to field)

In the light of above discussion, the group decided to evolve a model proforma of evaluation specifically with reference to two fields namely, Personnel Management, Industrial Relations and Labour Welfare, and Medical and Psychiatric Social Work. For this purpose the group was guided by the objectives of evaluation evolved in the process of discussion. Initially the group focussed its attention on the first objective, namely, "to assess the knowledge and understanding of the field". When the group was discussing various elements that needed to be highlighted in order to evolve, as fas as possible, a sound criteria of evaluation for different fields, it found itself meeting at the same point more than once from different angles and for different fields. Because of this experience the group decided to evolve a proforma of evaluation which would be applicable to all fields. The proforma was developed as follows :

To assess the knowledge and understanding of the field

(a) Student's ability to understand the history and administrative structure of the agency/factory.

(b) Student's ability to understand the different functions of the agency.

(c) Student's ability to understand the policies and programmes of the agency/factory.

To assess the ability of the student to integrate theory and practice

(a) Use of the guidelines.

(b) Interiorisation of theory.

(c) Use of guidance.

To assess the ability of the student to make use of specific methods

(a) Use of methods of social work.

(Note : It was observed by the group that the use of case work, group work and community organisation was rather remote in the industrial setting and therefore the supervisor had to take into consideration the scope of methods of social work being used. A student of medical and psychiatric social work or community development however might be able to use methods in the field situation. In this case therefore this part of the proforma would play a major role in the process of evaluation of field work performance of the student.

(b) Manner of application of methods.
(c) Use of principles of social work.

To assess the ability of the student to write records

(a) Ability of the student to write clear and concise reports.
(b) Ability of the student to record emotional involvement, feelings and non-verbal behaviour of the client.
(c) Regularity and punctuality in submitting reports.
(d) Ability to express his feelings, attitudes and so on.

To assess the supervisory inputs and contributions

(a) Student's attitude to and acceptance of field work and supervisory instructions.
(b) Student's preparation for conferences.
(c) Acceptance of suggestions and criticisms objectively.
(d) Use of supervisory guidance.

To assess the student's ability to plan and act

(a) Ability of the student to identify and to articulate problems emerging out of the work situation.
(b) Ability of the student to make intelligent choice of methods in dealing with specific problems.
(c) Ability of the student to develop programmes according to the needs of the agency.
(d) Ability of the student to work as member of the professional team and in collaboration with the staff of the agency.
(e) Ability of the student to work within the limitations of the agency.
(f) Ability of the student to adjust to the rules and regulations of the agency.

To assess personal and professional growth

(a) Skill in assessing the problems, needs and limitations of the agency.

(b) Skill in assessing his own performance, prejudices, and biases.

(c) Skill in establishing and maintaining professional relationship with client, staff of the agency, and community.

(d) Skill in identifying and mobilising resources for the purpose of learning.

(e) To assess the skill and the capacity developed by the student in shouldering professional responsibility.

(f) To assess the student's development of confidence, initiative. motivation, and other personal qualities.

Evaluation according to methods of social work

The group listed the following issues pertaining to evaluation :

1. The question of doing full justice to the student while evaluating him was upper most even in those areas where one was not present always and one had to depend on records (self-reporting).

2. Should evaluation involve supervisor and supervisee ? Or should other staff of the college, external examiner, community and client be included ?

3. Did one evaluate the learning process or task achievement keeping in mind the background of students ?

4. Evaluating the effort made by student and factors that influenced this (for example persons with a disadvantaged background) might put in more efforts and show less results.

5. How often should evaluation be done ?

6. When and how should supervisor's evaluation be communicated to student ?

7. How objectives were the present methods of evaluation ? Could they be made more objective ?

8. When should criteria of evaluation be communicated to the student ?

9. How did one evaluate those students whose agency and supervisors were changed ?

Field work evaluation

Field work evaluation was a continuous and realistic assessment of a student in terms of his efforts, abilities, work done, learning, use of guidance, and personal-professional growth (or the lack of these) in a particular situation of the field. This was periodically conveyed to the student, with an educational objective, and which ultimately was instrumental in the award of marks or grades for his overall performance in field work.

The group attempted the following questions :

What is evaluation ?

Field work evaluation was a periodic assessment of a student which ultimately led to the award of marks or grades or making a formal statement on his performance.

Elements listed in evaluation were

1. Formal statement of marks/grades communicated to the department.
2. Assessment of work done.
3. Assessment of personal growth and learning within a stipulated period specified by the school for assessment.

Why evaluation ?

(a) To review student's educational and personal growth,

(b) To award marks or grades or make a formal statement as required by the school.

One member felt that evaluation could also be used for the moderation of biases.

Later the group prepared a format for evaluation on the basis of the methods of social work, particularly social casework as an illustration for other methods.

Format for evaluation on the basis of methods (social casework)

Criteria	*Weightage*
1. *Adaptation* to the agency/field	2 points
2. *Understanding* critical understanding of the	

agency/field, policy/programmes/procedure 2 points

3. *Exploration and study* of needs, problems, locating a person who needs help 3 points
4. *Relationship* establishing and sustaining relationship. Communication skills, in interviewing, collatoral contacts 5 points
5. *Assessment* of personality, personal history, analysis of the dynamics of family and environment in relation to the problem, person's own effort to deal with his problem, resources available to the person, client's motivation, capacities, opportunities and prognosis 5 points
6. *Formulation of goals* involving the individual in the formulation of goals, enhancing the capacity of individual to deal with the problem involving significant others 5 points
7. *Planning and implementation* of goals, plan of action, assessing potentialities, assessing the role of worker and agency, planning the sequence of action, planning the use of resource, use of appropriate method 4 points
8. *Evaluation* Assessment of case, planning process, worker's skills in inter-personal relationship. Worker's skill in using external or community resources, and others on the implementation process 5 points
9. *Recording* Relevance, type (process record, summary record, description) and understanding of the client from record, analytical interpretation, analyses of client-worker interaction, interview as a tool for relationship 4 points
10. *Responsibility* Punctuality and regularity 2 points
11. *Consistency, motivation, commitment* 4 points
12. Inculcation of professional attitudes—non-judgemental attitude, client as unique person, client's ability to change, inherent dignity and worth of individual, attitude towards self 4 points
13. *Conscious and disciplined use of self* awareness of self in terms of feeling, attitudes, capacity,

sympathy, warmth, sensitivity and perceptivity, also awareness of strengths and weakness — 5 points

14. Supervision — 4 points

	Supervisory input	Use of supervision by the supervisee
1.	Helping student overcome anxiety in relation to supervision	Acceptance of supervisor and supervision
2.	Preparation for supervisory conference. Reading of records	Preparation for supervisory conference
3.	Encouraging student to express feelings and opinions	Participation in supervisory conference
4.	Study of field work situation, giving suggestions and offering criticisms	Use of suggestions and criticisms
5.	Availability and regularity	Using self (supervisor's) as a resource
6.	Individualized plan for student's work	

REVIEW SESSION

Review session was intended to discuss such problems which were not raised in earlier sessions, or which needed more discussion. These are presented below :

Administration and organisation in terms of work load of teachers in field work

The group felt that it was very difficult to fix criteria regarding the work load of field work since it varied from University to University. In one school, teachers did not act as field work supervisors at all. It was pointed out that in those schools where there were separate field work supervisors, the teacher should consider taking voluntarily the responsibility of field work considering its importance as a core programme of professional education.

Duration of field work

Number of days of field work per week (and the number of hours) was the other question discussed by the group. The following suggestions were made : (1) One member suggested that field work should be scheduled for two days a week for the first year and three days a week for the second year students. He supported this idea by emphasizing the need for more skill development in the second year. (2) Another member suggested that two days' continuous field work would be desirable in community development setting. Finally, majority of group members felt that two days' field work in both the years would be reasonable, with a minimum input of 15 hours per week (or 50 days per year). The student however should not be allowed to show more than two hours per week for report writing. Group also felt that it was not desirable to fix field work timing and it should be flexible according to the situation. This arrangement would be more appropriate since the workshop was giving almost equal weightage to the number of hours that is, 16 hours for theory and 15 hours for field work in terms of time.

Minimum desirable number of field work conferences required

One member suggested that 24 conferences per year would be desirable whereas another member reacted that there was no need for fixing a minimum or a maximum, for the teacher was expected to be in close contact with the student. One member suggested that one conference per week would be desirable since there were 30 to 32 weeks in an academic year. But another member disagreed with this suggestion and held the view that it was very difficult to arrange field work conference per week because there were 40 to 50 students under one supervisor. This applied to such schools which offered under-graduate programme. Reacting to this, a member explained that individual conference could be taken even at the agency. If the agency did not provide any facility, this kind of conference could be taken even under the tree. Another suggestion was that the group conference could take place once in a fortnight. Besides this, the teacher should be available when the students needed assistance. The general consensus however was that a minimum number of field work conference was desirable and the same should be fixed by the school concerned.

Field work as a non-credit programme

The group felt that this kind of arrangement would reduce the importance of field work and might create other problems in the Indian situation. The field work therefore should be graded. The group however observed that giving more weightage to field work might lead to corrupt practices like over-marking for casual or sub-standard work.

RECORDING

The group deliberated in the plenary session on the content and types of records in field work. A good deal of time was devoted to examine the kind of records needed to be maintained by a student of social work in field work, irrespective of the fact whether one followed the traditional or developmental model. It was emphasised that records should be dynamic in nature, and should contain relevant factual information. Further it was felt that records should project a graphic presentation of events and incidents that took place during the process of intervention.

The group felt that good record should incorporate, among other things, rational thinking, and should indicate student's growth. Further, such records should be useful in supervision and research. It was recognised that a record was an effective tool in learning administration and evaluation. While discussing the nature of records it was visualised that a time had come when schools should deviate from a set pattern of report and incorporate information on process of structural change. The need for such record both by the student and teachers was recognized. The question of time for recording was also taken up. It was suggested that records should also include role analysis and evaluation at different stages of field work at the B.S.W. and M.S.W. levels. The group felt that plenary session could be divided into four groups: (i) Casework, (ii) Group work, (iii) Community organisation, and (iv) the fourth group could take up integrated approach. The format of records was also taken up briefly for discussion and it was decided that the sub-groups might discuss recording keeping in view the following points:

1. Purpose, objective and importance of recording;
2. Content of recording;
3. Various types of recording;
4. Expectations in recording;
5. Difficulties in recording;
6. Format;
7. Time allotted for recording; and
8. Supervisory input.

The reports were presented by the rapporteurs concerned which contained format/guidelines for recording at two levels that is, BSW and MSW A member of the group felt that the distinction made between BSW and MSW was only a patch-work without any details. So it was decided that a special group would be constituted with teachers who were teaching at the BSW level to work out the detail. More questions were raised by members on recording in the integrated method of social work, that is 'when to teach' and 'how to teach it'. It was pointed out that no hard and fast rules could be prescribed for this purpose.

While the workshop was to be divided earlier into four groups, it so happened that it could divide itself only into two sub-groups: One on community organisation and the other on Integrated Methods. On the intervention of the chairperson of the plenary session, and also others, some members from both these groups were drawn into the formation of a third 'offshoot' group, which was to work on casework and group work recording.

Recording in casework and group work

Regarding the purpose, objectives and importance of recording, there was general agreement in the plenary session. The group recognized that;

1. Recording was a tool of learning
2. It provided an opportunity to student to organize and present information, observation, reflection and action in a systematic manner.
3. It was useful for reflection on one's own role.
4. It was useful for administrative purpose and research.
5. It was a tool for supervision and evaluation.

The group outlined the following contents of recording :

(i) Factual information,
(ii) Purpose of intervention,
(iii) Contract,
(iv) The process of establishing and sustaining relationships and analysis of the interactional dynamics including the identification and interpretation of verbal and non-verbal communication,
(v) Assessment of intra-personal, inter-personal and situational dynamics,
(vi) Process of need determination,
(vii) Planning for future intervention,
(viii) Understanding of the field situation and worker's own situational limitations,
(ix) The worker's own role in intervention. His initiative, efforts made ; use of self as a resource and use of other resources,
(x) Understanding and use of knowledge base, principles and techniques,
(xi) Supervisory inputs.

The following formats were evolved by the group for casework and group work recording.

FORMAT FOR CASEWORK RECORDING

The student would be expected to write social histories wherever needed or required. Apart from that the student would also be expected to write records in the following format :

A. Brief introduction with basic identifying data and purpose of work.

B. Interaction with field person/situation—details of interactional dynamics (action-reaction in terms of verbal and non-verbal communication and so on)

C. Assessment :

—of the need

—of why the need had arisen :

(a) personal factors

(b) inter-personal factors

(c) situational environmental factors

—of strengths and weaknesses; of motivation, capacity and opportunity

—of earlier efforts made by the person

—of resources : (i) of the person himself (ii) other human, material and situational resources :

—expectations of the person from and reaction to the worker/intervention

—reflection upon the situation with a developmental perspective

D. Plan :

—future strategy of intervention comments about prognosis

E. Self-evaluation :

—students' role; rationale for action; analysis of his feelings and attitudes ; his learning

FORMAT FOR GROUP WORK RECORDING

A. Introduction with the purpose of group formation, the process of group formation and basic identifying data of each individual.

B. The interaction—the extent or level of participation, quality of participation; sub-groups; isolates, dyads, triads, cliques and so on; leadership pattern; decision-making in the group; levels of acceptance of individuals by other members; shyness; domination, potential leadership in members etc.

C. Assessment —Observations on the needs and capacities of individuals; motivation(s) for joining the group; individual's and group's perception of the worker; conflict-resolution; group cohesiveness and effectiveness.

D. Plan of action —Programme planning/development with reasons

E. Self-evaluation —The worker's role and approach vis-a-vis the group; vis-a-vis individuals within and outside the group situation; his learning etc.

The group felt that in any form of record, the supervisory inputs, that is, how in the student's perception the supervisor aided him, must be periodically conveyed.

While working on the format of casework record, point under 9 was initially entitied "interview". However, it was pointed out that this was a very narrow view of casework situation and also that it reflected conditioning by the past. Working with individuals did not only mean one-to-one situations, and also, all one-to-one situations in the process of work were not 'interviews'. Hence it was collectively agreed upon to replace the phrase "interview" by 'situation' or 'meeting' or even 'interaction with the field'.

The group preferred to use the word 'assessment' to 'diagnosis', as it was felt that the latter reflected a pre-occupation with the 'medical model'. Further, the term 'assessment' was more appropriate in the context of analysis and evaluation of interactions and transactions.

While discussing the format of group work record, the term 'programme planning' was rejected in favour of 'plan of action' because the latter subsumed the former and meant even more in terms of future strategies and approaches.

Types of records identified by the group were similar to those made at plenary session : Narrative records, process records, role records, summary records, administrative records, and abstracts. It was pointed out that summaries could preferably be 'topical summaries' on the basis of a prepared format.

Also, there was discussion on the point whether student's observations, analytical comments and comments about his own role and approach could be interwoven with the description of interaction with the field. It was felt that they needed separate mention under 'assessment' and 'self-evaluation' for more systematic presentation and also to enable the student to reflect upon and understand these aspects more specifically.

It was also felt that the narrative, process and role records could be seen as a continuum with increasing amount of 'purity' or 'selectivity' in recording as the student moved from narrative to role recording.

While discussing expectations in recording at different levels of social work education, it was felt that at the early BSW level, narrative, journalistic records should be expected from the student and that he should take up only such cases where problems were of a rather simple nature with sources largely in the environmental. The student should, by the end of second year, be able to assess simple cause and effect relationship and observe the feelings and emotions of the person concerned. By the end of third year of BSW, analytical and interpretative element should increase and the student must develop some capacity for self-evaluation. The records then should reflect a certain amount of conscious use of self. The possibility of some outstanding students giving evidence of a perspective in their records was not ruled out. At the post-graduate level, a more rapid movement towards clarity in recording would be needed. The student must be given experience in writing various types of records.

While discussing recording at the BSW level, a member pointed out that in some places, the BSW students were asked to write only 'case studies' without taking up any intervention. One member felt that the intervention component must be included.

A member suggested that in spite of a variety of practical

difficulties, placing the BSW-I students with good MSW-II students for a few hours in a week on an experimental basis could be tried, so that even though he did not take direct part in intervention, she gathered factual information and also learnt about it by observation.

The group also noted some difficulties in recording :

(a) Language deficit
(b) Emotional blocks
(c) Inability to put feelings and reasons for one's own action into words
(d) Lack of experience/exercise
(e) Time-constraint

It was felt that although a number of students faced difficulty in recording due to various reasons, yet, the importance of recording as a tool of evaluation should not be minimized, as it was the only concrete evidence of a student's performance for a person other than the supervisor. Also, minimizing the importance of recording would mean less inputs in it even by the good performers. Therefore, what was needed was to enable the student improve his records. Use of earlier student's records could be made for this purpose.

Recording in community organisation

Before the commencement of the proceedings, there was a discussion on field work record in the plenary session which gave certain guidelines. Keeping these in view the group evolved the following outline for its deliberations :

1. Nature of recording in community organisation,
2. Purpose of recording in community organisation,
3. Traditional and developmental perspectives in recording
4. Contents of recording,
5. Types of recording,
6. Difficulties in recording,
7. Preparation of a format on recording at BSW and MSW levels,

(i) Recording in relation to work done in the field
(ii) Reporting in terms of linguistic difficulties of the students

Nature of recording in community organisation

The group defined recording as follows :

Recording was a written document of work (action-reflection-action) done in the field (community) by worker (student/agency/supervisor/other members of the faculty) for the purpose of learning to work with people and to facilitate the professional growth of the worker by way of helping him plan, implement, evaluate his work and to maintain continuity in practice.

The group took up for consideration the next point and visualised following purposes :

Purpose

(1) To record the actual work done in the field;
(2) To reflect on the work highlighting its various dimensions;
(3) To record social change(s) taking place in the community;
(4) To maintain continuity in work;
(5) To help develop a built-in mechanism for research and evaluation by student, field work supervisor and the faculty;
(6) To use it for follow-up and future planning;
(7) To develop teaching materials (indigeneous);
(8) To use it as a reference;
(9) To verify self-accomplishment;
(10) To locate strengths and weaknesses of the student ; and
(11) To ensure accountability.

Perspectives

A view was expressed that the perspective in recording depended on the perspective in social work. For example if the approach to social work was developmental, the same would be reflected in recording.

While the importance of traditional approach to recording cannot be minimised, or totally ruled out, the recording should also reflect the developmental approach to community—organisation as a method of social work.

Further the group discussed at length the traditional and developmental perspectives in recording. The consensus was that these two were inseparable phases and on-going processes.

It was also pointed out that the set pattern of record-writing could be termed 'traditional' and the records incorporating recent trends like advocacy and social activism could be taken as 'developmental'.

Contents of recording

On contents of recording, the group prepared a face sheet of community organisation record which is given at the end of this section.

Types of recording

At this point the Director of the Workshop intervened to say that the group could not afford to forget the relationship between community work and inevitable political aspects of such practice. He emphasized that community work and social action had a different dimension in developing countries. If this was the reality, it should be reflected in the records.

The group took note of this remark and after a discussion arrived at a consensus that community work demanded intervention on the part of worker on many occasions as the situation demanded. In this sense community work turned out to be social action. In developing countries particularly group and political pressures could not be ruled out in community work. The following contents of recording were listed :

Structure/function

(a) *Physical* : Factual data on nature of the community etc.

(b) *Social* : Social groups—formal, informal groups, institutions, organisations, religious groups of the community etc.

(c) *Economic* : Occupation, classes, income groups, land ownership etc.

(d) *Political* : Power structure—caste, different groups,

participation in political process, relation between power centres and the people.

(e) *Educational* : Formal and informal, level of literacy, education and professional education etc.

(f) *Cultural* : Cultural background of the community incorporating its social, moral and aesthetic aspects.

Need-resource, gaps and deficiencies—identification

Need-resource—problem, methods used in identifying needs, and determining priorities.

Interaction

— Areas of interaction and priorities;
— Communication skills, strategies for sensitization and self-awareness, rapport establishment skills;
— Involvement of people/community and their participation ; level and duration of relationship;
— Leadership pattern;
— Group and sub-group dynamics;
— Disguised factors—opportunities and hinderances;
— Capacity to absorb shocks and frustiations, setbacks, and
— Gradual self-realiance and assertion of community leaders, leaders trying to be self-reliant.

Attitudinal change

Appropriate attitudes towards the community and oneself.

— Supervisory inputs—guidance in the area of programme development; relating theory to practice; decision-making : resource utilization—tangible and intangible identification, mobilization and utilization of resource; co-ordidation, inter-agency work, prevention of wastage and duplication.

Activist role

Community issues : Civic, political, social, economic, linguistic, regional, religious and cultural issues.

Types of recording

Phases in recording	Types of recording
i. Primary	Narrative, descriptive
ii. Inter-actional	Process-analytical
iii. Terminal and trend	Trend, analytical and summary

Note : Aids to Recording : Charts, diagrams, graphs, tables, pictures etc.

Difficulties in recording

Problems

1. Lack of insight in analysis and planning,
2. Inability to grasp and express due to language problem,
3. Lack of adequate supervisory guidance,
4. Fear of being compared and/or criticized, and
5. Cultural constraints in articulation.

Preparation of a format :

1. Introduction,
2. Actual work process,
3. Responses and reactions,
4. Observations and interpretations,
5. Analysis and assessment,
6. Future plan,
7. Summary.

Recording should be precise, specific and sequentially expressed in simple, clear, and unambiguous language. Abbreviations should be meticulously avoided. The group further discussed the format of recording in community organisation for different levels of training in social work. The group evolved the following format :

Level of training

Format	*BSW*	*MSW*
1. Introduction	Guided-more supervisory input	Less supervisory input

2. Actual work process	Interpretation	Inter-action and intervention
3. Responses and reactions	Peripherial level observation	Observation, and analysis of responses
4. Observations and interpretations	Theory-based ; simple interpretation	Self-acting, more involvement, relating theory to practice
5. Analysis and assessment	Comprehension guided and peripheral	Insight oriented and in-depth
6. Future plan	Short-term	Short-term and long-term
7. Summary	—	Edited reports

Contents of recording at different levels of social work training :

Bachelor of Social Work (BSW)	Master of Social Work (MSW)
1. Strong foundation for interdisciplinary learning (Theory)	Stabilisation of such learning
2. Exposure to realities in the community	Mobilisation and utilisation of community resources and potential
3. Specific task-oriented	Process-goal oriented
4. Learning to apply theory in practice	Testing and synthesizing theory
5. Strategies planned through supervisory input	Self-evolved strategies
6. Less experimentation	More experimentation
7. More effort-oriented	More dynamic and creative
8. Review	Evaluation
9. Learning on a continuing basis	Capacity to generate new ideas
10. More traditional and factual	Developmental and perspectival
11. Less importance to style and presentation	More importance to language, presentation, analysis.

Recording in integrated social work practice

The group, first of all, clarified the concept of integrated approach as follows :

Integrated method—a conceptualization

1. Integrated approach was a holistic approach to social work practice which took into consideration the use of all the methods of social work in a given situation and tried to effect integration of theory with practice as far as possible.

2. Integrated social work practice meant application of an integrated approach according to the demands of a given situation, the purpose of which was to answer the needs of any situation that could arise in the process of human interaction.

3. Integrated method gathered importance in a field where the individuals and groups were conceived of not only as products of the social environment but also interacting processes therein. The help was offered through a combination of methods and the focus of practice was both individual and situational.

In the integrated approach, the role of a social worker would not be that of a professional only who attempted to influence a given situation but also of one who belonged to the change agent system, which called for be interdisciplinary work.

Application of integrated method to school setting : An illustration

The school setting, like others, offered a wide scope for the practice of integrated social work methods in which the child, school, parents, teachers, community and social worker were equally considered important in the process of dealing with the problems of children.

Process of identification of area of work

1. Identification of the child,
2. Identification of educational and adjustment problems of children in the school,
3. Knowing the reactions of administration, teacher and parent groups towards such problems.

Selected area of work

1. Educational adjustment problems of children,
2. Individual or groups of children in need of special services,
3. Work with parent and teacher groups,
4. Referral services,
5. Bridging of cultural gap between parent and teachers.

Services rendered by the social worker

Various services could be rendered by the school social worker in a school setting which were as follows ;

1. Child guidance services,
2. Organised recreational services,
3. Parent-teacher meetings,
4. Extension education activities,
5. Rendering organised services in the community,
6. Work with school drop-outs and other underpriviledged groups,
7. Physical and mental health activities,
8. Co-ordination between educational, and other services.

Types of records expected

1. Casework and group work records
2. Minutes of meetings
3. Narative and process recording of work with individuals/ groups
4. Periodic summaries
5. Monthly and annual reports
6. Notes on methods applied and found effective

After having discussed the concept, the group took up the following aspects of recording in field work:

PURPOSE, OBJECTIVES AND IMPORTANCE OF RECORDING

It was agreed by all that the purpose of field work recording should relate to the following areas :

1. Learning,
2. Teaching,
3. Evaluation,
4. Administration,
5. Professional contribution.

In view of these, the following objectives of recording were listed by the group :

1. To project the growth of a student in terms of knowledge, attitudes, professional learning, feelings and blocks;

2. To reflect the approach adopted by the student and work done ;
3. To help the student communicate with the supervisor ;
4. To assess the need of the field ; and
5. To analyse and interpret the situation.

Types and content of recording

After serious deliberations, the group arrived at a consensus on various types of recording which were as follows :

1. Narrative recording,
2. Process recording,
3. Summary recording, periodic summary and evaluative summary,
4. Administrative recording,
5. Field project recording,

The group also discussed and agreed upon the content of each type of recording as follows :

Narrative recording

The narrative recording was a base for the study of a given situation. It included :

(a) First-hand information
(b) Factual data
(c) Observation
(d) Sequence of occurrences
(e) Mobilisation of resources

Process recording

The purpose of this recording was to show the process of development and use of relationship between the worker, supervisor and the field. Such records would include the following ;

(a) Goals of field work;
(b) Record of facts, observation, analysis and interpretation;
(c) Critical approach to the role of worker and field situation;

(d) Plan of action;
(e) Professional inputs, implementation and evaluation of work done;
(f) Raising questions and seeking clarifications; and
(g) Projecting feelings, attitudes, frustrations and blockings in learning while working in the field.

As students gained experience, they were more able to think and recall in terms of larger areas, and so they recorded only what was essential and significant.

Summary recording

(a) Periodic summary
(b) Evaluative summary

The periodic summary recording could be done at every mid-term/mid-semester, and evaluative summary could be made at the end of every semester/year.

Content

(a) Period spent in the field
(b) Professional thrust in terms of fact-finding, analysis, plan of action, implementation and evaluation
(c) Summary of the work done
(d) Programme summary
(e) Evaluation of professional self
(f) Evaluation of field
(g) Evaluation of work done, field/agency and significant others including the supervisor
(h) Any other supportive activity
(i) Future plan

Administrative recording

Content

(a) Face sheet (intake sh eet)
(b) Case papers
(c) Filling up registers
(d) Cardex
(e) Clinical records

(f) Reports on area referred

Field project recording

Content

(a) Gathering information—fact-finding
(b) Drawing conclusions
(c) Preparing plans and action phases
(d) Implementation
(e) Evaluation of work

Expectations in recording from various levels of students

The group decided to discuss expectations in recording at the under-graduate that is BSW-I, BSW-II, and BSW-III levels and the post-graduate that is MSW-I, and MSW-II levels. The following points emerged :

UNDER-GRADUATE LEVEL

(A) BSW-I

Observational visits

The BSW-I students were expected to observe the field situation and give their views in a narrative form of recording. It was suggested that they might emphasise more on the following points while preparing their records :

(a) Organisational structure
(b) Historical background of the organization
(c) Aims and objectives
(d) Programmes and services
(e) Administrative pattern
(f) Beneficiaries
(g) Students' own observation, impression, suggestions and comments

It could then be followed by discussion in the conferences. It was further felt by the group that since observational visit was an exposure to a new-comer, one should not expect too much from him, because such visits were arranged to make the student aware of existing problems and services.

Secondly, since no specific method was adopted in observational visit, it could be taken as an important part of an integrated approach.

At this stage a member raised the point whether one should show the previous records to a new-comer. On this it was commonly felt that it might not be advisable to show previous records at this level because there might always be a danger of imitating them. It might also block the progress of the student.

Programmes in the community

The following points were considered important while recording the programmes in the community:

(a) Early contacts, study, initial interviews, discussions
(b) Identification of need
(c) Understanding of the limitations of field work programme
(d) Understanding of very elementary project work such as health, recreation etc.
(e) Understanding the value of programme in terms of agency situation
(f) Identification of learning content

(B) BSW II level

The BSW-II students were normally placed in the field for family level work in the community and thus were expected to bring out the following points in recording :

(a) Socio-economic background of the community
(b) Analysis of socio-economic data
(c) Study of intra-family relationship
(d) Information related to associations within the community
(e) Information on formation of groups
(f) Information on group and community problems, needs and resources and methods of mobilising resources
(g) Information on efforts made by the student

(C) BSW-III level

Expectations

(a) Knowledge of methods of social work
(b) Application and workability of social work techniques and methods in a given situation
(c) Description of the field situation
(d) Identification of the problem areas
(e) Assessment of group interaction, and its development
(f) Information on work done by the student

Post-graduate level

(A) MSW-I

At the MSW-I level, the students were expected to bring out in their recording all the points that were discussed above at BSW-I, II and III levels.

In addition, they were expected to focus on the following aspects :

(a) Critical analysis of the field situation;
(b) Interpretation, exploration, plan of action and resources use; and
(c) Implementation and evaluation.

(B) MSW-II (Integrated method)

(a) Knowledge of the field and its relevance to social work practice
(b) Record on procedural aspects
(c) Identification and formulation of problem
(d) Identification of areas of work
(e) Worker's role—process of intervention
(f) Reflection on the work done
(g) Critical review of own approach
(h) Analytical process and summary recordings with interpretation of strengths and weaknesses

TIME REQUIRED FOR RECORDING IN FIELD WORK

The group suggested that the student might be specified a time limit for writing records with proper safeguards that this was not misused. The record received from the College of Social Work, Nirmal Niketan, Bombay on 'Work in Slum Communities' was discussed by the group.

The record showed elements of working with individuals and groups at a minimal remedial level and to some extent preventive aspects were also taken into consideration. It was noted by the group that other communities were also contacted and made aware of eviction so that they could resist it. It was however felt that the record did not reflect the holistic approach in the true sense of the term.

Note : This section on recording could be used by educators and practitioners to identify the content of field work at different levels to appreciate the interlinkage between under-graduate and post-graduate programmes; and, more importantly, to highlight the gradual progression of field work process and its place in teaching and learning skill, acquiring attitudes, and developing a perspective.

STAFF DEVELOPMENT

The first reaction on the topic of discussion related to the attitudes of staff towards staff development. Some felt that the very concept of staff development had an element of insult in it. Secondly, instead of volunteering for such programmes there was the practice of 'deputations' by some one from above which added injury to insult. Some took staff development positively; others felt that they had learnt enough and so there was nothing more to develop; and some liked it only for the sake of pleasure trips. Members of the group raised doubts about the effectiveness of any staff development programme. For example, after undergoing a staff development programme if a member returned with new ideas, what then was his role in the school ? What would be the guarantee that his organisation would give him an opportunity to experiment all that he had learnt in the staff development programme ? It was thought that once again this was related to the attitude of colleagues towards staff development.

It was pointed out that members of staff who attended a staff development programme should not at once build counter-groups but should work slowly to bring about changes.

Another problem in connection with staff development was that of having non-professionals as heads of departments who did not realise the importance of it. What was the solution to such problems ? It was felt by some that two modelities could be tried : one for administrative purposes where a non-professional might act as head of the department; and the other for academic purposes where a professional headed the department. The practicability of this suggestion was questioned by others and the consensus was that professional person only should head the schools or the departments of social work.

Another question was : What would be the possibilities of a school devising its own system of staff development within its structure ? A member gave an example as to how his department had devised its own methods, like establishing its own agencies for field work and making each member of the staff incharge of one of them so that it might give him an opportunity to experiment and to learn. Secondly, change of subjects of a teacher from time to time was another method.

Other suggestions included regional seminars, presentation of papers, and use of local resources. The services of educators and practitioners visiting the school might also be used for the purpose.

The group was told by the resource person at this stage that staff development meant two things :

1. The professional and personal development of the staff; and
2. Adequacy of staff.

According to him "work study" could be conducted in every school to identify the present level of development and to find out method of maintaining and promoting standards.

METHODS OF STAFF DEVELOPMENT

1. In service training programme could be organised on the basis of needs, levels, and service records of the staff. Examples from both the medical and psychiatric fields were cited.

2. Case conferences and group conferences in which students, staff and experts from outside might take part could be organised.

3. Presentation of papers on a theme and demonstrations on the same (e.g.) psychodrama could be tried.

4. Weekly seminars either during working hours or later could be held. It was stressed that staff development was the professional and moral responsibility of all the schools of social work.

5. Evaluation of the staff by students could be introduced although its use was doubtful in the existing educational system.

6. The concept of field work-by-objectives should be introduced on the lines of management-by-objectives.

7. The concept of field work-by-objectives should be introduced on the lines of management-by-objectives.

8. Individual-informal-conferences where head of the department reviewed the work of the staff and enabled them to do better would prove useful. In this connection it was observed that groupism and politics were bound to be present in any school; nevertheless such reviews should be conducted.

9. Recorded appreciation of work proved a source of encouragement.

10 Study-leave-benefit for staff development programme should be provided every 3 or 5 years and financial resources should be provided either by the school or the university.

11. Direct implementation of such projects as Integrated Child Development Scheme could be undertaken by the schools of social work. It was pointed out that the Universities have been provided with the posts of Director/Dean/Chairman of College Development Councils to promote staff development and this resource should be used properly.

12. The place of M.Phil. and Ph.D. programmes in staff development was also discussed and the problem of non-availability of 'guides' was highlighted. A member suggested that an orientation programme could be arranged for heads of departments but a doubt was expressed whether they would be receptive to the

idea. Another member suggested that the deliberations of the present workshop could be sent to all the heads of departments so that they could be implemented.

13. Rotation of the post of the head of the department in a school every three years or so would contribute to staff development in terms of new inputs by the incumbent. In this connection, strong objection was raised to the status of non-professionals being the heads of departments, not only from the point of view of staff development but also from the point of view of the growth of profession itself.

14. An orientation programme was considered essential for new supervisors and the agency staff.

BLOCK PLACEMENT

Detailed discussion was held on the existing pattern of block placement. The pattern followed by different schools was as follows :

1. In many schools the duration of block field work varied from three weeks to three months.
2. One department distributed the period of one-month placement over three phases that is, (a) exposure for 2 weeks to a tribal areas; (b) one week in an agency; and (c) one week's experience in conducting research.
3. In most schools, the final examinations were conducted before the block field work. A favourable report from the agency was a requirement for declaring the student successful.
4. In most of the schools/departments the block placement did not carry any marks.
5. A few schools affiliated to one particular University allotted 150 marks for block placement, though the pattern of placement differed. One school allotted 25 marks out of 100 reserved for field work in the fourth semester/term.
6. Social work departments/schools offering specializations in various fields, placed students according to their fields of specializations, whereas those offering generic

training kept in mind the choice of the students, and also their area of interest, and desire for a new field experience.

The need and rationale for block field work was discussed by the group as under :

1. Pre-employment experience
2. Induction to the expected role change that is from student to prospective employee
3. Intensive training in the field
4. Opportunity for integration
5. Opportunity to work independently
6. Reinforcement of concurrent field work experience, and
7. Help in developing public relations through which the schools'/departments' image was projected to the community.

It was pointed out that though a number of students felt that block placement delayed early employment opportunities; an equally large number felt that block placement helped in learning more intensively the methods of social work, and therefore suggested a longer duration of block placement.

It was strongly felt by the group members that block placement as part of social work training needed to be strengthened. Innovative situations for students' placement needed to be explored in order to make block placement an important part of developmental field work.

It was suggested that proper orientation must be given to students to make them aware of the need for block placement. Some members were of the view that certain norms for block placement could be developed to suit the requirements of social work education.

A suggestion was made to make block field work voluntary. But it was pointed out that such a step might indicate lack of importance given to block field work.

Regarding the question raised about remuneration/stipend paid to students, it was felt that if demands were made on the part of the student/school for remuneration, it might weaken educational programme of the school for, the school might have to adhere to the programme of the agency.

In response to a question on the duration of block placement, one member suggested a period of three months or more, while another suggested a placement of two months (one month during the semester, and one month after the completion of the course). Regarding the suggestion for a three months' placement, it was pointed out that it would hamper employment prospects of the student and might also make detrimental impact on the student's plans for further studies. Another suggestion that a three months' placement could be followed by granting exemption to those where early employment was available was not found acceptable.

Supervisory input and its extent also drew the attention of the group. It was expressed that even in a developmental field setting, a well-motivated student might not require very close supervision. Only a student with lack of motivation needed supervisory control either by the agency supervisor or by the faculty supervisor. It was also suggested that in cases where trained supervisors were available at the agency, there was no need for faculty supervision.

Proper selection of field agencies for block field work was impressed upon by the group. It was suggested that intership on the lines of medical profession could be introduced and that the Association of Schools of Social Work in India should take up the initiative to co-ordinate and establish academic relationship in developing intership, and similar other programmes for the development of the profession.

NEW AREAS OF FIELD WORK PRACTICE

The areas mentioned by the workshop were :

(1) Trade unions; (2) Missing children's Bureau; (3) Courts, and police stations; (4) Sub-registrar's office/BDO's office; (5) Consumer Welfare Societies or organisations; and (6) Human Rights and social or environmental activists.

A point was raised about the role of social workers in communal tensions, and apprehensions were expressed about involving students in direct intervention during tense time of strife. However it was felt that social workers could be involved with National Integration Committees at the University, College, School or community levels, could work with peace committees, and work for a variety of preventive programmes for the promotion of communal harmony.

Relief operations in times of riot, other tensions and natural calamities were also pointed out.

People's co-operatives

At this point the Director of the workshop stated that the placement situation or the field could either be "relatively stable" or fluid (for example : strike, ferment, riots and so on). He added that if the professional role was found to be restrictive, than at least social workers could play the citizen's role. The group was of the view that only selected students under selected supervisors should initially be placed in unconventional areas.

Other areas suggested were working with legal aid societies, women's organisations, housing societies etc.

Banks

An experience was shared by a member where a social worker had organised rickshaw-pullers and acted as liaison between them and the bank. He helped the rickshaw-pullers to take loans from the bank to procure their own vehicles and at the same time helped the bank in the recovery of loans.

Occupational groups that is, rickshaw-pullers, hawkers, vendors, skilled and semi-skilled labour were also identified.

In the end it was suggested that case studies of such field work experiences should be prepared and they should be circulated among other schools of social work.

Experiences were shared in giving developmental focus to the adult education programme by involving the community on a large scale for organisational, educational and income supplementation work.

Another interesting experience shared was on giving school social work a developmental dimension. Here the social worker involved school children in community service as part of the curriculum under "socially useful and productive work" (SUPW). He provided non-formal education to adults in slum communities. Experience of developmental work through the programmes of the National Dairy Development Board was also recounted.

Another potential area suggested was work with activist groups involved in social-environmental movements, that is chipko movement, Mithi Bachao Andolan at Hoshangabad, Movement to protect the Silent Valley, organisations like Kashta Kari Sangahatana, small farmers, marginal farmers and agricultural labours. Here students could act as observers, propagators of information; documentors, and possibly initiators of action on similar lines. One member pointed out that the method of work would evolve out of the field situation itself in unconventional fields.

DEVELOPMENTAL FIELD WORK

Initiating the discussion a group member pointed out that there was a great deal of confusion about the concept of developmental approach and therefore there was a need to clarify what was actually meant by the term. Reacting to these a number of members pointed out various aspects of developmental approach. They were as follows :

Developmental approach was need-oriented rather than problem-oriented; it was holistic; had a broader, national, macro and long-term perspective; had anticipatory and preventive aspects; it laid emphasis on class in preference to case; it was promotional; and it encompassed social action, and social change components.

Finding the group making comparisons between the traditional and developmental approach it was pointed out by one member that 'developmental' should not be considered as against 'traditional'. Apart from system-maintenance functions, social welfare with developmental approach assumed system change roles also.

After some discussion it was agreed that developmental approach was not against the residual approach (which the group called traditional approach). It was not the question of traditional versus developmental but of traditional and developmental.

The latter had a perspective; it worked for planned change; and it was goal-oriented. It stressed equality and discouraged inequality in all forms. Developmental approach focussed on the weaker and the weakest sections, and helped them to get rightful share in the resources and services. It called for the redistribution of incomes, statuses and decision-making power. In the developmental approach oppositional practice (political components) could not be over-looked. A member posed the question whether developmental approach was applicable to advanced countries ?

At this it was pointed out by a member that to the extent developmental approach worked for lessening inequality, it was applicable to the developed countries also. Examples from the USA and Germany were given in this regard.

During the discussion some examples of the practice of developmental approach in field work setting were given. It was said that in a hospital (or broadly the health service delivery system) there were class, ethnic, and linguistic biases in the provision of services. The students therefore could identify new tasks to lessen or remove these biases. Even in the casualty departments of the hospitals, these discriminatory practices prevailed.

Another example was given in the context of school social work where a social worker, going beyond his usually accepted role and function, had initiated a programme to involve school students in providing non-formal education to pupils in various slums.

In this connection it was pointed out that one social worker lost his job because she refused to work for motivating the neighbourhood slum children to come and study in the school premises and to provide coaching to them. The school concerned had provided for the place and had arranged for teachers on rotation basis for the above purposes. The discussion ended with emphasis that social workers must prepare themselves for change; accept new role and function; and re-order their priorities.

Observational visit to T.B. Hospital, Delhi

The resource persons posed the following issues for consideration:

1. Was T.B. Hospital only a single-function case-work agency ?
2. What was the role of a social worker ?
3. What was the social work programme of the T.B.

Hospital in the context of social welfare goals ?

The group noted that the field provided scope for work in the following areas :

Work with the families of the patients
If a male member of the family contacted the disease, there was a financial crisis in the family (as he was usually the only earning member) and many problems arose on account of it. In the case of female member being a patient, the domestic routine was upset and children suffered. The stigma attached to the disease led to further social, psychological and emotional problems for the patient and his family.

Work in the community
The scope of work was outlined as follows :

(i) Creation of awareness about the highly infectious nature of the disease and the medical fact that disease was curable if treatment was taken regularly.

(ii) Motivational work in terms of screening for T.B. for persons in the family and neighbourhood of the patient.

(iii) Preventive work for control of the disease; and

(iv) Identification of community resources for prevention, treatment and rehabilitations of those affected and also their families.

The field was considered to be a multifunctional one and the work done at the T.B. Hospital, Delhi, was regarded as developmental.

Social work at the micro-level
The following functions of a social worker were identified by the group :

(i) Motivational, supportive and rehabilitative case-work with patients.

(ii) Work with patients' families.

(iii) Dissemination of factual information about the incidence, spread and control of disease and also correction of some faulty notions about the disease in the community through film-shows and campaigns.

(iv) Reference in this connection was made of the talk by the medical superintendent of the T.B. Hospital in which he said that approximately 90 lakh persons were suffering from T.B. in India but the country had got provision for hospitalized treatment for 42,000 patients only. The group felt that in such a situation a social worker should work to emphasize domiciliary treatment of the non-emergency and economically well-off cases. The social worker, amongst other things, must also ensure that the patients took treatment regularly.

(v) Mobilisation of resources for treatment, rehabilitation and preventive programmes. The group observed in this connection that there was no paucity of funds but there was paucity of committed workers.

(vi) Health education in the community. It was also observed that the thrust of field was socio-medical as contrasted with medico-social which meant a new focus from traditional to developmental social work.

The efforts made by the social worker at the T.B. Hospital were appreciated by the group. In this connection the role of professional social workers in eradicating poverty was also referred to.

The Director of the workshop then gave a brief historical account of the Child Guidance Centre, Delhi School of Social Work and highlighted its changing orientation over a period of time, and fluctuation in perspective from traditional to developmental social work. It was also brought to the notice of members that a programme which started as a developmental programme might revert to the traditional pattern depending upon the attitude, perspective and commitment of the staff.

MEASURES TO STRENGTHEN FIELD WORK

The resource person summarised the way field work was done at the Department of Social Work, Delhi University, Delhi. It was pointed out that field work was considered to be an educationally meaningful and a socially relevant process which was directed both at the micro and macro levels.

Giving an idea about the working of the Department of Social Work, Delhi University, the resource person added that there was no hierarchy in the field work organisation. The Director of field work was appointed by rotation which did not take into account the designation. The teachers were assigned 8/11 students each and through collaborative effort it was ensured that students were properly helped. He summarised the educational and administrative aspect of field work starting with orientation to that of final evaluation. It was pointed out that the final evaluation which was done at the end of the year involved experts from other universities. The school had evolved a comprehensive guideline to evaluate the student ranging from understanding the community, establishment of support, ability for the identification of services to professional growth of the student.

The group then raised questions regarding gradations and numerical assessment of the student at the end of the year. Regarding placement in agency/field (whether concurrent or block) problems were briefly discusssed.

The resource person emphasised that there was a need to have a guideline for field work in the absence of which it would be just "random wandering".

A doubt was expressed by a member about the supervisor's personality and the age difference between students and supervisors. Another member pointed out that age/or personality should not hinder normal field work programme and what was essential was insight, introspection and interest in the work assigned. Further, it was strongly felt by members that there was no instructional guideline for the teacher-supervisors. When the resource person suggested that a commonality should be evolved, it was endorsed by another member. This would, it was felt, require schools to come together to evolve the basic guideline involving staff and agencies.

The chair-person posed the following questions about the advisability of a detailed guideline. Routine nature of work, time factor, work-load, and likes and dislikes must be looked into to avoid pitfalls. In any case the guideline would serve as a functional device to support the supervisory input. The resource person cited a few lines from his write-up—From Field Work to Field Instruction—Need for Shift in Perspective for the Supervisory Process, highlighting the need for constructing referrants and need for empirical evidence. He made this point by displaying a chart which was evolved by agency and school supervisors. Some members felt that the guideline may hinder the creativity of supervisor and may also leave room to vagueness.

In the review session which followed a member raised the question about study tours and camps not being given due importance in the workshop. The other issue put forth was placing students in non-structured agency than structured agency during first year where they could have ample opportunity to learn case-work, group work and community organisation together. In the second year students could be placed depending upon specialisation, if any. Another member pointed out that non-structured agencies should be preferred to the structured ones. Some members felt that conflict had arisen due to the placement of student made by the Institutes of Management and others to the same agencies where MSW students were placed. About study tour a member strongly felt that at the MSW level it gave students an opportunity to think, and organise experience properly which would otherwise not be available.

REPORT OF THE WORKING GROUP ON FIELD WORK AT BSW LEVEL

The focus of the working group, consisting of six members, in preparing these recommendations was to suggest a scheme which would prepare a student to take up direct field level practice responsibilities after the BSW programme.

During the first year of field work the student would be given an exposure to the social reality and to the field of field work. Observational visits may be made to a variety of settings (welfare institutions, slums, communities, court, police station, municipal corporation, people's organisations etc.)*. The student would also be equipped with elementary skills of relating to people. A village camp was felt to be a good opportunity at this stage. The field work would stress on developing civic consciousness, attitudinal change and a sense of social responsibility.

* Reference could be made to the report of the session on New Areas of Field Work Practice of the Workshop.

In the second year of field work a BSW Part II student could be placed in a community setting, where understanding and adjustment to the setting, exploration, work on specific programmes and development of holistic approach to situations may be emphasized.

In the third year the student might be given experience in any two of the structured settings : hospitals, schools, and welfare institutions. In such settings, the student would not only work within the institutions but also identify areas of work outside the institutions.

A few selected students could be placed in unconventional areas of work also for the second placement in the third year. A block placement for students after the third year for at least two weeks was considered desirable.

The working group noted a great deal of variation in the BSW programme in the schools of social work.

It was observed that schools would of course need to take into account local needs but the approach should be rational. For example, schools in the rural areas could consider placements on the agricultural farms and in the community blocks.

The recommendations of the working group are as follows :

BSW-I : CONTENT OF FIELD WORK

At this level ten hours in a week should be devoted for field work in welfare institutions, communities, hospitals, courts and police stations etc.

Observational visits

Fifteen visits with guidelines should be organised which are followed by group discussion and report writing.

Knowledge of group games
Recreational group activities
Art of story-telling
Preparation of charts, graphs and audio-visual aids
Preparation of scripts and preparation of experimental dramatics
Teaching elementary craft skills

Field work camp in rural areas
Duration 7 days. Understanding various aspects of village through community contacts, experience in group living, discussion with local leaders, panchayats and others, involving village, women, children and youth in games and other social, cultural programmes, involvment in manual/labour work with local people.

BSW-I : SUPERVISORY INPUT

Selection of a variety of settings for observational visits
Contact with agencies
Briefing students about the purpose and procedure of field visits
Guidance for observation and discussion, purposeful group activities, discussions and demonstrations to help students prepare charts, graphs, audio-visual aids, and scripts for street corner plays with social educational themes; performance followed by discussions, arrangement for teaching art and craft.

Field work camp in rural area
Selection of area
Preparation for the camp (committee work)
Orientation to the camp
Discussion of work plan
Evaluation of day's work and plan for the next day (2 hours)
Guidelines for report-writing
Use of audio-visual aids

BSW-I : RECORDING

Narrative recording of the field situation, organisational structure, historical background, programmes and services, beneficiaries, students' own observations.

Recording of use of street corner plays, arts, crafts and mass media.

Recording of camp : Diarizing on the basis of a guideline.

BSW-I—EVALUATION

Evaluation of student would be periodic, and final evaluation should be based on the following :

Skill in observation; participation in group discussion ; use of games, arts, crafts and audio-visual aids; participation in camp; and recording.

BSW-II—CONTENT

Two days a week (12 to 15 hours)

Placement in community

Understanding of the field situation, structure, function, and characteristics (class, caste, religion, education, occupation, civil and welfare facilities, etc.). Need identification—expressed or unexpressed through contact with family members. Carrying out of specific programmes in response to need. For example, recreational group activities, social and cultural functions, health exhibitions, nutrition programmes, demonstrations etc.

Observation of group members' participation, identification of leadership and groups, working with formal-informal leaders, Working with children, women, adults and youth. Analysis of community leaderships pattern. Writing of social histories of individuals in need of help. Organising local groups to mobilize and use resources. Preparation of a plan of action for work with community. Field work related elementary research experience.

BSW-II—SUPERVISORY INPUT

Information about the community. Support and clarification. Exchange of views. Information to student about achievements and limitations of his work. Help in the identification of need and determination of priorities. Help in building and strengthening relationship. Help in planning of programmes: on-the-spot supervision (being an observer as well as participant). Help in locating leaders and groups and how to approach them. Providing guidelines to write social histories, to organise and conduct meetings etc. Identifying areas where research can be taken up. Help to student to prepare a short interview schedule/questionnaire and collect data. Instruction on interviewing.

BSW-II—RECORDING

Narrative recording with analysis of community characteristics. Information on formation of groups, community problems, needs, resources and methods of mobilising resources. Information on efforts made by the student. Identification and ordering of needs. (Approach to be described). Process of programme planning, implementation and evaluation. Process of group formation. Recording of interactions with analysis. Preparation of social histories. Self-evaluation. A brief report of survey with major findings.

BSW-II—EVALUATION

Student's understanding of the situation, his ability to identify and study basic components. Analysis and identification of needs. Ability to identify formal and informal leaders and their involvement in activities. Process of contacting, programme planning, tapping resources, implementation and evaluation. His role in group activities and group interaction. His ability to write relevant social histories. Work done with groups of his interest and plan of action. Survey work experience : clarity of objectives; methodical work; understanding of various tools for the presentation of data; ability to use research.

BSW-III—CONTENT

Two days in a week (12 to 15 hours)

Placement in any two of the agencies—welfare agency, school or hospital.

Orientation phase

Understanding the agency, nature, objectives, administration, staffing pattern, finance, organisational structure, programmes and procedure, problems and limitations. Understanding the role of social worker in the agency.

Exploration-Assessment-Action phase

Carrying out specific tasks assigned by the agency supervisor and undertaken by oneself which evolved out of exploration of the work situation within and outside the agency. For example :

Hospital

Conducting home visits to fill gaps in information about particular clients, interpretation of health charts, graphs etc. Administrative functions, correspondence, conducting of survey of the health status of community, arranging special diagnostic and treatment camps, immunisation programmes etc.

School

Educational and recreational programmes, organising outing and various talent competitions, programmes of health check-up, nutrition, identification of cases of absenteeism, truancy, aggressiveness, scholastic backwardness, home visits, work with the family, acting as a link between teachers and parents, referral work.

Welfare agency

Preparing social histories of inmates, working with children in need.

BSW-III—SUPERVISORY INPUT

Orientation phase

Explaining the process of supervision; Introducing the student to the agency; Explaining client system to student; Establishing supervisor-supervisee relationship; Informing the student about phases or stages of recording.

Exploration-Assessment-Action phase

Helping the student to identify needs and resources, to evolve work assignments and to carry them out; clarifying doubts and help in problem-solving; sharing experiences of the supervisee; analysis of the feelings of the supervisee; support; fostering growth and awareness in the student; on-the-spot supervision; developing relationship between the agency and school.

Evaluation phase

Explaining the process of evaluation; Helping the student to evaluate himself; Periodic evaluation followed by final evaluation; self-evaluation by the supervisor.

BSW-III—RECORDING

Detailed profile of the agency; Detailed social histories; Experience in writing administrative and summary records; Selective and process recording; Recording with the help of a format :

(a) Brief introduction of the client or client system
(b) Interaction with the client or client system
(c) Assessment of need and formulation of goals
(d) Plan of intervention
(e) Evaluation
(d) Self-evaluation
(e) Field work survey reports.

BSW-III—EVALUATION

Student's understanding of the agency
Student's understanding of his role in the agency
Ability in establishing and sustaining relationship
Communication and interviewing skill
Ability to analyse the dynamics of situations
Resource utilisation, formulation of goals
Planning, implementation and evaluation
Selective and relevant recording
Analytical records and reports
Application of theory
Professional growth

EVALUATION OF WORKSHOP

EVALUATION BY GROUP A (NUMBER OF MEMBERS 10)

Organisation

This aspect was evaluated at two levels: (i) Academic, and (ii) Physical facilities.

(i) *Academic*

The group appreciated the procedure adopted by the Director of the workshop for using resources mainly from amongst the participants themselves than from outside.

Organisation of the workshop was such that tension of work continued for the first seven days. Some of the participants could not get adequate rest during that period.

Plenary sessions helped a lot in providing food for thought, and framing and sharing of issues. These however also witnessed occasionally time-consuming lectures of some of the participants and unnecessary discussion that ensued therefrom.

Formation of sub-groups was really helpful in making the participants more active. However, the tasks given to sub-groups were rather demanding.

The democratic method adopted by the workshop was highly commendable. This provided ample opportunities for all the participants to assume responsibilities as chair-persons, rapporteurs, and resource persons.

Even though guidelines had been given for discussion, it was always left to the group(s) to evolve own guidelines and issues for discussions. The group considered this as an example of developmental approach.

(ii) *Physical arrangements*

The group was highly appreciative of the selfless service given by the N.S.S. Programme Officer of Rajdhani College. Better accommodation however could have been provided. The Director had however explained the position in this regard in his letter to the participants. The group placed on record the excellent arrangements made with regard to transportation and food.

Content of the workshop

The workshop covered almost all the aspects of field work, and discussions have led to an indepth analysis of each issue.

Participation

Though participation in the plenary sessions was limited, the climate of sub-groups provided for the wholehearted participation of all the members.

Outcome

The group was of the view that in general, the material generated in the workshop was very useful for future reference and for the improvement of field work programme in different schools.

The workshop was very helpful in giving the participants a developmental perspective of field work. The discussions also facilitated a kind of introspection of what is being attempted in different schools. Participants could compare the adequacies or otherwise of their present programmes and find themselves better equipped for effecting change in field work programmes of their respective schools.

Suggestions

1. More time could have been allotted for each session.
2. It would have been proper to organise cultural programmes for and by the participants which would have reduced the tension created by exacting assignments.
3. More agency visits, increased use of audio-visual aids, concurrent evaluation and the participation of the members would have enriched the workshop.
4. A daily process recording of the entire group would have brought out the dynamics of the workshop and groups.

At the end, the group as a whole expressed its appreciation for the skillful and able conduct of the workshop for the benefit of social work educators.

EVALUATION BY GROUP B (NUMBER OF MEMBERS 14)

In the light of the objectives outlined it was unanimously felt that the workshop on Field Work was a tremendous success. Most of the objectives had been achieved to a great extent.

On various aspects of the workshop the following observations were made :

1. The topics on Review, Organisation and Administration were dealt with satisfactorily.

2. Content of field work could have been discussed keeping in mind the different levels of social work education. Much emphasis was laid on MSW thereby rather neglecting the BSW programme.

3. The session on supervision could have been given more time. Certain areas discussed under supervisory inputs were found to be repetitive.

4. Evaluation was discussed fairly well and so were recording and block field work.

5. The topic New Areas of Practice was very lively. Had the role of social workers working in new areas been emphasized, it would have added to the value of exchange.

6. The discussion on Developmental Field Work was at a very abstract level. The concepts were not clear. This could probably be due to the paucity of material. Besides, it could have been discussed in sub-groups as well.

7. Measures to strengthen field work was another area which could have been attended to more adequately.

8. Staff development was however discussed elaborately.

General evaluation and impressions

The group was just the right size for a workshop of this kind. The participants appreciated the fact that they were given freedom to form their own groups and sub-groups which facilitated discussion.

2. Discussion on Block field work at the plenary was welcome as it was a timely movement from sub-group sessions. This was an indication of effective planning.

3. One of the members observed that the Director was rather demanding during the first week. It looked like he drew whatever he wanted during the period. However the sincerity of the Director deserved appreciation.

4. While some members were of the view that prior

intimation should have been given to the chair-persons for effective handling of the sessions, others felt that since it was spontaneous, it was a good experience for those chairing the sessions. The younger members of the group were found to be very good both as chair-persons and as rapporteurs.

5. There were times when the participant had to rush through the sessions just for the sake of completing the discussions. More time therefore could have been allotted for group discussions.

6. The efficiency and promptness in which the materials were typed, cyclostyled, and distributed deserved to be appreciated.

7. One participant felt that BSW programme had not been discussed adequately. This was primarily due to the fact that the majority of the participants were teachers at the MSW level. A suggestion in this regard was made that a similar workshop could be conducted wherein only the schools offering BSW courses could be invited.

8. A few members felt that the workshop was more of sharing of experience and more like a refresher course. Vital issues should have been given due consideration.

9. One of the members felt that instead of viewing them as learners they could have been regarded as persons with experience and some more time could have been devoted for the discussion of actual problems faced by the educators.

10. Some members felt that issues related to poverty and political situation in the communities where students were placed for field work could have been discussed in detail. Also, in a workshop of this nature more opportunity could have been given to the participants for introspection as supervisors. This could have perhaps been achieved through transaction analysis sessions, simulation games, sensitization and so on.

11. It was felt by some that a review of earlier workshops could have helped in making participants aware of what had been done before. The group felt that it would be beneficial for all the schools if the consolidated report of this workshop was sent as early as possible.

12. The workshop was a success in so far as it could tap the resources from within the group. However it was felt that

external resource persons could have contributed more if they had "journeyed along with the group".

13. Some felt that for a workshop of this type people of the same level with approximately the same number of years of experience should have been invited. However there were others who felt that it was always more beneficial to have a mixed group.

Lastly the workshop was an exercise in co-operative group endeavour and in the utilisation of human efforts towards investment in the profession. Thanks to the untiring efforts of the Director and the participants of the workshop.

EVALUTION BY GROUP C : (NUMBER OF MEMBERS 6)

To start with, the group decided to list the following important areas for the evaluation of the workshop :

(i) Felt-need of the workshop
(ii) Organisation
(iii) Accommodation
(iv) Participation and communication
(v) Content
(vi) Limitations and
(vii) Suggestions

Felt-need of the workshop

1. Field work is an integral and important part in the programme of social work education. It has got varied patterns in different schools of social work.

2. Therefore there was a need to share common experiences, and to identify new avenues for social work practice. In this sense the workshop was very timely and welcome.

Organisation

The planning of the workshop was well-thought out in terms of time, place, session, and purpose. The workshop provided an opportunity to all the schools of social work in the country and adequate time was given to the participants to come prepared.

The workshop setting and other arrangements were good.

Flexibility in the time schedule and discussions was adequately provided. The cyclostyled materials arising out of group discussions and other materials were substantial and were distributed on time.

Accommodation

Even though the place was far off from the workshop venue, participants did not find difficulty due to school's transport. Food was good.

Accommodation gave opportunity to participants to know each other personally. In short board, lodging and transport were adequate.

Participation and communication

Division and sub-division into groups, rotation of chair-persons, resource persons and rapporteurs gave opportunity to everybody to share responsibility. These exchanges of views and opinions provided unique learning opportunities and imparted developmental perspective to the workshop. The workshop gave real insight into the various aspects and dimensions of field work. It also helped to draw out individual potential, resources and capabilities. Individual members through participation gained confidence and a sense of achievement.

Content

The subjects of the workshop were very relevant and every aspect of field work was discussed. The group can say confidently that the workshop helped members to understand the concept of field work and its different elements.

The resource from within the group was well utilized.

Limitations

1. The extension of daily work schedule continuing even after dinner spoke for the need to provide a few more working sessions for the workshop.

2. Involvement of student representatives would have supplemented the deliberations of the workshop and made it more broad-based.

3. Two members of the group had a feeling that a few

resource persons and participants with a number of years of experience contributed, at times, more than what was necessary for the deliberations.

Suggestions

1. Such workshops should be organised by rotation in different parts of the country.

2. The recommendations of the workshop should be reviewed every three years.

3. As a continuation of the workshop, a news-letter could be circulated occasionally in order to maintain a link for the exchange of information on field work. The news-letter may be given the title 'Developmental/field work in social work'.

4. All the participants should make efforts to implement the recommendation of the workshop in their respective schools. In this connection, school/department may prepare and implement a two-year plan on field work.

5. The deliberations of the workshop might be sent to all the schools/departments, the Indian Association of Trained Social Workers, and the Association of Schools of Social Work in India.

The Director of the workshop took tremendous pains, and provided all possible care to ensure the smooth functioning of the workshop during its various stages. His untiring, unfailing, and above all, timely and friendly intervention set a pattern for all the participants to emulate in organising such democratic group discussions in future.

The remarkable feature of workshop was group discussion, participation, involvement, clarification, raising of issues, and checking and cross-checking of questions both in informal and formal settings without any acrimony, bitterness or bickerings.

The workshop was a unique experience for all the participants.

DELIBERATIONS OF THE WORKSHOP AND THEIR IMPLICATIONS FOR HUMAN SERVICE PROFESSIONS : AN ANALYSIS*

Deliberations of the workshop were carried out through plenary and group sessions. While the plenaries provided opportunities to discusss broad areas of field work, to arrive at a consensus, to evolve guidelines for working groups, and to reconcile or appreciate differences, to the extent possible, the working group sessions reflected both commonalities and differences in approach to field work. Even though the same guidelines were used by working groups, perceptions of the problem or approaches varied. In some cases guidelines were evolved by the groups themselves, thus making a departure from the general guideline(s). This approach is reflected more in the area of supervision.

The objectives of field were broadly agreed upon in the plenary session, but these were further re-defined by the group subsequently, and the stress was laid more on purposeful learning experience, fostering of attitudes, development of skills and application. Thus, development of ability to perceive and appreciate social situations, assistance to the client-system, and personal and professional growth specifically listed as objectives of field work in the beginning appear to have been either subsumed by or implied in re-definition. However the objectives of field work, in whichever order they are listed or stressed upon, are the perceptions of educators only and it is empirically not yet known as to what actually happens to the student during and at the end of a structured field work process. It is likely that the responses of students obtained through a well-designed longitudinal study (action-research preferably) may correspond with what has been assumed so far by educators, but this is an area yet to be explored systematically, including educators' observations and experiences.

On the organisation and administration of field work, the

*By the Editor

two groups of the workshop chose different set of questions, and in the process they have complemented their efforts. While discussing contents of field work, the two groups have again tried to strengthen and supplement each other's effort, but in the delineation of phases of field work, they seem to differ markedly. Group A worked out the content on the basis of four phases of field work whereas Group B visualized the evolution and development of field work process through six inter-connected phases. Though one may find similarities between the approaches to phases of field work of the two groups, the fact that the third phase of Group A, namely, 'exploration-assessment-action' was spelt out further by Group B into three distinct phases, namely, induction, exploration-identification and planning-implemention is important for its emphasis. Differences exist between the two groups on community field work in their illustrations more than on field work in an agency. This only shows that introduction of 'dead uniformity' in field work is neither possible nor desirable, and that guidelines should be treated only as *suggestive*. They should be adapted to emerging situations in which the schools of social work function. Therefore, there is no final guideline on field work, and this needs to be developed and improved upon through faculty dialogue on a continuing basis.

The approaches of the two groups on selection of agencies and placement of students also show uniqueness and variation in their respective approaches. While Group A chose to discuss concerns of social work educators and practical issues, Group B seems to have dealt with the topic more objectively and developed some criteria for both the areas. Group A's contribution on the definition of the field, its properties, and typology, though useful, did not preoccupy Group B's thinking. Both the groups worked independently of the other but enriched each other's contributions.

On supervision again the two groups show distinctiveness in their approaches. Group A addressed itself to the problems faced by supervisors, and laid more stress on the educational component of supervision ; Group B dealt with the topic component-wise, and laid stress on *educational objectives* as well as the *needs* and *type* of the learner. This is clearly reflected in the definitions of supervision given by the two groups.

Approach to evaluation by Group A, appears to be more broad and general although it did work out a scheme of weightage by the level of education. Objectives of evaluation have been perceived as common by both the groups except for inclusion of 'arresting growth neutralising element' by Group A. Group B has preferred to approach the problem of evaluation in relation to the *field* and *methods*, and has worked out an elaborate scheme of weightage for students' work. In this scheme the stress is also on the evaluation of supervisory input.

Recording is the area which has shown striking similarity between the two groups and therefore instead of presenting their reports separately, a comprehensive report incorporating group reports has been presented in the proceedings.

Evaluation of the workshop by the three groups can be called an exercise in 'participant evaluation'. The three groups looked back and reflected upon the entire process in terms of what they contributed to it and also what they received from it. They developed their own guidelines, and through approaching the theme from different angles, that is, general remarks, structure and content-wise detail, and focus on felt-need, they succeeded in highlighting all the aspects of the process without any pro-forma. This indeed was remarkable.

Developmental field work has the Achille's heel of the faculty development workshop, the input by the organisers and resource persons on the subject notwithstanding. Only some headway could be made in this area. But this was not unanticipated, especially when one surveys the library resources of the schools of social work, the availability and generation of indigenous material on the subject, exchange of field experiences, generic-specialization controversy, and lack of opportunities for staff development through inter-disciplinary interaction. Nevertheless whatever little could be achieved was satifying to quite a few of the participants.

One thing which the workshop experience made abundantly clear to most of the participants was that in the provision of services by human service professions and in the preparation of trained manpower, approaches are varied; and within the framework of a profession's goals, they should be tried. For example, effective entry into the area of health may be possible through welfare and/or education; in the area of education through welfare and nutrition; in the field of social welfare, both through education and health and also through law; and in the field of community development through professionals, para-professionals as well as through people and their organisations. Case studies on such experiments in different areas are now available to show that human service professions need to transcend their boundaries and seek or forge alliances with other *professions* and with the *people* in order to meet the twin challenges of social development and change in developing societies. Perception of human problems and approaches or alternatives to deal with them within a holistic framework was the main thrust of the session on developmental field work. To an extent this awareness and appreciation is reflected in the deliberations of the workshop. However, this proved to be a difficult area because it challenged own training background, participants professional convictions, attitudes and orientations, and the existing pattern of professional education of which they are a part. Also the theme's yet undefined boundaries, and exacting demands on the educator in the area of study, practice and reflection made its acceptance difficult. Such a challenge is not a unique experience for social work educators only; it affects other human service professions as well. In fact it brings into focus a conflict between tradition and change, and between new orientation and old practice in the development process within and between the human service professions, and their slowly changing response to emerging needs.

The deliberations of the workshop reflect throughout the concern of the group(s) with rationality in approach towards understanding human predicaments and to the provision of human services in contradistinction with uniformity in these areas; with the trying out of plurality of approaches against their singularity and prescriptivity; and with the continuing learning and evolution of negotiated efforts as well as solutions against their finality. Thus, while identifying the phases of field work and working out details the groups were acutely conscious of their interlinkages and overlaps but they undertook this exercise in order to rationally identify distinctiveness of the process of field work so that educational guidance could be consciously and meaningfully directed and balanced. Thus application of rationality and humanism characterized the ethos of the workshop.

The trend of discussions reflects the concern of the group with *form* and *structure* of field work more than the *process*. Although phases of field work identified by the groups and their inter-relationships do imply the processual nature of practice, recording, content, evaluation, supervision, and selection/placement of students clearly dominate the deliberations. (Reports of the schools were also activity-and form-centred, projecting field work as a compulsory, in some cases even peripheral, and useful activity than an integral part of professional education). One of the factors which appears to be responsible for such a trend is that even after 48 years of professional education, the goals, forms, and boundaries of field work (the basics) have not been *clearly*, *conceptually*, and *integrally* established, and therefore participants tried to evolve guidelines to consciously direct this process. The other factor appears to be the heavy demand placed upon the educator by the process approach than by directed instruction. The former requires a holistic perspective, acquisition and application of social work knowledge as well as knowledge relevant to social work, innovation and experimentation in educational guidance and selection of assignments, interaction, reflection, and participation with the learner, individualisation of goals, content and structure of field work to meet the educational needs of the learner within the broad framework evolved by the concerned school of social work. The third factor perhaps is linked with authoritarian approach to professional education, and form and structure of this system as a means to exercise direction and control over the learner whereas the demand of field work process gravitates more towards the cultivation of a kind of 'liberated rationality' through mutual growth, dialogues and sharing. It appears from the present trend that this aspect of professional education will take more time to evolve in a traditional society. The contribution of the workshop however in the area of form and structure is commendable indeed, and it needs to be worked through, and modified accordingly with a focus progressively on the process. Also, the materials generated by the workshop, especially on community work, adequated highlight the importance of developmental approach and the application of integrated methods which has hitherto a remained rather neglected area in social work education and practice.

RECOMMENDATIONS OF THE WORKSHOP

The workshop held fourteen plenary sessions and twenty group sessions between 16th and 29th March 1981 at the Delhi School of Social Work. The recommendations are as follows :

Parity of field work with theory courses

Field work is an integral part of the curriculum of social work and hence it should be treated on par with theory courses.

Orientation of students

There is a need for orientation programmes for students at different levels of social work education. Serious efforts should therefore go into the planning of such orientation programmes.

The field work co-ordinator should necessarily be present throughout the orientation programme in all the sessions.

Further, since it is usually the first encounter of students with professional social work, it is not necessary to involve all the members of the staff in the orientation programme.

Placement

Students should be placed in the field which showed potential for positive learning and teaching.

Organization and administration

(i) Since field work is accepted as an integral part of social work curriculum and involves a variety of tasks, it is necessary to have a structure or nucleus for co-ordinating field work. This should be a functionally distinct unit within the set-up of the school or the Department. A full-time and experienced member of staff should be assigned the responsibility of co-ordinating field work. The head of the institution should not ordinarily assume the responsibility for field work co-ordination because such an arrangement will impart field work an administrative rather than an educational focus. The responsibility of field work co-ordination must rotate amongst the members of the staff.

(ii) Work of co-ordination should be a delegated responsibility and therefore the field work co-ordinator should report to the head of the institution. Crucial or sensitive decisions however must be conveyed to and approved by a larger body constituted for the purpose. It may be the entire teaching staff, an academic committee, or a sub-committee.

(iii) On account of his additional responsibility, the co-ordinator may be given some concessions, (not honorarium) in terms of lesser number of students to supervise and also compensatory leave for the work done during vacations.

(iv) The co-ordinator should also be given necessary secretarial assistance right from the phase of pre-admission through that of post-evaluation.

Definition of field

The workshop recognized that the 'field' in field work had not been clearly defined as yet and there was a need to do so. Deliberations of the workshop led to the following definition of the field : "The field consists of a situation in which social work has got a deep and abiding professional concern and which provides opportunities for positive learning experiences through guided interaction in the areas of need, problems, resources, and requisite action".

Content

The content of field work must be worked out according to the identified phases of field work, namely—orientation, placement, induction-exploration-assessment, planning-implementation, and evaluation.

Developmental perspective in field work

Field work and field work instruction should adopt a developmental perspective.

Interlinkage between under-graduate and post-graduate programme

Emphasis must be placed on the common core of field work practice and on the linkage between the BSW and MSW courses.

Integrated approach

The essential underlying unity among the methods and fields

of social work practice must be recognised and such recognition should lead to suitable modification in the approach to field work instruction.

Supervision

(i) Every social work teacher must necessarily take up field work supervision of students and there should be no separate posts of field work supervisors. The heads of the departments/school institutions must also supervise a few students.

(ii) Only teachers with two years of post-graduate education in social work should supervise students' field work.

(iii) Field work supervision in social work must endeavour to use the integrated and developmental approach to social work practice.

(iv) Field work supervisors should be enrolled as full-fledged members of the staff council and should participate in all the staff development programmes. The field work supervisor should be accepted as internal examiners and also serve on the panel for viva-voce examination on field work. He should also be given opportunities to represent the profession in regional, national and international conferences, seminars and symposia.

(v) Field work supervisor should get all facilities on par with the teaching staff for undertaking any study or research project of own choice and of professional importance.

(vi) Two hours per student per week must be spent on supervision by the teachers.

(vii) Weekly individual conferences must be held, and group conferences should also be conducted periodically. Supervision is a serious work which requires certain preparation and therefore, casual or "roadside" supervision should not be practised.

Evaluation

Evaluation of student's work should be periodically done and communicated to the student. Necessary records should be kept for this purpose.

The supervisor who supervises the student should play a

major role in evaluation. However in cases where a review is necessary, moderation should be done by a Committee consisting of the head of the department/institute, external supervisor(s), the Field work Co-ordinator and the concerned supervisor.

The question of associating external examiners in field work may be examined by the individual schools of social work. The observations of external evaluators in field work should be passed on to the supervisors concerned for reference and improvement.

Field work time

The time allotted at present for field work in a week includes time spent on individual and group conferences, and in recording. Although students may actually spend more time in recording, care should be taken to see that recording does not become a substitute for actual work. Therefore two hours out of fifteen per week should be assigned for recording.

Recording

Analytical and interpretative content in records should be encouraged with the progression in student's learning.

Visits

Surprise checks/visits reflect supervisor's own inadequacy and therefore usually these should not be conducted or resorted to.

Block placement

Block placement must be compulsory for the post-graduate students in social work. Orientation should be given before block placement and the period of block placement should be at least from four to eight weeks.

Staff development

Heads of the schools of social work should make efforts for staff development and should remove such hindrances which might arise in the organisation of such programmes.

New areas of field work practice

Serious effort should be made by the schools to utilise new and unconventional field situations for field work placements, that is, activist groups involved in social, human rights and environmental movements, relocation areas, citizens' groups and so on. Only selected students under interested supervisors should be sent for such placements initially.

Need for workshop at the under-graduate level

Since the under-graduate programme of field work needs to be discussed at length, another workshop for only those schools which offer under-graduate courses should be organised.

PART TWO

3

FIELD WORK PROCESS IN SOCIAL WORK

R. R. Singh

"Awareness is imprisoned in every human being. The educative or conscientizing process leads to expressing this awareness, much the way a certain temperature hatches an egg to bring forth the little bird . . . ." Experience is a cruel teacher, it punishes first and teaches later.

BABA AMTE

I

NATURE

FIELD work process in social work is a dynamic, rational,* educationally planned and guided, interactive, intuitive and an integrative process. It is a continuing interaction between socio-educational goals of the profession, and the selection of meaningful learning experiences in the field. It is an interaction between the learner and the educator; and between the *actor* (subject) and the *acted upon* (object). Feelings, perceptions, values, knowledge, attitudes, skills, and perspectives of the learner and that of the educator are affected by this process. The learner, the educator, the field, the system (environment of professional education and the relationship of the profession with other professions and the larger society) constitute its dynamic elements. These elements are continuously interacting, evolving, developing, and changing

* Consideration of non-rational dimensions of a social reality or field is implicit in the rational approach.

with new *whats*, *whys*, and *hows* added to them in time and space. The process is composed of varied and inter-related situations which are inherently consensual, conflicting and even contradictory; and therefore it calls for multifaceted practice and innovative approaches.

Evidence

Confirmation of the multifaceted nature of the process is borne out by empirical evidence. It was found in a study[1] that students intervened in a wide range of target systems . . . use of methods paralleled the range of target systems, and there was a striking consistency in the rankings of target groups and methods across field . . . (for) social work in every field of practice includes a broad range of target system and utilizes a similarly broad range of intervention methods . . . . A focus on one method would not meet the demands of these fields (In fact) demands of actual practice in a field are broader and more complex than single method approaches, and a potential gap is noticed between conceptions of practice and the actual practice of social work.

Professional socialization

Thus, field work process is not a 'universalistic' form of practice experience; it is a holistic and individualizing, and professionally socializing process ; a form of creative and complementing endeavour through fellowship. It seeks to develop humaneness, compassion, caring and a readiness to share, to respond to and to experiment with human and environmental needs/situations to bring about desired change(s) in them. It is a kind of bridging of *common* knowledge and *professional* knowledge[2] ; a method of acquiring knowledge, and experience by entering into a concrete relationship with real objects and processes.[3] The quality of encounter in it is more important than scholarly knowledge.[4] The interaction of the various components of field work process could be illustrated briefly by the reactions of two students who were interviewed on their field work experiences. One narrated his experience of community work. After he was given orientation where he was told that children are the entry points to reach adults, he went along with others to the community; "started on his own" ; "roamed about", and was plagued by such questions as What to do ? where to go ? whom to talk ? After some time he decided to go to people who were sitting and gossiping. They were surprised to see workers who introduced themselves as students of 15th class (and not M.A.) and came to the community for their practical work. Residents were satisfied with that explanation. When asked to tell about themselves, some responded while others did not . . . . Since there was nothing else to do for the time being workers played with children. Their parents were happy . . . . By experience students learnt that certain projects were ambitious and so they selected individual cases, organised recreation programmes, (picnic and film show) and taught children. This led to the formation of a youth club, and to the diversification of their activities which were educative and meaningful.

The other student felt that she, being a 'lone' worker, worked for people and not with them, found it difficult to mobilise resources and to organise people collectively and wondered whether field work in community was an exercise for failure ! Why do not social workers live with people because they do not know them well enough ? Due to disappointments, own limitations and lack of experience, case work in her case predominated other forms of social work in the community.

One can see from the above that between entry and exist when a student is engaged in a guided action, changes occur in his *self* (feelings, attitudes and orientation); his *method* of working; *nature of work* and *selection of goals* (his perceiving, knowing and thinking), the people he works with; and the experiencing of the entire process. This interaction could be conceptualised as follows :

Uneven process

It may be added here that the above framework is not so neat and smooth in practice as it appears. Discontinuities in action, lack of information and awareness, miscommunication, misunderstandings, inappropriate action, ambitious goals, groups' resistance, professional rivalry, inadequate resources, differences in perceptions etc. often occur, and add to the complexity of the field work learning. They also interfere with the smooth progression of the process. Since the field work process affects

Dynamic interaction between the components of field work process

Field work process (Màcro dimensions)	Field/situation for educational experience (Micro dimensions)	Students field work learning	Educationally planned and guided experience
Priority area of human-environmental needs	Characteristics of the chosen field and its relationship with other need situations	Self of the learner : motivation attitudes, knowledge, skills, capacity, assets and liabilities	Evidence to learner in self-awareness and introducing him to a theoretical framework for professional practice.
Translating need situations into service and educational goals	Specific service/educational goals in the chosen area	Opportunities and demands of the field situation and expectations of the profession; goal-setting	Definition of field situation and professional role in relation to field; anticipation of problems; teaching when class instruction does not parallel field work demands
Identification and selection of specific area/need	Identification of specific situations	Matching the self with field work, tasks and goals, selection of stimulating and challenging assignments but not overwhelming ones	Help in the judicious selection of areas of need/tasks/units of work, and approaches in relation to practice and educational goals; help at all stages ranging from exposure to integration
Possibilities of professional intervention for change through external and internal efforts within a theoretical framework	Exploration of action potential, resources, and participation by individuals/groups application of professional knowledge and anticipated problems		
Determining and evolving approaches and marshalling recources—internal, external intra-professional	Determination, phasing and initiation of action and modification thereof. Review of goals, tasks and approaches	Mutual exploration/determination of assignments, theoretical inputs, likely blocks	

Planning, phasing and inter-linking of interventive action by own and other professions	in relation to practice-theory. Meaning of field work experience and its macro and micro implications	Exploration of resources and determination phasing/ initiaion of action by learner	
Review of need situation and approaches in a macro-perspective.		The action process-planning, continuation and termination. Review of change in specific need situation, the learner, practice-theory, integration of learning	Information on resources Sequential structuring of tasks/actions and their continuity Help in planning, organisa-tion, inititation and termi-nation of action/application of knowledge Help with dead-ends—through demonstration, suggesting alternatives, participation, reading references; help in relating/ integrating. Evaluation in terms of self-growth, change in the field, interaction between worker, field and other professionals, and links between macro and micro perspectives

knowledge, skills, and attitudes of the learner, a few examples in these areas will be in order.

Changes in knowledge, attitude, and skills

Only by practice the learner knows and appreciates that social work interview[5] is concerned with personal interaction and it is a mutual and purposeful talking; communication involves both monologues and dialogues, is concerned with proximics, kinesics, paralinguistics, oil factory channels, tactility, visual sensations, postures, voice etc; one does not accept a thing which is good or bad but real; coverage of territory means less depth; beginning interviewer asks more question at a time; asks *why* more than *what*; that interview transitions need to be dealt with skillfully; hearing is different from listening—the former being a physical and the latter a mental—emotional process; and pauses and silences are not the same and these should not embarrass the worker. In the interview[6] the client brings his problem, experiences, feelings, attempts, attitudes to help seeking, and all these should engage worker's attention. It is through field work process that a learner appreciates differences (31 of them) between the beginning and advanced interviews[7], that, is beginner focussing on concrete needs whereas advanced student on emotional and feeling aspects of concrete needs. The beginner also learns that he focusses on structured approach, direct questioning and stereotyped introductions, whereas the advanced student adopts flexible approach, selective questioning and varied introduction. Through practice he learns that any group may not serve the purpose of social work group, and that a group passes through several phases[8] : pre-group phase, group formation, integration, disintegration, reintegration/synthesis, and termination. The size of group, space and time determine the type and quality of interaction and pattern of communication. This knowledge has got both skill and attitudinal dimensions.

Learning in the area of skills occurs[9] through observation, listening, understanding, asking, explaining, advising, preparing, limiting, confronting, anticipating, interpreting and reviewing while in a work situation.

Attitudes[10] of listening, understanding, positive and unconditional regard, rational approach, readiness to creatively respond, and to participate develop through direct confrontation with reality. Questions on historical appreciation of need—situation, its direction and links with other situations, adequacy of professional efforts, obstacles to these and people's efforts which arise in the mind of the learner shape and broaden his perspectives. These can be structured as part of educational guidance.

In the light of the above, field work should not be treated as given or assumed; or a set pattern to be repeated mechanically year after year with new batches of students. Each area of practice should be examined in terms of societal goals, its relevance to the goals/functions of social work profession; possibilities of educationally planned intervention and practice opportunities; and its growth potential in the area of social development, and inter-professional collaboration. This calls for a continuing dialogue between educators on the selection and use of field/agencies every three or five years, and introduction of new agencies or educational content which strengthen field work process.

Development or change of knowledge, attitude, skills, and perspectives are interrelated occurrences and experiences in professional education and practice. This will be clear from the examples that follow. A final year student after she learnt about her client's diagnosis as a case of terminal stage cancer, was so shocked that she felt nothing could be done by her in the matter, not even communicating the diagnosis to the patient and her family. The supervisor shared his experience, and also that of his professional colleague who was wrongly diagnosed twice as a case of leukemia and who had even taken a life insurance policy thereafter. Literature on the subject was referred, and the student was asked whether as a professional worker she could be "choosy" while intervening in need situations. This made her to review and ponder over her initial reactions and attitudes. Her co-worker in the area was planning to make further contacts so that she could know the block *completely* before starting action, only to be told by the supervisor that no social worker can claim to secure complete knowledge of the field which is always changing. The student appreciated this point and felt that she was probably doing so because she was yet unsure of her actions in community work.

Another student, who was placed in the community chanced to visit a family of low repute during her contact and listened to its multiple problems. She was later told by her new acquaintances that women in that family were prostitutes. She was shocked to know the "truth" which was concealed from her by the family as it was not shared in the first contact. Student's parents were also against her continuing with this case, and she was feeling insecure and ambivalent. In the conference she was inclined to help the family with part of its problem on a *rational level*. She was however finding it hard to overcome the reactions of community members who were likely to be alienated from her, and also the parental pressure. The student was advised not to sever contacts with the family; keep a low profile; equip herself adequately to work with the multi-problem family through the review of relevant literature; and prepare ground in the community so that her identity and intervention were not mistaken by people who were co-operating with her in other programmes. By this time it was hoped that her parents would also get over their initial reactions through assurance that she would be safe.

The response of a first year student was indeed typical. She cursed god for being cruel to children who were mentally retarded when she visited her field work agency for the first time. She was helped to see how she could help these children through love, understanding, and action by accepting the reality as it was.

Problems

Problems or discontinuities in the field work process arise because of inadequate educational planning by a school passive or casual role of individual supervisors which reflects a split between preaching and practice, the educational environment, and the nature/functioning of the field/agency. Examples of inadequate educational planning and supervision are legion. Cases of students being placed in 3-4 agencies or with supervisors in an academic session, assignment of more cases without due regard to work load when a student has already got six of them, asking a student of the first year to do cost-benefit analysis of three years in the first fortnight and insisting upon the same without mentioning about guidance given and its outcome at the end, assigning student to practise social work methods whereas he undertakes a variety of useful activities, stress on case investigation and group activities rather than on casework and group work, imbalance in supervisory input—introduction, information, reporting of students work, guidance, evaluation and so on, uneven periodicity of fortnightly reports and their sharing with students, expectation of clarity of own role by student in the first fortnight (supervisor found considerable vagueness but student held the view that role was clearly mentioned)[11] are but indicative of an educational process which is inadequate, *ad hoc*, arbitrary and unplanned. Inadequately planned and guided field work converts even a motivated student into a marginalised one. In a statistical analysis of nine components chosen from supervisory conference records, planning and decision-making, review and analysis, and discussion of theory of social work and allied disciplines were referred to most frequently in that order, and other components like information, psycho-social aspects of the situation, students' conscious preparation, feelings and attitudes, constructive criticism etc. were least referred.

In another study[12] descriptive, and problem-centred comments far outnumbered those on guidance, evaluation, information, and suggestions about reading references in the fortnightly records maintained by the supervisors. Therefore there is a need to consciously review the field work process, and plan it adequately in order to provide a meaningful educational experience to students. This should include provision for 'compensatory guidance' when field work is affected by disruption of one kind or other in educational institutions or the field.

Details on the structure of field work, supervision, evaluation and recording have already been given in the proceedings of the workshop, and the contributions made by the educators in this volume. Two illustrative materials in section II of this paper present the student's and the supervisor's view of *progression in learning through field work process along with comments, wherever necessary.*

II

PROCESS OF LEARNING IN FIELD WORK* : A STUDENT'S VIEW

Placement

I have been placed in Trilokpuri resettlement colony which is situated across the Yamuna. The colony like other colonies (resettlement) was set up during the Emergency period having an assembly of people from all castes, creed and religions in its 25 blocks.

The tools of a service-oriented discipline

The most important tool at the disposal of the social worker is his own person—his own 'self'. He uses his self through a unique relationship with the client and others in his (client's) environment.

Demands on the self

In social work learning, however, the learner has to develop self awareness to a far greater degree than is required by other professions. The demands made on the 'self' are in four areas of 'feeling', 'knowing', 'doing' and 'being'. The practitioner has to assimilate a body of knowledge to equip himself for practice, so a demand on the 'knowing' aspect of self is unavoidable. This process of 'knowing', 'thinking', 'doing' and 'being' is a product of one's continuing orientation.

Progression in field work learning *The first stage*

Last for a period of two months and proceeded from, in the social work jargon, rapport-building to ascertaining needs, and finally to priority-determination. Needs were sensed with eyes where the retina would picture everything as economic (myself being from an economics background). The underlying cause

* Edited by the author from the group conference paper, presented by Hemant K. Sarma, M.A. (Previous) student on January 22, 1982. The student at the time of presentation had been exposed to about 30 days of field work over a period of four months. The author was also his field work supervisor.

of all evils was economic. The follow-up action was also on the same lines with a view that problems would ease if sufficient income could be generated. Although this approach had been critically commented upon in the supervisory conference, I wanted to test it out myself. The supervisor gave me freedom to do so.

I proposed to get resources from governmental and non-governmental agencies without even setting up a proper base in the community. Folly was soon realized and amendments were made which marked the end of this stage. Factors which came to light were : (1) absense of any institutional back-up—no proper and satisfying answer to questions like who are you ? Why have you come here ? and (2) generation of enormous expectations through the courtesy of government and other agencies resulting in the gratification of needs from external resources without even an iota of effort on people's part. Statements like get me a job ? etc illustrate this situtaion.

The second stage was characterized by work in the community amongst a selected group of people (target group) with the conviction that community can develop capacity to deal with its own problems. This led to further exploration of the field with a new vision. Economic vision was gradually replaced by social.* I was able to see during this process that the field is very dynamic and it generates its own resources to meet needs. I, therefore, with the help of the supervisor, redefined my earlier role. Previously I thought that the only possible way to meet unmet needs was to procure resources from anywhere. Now when I saw that the community had enough resource, my role was confined to only channelizing it through the introduction of a

* Another student, who espoused the cause of liberation of women and their economic independence, discovered from her field work in the Anti-Dowry Cell that an educated and employed woman, now living separated, and whose salary of Rs. 700/- per month was equal to that of her husband, was still hoping that she would be reunited one day for the sake of her two young children. The student said, "If I were in her place, I won't have cared for him. But in this case and similar others I realise that economic approach to women's development alone was not the answer to their problems which were structural". (See also Neerja Chowdhary's write-up on "Daring To Stay Single". *The Statesman*, February 18, 1984).

scientific approach with 'constructive' work.

I then thought of and started a humble project of making paper bags with a selected group of people. It was started with least of resources on the principal of 'plouging-back profits'. I learnt the job myself from a vendor in another block. Currently four people are gainfully occupied in this project. Important features of the project are :

1.	Production (target)—2500 bags per day per person	
2.	Income per 80 bags	Rs. 2.50
3.	Total income per day	Rs. 7.80
4.	Less cost, like transportation, glue, etc.	Rs. 2.00
	Net profit per day	Rs. 5.80

These calculations formed the basis to organise a group of interested residents to work with them; and in the process to experience the dynamics of interaction both frustrating and rewarding—between members themselves, between members and work, and between the worker and the group.

LEARNING THROUGH FIELD WORK PROCESS : A SUPERVISOR'S VIEW

The following is a brief description of the fortnightly reports (edited) given by a supervisor on field work of an M.A. final student who was placed in the home for healthy children of leprosy patients :

THIRD TERM

1. Student met the officials; got acquainted with the set-up and organised his work schedule.
2. Met children individually and in groups; discussed assignments with agency supervisor; fair perception of role; he is to formulate specific work plan.
3. Change of field work time to enlarge helping role; assumed the role of caretaker at the time of meal distribution; seems to have found a "footing"; is sensitive.

4. Contact with staff, and with other institutions ; is receptive; took classes for children.
5. Is responsible and involved; needs to improve quality and content of record; working to improve library facility of the institution.
6. Improvement seen in recording; individualising situations; stress on interpersonal relations in group/ situations; purposeful observation in records; agency visits; reading suggested; application of readings.
7. Improvement in recording; organised games competitions; positve attitude to work.
8. Took leave; active involvement; motivated; to study the role of case work service in the agency; preparing interview guide.
9. Active and busy; organizing a trip; individualizing situations; taking classes; made good collection for library.
10. Excellent working relationship ; tour for 20 children.

FOURTH TERM

1. Presented group conference paper; integrating theory; reflection on group activity; maintained contact during vacation.
2. Worked on extra-days; active in group conference; engaged in routine administration; approach purposeful.
3. Supervisor observed interest of student in children on the day of visit; is quite clear of objectives.
4. Took leave; reflective on programme media in group as an educational process; aware, insightful and objective; evidence of professional maturity.
5. Useful/class sessions; informal group sessions; preparing an assignment on casework.
6. Class teaching, analytical and introspective; good write-up on casework.

Analysis and application

The above presentation gives an idea of the perceptions of a supervisor in field work learning. The supervisor's role however does not show a "sequential structure and continuity" in guiding field work learning through 'active supervision' and sharing of field work experiences. Objectives for the student in field work do not seem to have been jointly and specifically evolved and guidance given accordingly. Supervisor's comments do not adequately give an idea of the gradual and systematic evaluation of tasks in field work, and their planned termination in the two terms. All the activities listed, though useful, could have been woven around stipulated objectives, and conscious attention could have been paid to children's emotional and social needs through specific individual and group tasks over a period of time. A balance could have been struck between child-centred social work tasks; educational, administrative and survey work (supportive tasks), and co-ordination with other centres or resources. Developmental dimensions could also have been introduced in the process through references to preventive and rehabilitative work in the area of leprosy control, socio-economic background of victims, distribution and use of health resources, 'vulnerable' geographical areas, social and health care policies, and adequacy or otherwise of professional organisations in the field of human services. The sequence of reported aspects is *ad hoc*; and activity rather than goal-and process-centred. It gives an impression as if the student was left largely on his own with supervisor playing only a passive role in the entire process. Nevertheless the account does give some idea of progression in field work learning, professional growth in the learner; definition and assumption of professional tasks/roles; and also role of the supervisor in the process. Since the records maintained by the supervisors are not exhaustive, limitation of analysis from such data is obvious.

Bartha Raynold's[13] five stages of learning in social work practice, namely, acute consciousness of the self, sink or swim adaptation, understanding the situation without power to control one's activity, relative mastery, and learning to teach could be seen from the above descriptions. Such entries as perception of one's role, formulating a specific work plan, finding a "footing", progressive involvement, individualizing of situations, integration of theory, clarity of objectives, professional maturity etc. are evidences of an orderly progression in learning.

Also clear is the evidence of conscious attention . . . groping, experimentation through trial and error . . . and repetition of adequate behaviour pattern[14] found useful in the growth cycle by the student. The account given by the student of his experience also reflects the above characteristics in his field work learning.

It may be clarified however, that any regular and socially useful activity, consciously planned or incidental, should not be confused with field work process which, on the contrary, is characterized by the consciousness of educational goals, definition of the situation, purposiveness, planning and phasing of interactional inputs, continuation of reflective-action shared and supported by educational guidance to achieve stipulated objectives, experiencing of desired change in the self and/or the situation through participation and action, and critical review and integration of such an experience. Field work process is thus marked by a beginning, an unfolding and a termination. While field work activities may be terminated or suspended, the process as such may go beyond a specified period in the form of review, reflection, integration and even new forms of intervention. The process demands from both the student and the supervisor to approach the situation as learners, while the completion of activities, tasks, or programmes continue to enrich their professional experience. This dynamic, integrative and inter-related nature of the process would also become clear from the outline of a course on social work methodology which is given at the end of this section.

Conclusion

In summary, field work process receives from and contributes to educators and students when an interaction takes place. Learning in this process is differential. Marginal students (unmotivated, uncertain, uninterested, insecure, cynical and disillusioned students who secure admissions for reasons other than social work, and only some of whom develop positive helping attitudes), and motivated students receive varying degrees of guided learning experiences. Some receive only exposures; others become interested and go beyond administrative and routine approach to individualising situations socially and emotionally; still others get into the domain of progressive involvement, integration, and commitment; and some are able to develop a broader perspective through planned and individualized educational guidance which is also a form of projecting the commitment of an institution to the field work process.

Field work process acts upon the individual learner differentially over time, and also upon different types of learners. It exposes learner's motivations and limitations; unfolds as well as threatens his self; challenges his capacities and abilities; and sustains his interests through varied opportunities for engagement. This differential 'acting upon' evokes a whole range of responses, that is, withdrawal (dropping or falling out), marginalization, secondary socialization (only formal and minimal adjustment for the sake of survival, and internalization of different realities without identifying with them), intellectualization, primary professionalization, and creatively shared participation with growing conviction and commitment. Therefore in order to foster positive responses, a guided individualized, and selective practice experience becomes an integral part of field work process.

Field work in social work is not concerned only with the completion of tasks or specific assignments as has been practised generally. It is designed to help students develop an orientation through action-reflection. Completion of tasks therefore is less important than the appreciation and experiencing of the process with an accompanying development of a point of view in the learner which helps him 'own' and individualise the process. Such an experiencing is concerned with observation, reason, intuition, intuitive rationality[15] and rational certainty[16] which are mutually supportive, and which foster the development of professional attitudes, skills and a holistic perspective. Both the educator and the student learn from mistakes[17] ; develop a critical attitude which replaces the dogmatic[18] ; begin appreciation of interconnections thereby transcending Cartesian divisions[19] of atomic physics which makes a sharp distinction between the observer and the observed. The entire experience is seen as an interconnected and interacting whole.

A COURSE ON SOCIAL WORK METHODOLOGY*

Nature of social work task, the practice context, the rationale for new approach, holistic nature of the field, contribution of social, psychological and bio-medical sciences and other human service professions to the understanding of the field, implications of relevant concepts for professional practice and social work task.

Evolution of different methods of social work in response to human needs, their professionalisation, compartmentalisation and inadequacies, plea for generic approach, traditional-generic and generic—developmental continuum, controversies.

Changing perceptions of human problem, manifestations of problem in primary and secondary groups ; family life, work place, leadership ; dimensions of human problems, human living and environment, emerging social work roles ; perception, preparation and performance. Myth of primary and secondary setting.

Micro and macro level intervention as a continuum, linkage between policy practice and field practice, developmental social work practice : collective perception and identification of human needs, definition of human need situations for intervention, determination of priorities favouring the deprived, the disadvantaged and the powerless, assessment of resources and strategies, negotiation and phasing of micro/macro level strategies, collective action, review and reflection of change in the need situation ; selected need situations and their dimensions for developmental social work practice in developing societies as distinct from generic, traditional and non-developmental.

* This course was submitted by the author to the Academic Committee of the Departmental Council in 1983 to replace the teaching of basic methods' courses. It takes a holistic and developmental view of the social work process, and is in accord with the deliberations of the Faculty Development Workshop. Since any change in field work orientation will necessarily affect the existing arrangement of theory courses, the draft course on Social Work Methodology may serve as a guideline to the schools of social work in their revision of the curricula. This draft is still under consideration. Author is grateful to Shankar Pathak for his suggestions in drafting this course.

Politicization of human and environmental needs and of professional practice, developmental social work practice and other human service professions.

NOTES AND REFERENCES

1 Robert Constable *et al.*, "A Study of Common Dimensions of Social Work Practice in Field Instruction," *International Social Work*, Vol. XXVI, No. 4 (1983), pp. 40ff.

2 Dominique Desjenx, "Development As an Acculturation Process" *Ideas and Action*, FAO, 195 '83, 314 (M/Q 23701E), p. 14.

3 *Ibid.*

4 Carl Rogers and Barry Stevens, *Person To Person : Problem of Being Human* (New York : Pocket Book, 1971), p. 86.

5 Alfred Kadussin, *The Social Work Interview* (New York : Columbia University, 1972), pp. 14, 27, 38, 50, 142, 161, 172, 174, 187, 193, 262-269.

6 See *Interviewing in Social Work Practice* by Margaret Schuber (Council on Social Work Education, New York, 1971).

7 Suanna J. Wilson, *Recording : Guidelines For Social Workers* (New York : Free Press, 1976), pp. 26-32.

8 Margaret E. Hartford, *Groups in Social Work* (New York : Columbia University Press, 1972), p. 67 ; Also Virginia Satir, *People-making* (California : Science Book and Behaviour Books Inc. 1972).

9 Margaret Schubert, Opcit, p. 64.

10 *Ibid.*, and Carl Rogers, op cit, p. 18.

11 R.R. Singh, *Field Work in Child Care Institutions* (Delhi : Department of Social Work, 1984). Unpublished, The Study is based on the field work reports, and records maintained by supervisors and covers a 5-year period of work done by 59 students in Child Care Institutions.

12 R.R. Singh, op cit.

13 Bertha C. Reynolds, *Learning and Teaching in Practice of Social Work* (New York; Farrar and Rinehart, 1942), pp. 69-85.

14 Charlotte Towle, *Learning In Education for Professions* (Chicago : University of Chicago, 1954), pp. 33-34.

15 Karl R. Popper, *Conjectures and Refutations : The Growth of Scientific Knowledge* (London : Routledge and Kegan Paul 1963), p. 4.

16 *Ibid*, p. 51.

17 *Ibid*, p. vii.

18 *Ibid*, p. 49.

19 Fritjof Capra, *The Turning Point : Science, Society aud Rising*

Culture (Flamingo, 1982), p. 77 ; Also see Roberta Wells Imre's "The Nature of Knowledge in Social Work" in *Social Work*, Vol. 29, No. 1 (January-February, 1984) p. 41ff, which mentions the limits of logical positivism or empiricism in social work practice.

4

FIELD WORK IN SOCIAL WORK EDUCATION
A Developmental Perspective for Human Service Professions

R. R. Singh

. . . But I have not abandoned my faith in humanity. Mankind may err. But mankind is still the only source upon which we can depend for social regeneration. If the instable condition of the world today is directly attributable to human failure, the stabilization of society can only be accomplished through intelligent human effort. As social idealists we are faced with a tremendous task—a task which is by no means lightened by the apathy and pessimism of so many of our fellow-men. But I am firmly convinced that if the thought . . . could be given to morally creative efforts towards mobilisation for social welfare, our problem would be solved . . . if we can play but a small part in this process, our training here shall not have been in vain.

CLIFFORD MANSHARDT
June 20, 1938

FIELD WORK IN A HISTORICAL PERSPECTIVE

THE education for professional social work started in India in 1936 with the establishment of the Tata Institute of Social Sciences (then known as Sir Dorabji Tata Graduate School of Social Work). The school came into existence after 10 years of practical social work in a neighbourhood of Bombay[1] which brought out the need for professional training into bold relief. The intellectuals of the time were engaged in fighting for social, religious and political causes although they were in a minority.[2]

The effort was to influence conditions around them, and in the establishment of a community centre at Nagpara "an impossible was being attempted" which did materialise.[3] There was an inspiration, an idealism and a perspective which provided sustenance to the early pioneers of the new profession.

In the growth of any human effort, and also professions for that matter, if the inspiration becomes routinised and ritualised, it breeds a sense of despondency. Therefore for its nurture, exploration and idealism are always necessary at different stages of growth. On the occasion of the opening of the school, the dangers and uselessness of modern social work ideas imported from the west had been clearly pointed out, and the advice had been given that the real power of the new institution and of the emerging profession would lie in influencing the people who had lived and worked in the neigbourhood. The spirit of service, and deep and profound practice experience was emphasized on this occasion.[4] The school therefore while aiming to uphold high academic standards also sought to be *eminently practical* and endeavoured to apply the best of modern *social thinking* to the solution of social problems.[5] The field and the ferment of the time charted the course for the nascent profession. Even though the model of neighbourhood work, and later, social work education was western, it could not remain unaffected by such developments taking place in a traditional industrializing society as the Factory Act of 1891 (amended in 1912, 1923, and 1934), Industrial Commission 1878, The Workmen's Compensation Act 1923, The Payment of Wages Act 1936, series of Provincial Maternity Benefits Acts passed between 1929-40, Labour Enquiry Committees 1937-38, Organisations of Trade Unions[6], the Report of the Royal Commission on Labour in India, 1931, the Bombay Trade Disputes Act of 1934, The Children Act of 1920[7], and the demand for workers in the juvenile courts. These developments led to the institution of special courses in labour welfare and correctional administration then. The growth of the new institution thus was abundantly influenced by the pioneering, dynamic, and interdisciplinary approach to professional social work. The other schools which came into existence under the auspices of the Christian Missions also were preceded by years of practical experience, but later, this trend was reversed; and the university and college departments were established without any tradition of practice. Although these institutions were modelled on the lines of their predecessors, inspiration and idealism in their cases were lacking. Routinised and stereotyped academic focus was predominent which did not prove helpful to explore the field and to pioneer new ventures depending upon the needs and problems of the area and the challenge of the time. The first school of social work was established during the colonial period. But the institutions which were established after Independence*, more or less, followed the pattern of professional education adopted by the first school. Therefore history instead of teaching a lesson for change, has proved to be a burden in the growth of profession, and has been unscrupulously distorted to further narrow career interest of the professionals. In fact it has been made to repeat itself blindly with great speed.

Even after 48 years of existence, the individual schools and the professional associations are yet to define the goals of social work education and field work in a society which is wedded to the ideals of socialism, secularism, social justice and democracy. The Second Review Committee Report also has not spelt out in clear and precise terms the goals of social work education although it has given description of its needs, functions and the direction that it should take. The Second Review Committee on Social Work Education[8] appointed by the University Grants Commission suggested for the constitution of a sub-committee to draw up the course content of field work. The secondary importance given to field work by the Committee is clear from the fact that while it found time to make recommendations on theory courses extensively, it disposed of field work in a few pages leaving it to the professional associations and the schools to give serious thought to this important aspect. The syllabi, and the prospectuses of the schools of social work do list the aims and objectives of their institutions but the results of the content analysis of these objectives gravitate towards the residual-traditional careerist functions of social welfare, and the developmental

* The Post Independence period has been marked by the adoption of the Constitution (especially its Directive Principles of State Policy), launching of development plans, and enactment of spate of social legislations.

and change perspectives are conspicuous by their absence. These listings do not give any evidence of serious thinking, and under the goals of professional education whatever seems to have attracted an institution as a social work function has been added as an objective.

GOALS OF SOCIAL WORK EDUCATION

The education for social work in a developing and changing society ought to direct itself towards the following goals :

1. Organisation of teaching and practical experience in order to provide professionally trained manpower in social welfare and allied fields to ensure effective service delivery, and to create support systems specially for the underprivileged population groups or areas.
2. Development and dissemination of scientific knowledge in regard to welfare and developmental needs, tasks and services.
3. Deepening of understanding, acquisition of skills, and inculcation of a perspective for bringing about improvement in the human-environmental situation and services through institutional change and organisations of people.
4. Promotion of close collaboration among different disciplines for a better understanding of human problems, services, issues of social development, and also for initiating corresponding action in these areas.
5. Ensuring better integration between scientific social theory and practice in the field of social welfare, social policy and social justice.
6. Development of positive attitudes, values, critical stance, professional leadership, social commitment and holistic approach to deal with socio-ecological issues.

Since social work profession places heavy reliance on practice, professional education is both learning (knowledge) and service (achievement) oriented. In this sense it is dialectic in nature, and such questions of priority as individual versus group, service versus reform, case versus class, field versus theory, stability versus change are bound to raise controversies which remain unsettled for good. The field of practice therefore in terms of time, space and person is indivisible; it keeps changing and is constantly changed through myriad forms of interaction. Its dimensions are structural, functional, need-resource, interactional, and also social issue-based. And these constitute the area of field work practice in their inter-relatedness.

OBJECTIVES OF FIELD WORK

Field work in social work education therefore has got specific educational and service objectives which are related to the areas of knowledge, skills, attitudes, perspective, and action within a dynamic theoretical framework. The objectives of field work therefore could be identified as follows :

1. Acquisition of knowledge and understanding through educationally planned exposure to and experience in real life situations with reference to welfare and development needs, problems and resources at the micro and macro levels.

2. Acquisition of knowledge of process-oriented approaches and selective use of integrated methods of social intervention to solve human problems, to effect changes in policy, and to undertake preventive, remedial and developmental tasks through institutional, multi-organisational*, and people-based systems.

3. Acquisition of professional action (practice) skills through field learning in problem-solving : study, analysis, assessment, action-reflection and organisation at micro and macro levels.

4. Development of self awareness, social and professional consciousness, leadership, values, commitment and a perspective to intervene in human situations of need as inter-disciplinary group, and to develop skills of critical evaluation of own actions and systemic processes.

5. Planning, organisation and initiation of such action strategies through individuals, institutions and collectivities which are designed to effect change in the existing conditions of the clientele group, area, human populations, or in the method of service delivery.

* Multi-organisational also includes the cluster of schools of social work in the town, and implies co-ordinated efforts in curriculum planning and field work by them.

6. Examination of the relationship of theory with practice and conceptualisation of practice-experience to build or modify social theory.

Since the objectives of social work education are broadly directed towards the twin goals, namely, of education and service action, the following would suggest as specific sub-goals under them :

Educational goal	*Service goal*
1. Knowledge of a human situation or system through participation in action	1. Identification of an area, institution or group
2. Exploration of alternatives or solutions, if possible, in the determined 'field'	2. Preparation of a profile as bench mark or reference point
3. Use of individuals, groups, institutions for planning and action for self-growth and confidence, fostering of democratic action, leadership, and group growth	3. Knowledge of needs, problems, potentials, resources, and agents
4. Relating the acquired practice experience with the subject of study (theory) if possible	4. Conscious, planned and sustained action in collaboration with beneficiary and resource groups, and search for alternatives
5. Self-and group—evaluation of such knowledge and experience with regard to its relevance	5. Use of own and clientele resources for meeting obstacles faced in the delivery of services, search for innovations, and re-orientation of service strategy in case of need
6. Appreciation of the generic and specific nature of knowledge and experience in relation to other areas or subjects	6. Assessment of the use and impact of service

7. Redefinition of the human situation or system under reference for further action, reflection and conceptualization.	7. Plan for termination of action or service, redefinition of situation under reference, or continuation of earlier effort with local volunteer group(s)

Definition of field work

It has already been pointed out that the field work programme at the first school of social work in India evolved through pioneering and exploration and in response to the needs as perceived by the professional elite of the time.

Field work carries different connotations in social sciences[9] and in social work. In social science it refers to the observation of people *in situ* whereas in social work it is concerned with changing people, situation or both. Observation in social science is meant to make a contribution to knowledge. Social scientist possesses a different attitude to social facts. While he analyses them to see their relationships in a theoretical context, a social worker discovers social facts of and in a situation either to participate in it or to offer help.[10]

Field work in social work is carried out in and through social welfare agencies and communities, where the student learns skills and tests out knowledge according to an educational plan.[11] The whole programme is student and field-specific. Field work training is supervised practice of social work under the guidance of a trained social work educator, or a field personnel. It has been defined as an educationally sponsored attachment of social work students to an institution, agency, or a section of community, in which they are helped to extend their knowledge and understanding, and experience the impact of human needs. Such an experience is deliberately arranged on a whole or part-time basis.[12]

The drawback of the above definition is that it limits the function of the professional social work to that of a support to or a means of delivery of a specific service *only* and it falls short of recognizing the change functions of social work in a society. It assumes agency and client systems as "given" whereas these are always in a state of change.

Field work in the developmental context therefore may be defined as an educationally planned and professionally guided programme of interaction of a student with the real life situation experienced through welfare, institutional, multi-organisational and people-based systems in order to help him perceive, understand and appreciate existing human condition(s) and work to bring about desired improvement and change in them. The improvement or change in the situation is effected through conscious and critical application of professional (and scientific) knowledge, and method. The real life situation chosen is deemed to be one which reflects the concern of the profession and warrants intervention by one or more professions, disciplines, or organisations. The level of social work intervention may be a unit, an institution, a human group in an area, a system, or a policy on an important social issue. In a given political and ideological context, field work also implies a process of declassing and ideological remoulding through field work. . . . It is a means to mould outlook of an intelligentsia . . . and is directed to teach the masses clearly what has been received from them confusedly. Living with the villagers, sharing the joys and sorrows becoming an insider . . . observation, combined with questioning attitude with basic sympathy and respect, are the ingredients of genuine field work.[13]

Social practice is another name for field work. According to Mao Tse-Tung, "social practice" encompasses "class struggle, political life, scientific and artistic pursuits" . . . man's social practice alone is the criterion of the trurth of his knowledge of the external world. Theory therefore is based on practice and it serves practice. Social practice begins with the perceptual stage of cognition. Gradually concepts are formed and these lead to the stage of rational knowledge. *Logical* knowledge differs from *perceptual* knowledge in that the latter pertains to separate aspects whereas the former reaches the totality of it. From rational knowledge may emanate revolutionary practice. Knowing a thing therefore means coming into contact with it . . . living in its environment . . . and personal participation. There is a historical unity between theory and practice. Truth can be discovered through practice and practice can further verify truth, and develop it.[14]

On the structure of Scientific Revolutions, Kuhn also mentions about the rejection of time-honoured scientific theory in favour of another. . . .He adds that no theory ever solves all the puzzles . . . nor are the solutions already achieved often perfect. On the contrary it is just the incompleteness and imperfection of existing data—theory fit, that at any time, define many of the puzzles that characterize normal science.[15]

While one may note that professions by nature are conservative, and they do not (and cannot) offer training for revolutionaries (who train themselves or are trained by the field), the approaches outlined above do have significance for practice in human service professions. Field work should therefore aim at the development of *social practice and logical knowledge* from out of the altruistic and the perceptual. Development of logical knowledge invariably requires a comparative study of the community structure of the professions in order to adequately inform professional practice.

Definition of the field

Field in social work, in simple terms, is a community of human beings. The entry of a student or trained social worker in such a field is more like a stranger[16] and it involves participation and assumption of a role(s), and its performance in a changing milieu. Sometimes the worker finds the field whereas at other times the worker is found by it.[17] There is no *typical*[18] field as such in social sciences. One may hit upon a field[19]; spread thin for exhaustiveness[20]; or may come across unexpected material which may change one's focus.[21] The field is dialectic; contradictions co-exist in it. For example, there are proximate versus ultimate goals, self-directed versus other-directed action, individual versus organisational action, direct versus indirect action and so on. The properties of the field continue to change. One time accepted workers may be rejected by the field if they fail to meet emerging needs and aspirations of those they serve. Like history[22], the field is in a continuous process of interaction between the situation and the worker, and this interaction may lead to radical modification in the outlook of the latter. The field therefore is always in the process of change and development, and in point of time it may be viewed as a struggle of man by exercise of reason to understand his environment and to act upon it[23] with or without the intervention of a profession. It provides *social feed* to the workers and in turn is fed by them. Different disciplines approach the field from different angles but in reality it is indivisible, and therefore calls for a rational and holistic approach on the part of the professions. The field may consist of individuals, families, population groups, welfare systems and peoples' organisations. Thus the structural units of the field may be relatively *stable* or *transitional*, or *fluid*. The focus of professional intervention may be one or more of these units. The one time 'external' field should become the *psychological field* for a professional/functionary with or without training so that its dynamic properties are recognised through interaction with target groups either directly or through their *represented presence*.[24] In this sense the psychological, group dynamic, and organisational approaches[25] converge in a field and their operational dimensions become socio-ecological. It is this dimension which is to be identified and re-identified by the human service professions including that of social work in a developmental and change context. The disciplines or professions which are action and change oriented pose a problem (even danger) when they identify with normal sciences, or with social sciences which have not yet developed their applied or application dimensions.

It may be noted that the field and the educational institution may not always experience harmonious relationship.[25] This relationship may be characterised by harmony, conflict, re-enforcement, competition and redirection. A beholder may not capture all the dimensions in point of time and space. The field is perceived, identified and rediscovered differentially; it grows, changes, ossifies and decays. If such is the inherent characteristic of the field, an educational programme must take this into account, and if these characteristics and contradictions of the field do not agitate the minds of practitioners and educators, one may say without much hesitation that the field has neither been perceived, nor experienced adequately. The concept of a 'permanent field' for professional practice therefore is limiting and smacks of social determinism. The field must be identified anew over a period of time, and should guide social practice in a programme of professional education. The approach, that once selected agencies remain permanent social laboratories, is retrograde for field learning or social practice. Looking at the field from this view point, or against imported models may prove dys-functional. It reflects badly upon such schools of social work which have discontinued the programme of field work at the bachelor's level. This also gives evidence of the fact that their recognition of the field (and approach) was defective, and therefore their educational programme collapsed under the weight of sheer numbers. Abandoning the field is therefore no remedy to problems which are experienced by human service professions. In one perception the field may range from being highly structured to its being nebulous. Nevertheless, it has an underlying unity and it provides a challenging opportunity for interaction between the learners, the educators and the self. Dynamic properties of the field demand restructuring of the calendar of schools of social work in that the planning and investment of social time is a major resource which influences the field.

If one looks at the allied professions (medicine, law, education and nursing) and examines whether the concept of field work and the field as conceived of for social work above would be applicable to them as well, the answer is more in the affirmative. All these professions stand to gain by adopting a developmental (from case to class) perspective. Medicine and public health now cannot effectively deal with 'diseases' and 'patients' on a mass scale without paying attention to social, economic, and even political factors. Education likewise will be severely restricting its scope if it focusses only on the scholastically backward, drop-outs, truants etc. as 'cases' without effectively intervening in the 'catchment areas' which give rise to these problems. Law is, of late, under severe pressure already to view the problem of rape differently. It may also find it difficult to deal with prospective divorces as 'clients' without paying attention to systemic and structural factors. On the lines of social, preventive, and community medicine, nursing can also discover a new area of service with a community thrust. All the professions thus are in the process of discovering their fields; and if their response is not adequate to the emergent situations, the field will discover other profession(s) to meet them.

WORK IN FIELD WORK

Becasuse of the complex nature of the field, and feelings of inadequacy and uncertainty about their actions, beginning students, tend to skirt around human problems or needs and take time to focus on issues, and on planning and action strategies. Sometimes deliberate postponement of specific issues is resorted to gain more time to confidently deal with the situation. This problem requires from the supervisor an understanding, encouragement through guidance, joint critical review and even prodding. Since specific assignments—undertaken or given—become the bench-mark for final evaluation, marginal (uninterested, defensive, and insecure students) and even motivated students struggle to define their tasks, obviously for different reasons. The marginal and the unmotivated allow this stage of learning to linger so that they are not caught too soon for not discharging their role properly. Their response to the situation is tactical. The motivated students, on the contrary, find critical examination, reviews and specific details bothersome, mentally taxing, and even obstructing the flow of their hitherto altruistic urges into meaningful, satisfying and useful activities. They realise only after a great deal of effort and practice that planned and reflective intervention in fact doubly directs the flow of their urges in the helping process, and reinforces their sense of accountability and commitment.

The perception and definition of a problem or need, and its conversion into a task, goal or a designed learning and interactive process is crucial in unfolding the potential of a student. The setting however determines its direction. In a structured agency, field work tasks are normally known and they are generally assigned to students although some of them do get opportunities to pursue other tasks of interest on their own initiative, or with encouragement from the agency supervisor. Such a setting provides a rather secure place to marginal students, who (even though lacking in interest) are asked to do a piece of work. Field work thus becomes (and remains) a task or job for them to be done at the agency's biddings, thereby making it an apprenticeship or training programme rather than an educational endeavour. Such a structure however proves occasionally frustrating to a motivated learner who strives to go beyond in order to gain further experience (with a perspective). For either category of students field work tasks form a continuum with wide-ranging interrelated components : directed assignments; selected assignments; directed/selected assignments with or without opportunities for individual initiative; consciously negotiated assignments between the student and the supervisor; and evolved assignments —both the surpervisor and the supervisee exploring and working on them jointly. The last component of the continuum is an indication of the higher level of progression in field work learning. Consciously designed interactions between the supervisee and the supervisor provide rich, varied and challenging experience to the former in appreciating and owning the field work process, developing one's social potential (relevant knowledge, skills, attitudes, and perspective in helping), and experiencing its investment in and returns from the field.

The unstructured setting makes both types of learners—marginal as well as motivated—apprehensive and insecure initially. But the latter overcome this stage soon and begin to set their lenses for exploration, planning and action. Field work process in this setting also is characterised by a range of tasks from assigned to evolved ones as mentioned above. In the case of marginal and scholastically backward students, the supervisor who finds himself at his wit's end may design a programme to complete simple tasks : that is, immunization, school drop-out, use of volunteers, assistance to the sick and the needy and so on. In the case of the motivated students, he may encourage and even challenge them, for example, to enter into the intricacies of the power structure in the community, and judicious use of it in the helping process. In fact how field work tasks are given, selected, evolved and owned can be used as an indicator of growth in learning, development of professional self, and differential use of supervision. In both the settings the learner passes through distinctly interrelated phases of gestation, take-up, sustained action, accomplishment, and reflection in varying degrees in the process of selecting or receiving 'assignment' in field work.

In all the human service professions, evaluation of a student is currently done more on the basis of what he has learned through the completion of assigned tasks, rather than what his role has been in their exploration and selection within a theoretical or practice framework, and how these tasks have been evolved, executed, modified, and reflected upon in the process of learning. It is this aspect which requires to be given as much (even more) importance as assigned work performance if the human service professions aim at preparing functionaries who are capable of meeting adequately the challenges of social development and change through role-sets imbibed during training, and who are also able to act as path-finders in the formidable task of alleviating human suffering and enriching the environment.

FIELD WORK AND THE SCHOOL ENVIRONMENT

The educational programme at the schools of social work is conducted either in the departments of the colleges, universities, or at the autonomous institutions. The students who join social work are influenced by the educational environment of these institutions. It also happens that students rejected from one school succeed in getting admission to another school although the schools have tried to develop admission criteria to select the best socially educable students. The very fact that a student rejected from one school is accepted by another proves that the criteria of selection are not scientific, nor can they be made so. The second aspect in this connection is that of the relative youth of students and specially of those who join the professional course without social science background or practical experience, and who come through a didactic stream of higher education.* The third aspect is linked with the problem of educated unemployment. In the developing countries since this is an acute problem, all those who join a school of social work are not necessarily motivated or committed to profession. Some do imbibe positive commitment during the course of training whereas a few others who come with motivation also leave the portals of educational

* The students experience conflict between passive learning of the class and active learning demand of the field. No wonder then that declaration of holidays on field work day are welcomed by students. Such reactions are indicative of marginal or major involvement of students in field work and also the seriousness with which field work is taken by an educational institution or individual supervisors.

institution with disillusionment, frustration and cynicism. Since the life (career) goals of students are uncertain, this influences a great deal the extent to which a student invests himself in the programme of theoretical instruction and field learning at a school of social work.

The behaviour of teachers in a school as role models also influences to a large extent the participation of the new entrant. In most of the schools, consciously or unwittingly, a role model is projected which is residual and traditional, method or field-oriented, or which is without any orientation because in the latter case teachers in schools may be as disillusioned or cynical as a prospective student can be. Even after a couple of weeks of the supposedly finalised and approved field work assignments, some students, though intellectually conscious of them, are found to be unsure of themselves and take time to emotionally accept them. The process of emotional acceptance from that of the intellectual one is also a phase of field work learning which required planned guidance. This phase is characterised by change of references in assignments, modifying or dropping them when their implications are gradually appreciated, re-grouping or interlinking them, or their further expansion. The following illustrations show the characteristics during this phase. A student wished to drop one area of work on grounds which were not found convincing by the supervisor, and she also wished to change a qualifying work (replacing 'withdrawn' by socially adjusted children' for group work) in another of her assignment. During discussions in the conference she admitted : 'Frankly speaking now we know what we are doing'. In the opinion of the supervisor however she was yet to reach that stage after overcoming her ambivalence. Another student wrote in her report : "Proposals on field work assignments which have been submitted will undergo change depending upon the situation in the field". A third wrote saying : that "the submitted proposals on assignments will be further developed in the subsequent reports". These examples adequately show that selection of assignments, making up one's mind to pursue them systematically, their finalisation, approval, intellectual and emotional acceptance, and action thereon create anxieties and uncertainties among students and these require due attention. However when tasks are assigned to students without allowing them freedom or time to choose or develop them, a very important learning opportunity is denied or lost, making the learner dependent upon directives, and thereby curbing the very initiative and self-growth which the field work process should engender and promote.

Nearly all the schools of social work are co-educational, and this in itself becomes a new experience for students coming from diverse urban, rural, ethnic, and linguistic backgrounds. Majority are quite young[27] ; some of them are shy. Quite a few students find it extremely difficult to make responsible use of freedom permitted in the schools of social work. While freedom aids a student's learning, it also impedes it in that personal, inter-personal and personality problems interfere with the educational achievement of the otherwise motivated students resulting in their failure or poor grades. In some of the universities and colleges involvement of Students' Unions on all matters of educational administration and picking up of issues only for maintaining a following through pressure group tactics also affects adversely the programme of social work education.

There is however another side of the involvement of students in educational administration. The Students' Union of a school of social work once considered the question of curriculum and field work at length.[28] It found placement in field work "unscientific", and recommended : (1) agencies should be "classified by methods" ; (2) student should enjoy the "right to raise problems connected with field work placement" ; (3) since "community organization was an extension of group work, students should be asked to practise casework and group work more than community organisation"; and (4) students in the field of labour welfare should be placed in the first year in "labour colonies". The students found the supervision of field work a "mere formality" . . . which was "more regular and less purposeful" and "evaluation was impressionistic, subjective and unscientific". The Students' Union of the same school had later started bringing out a periodical *SWS view-point* during 1979-80. Some of the issues of the *view point*[29] contain articles on field work which have brought out the following problems : evaluation shows marked discrepancies in grades ("worked equally well . . . was unequally graded") ; students with high and low grades feel about inequality the same way; field work in the communities was "frustrating" . . . and sometimes students were "pressurized prematurely to act and to achieve" ; and students feel the "impossibility of relating theory to practice". The students should be "given knowledge first, (allowed to parenthesis) know people and live with them before work in the area."

While one can note the fallacy in students' their observations and lack of understanding on group work and community work, scientific evaluation, and theoretical knowledge first ; one should also note the validity of their observations on evaluation, supervision, and premature pressurizing. These only prove the need for more effective communication between the staff and students, and adequate preparation of staff to impart a proper perspective through consistent practice.

Another problem which the student experiences is between the social and bureaucratic orientations. While the school stresses the former; agencies practise the latter. An example will suffice in this regard. A student was doing community work in the first year of social work was selected as 'Management Trainee'. She preferred social work to management and therefore did not want to join it. Parental pressure however compelled her to leave the school. Since she was quite used to relating to high and low in the community without any distinction, she was also conversing with peons and watchmen 'spontaneously'. She was told by others of the group to "cut down her talks as she had become an officer." The student was experiencing acute conflict and felt that she may have to return to social work after 'wasting' a year in management. Such conscientious students also experience a sense of guilt when they find the reality too overwhelming, and their efforts far too feeble. It is here that timely and adequate supervisory input through supportive relationship helps the student to discover the *real* field.

These aspects, together with the student-teacher ratio, can not be ignored in discussing problems in field work. The greatest barrier to be overcome is that of the limited number of "agencies". If one goes to select "agencies" in developing countries by applying the "good agency model" of the West, one's exercise would end in futility. The field therefore needs to be defined from the point of view of developing countries, and the placement arranged accordingly so that it is educationally meaningful and socially relevant.

SELECTION OF FIELD AND PLACEMENT OF STUDENTS

The criteria for identification of field in developing countries therefore should be evolved and the agencies should not be considered only to lie within the four walls of the multi-storeyed buildings. Once the goals of social work education, field work, and the properties of the field in accordance with these goals have been clearly outlined the question of placement of student in field work either on a concurrent or on block basis should be determined. Some schools do follow certain criteria in placement even under the traditional pattern of social work; other schools do not follow any criteria and they go by convenience; still others adopt informally certain criteria which also include the interest of students. Whether a school follows traditional or developmental model of social work, it may develop some criteria as a guideline but all the criteria so evolved may not be applicable. If one assumes, for example, that a placement has been made taking all the criteria into account including that of the preference of students, changes in the field situation subsequently, or progression in the student's learning and orientation may show divergence, thus creating in the process a situation of 'mis-match'. In another case a mis-match in placement on account of the constraints of an educational institution may later turn out to be an educationally satisfying experience. Moreover during a particular placement the area of a student's interest may show variation. A student who was placed in a particular block of a resettlement colony perceived that the clientele was too demanding and dependent on social worker because they were asking her to solve all their problems without any involvement on their part. She attributed this situation to the heavy input of the last year's student who in the community mainly focussed on case work. When asked the reason, one client remarked : "This may be because when she takes patients to the hospital, she talks in English; approaches the doctor more easily than they can do themselves, and hence they feel more secure to go with her." The new student therefore feared that her practice of community work would be affected badly if she continued work in the allotted block. It was therefore agreed to change the placement to an adjoining block of her choice where she felt more comfortable although she found later that she had "ended up with casework practice more than with community work". In this case, before the field work tasks could stabilize, student effort was marked by selection of block initially, change to another block, choice of such areas which fitted into the student's idealism, (and also her interest in the use of social media in social work), conflict between social media and social work, her efforts for the self-employment of women, and reversion to case work on account of poor health with added 'frills' (a phase of destabilization) like eye camp to make the whole process *appear* as community work. In fact social case work happens to offer a secure foothold initially to all community workers, and sustains their interest in work through a sense of achievement of having at least done 'something useful' during field work. Intra-group tensions and rivalries also affect the field work process and its output both in the area of learning as well as achievement, and attempts to forge unity (or a facade of it) by the supervisor or enthusiastic members of the group, prove counter-productive eventually.

On account of these factors some element of "hit-or-miss", accident or contingency is bound to affect the placement of students, and the selection of the field. The latter may appear to offer a promising ground for social work practice but only later it may be realised that the reality is different. Change of workers is known to have affected even such programmes of agencies where students have been working for a number of years. It is advisable therefore that the schools approach placement from two angles : (1) placement of senior students, (2) placement of new students. Every year the staff of the school should review as a matter of policy the nature, programme, resources, and other dimensions of any field, old or new, for the purpose of practical training. In the case of second year students their field work experience profiles could be examined by teachers. On the basis of this review (and also the review of opportunities to be offered by the new field) the placement should be effected.

In case of new students however this practice cannot be adopted for it shall be based more on their bio-data and initial observations of teachers. It may be noted that when such is the dynamic nature of the field, frequent changes in placement or multiple placements for providing varied experiences shall only impede the learning of student. Placement of student therefore shall always pose a dilemma for educators. A fear has been expressed that while community work may prove to be rather a difficult field assignment for the first year students, agency placement in the second year with emphasis on tasks and concrete achievements may reinforce traditional approach in social work. However, one cannot say with certainty that community placement in the second year *ipso facto* shall impart developmental perspective to students. There is much more to developmental social work than meets the eye through community placements.

Content of field work

The content of field work at different levels and in different "fields" should be determined in accordance with the goals of social work education and of field work as identified by the schools. Variations in this area again are bound to occur between institutions and even within an institution over a period of time. The content therefore may relate to induction to the field, its exploration, assessment, action, and review of learning in terms of knowledge, attitudes, skills and perspectives. Whatever the pattern—traditional or developmental—field work programme can be structured on a semester/annual basis. The educational and service objectives given earlier as specific sub-goals of social work education may serve as guideline for field work assignments under any pattern. The student* may be given cases, groups, situations, programmes or projects in an agency or area, multi-agency network, or a community, and he may be led through several phases of field learning beginning with introduction,

* Some students select tasks to meet *their interests and needs* rather than those of *clients* they are supposed to serve. Instances of 'teaming', sharing or withholding information, level of experience, perception of one's self and so on are known to influence their selection which could be changed through proper guidance.

perception of situation, exploration, description, understanding and analysis of interaction, review of action, and change in the task(s) and strategies. In this way the progression in learning may move from simple to complex situations. The content of field work and principles of learning followed in it, as seen in social work literature have been largely influenced by psycho-analytical model[30] which emphasizes simple cases who are victims of situations to be assigned or taken in the first year, and cases manifesting deeper psycho-pathology to be assigned in the second year. When one looks at the dynamic property of the field, its structural, functional, interactional, inter-organizational and developmental attributes, this model proves positively unhelpful. Assuming for a moment that field learning is programmed, structured and guided, it is inherent in the property of the field to throw up "surprises" which the student and the supervisor must deal with as they go along. Therefore even though the content of field work has been determined for the student and tasks have been phased for each stage of learning, they must be constantly reviewed by the student and the supervisor, and re-adjusted accordingly by applying the criteria of rationality to the extent possible. Field may reactivate the past experiences of the student.* Two high or too low expectations may also affect learning and performance. Students generally start with expecting answers to questions in practice before they move on to raising questions and then finding answers which they can claim as their "own". Depending upon the collegial relationship, the opinion of the former supervisor may or may not be considered by the new supervisor as a proper guide to him in his work. Some students may require "social feed" to minimize their starvation; others face such problems as lack of knowledge, inability to satisfy clients, emotional reaction to clients, reaction to being a student or being supervised**, and supervisor's reaction to

*A student who had a schizophrenic mother and sister at home found it extremely difficult to adjust to her field work placement and needed continuing support from the supervisor for doing so.

**Individualized teaching and guidance, though necessary, have proved *threatening* to some students who are accustomed to be treated 'as one among many in a class' for several years before joining social work, and they feel *too exposed* to feel comfortable with closely supervised tasks with the result that either they drop out of a course, or the post-graduate programme itself.

student's approach. Some students use ideology as defence against new learning. Guidance to student therefore from the stage of superficial overview, to breaking down into parts for specific learning, and then to reassembling parts into a whole[31] is a difficult and challenging task for any sincere supervisor, let alone the duality of the intellectual process[32] which is being experienced by the student within himself.

THE SUPERVISORY INPUT

The supervisory input similarly may be determined for the beginning, continuing and terminal phases of field work learning or for the following well known learning stages[33] : the stage of acute consciousness; sink or swim adaptation; understanding the situation without power to control one's own activity ; stage of relative mastery; and learning to teach. The concept of field being dynamic, its content and task should be broadly worked out for the whole or part of the year. Supervisory inputs should also be outlined for different stages and evaluation criteria evolved accordingly. Provision of fixed time for conferences helps the supervisee and gives him the feeling of his "own" time. Apart from this, there always remains the need for "emergency help".

The focus of conferences may be needs of clients, resources, individual and group dynamics, student's reaction to clients, own approach, the supervisor, use of supervison, content of programme, support, direction for future, personal problems, application of integrated approach, interlinkage between theory and practice, appreciation of a broader perspective. These may need to be judiciously linked with the goals of field work. Conferences may also stress upon innovations, and the student may be told clearly that innovative professionals are marginal persons[34] in the positive sense of the term.

Depending upon the content of field work and the phase of learning, supervisor's comments on field work reports should reflect purposive guidance. For example, comments in the first quarter may be supportive, and task-centred; then questioning, appreciative, 'field-learner-approach' centred; and still later, interpretative, analytical, critical, reflective, and integrative.

These again may be seen as distinct phases showing increase in field work demands, with enabling, support, and guidance elements held constant at all the stages. Analysis of comments of a supervisor over a period of time on student's record may reveal his self in terms of focus, perspective, extent of helpfulness, clarity of goals, understanding of field situation, application and the growth of the learner in a highly individualized situation. Negative comments, like-wise, may yield another set of data on the field, learner, supervisor, and the process. Such studies need to be undertaken as part of staff development, and also to improve supervisory and field work inputs. No comments are equally significant if they are deliberate. These reflect the level of the learner and also the preparation of the supervisor. Only such comments are made in the reports or conferences which could be 'digested' by the student and which are facilitative. Supervision in this sense is a kind of selective nurture. While the supervisor may have observed the directions of development in learning, he need not comment on all of them, and in all cases, at least formally and in writing. These however may be shared as and when thought necessary during the conferences. In one case when a student was struggling to strike a balance between social media and social work at the end of the year but was being pulled more by the former, this aspect was only hinted at, and not recorded in the fortnightly report. This was nevertheless shared with the student at the time of evaluation in an overall context of field work. When asked by the student the reason for such a step, she was told that only three weeks (5 days) were left for field work and such an observation would not only have been inopportune but also frustrating. Therefore adequate time was given to the student to see through her effort rather independently and then ponder over it. The student could then appreciate the meaning of social feed and nurture in supervision and how it was a consciously planned educational process.

During a normal year, a student attends 35-40 individual and group conferences. This input of time and resource needs to be planned with the student within the first few weeks. At present conferences are left to deal with situations as they arise in the field every week or fortnight. Since the learner and the field are in a constant stage of change, a certain amount of flexibility and dynamism will be required on the part of the supervisor. For a normal year a guideline for 'minimum-optimum' conference input should also be worked out.

The supervisory process in both the traditional and developmental approaches to social work will be similar except that of change in the latter's focus which is holistic, and the stress on participant role by the supervisor. However even a developmentally oriented supervisor may have to identify traditional tasks for a particular student and help him in this field learning if he finds that the capacity of student to appreciate the new perspective is limited. This only shows how the two approaches are inter-related phases, and they are not dichotomous in practice as they appear to some in theory.

RECORDING IN FIELD WORK

Records in field work are maintained in all the schools of social work. If one looks at the goals of social work education, and field work, the properties of the chosen field, changing content, task and supervisory input at different stages of learning, the records should truely reflect these elements. What is however found is the practice of descriptive or process records in field work and that too for all situations, and methods of social work. This is contrary to any rational approach in professional education, and may be regarded by some as a capitalist, individualistic, psychoanalystic and neo-colonial hang-over. The beginning student, for example, may be required to write descriptive records and may follow journalistic style. Later he may be introduced to write process records. Later still, the process record may be further "processed" to report significant interactions of the field situation, the roles of key participants and the roles of social worker. This may be called "role recording".[35] From here the student may be aided to prepare records which are evaluative, reflective, and analytical. The perspective component may be gradually built into them. Assuming a 5-year period of social work education from BSW to MSW level, outlines of the type of records may be prepared to help students.

Depending upon the stage of learning, and also the intellectual and emotional equipment of the learner, and the supervisor, the input by the latter should vary in helping the student from one type of recording to another. Recording is not a report on the field situation to be prepared somehow "for submission on a stipulated day for the purpose of conference with the supervisor". It has a beginning, continuity and an end. And these may be seen as phases of learning inextricably linked with the content of field work in a given field, perception of the situation by the student, goals set, and approaches followed by him.

Students find difficulty in recording because they may not be clear of what is expected of them ? What they are doing ? And how ? The dynamic interaction of field is difficult to grasp initially. Students also fear self-exposure, or record scantily because of other underlying causes, that is, lack of systematic habits, motivation, conflict between idealism, altruism and routine; language proficiency, lack of self and social discipline etc. These factors need to be recognized by the supervisor in order to be helpful to the student in recording.

Even the most articulate students in the first year of community work avoid *project formulation* for action in their records, supply and discussion of the guidelines by the supervisor notwithstanding. They prefer reviewing their weekly 'hand-to-mouth' experiences as it were, but find sequential and analytical approach to a situation very difficult. They tend to give a suggestion, or an idea, but face difficulty in developing the same until the year-end. The fear of being evaluated against an approved proposal or plan creates further difficulties in this area. This also demands a degree of social discipline the student is not accustomed to. Besides the need for adequate preparation through field work, connected reading assignments in such cases overwhelm him. With proper support and guidance, some students have been helped to prepare good summary records of their work and experiences. Such assignments however should be phased between different stages of field work learning.

EVALUATION OF FIELD WORK

The evaluation of field work, perforce, makes one look at the objectives that a school seeks to achieve by imparting social work education, and the objectives it has set before itself for field work. So far field work is an area where no course outline is followed by the schools of social work. Interpretation of field work tasks ranges from observation and participation to bringing about development and change. On account of these interpretations, the method of evaluation, its nature and content, supervisory conferences and importance given to field work in general vary. Some schools however consider failure in field work as failure in theory papers also and the student is required to reappear in all the theory papers while repeating his field work. Cases of failure however are rare. Some schools, for fear of student agitation, generally award passing grade to irresponsible students in field work. This is also done to get rid of the undesirable student as soon as possible, and preferably, within two years.

The content analysis of the objectives of field work of the schools shows that while one school places more emphasis on traditional social work approach, the other emphasises the importance of inter-disciplinary and developmental approach, at least in theory. In such a situation, and in view of wide variations, it becomes rather difficult to develop a standard guideline for evaluation except that the nature and quality of work, supervision, use of placement, community resources, professional groups, and acquisition of professional attitude suggest themselves as 'core', or common denominators. These again are subject to varying degrees of interpretation between the schools, and the field work supervisors.

The above description also suggests that the content of field work in different schools of social work, its pattern, and the school's orientation to traditional-remedial and/or developmental aspects, will make for differences in evaluation. As has been stated earlier, from the point of view of the principles of learning followed so far, students in the first year are expected to deal with cases who are, in the first place, victims of circumstances. Thereafter they deal with such cases or situations which are both the products of interaction between the individual and his environment, and also where victims are plagued by intrapsychic problems. Such an orderly arrangement of cases however does not occur in the field especially while working with groups and communities. Sometimes old cases are given to students which have been helped by the school, and/or the agency supervisors, and these create anxiety in them. At other times new cases are assigned or picked up without any anxiety of having achieved less than what the supervisor or the former student had been able to achieve earlier. In both the situations the supervisor uses, directly or indirectly, his social power through expertise, position, 'coercion', and reward to help the student, and provides a kind of 'protected' or 'sheltered' environment. The cumulative performance of students under this arrangement can be taken as a crude index of a school's achievement. Similarly, the supervisees' achievements under a supervisor reflect upon the quality of investment of the supervisor concerned during the year. It is common knowledge that there are popular supervisors, casual supervisors, sincere and serious supervisors, administrative supervisors, and therapist supervisors. These determine the emphasis in the evaluation of field work.

Type of evaluation

As has been mentioned earlier, evaluation of students, is bound to vary from school to school anywhere, and even within a school between supervisors. The problem of correspondence of field work marks with theory is always a matter of lively controversy. Therefore some schools have provided for separate divisions—first, second, and third—in theory and in field work; others have provided for these by combining the two but proper (?) care is taken to see that field work marks do not unduly influence theory marks upwards. It is accepted in principle by all that a student who normally secures good marks in theory may not be a good field worker, and vice-versa. In practice however it has been found that in the majority of cases, field work marks generally favour students more than theory marks in their final grades. This is interpreted by some as normal because students devote more time in field work than in a particular theory paper, and secondly, mild and popular supervisors tend to award 'satisfying' grades perhaps with an implicit understanding with students towards that end.

Another pattern which requires students to prepare a case[37] on a given guidelines, and explain different aspects of it during the viva-voce has not been adopted so far in India. Further, viva-voce may be held for all the students, or it may be conducted only for those who fall on the border line, or in the distinction categories. In this pattern a report is obtained from the student on a case he has worked with; he is given a hypothetical case to diagnose and work; or he is asked to pursue a case in his field work as an "examination case"; or still, he is assigned a client who reports to the agency on the day of the viva-voce.

All these options resemble the clinical-medical model which has obvious limitation as a criteria for evaluating performance of a student in social work who is not only expected to deal with *cases* but *classes* or *situations*, and the latter may not be so controlled or contrived. (In fact even in medicine, law, education, and nursing, emphasis on preventive aspects, of late, is compelling professionals to re-orient their approaches to deal with *class* situations. However the functionality of graduates in this area is rather limited).

In yet another pattern a student is asked to apply the personal construct theory[37] and rank-order 8 to 12 clients with whom he has worked, that is, client liked most or least, clients seen more frequently or less frequently ; clients with whom the student has been, or rather will be successful or otherwise; client most or least motivated; client close to one's social class or farthest from it and so on; and indirectly learning achievements are evaluated by obtaining the responses of students on these cases. This method again is rather over-standardized for capturing the dynamic situation of the field and of learning, its quantitative and clinical focus besides.

Further, a thumbnail sketch of clients is obtained from the student and his performance is evaluated on this bases. Mock examinations[38] have also been suggested to develop evaluation pattern by some. Suggestions have been made for the development of scales of measurement of empathy, non-possessive warmth, genuineness etc. Some schools have used check-lists to assess field work performance. But the question arises again whether the over-lapping aspects of the students' progression or otherwise in learning and work could adequately and strictly conform to the description in the check list.

The use of observation and recording, interviews, questionnaires, and projective techniques has been suggested. No study however has been conducted in India at any school so far to standardise the system of evaluation and effect modification in it over a period of time. The students have complained that internal supervisors favour some students against others. Complaints have also been made against external examiners who do not know the total performance of students from close quarters as the supervisors do, and therefore their evaluation is not considered valid; or they are influenced by internal examiners, for, the head of the department may have recommended such names to the University for examinership who will be favourably inclined to make assessment of the students' work by giving due consideration to the informal opinion of the head during or after the viva-voce.

Criteria of evaluation

On account of the dynamic nature of learning, the field situation, supervisors' and students' personality, and attitudes, the subject of evolving a criteria is always difficult. Therefore the problem whether the student's learning, or client's satisfaction with the help offered by the student (achievement) should be evaluated always remains. Questions are raised whether the student should be assessed for his knowledge, understanding, work, attitudes, skills or on all these counts together. Some educators hold the view that considerations of personality and attitudes introduce elements of prejudice and subjectivity and therefore they should be avoided to safeguard students' interest. Only the knowledge and work performance of student should be evaluated. This type of evaluation includes grasp of the factual material of the case, intuitive understanding of the situation, interpretation of data, problems-material, social and psychological, and management by the student of client-worker relationship in the practice of traditional social work. In spite of the fact that this pattern emphasises factual details, such areas as intuitive understanding, and managment of relationships do introduce personality and attitudinal dimensions which are subjective.

Some schools of social work consider the following criteria important for field work evaluation : (i) philosophy of social work, (ii) adjustment to agency, (iii) development of social work skills, and (iv) use of supervision. Detailed evaluation guidelines for first and second year students have been prepared. These include understanding of the community; establishing rapport and developing skill ; helping process and action, and professional growth as criteria for first year students; and understanding of individual and group dynamics, diagnostic assessment and skill, helping process and action, and professional growth for the second year students. In addition, the students in the first and the second years are evaluated in such areas as self-discipline, adjustment to the community/agency, quality of recording, and use of supervision. The assumption in this pattern is that the first year students will be placed in the community, and the second year students in the agency settings. A mixed pattern of placement has also been followed by some schools but the differential operation of the same set of evaluation criteria at different levels of training is yet to be known.

The schools following a generic pattern make the common mistake of regarding community placement and the practice of integrated methods as developmental social work. They have introduced this pattern without identifying the content of field work and supervisory input. The evaluation criteria of earlier years have also continued only with the substitution of term 'community' for 'agency' without much change in the orientation of teaching, identification of field, corresponding supervisory preparation and input, and content of recording.

This can be known from the written evaluation reports of students, and supervisors which are shared. It would be interesting indeed to see how evaluation reports of experiences in community and agency placements are similar or different. In fact if the student and the supervisor have invested themselves in work, their evaluations would remain similar although they would approach it from two distinct angles. The student's report would generally be task or performance based, whereas that of the supervisor, learner (growth in learning) based. If the supervisor's evaluation is also mainly performance based, it raises a question whether the student has been supervised properly ? Moreover supervisee's self-evaluation report may not be a 'free' and a 'relaxed' one. When asked the reason why the evaluation report was not lively, a student confessed that she thought of evalution as a technical matter and therefore her style was different. However for a supervisor who has invested in supervision as a sharing, mutually educating, and a 'life-process', such interactions (positive and negative) should be reflected in the evaluation report with *courage*. Neither supervision nor evalution can be approached mechanically, for, in order to be effective these need to transcend formalism and routine.

These factors need to be considered seriously in developing evaluation criteria because intellectual acceptance of a new approach yet remains to be emotionally accepted, and practised. The evaluation criteria therefore remain clinical, neo-colonial, and traditional with their emphasis on relationship, adjustment, method's trichotomy, and skills; without much regard to a rational and holistic orientation towards the problems of a developing society with its age-old traditions. (See Appendix I).

In the developmental context such criteria (tool or skills) as articulation and resolution of conflict of interest and commitment, maximisation of associative processes, mobilization and use of resources, people's education and organisation, reflective action, evaluation, and administration need to be emphasised increasingly. It is not expected that the student will gain direct experience of all these but through his involvement he should develop a critical stance and a perspective for his actions through properly designed field experiences. He can be given experience in such related areas as building, use and management of relationships, inter-personal transactions, organisation, management and administration, and experience in interpersonal and environmental strategies.

SUPERVISION—EVALUATION PROCESS : A CASE ILLUSTRATION

This section deals with the pattern of supervision and evaluation in a school of social work. It may be noted here that although the evaluation procedure is quite formal, substantive differences occur in its operation. Such differences arise on account of the supervisor's orientation, involvement, interest in field work, and his professional commitment. The student is placed at this school under a school supervisor who is also a member of the teaching staff. The student is placed in the community setting in the first year, and in the structured setting in the second year. (Now mixed placements for both the previous and final year students are being tried). In the first year, there are no agency supervisors to guide the student, whereas in the second year, the student is mostly guided by the professionally trained agency supervisors in addition to the school supervisor. In the first and third semesters, weekly individual supervisory conferences are held; and in the second and fourth semesters fortnightly conferences are held so that the student is less dependant upon the supervisor, and works more independently in the field. In addition, the student is expected to present a case during each year narrating his experiences in field work at the group conferences. These conferences are held with a group of 10-12 students and 2-3 field work supervisors every fortnight. During a year a student attends on an average 35-40 individual and 6-8 group conferences. In the second year although the student has two supervisors, the opinion of the agency supervisor is not formally obtained for evaluation in writing. There is another reason for this. Some of the agency supervisors may not be even graduates, and the criteria for appointing examiners in the Universities are based on academic qualifications. The school supervisor makes fortnightly visits and shares with the agency supervisor the progress of student's field work and ascertains the views of the agency supervisor in the process.

All the supervisors are expected to record their observations on supervisees in the fortnightly reports. These reports are signed by the student concerned, and if he disagrees with the content of the report, he is asked to record the same in writing. Generally, students do not like to confront the supervisor directly. Either they tolerate unfavourable reports or record their dissents only reluctantly for fear that they will be punished for it. The student and the supervisor both write their evaluation reports on the same proforma and sign each other's report by recording their differences, if any. On the basis of these evaluation reports, field work report, and the fortnightly reports, evaluation conference is held with the student by the respective supervisor. After the conference a final award is given by the internal supervisor without disclosing the grade to student. External examiners are also appointed for field work evaluation and they are given all the field work documents. After careful reading, they award their grades separately. The average grade thus becomes the final award for the student. In case of differences of over 10 marks between the two internal and external examiners—a third examiner is appointed, and the average of all the three becomes the final award for the student. External examiners do not conduct viva-voce for the student.

The fortnightly reports, which should more or less cover the areas which are included in the outline of the final evaluation report vary from supervisor to supervisor. Sometimes they are summaries of work done by the student; at other time, they emphasise attitudes, personality and skill; or they emphasise such routines as attendance, punctuality and so on. The following is an extract of a fortnightly conference report of a first year student placed in community setting which was written in the second fortnight of her field work.

Content of the fortnightly report

Mention of insecure aspects of personality of the student was made. The student reacted sharply to the use of the term insecurity. The supervisor explained in the conference, and again in two other consecutive meetings, the purpose of the individual conferences, and fortnightly reports, and added that they were meant to help the student in work, and learning, and that they should not be treated as threats. The student asked the reason why she was considered insecure. The student's problem of anxiety was mentioned (without using the term) generally by the supervisor which spurred her to work at great speed. The student's negative approach to situations/problems was also illustrated and the need for exploring alternative ways was emphasized. Instances were quoted from the student's work, and reassurance was given. In spite of these efforts, the student remained undecided whether she should sign the report with her comments or without it. She asked for time which was given. In the next meeting it was pointed out that expression of disagreement should not be feared. This again did not prove reassuring. The fortnightly report also contained such positives about the student as interestedness, conscientiousness, punctuality and sincerity. It was also noted that records had shown improvement over the previous week. (The student however was found to be intolerant of any negative remark and showed uneasiness in social casework class which was taught by the field work supervisor).

Supervisor's assessment

Defenses of the student needed carefully handling so that she felt more open and relaxed. At present it is feared that due to the nature of exchanges, the defences are likely to build further. (Comment : The educational assessment made in the second fortnight on the role of anxiety remained valid throughout the year as the later events proved. Student's approach continued to be didactic. She preferred personal relationship to formal supervisory relationship and had at one time even suggested that the supervisor call her by first name. The supervisor however did not comment on this and continued to exercise caution with a view to see that personality problems were not aggravated or further re-activated, some reactivation was already in evidence though. The student used to come to conferences with tense and flushed face. Later the student reported to the head against the supervisor on a group conference paper which was corrected by him for major revision. The student mistook it for victimisation and she remained unduly attention-seeking and tense. Longer meetings were held but only a *frail working relationship* could be re-established because change of supervisor only for a couple of weeks was not considered advisable by the institution).

Students' comment on the fortnightly report after a few days

"I do not feel such kind of nervousness as my supervisor has written. I will not say anything in that context unless he realises himself." (This perhaps shows the defensiveness, and also the helplessness of the student. One may also note the comment "my supervisor" for a positive identification with the supervisor initially. Although the level of this type of discussion in the second fortnight itself may be questioned, there does arise the need to determine as to how and when such information be shared with the student in exceptional cases. Further, such students can only be helped marginally to learn traditional approach, let alone imbibe a holistic perspective which demands growth beyond the self).

Content analysis of the report

The content of the above report includes personality, approach, explanation of purpose, therapeutic help, etc. The report is more qualitative than quantitative and factual. The contents of the final evaluation report will require space and therefore they are neither being presented nor commented upon. The supervisee interestingly did not record the dissent in the final evaluation report.

The supervisory conferences, and even evaluation reports at times become game sessions where two partners are at play. Positive 'strokes' are generally used by the supervisors to get maximum work from students and by the students to get maximum marks from the supervisors. Such practices are also resorted to when a student has been only superficially supervised.

On the basis of experience one cannot say definitively that field work evaluation should (and can) be 'objective' and should include facts connected with work only. At best a conscientious supervisor can write only an 'objectively subjective' evaluation report in the sense that he may try to remain as objective as possible. Some element of subjectivity however will always creep in for, both the supervisory and the evaluation processes are inter-personal, involved, least neutral and more experiential. These therefore cannot be made wooden, 'technical', and totally objective. Positive and negative responses are bound to occur in the supervisory and evaluation conferences Moreover, a supervisor who has endeavoured to produce a "purely objective" evaluation report (?) may be regarded as one who has not been interested in the student, and therefore, has not supervised him well. Problems in evaluation also arise when the supervisor tries to compensate for his inefficiency; poses challenges without assigning challenging tasks, or begins to compare students performance with his own.

An idea of the nature of group conferences for field work which are one of the components of evaluation can be had from the following note prepared by a student :

Over-view of group conferences[38]

A general dissatisfaction with the group conferences has often been expressed, both by the staff and the students. In order to get the dissatisfaction analytically examined the worker interviewed a sample of staff and students of both the final and previous classes. This paper presents the views so gathered for discussion in order that the group is enabled to rectify the shortcoming and come closer to achieving the intended purposes of these conferences.

Expectations from the group conferences

According to the staff the aim of holding group conferences is to encourage analytical discussion on various problems, to enable students to organize their thoughts, and, to arrive at a synthesis of theory and practice through a mutual discussion of field work experiences. The students reiterated the expectations stated by the staff and felt that participation in group conferences encouraged professional growth.

Critical assessment of group conferences based on interviews

1. Stereotyped cases are presented, more as a routine, without any systematic analysis of the problem and without reference to the experience of the work in dealing with the problem.
2. There is a marked tendency to cross-examine the paper presenter on his handling of the case rather than analyse the problem as such by the group.
3. The group members are inadequately prepared for the conferences—a large number of them give the paper a cursory glance during the session only and therefore indepth analysis of the problem is not possible.
4. There is a tendency by some members towards dominating the group conferences at the cost of reticent members who need more encouragement in participation.
5. The chair-person plays a very passive role and he himself is unsure of his functions and is generally ignored by the members.
6. The formal structure of the group conference impedes

its effective working.

Suggestions by staff and students

1. There should be a syllabus outlined for field work to enable students to understand and seek the experiences expected of them.
2. The problems presented should be more broad-based. Fundamental issues relevant to social work practice should be raised for discussion rather than presentation of case records.
3. The role of the chair person should be activized so that h ɷ can direct the discussion effectively.
4. There should be an evaluation of the performance of the group members immediately after the conference.
5. The resource person should occasionally present papers that can serve as 'ideal type'.

(The staff council of the school concerned prepared an outline on topics for group conferences at the suggestion of a field work supervisor. Case presentations however continue to focus on processes, situations, and reflections on own learning experiences).

Problems in evaluation[39]

It is commonly held that only the student knows his real attitudes, feelings, and relationships with his clients; and generally, he endeavours to present a good front before the supervisor. Further student's uncertain future career roles* in the face of unemployment problem, and lack of agreement on the goals of social work education and field work effect learning and create difficulties in the evaluation of field work. Like the student, only the supervisor knows his real input in the supervisory and evaluation processes which are affected by his attitudes, interests and orientations. The supervisor's role as mild or strict, casual, expert, guide, educator, or administrator therefore matters a great deal. Some supervisors write their reports clearly while

*Francis Manis holds the view that students in the developing countries are motivated to serve the people.

others present them in such vague generalities that student may feel initially happy about them but the supervisor can interpret the same differently. Some supervisors find it difficult to write clear and honest reports because their stand can be challenged by the students in the existing University system. Therefore, non-committal statements, "strokes" and adjectives are used. Quite a few social work educators feel that one evaluation report may be conveniently used for other students just by changing the name. This is a matter which requires consideration. In fact, the supervisory and evaluation processes have been taken too much for granted and for too long. There is a need to study each and every aspect of these in order to improve field work. There is also a need to clearly define the goals and contents of social work education and of field work, and consciously establish an interlinkage between the two. The schools may then endeavour to follow a common outline. Besides, they may develop additional or supplementary guidelines to suit their individual requirements. Any evaluation can be considered adequate only when it includes the views of the student, of the concerned school and the agency supervisor, and also of the consumer of services. Each of these has its implications in relation to others. Such an evaluation is not being conducted at present. It will be of interest to pursue this ideal and to develop tools for evaluation which could adequately incorporate these elements. It is easy to do work by oneself but difficult to help others do the same. The supervision and evaluation processes seek to achieve the latter. The problems arise because field learning demands change in behaviour as contrasted with class learning which is an intellectual exercise. An individual's performance, for example, may be easily understood than the individual himself. And it is the latter which is the centre of investment in social work education.

Evaluation is not concerned only with learning or performance of students. It is also linked with other questions within a profession and a societal framework. These are : What kind of society is to be evolved ? What will be the role of social work in it ? What kind of preparation would be required of professionals to perform that role ? What should be the structure of social work education for such preparation ? and so on. One should admit that these questions do not lend themselves to easy and final answers.

FIELD WORK IN THE DEVELOPMENTAL CONTEXT : THE EMERGING PERSPECTIVE

The curriculum for social work should not only reflect the goals and concerns of the profession but also that of the changing society of which the profession is a part. The curriculum for field work which is the core programme of social work education should therefore be designed accordingly. Since the society is an ever changing system, the two components of social work education, namely, theory, and field work, should be kept in tune with change, visualize its direction, and work towards its achievement. The developmental (and change) perspective in social work education may be regarded as an orientation, and a strategy (study, assessment, action-reflection) which addresses itself to myriad forms of social situations between different systems and sub-systems. These may be broader socio-economic and welfares system and/or individual clients, groups, and service delivery arrangements to work through. The focus in this approach is to influence and change the clientele or service delivery groups as well as their 'catchment' (or feeder) areas. The approach in this sense is holistic, and systemic. It takes into account the socio-political, and economic dys-functionalities, discontinuties and even "dead-ends" of the various systems; and seeks to initiate a process of people-building, social change, and distributive justice through maintenance and reinforcement of existing relevant system, and establishment of new or counter-system. The approach may be built upon the existing traditional agency structure as an extension programme; it may involve change in its focus (priority) or approach; or it may imply establishment of new institutions—parallel or counter to the existing ones.

Developmental social work may, for example, take the problem of destitution as an institutional programme for a small number who meet the stipulated eligibility conditions, and in this sense it is remedial and rehabilitative in its emphasis. But when the problem of destitution is found to obtain widely in a region and which occurs due to *structutural inequalities* (inequitable distribution of political, socio-economic power and resources), shaping of socio-economic policies and re-orientation of political action strategies become its main concern. Another example can be taken of the orthopaedic handicaps caused by accidents. One measure of it is to provide victims crutches or artificial limbs (medical rehabilitation); the other is to plan urban development, reduce congestion, provide effective road safety measures, enforce safety rules, regulate the volume of traffic at peak hours, and spatially distribute social services and work centres.

It can be seen thus that the developmental orientation of social work subsumes remedial; and likewise, existing remedial programmes may be given a developmental thrust. These may be launched either through structured settings, politically and occupationally organised groups, special interest and citizen groups, or through 'floating' and 'open' community settings. The developmental perspective concerns itself with two major inter-related areas : (a) human resources development, and (b) environmental development. Human resources development may be achieved both for normal and under-privileged groups through services like formal and non-formal education, health, housing, nutrition, institutional services, and people-building. The environmental development may be secured through political, socio-economic, and community participation, and policies on land distribution, agriculture, population, labour and employment, urban development exploitation of natural resources, industrial development, policy on science, energy, technology, animal husbandry, agriculture, mass-media and communication net-work. Both human resource and environmental development in this sense suggest themselves as inseparable areas of social work practice.

It may be noted in this connection that any development programme within or outside a plan frame should not *ipso facto* be regarded as developmental. For example, a programme of poverty eradication may help the less poor or *non-poor*; or may help the poor but without arresting the system, processes or conditions which cause poverty. And in this sense it is not developmental. This aspect may be further examined in relation to the extent of destitution, overcrowding, congestion, consequent strain on public services, and perhaps, more accidents on roads.

Developmental social work is however difficult to practise, but not impossible, without a development plan which, in a way, provides for sectoral interlinkages at the national level. Sporadic local efforts may continue but their thrust will remain limited and weak. Sometimes even an *ad hoc* participant role may bring about developmental orientation. Conservative and casual actions by institutions may also create situations which may carry the seeds of developmental social work. The nomination of comparatively young teachers by the schools of social work for this Faculty Development Workshop on field work is a case in point. On the other hand, even though an institution may have adopted formally the developmental model, the 'split' staff, in spite of its minority character, may delay the emotional acceptance of new approach and its effective transmission to students. A study of the choices of block placement of students (1975-1980)[42] of a school of social work which has opted for the developmental approach since 1973, provides empirical proof for this statement and suggests the need for further efforts in presenting the new approach more convincingly through social theory and practice. Also, an institution may itself go through a cycle of traditional developmental phases contingent upon the change in leadership or staff composition, and therefore, it will be a mistake to assume that a developmentally-oriented institution over a period of time will never regress to a traditional model and *vice-versa.*

The pursuit of developmental social work also implies that trained social workers with traditional background may act, in some cases, as impediments, either because they do not appreciate the approach or they lack experience in this area. In fact the ultimate goal of social work which is 'helping people to help themselves' could be interpreted and applied traditionally and developmentally. The traditional-developmental approach is like a continuum which consists of contradiction, co-operation, conflict, and also integration between the two poles in their operation. The practice of this model of social work calls for associations with other professional and inter-disciplinary groups and even political and people's organisations without under-estimating own strength*. This is achieved through transcending, in some cases, one's professional boundaries because the latter prove restricting. In this sense it does not lend support to generic-specific, or 'method-field' controversies, although it does recognise the dialectic nature of human-environmental situation and the choices of strategies to improve it.

The field work programme in the above context necessarily requires experience in methods which involve articulation and resolution of conflicts (adversarial); maximization of associative processes (conciliatory); mobilisation and use of resources for human and environmental development; facilitation, education, evaluation, restoration and regulation. The target of work may be an organization, an association, a large collectivity, communities, or small client groups in relation to other systems in the environment. The experience may relate to relatively stable structures generally, but it may also provide for transitional and fluid situations (migrant or relocation groups, or riot-affected areas). The last two kinds of experiences however need to be planned selectively, with caution, and only for a limited number of students.

The student, in addition to knowing the traditional social work skills, needs to gain experience in the following skills[43] when he is involved in developmental social work :

1. *Relationship skills* : creation and use of relationship with individuals, pairs, families, groups and people in the environment ; management of relationship such as maintenance and development.
2. *Transactional skills* : skill in comunication such as observing, receiving, listening, interpreting, planning, responding, questioning, and summarising, etc. and in *overcoming* such problems as language, apathy, and problems caused by alienation of cultural and value systems.
3. *Organisational skills* : team work, collaboration,

*Developmental approach should not be regarded against career interest. Within the existing limitations of practice, it calls for the application of a new orientation even though the functionality of the same is limited.

consultation, and supervision, and social skills to initiate, support, supplement, and challenge a system, use of volunteers.

4. *Management skills* : clerical, reporting, recording, statistical and so on.

At the micro or unit level where coping behaviours are the main traditional concern, inter-personal strategies are resorted to; in the case of families, groups, communities, and institutions however which are confronted with life tasks, environmental stresses, and other demands, environmental and change strategies are preferred to that of the inter-personal. Action-reflection process acts as a guiding principle at both the levels.

In India, macro problems like youth unrest, unemployment, rural reform, atrocities against children, women and scheduled castes, large scale urbanization, national integration, human rights, ecology, regional imbalances, and development of backward areas may be considered as subjects of study, and social practice in the developmental context by the schools of social work. In case of the metropolitan cities like Delhi, the Master plan, the process of acquisition of agricultural land for urban development; and relocation of farm population with short-term and long-term provisions for their livelihood etc. would present as fascinating areas for testing and exploring social work action strategies. Such interventions demand training in planning, social theory and methods, social policy analysis, interdisciplinary project work, communication and feed-back, and methods of evaluation. Even if the schools of social work and other professionals undertake, for example, the task that they would make efforts to see that development grants allocated to a *block* or *city* during a given financial year are properly utilised and will not be allowed to lapse, this in itself becomes a specific project for field work. This task can be further delimited depending upon the level of training to focus only on the utilization of grant for education, literacy, development, legal aid, and/or health during a given financial year. For this purpose, a school may work with the concerned department(s), elites, political leadership, voluntary agencies and also consumer groups.

An important dimension of developmental social work is the

knowledge and understanding of the condition of the oppressed in the context of a social and economic structure with built-in system of alienation or exploitation. Such knowledge requires appreciation of political process and action and is likely to create occasions for confrontation with the vested interest groups, including own profession and bureaucracy. Participation in politics should however be distinguished from political social work. Political social work seeks to properly inform the concerned groups of their problems and how these could be solved through the use of available political avenues, or change of existing political machinery. It also helps to organize people for a dialogue with the political groups in power, including participation in non-violent demonstrations to secure distributive justice. (In the sixties a student—who was also a member of the Communist Party—was placed in the final year for field work in a Cotton Mill. He organised workers of a particular union which worked against the management on certain issues. The approach was partisan and the Mill withdrew permission for field work saying that the agency could not be used by the school thereafter. The student was replaced elsewhere for the rest of that academic session. The placement at the Cotton Mill was again revived with great difficulty after a lapse of 2-3 years when the Manager was transferred to another branch.) Political social work implies either effective linkage between the clientele group(s) and the political system, or exercise of "influence by the former over social, economic and political structures, including service delivery systems, and use of available resources. And such tasks cannot be undertaken as part of the curriculum *always* without risking the very existence of the concerned school of social work.* In some cases the school or the supervisor may be implicated legally by the vested interest, and this can happen even in traditional social work practice. The description that follows further gives an idea of the developmental aspects of field work in social work education.

This approach may range from remedial and rehabilitative, to

* A participant of the Faculty Development Workshop on field work who had received a telegram to appear before a lower court commented: "Developmental social work is not easy". In fact no social work is easy for that matter.

promotional, and preventive. Remedial approach would include; for example, assistance to patients, school drop-outs, alcoholics, cases of marital discord, delinquents and unmarried mothers etc. Some of these may be far too complicated for a beginner to deal with and it is for the supervisor to help student select situations which are within his learning capacity. The rehabilitative approach would include provision of artificial limbs to an amputee or a polio patient, or helping the blind to take advantage of a training programme, or finding a suitable job for an unemployed. Organisation of non-formal educational programmes, exhibitions on family life and planned parenthood, nutrition, education and demonstrations, environmental sanitation, publicity of social laws, small savings, and family budgets would suggest their inclusion under promotional approach. The preventive approach would consist of education in public health, preparation of the community for mass immunization, reaching out the potential drop-outs, delinquents, unmarried mothers, and expectent mothers. It can thus be seen that the status of unmarried motherhood after delivery will warrant remedial and rehabilitative approaches whereas, its earlier stage would call for preventive approach which, among others, may favour medical termination of pregnancy legally. Developmental approach would be concerned with all this and also with such aspects as activisation of the citizens' councils, preparation for, or active resistance to change, development of physical resources and proper land use, advocacy, political education, attacks on outdated community customs and practices, and action by the community to generate self-help efforts to deal with problems of development, and change[44]. These approaches are inherently overlapping and may as well be taken for possible action choices in field work in order to make it functional and relevant.

Like social work, if the profession of law, for example, begins to focus on such problems as class bias in the non-registration of crimes, grant of bail[45], operation of legal aid etc. and the benefit or otherwise of the system to the poor, the thrust will be considered developmental. If medicine, apart from its existing concern with the preventive and social medicine (the focus of which is traditional in that it does not enjoy high status in the structure of courses), decides to address itself to such aspects as social class of in-patients, duration of treatment, use of senior consultants' time, frequency of premature or early discharges, distribution of facilities i.e. X-Ray, medicine, and physiotherapy in relation to cases of under-statement of income to obtain them freely, proportion of time used by the medical and paramedical staff of different categories at the hospital and in the communities, and re-allocating resources accordingly to confer benefits to the underprivileged, the approach would be called social and developmental. In the field of education reports are already available on discriminatory use of existing facilities, extent of benefits derived by the scheduled castes and scheduled tribes, problems of stagnation, poor performance, and drop-outs. All that the profession is to do is to examine the extent to which the existing structure and function have been reoriented to remedy the situation. Such actions by the professions concerned may be taken directly, collaboratively, or through allied human service professions including social work. The focus in all developmental work is institutional, inter-institutional (professional) and systemic including the catchment areas which produce the clientele for different professions. Social development thus acts both as the proximate and the ultimate goal for all of them.

Depending upon one's ideological predilections in the profession, the choice of strategy may favour either an evolutionary or a 'revolutionary' approach. These two are generally seen as opposite poles which is not correct. In fact protests, and movements are an integral part of evolutionary process in any social system. While changing the system, the process itself undergoes change. Therefore the concept of developmental social work is generally applicable except for variation in its scope under different political, social and economic systems.

The learning of student in field work and the selection of individual or group of approaches thus would depend very much upon the educational objective of the programme, need of the client and target system, stage of the learner, orientation of the supervisor, policy of the school, human and environmental resource potential, and tasks to be accomplished for achieving desired change and human progress. These constitute the dynamic and perspectival field for social work education and practice.

Recapitulation

As the situation obtains, without clearly identifying the goals of field learning, and on the basis of past experiences only, field work tasks are assigned to students. Such practice disregards the potential of the learner and the field, because without a clear perspective he is expected to carry out certain tasks or apply method(s). A uniformity is enforced which may not be advisable in all cases. In fact, variation should be encouraged more in the case of 'demanding' learners than uniformity. At present, educational goals, field work tasks, supervisory inputs, expectations in recording, and evaluation appear to be so fragmented and disjointed elements that they do not constitute a complete whole in field work. This may be one of the reasons—and a major one indeed—why students find it difficult to appreciate holistic and rational approach. This in turn also affects their conviction in and commitment to the profession. Students and teachers perhaps favour fragmented approach unwittingly because the holistic approach conflicts with their old learning, and demands exacting work on a multi-disciplinary basis for developing new approaches in action, documentation, and theory-building. It questions the myopic determination of field work assignment or placement on the basis of a compulsory or an optional course because it disregards completely the dynamic nature of the field, goals of social work education, objectives of field work therein, and insights derived from social theory. In a programme of professional education, the *direct practice/service* component should be the determining factor in the choice of a field, and only such fields should be selected from amongst the existing or potential ones, which offer more opportunities for direct service (social practice), and thereby for the testing or formulation of practice-theory. Education for a profession is distinct from a programme of vocational training in that it is broad-based, liberal, liberating, and holistic. And it is these characteristics which provide sustenance to further growth and experimentation in any profession.

This is the challenge that field work of the kind outlined above poses for educators, the schools of social work, national associations, and allied professions. Exercises to establish a linkage between the field and theoretical instruction by the staff as a group therefore should be seen as continuing, and important where professionally trained workers, educators, and even selected untrained resource persons should reflect upon the field in order to determine relevant and meaningful educational tasks for students.

NOTES AND REFERENCES

1 Clifford Manshardt, *Pioneering on Social Frontiers in India* (Bombay : Lalwani Publishing House, 1967), p. 86.

2 *Ibid.*, p.v.

3 *Ibid.*, p. 37.

4 *Ibid.*, p. 87.

5 *Ibid.*, p. 87.

6 Shankar Pathak, *Social Welfare : An Evolutionary and Developmental Perspective* (Delhi : Macmillan, 1981), pp. 129-1982.

7 Manshardt, pp. 88-89.

8 University Grants Commission, *Review of Social Work Education in India*, (New Delhi : University Grants Commission, 1978).

9 Buford H. Junker, *Field Work : An Introduction to the Social Sciences* (Chicago : University of Chicago Press, 1960), p.v.

10 *Ibid.*, p. 1.

11 Council for Training in Social Work, *The Teaching of Field Work : Report of the Working Party on Field Work*, Discussion Paper No. 4, (London, 1971), p. 13.

12 S. Clement Brown and E.R. Gloyne, *The Field Training of Social Workers : A Survey* (London : George Allen and Unwin, 1966), p. 14.

13 M.N. Srinivas *et al.*, (ed), *The Field Worker and the Field* (Delhi : Oxford University Press, 1979), pp. 80-81.

14 *Selected Works of Mao Tse-Tung*, Vol. 1 (Peking : Foreign Language Press, 1967), pp. 295-308. The essay is entitled "On the Relation Between Knowledge and Practice, Between Knowing and Doing" (July 1937); Also Dorothy E. Pettes, *Staff and Student Supervision* (London : George Allen and Unwin, 1979), p. 24.

15 Thomas H. Kunh, *The Structure of Scientific Revolutions*, (Chicago : University of Chicago, 1970), pp. 6, 146 and 208.

16 M.N. Srinivas, pp. 1, 3, and 4.

17 *Ibid.*, p. 7.

18 *Ibid.*, p. 7. Also note on p. 5 that . . . situations arising in the field have their own dynamics and field worker is more often their servant than master.

19 *Ibid.*, p. 7.

20 *Ibid.*, p. 7.

21 *Ibid.*, p. 8.

22 E.H. Carr, *What is History* ? (Pelican Book, 1961), p. 30.

23 *Ibid.*, p. 134.

24 David Krech and Richard S. Crutchfield, *Theory and Problems of Social Psychology* (New York : McGraw Hill Book Company, Inc, 1948), p. 8. See also p. 11 for "peopled fields". The 'Peopled Fields' will change with changing perceptions and involvement of the worker. On the philosophical interpretation of the field, see the *Bhagavat Gita*, Chapt. VIII, Sloka 2 (*Khetra and Kshatragna*—Prakrati/Purusa or Mind and Matter).

25 *Ibid.*, pp. 13-23. Three levels of approaches outlined are psychological, group dynamic, and institutional.

26 Jack Rothman, "Development of A Profession—Field Institution Correlates" *Social Service Review*, Vol. 51, No. 2. (June 1977), pp. 291-93.

27 Faculty of Social Work, The M.S. University of Baroda, *A Seminar on Supervision* (Baroda, 1958), p. 10, and Delhi School of Social Work, *Field Work Supervision* (Delhi : 1957), pp. 10-11.

28 Delhi School of Social Work, Students' Union, Recommendations of the Seminar on DSSW : *Problems and Prospects in the Eyes of the Students* (Mimeographed, 1971).

29 Delhi School of Social Work Students' Union, *SWS View-Point*. Vol. 1, No. 4 (February-March 1980), and Vol. 2, No. 1 (September-October 1980), Mimeographed.

30 Charlotte Towle, *The Learner in Education for the Profession : As seen in Social Work Education*, (Chicago : University of Chicago, 1954P, p. 281, ff. Selection of Cases refers to (1) victims of circumstances, (2) victims of self and circumstances and (3) victims and self in that order for teaching purpose. Also See Dorothy E. Pettes, *Supervision in Social Work* (London : George Allen and Unwin, 1967), p. 68.

31 Georgia Tavis, "Notes on Supervision", *Australian Journal of Social Work*, Vol. 22 (June 1969), p. 29.

32 Charlotte Towle, *The Learner in Education for the Profession : As seen in Education for Social Work Education* (Chicago : University of Chicago, 1954), p. 106. Duality in intellectual process is marked by the co-existence of compassionate attitudes with dispassionate thinking. Also see Bessiokent, *Social Work Supervision in Practice*, (London : Pergamon Press, 1969), p. 75.

33 Bertha Capen Reynolds, *Learning and Teaching in the Practice of Social Work* (New York : Rinehart & Co. Inc., 1942), p. 73ff ; and Margaret Williamson, *Supervision—Principles and Methods* (New York : Women's Press, 1950), p. 33ff ; Also Virginia P. Robinson *Supervision on Social Casework*, (Chapol Hill, The University of North Caroline Press, 1936), p. 129 on individual differences in learning : first need for factual knowledge; second, greater understanding of people; and third, need to learn to use himself. The first is satisfied externally and intellectually; the other two involve

deeper use of self and changes in its structure.

34 Cecil St. George Henry, "The Application of Generic Principles and Theory to the Practice of Generic Social Work in the Field" *Journal of Education for Social Work*, CSWE, Vol. 10, No. 1, (Winter 1974), p. 79. And also Phelomena D'Souza, *Field Instruction in Social Work Education*. Ph.D. Dissertation (1978). Submitted to the Tata Institute of Social Sciences, Bombay, p. 514.

35 Francis Manis, *Field Practice in Social Work Education : Perspectives from, An International Base* (Fullerton, California : Sultana Press, 1972) p. 96ff.

36 D.W. Milland, "The Examination of Students' Field Work", *Social Work Today*, Vol. 3, No. 14, (19th Oct. 1972), pp. 13-14.

37 J. Wallace Mcculloh and Malcom J. Brown, "A Method of Assessing Field Work Students" *Probation*, Vol. 16, No. 3 (November 1970), p. 79.

38 W.D. Millard, p. 14.

39 See C. Towle on the portrait of an "uneducable learner" in *The Learner in Education For Professions*, University of Chicago, 1954. Also see Veronica Coulshed, "Why is Placement Failure So Rare ?" in *Australian Social Work*, Vol. 33, No. 4 (December 1980). Coulshed has referred to glowing report of a supervisor accompanied by summaries demonstrating ineffective work; objective tests of competence in addition to conventional reports; use of viva-voce, negative indicators, and minimum number of clients *required* to be helped by a student in some universities; prevalence of belief among students that good relationship with the supervisor will get a pass; and a stress on "how" rather than "what" to assess with a final question, "Would you accept this student as a colleague ?" She has offered suggestions to improve the reliability of assessments so that incompetent workers are not allowed to qualify.

40 Satinder Bolaria's Paper for Group Conference (1976-77). Also Poonam Chowdhary *Field Work in Community Setting* (1978), M.Phil Dissertation submitted to the University of Delhi.

41 Francis Manis, 49.

42 See the Statistical Profile of the Participants of the Faculty Development Workshop on Field Work (1981).

43 See Appendix-II on Block Placement of Students, Delhi School of Social Work, 1975-1980.

44 John Harris, *Skills and Methods in Social Work* (London : Constable, 1975), pp. 204-205; and also Background Material of the Faculty Development Workshop on Field Work, Association of Schools of Social Work in India, Madurai (Oct. 1978), directed by (Mrs.) Vera D. Mehta.

45 R.R. Singh (ed.), *Social Work Perspective on Poverty* (New Delhi : Concept Publishing Company, 1980), p. 258ff.

46 *The Stateman* (April 11, 1981). Also see the contributions of Ivan Illich on Education, and Medicine. He calls them 'Disabling Professions'. It may be noted that in its genuine concern for service to the underprivileged, and pursuit of developmental approach in its true sense, a human service profession may stand to rather lose economically in that it may not be able to offer lucrative positions to the majority of its members.

In order to effectively help people, human service professions will need to *grow out* of their present professional, and primary group narcissism. In the words of Acharya Rammurti, the scientific temper should replace the 'tribal mind' which is the greatest barrier to nationhood, secularism and democracy. (Inaugural address delivered at the Delhi School of Social Work, 1978 for the participants of the Workshop on "Perspectives on Youth Action".) Also see Dhirendra Mazumdar, *Kranti Prayoga Aur Chintan* (Varanasi : Serva Seva Sangh, 1979).

APPENDIX-I

CRITERIA OF EVALUATION*

Criteria	First year	Second year
1. Ability to form meaningful relationship	Formation of relationship, recognisation of differences, meaningful professional relationship with the supervisor, awareness of self, awareness of the necessity of working with different kinds of people etc. Use of conferences, increased ability, decreased dependency, and more freedom	Formation of meaningful professional relationship, relating to professional and non-professional staff, formulation of workable professional relationship, flexibility, willingness and ability to work with different groups etc
2. Understanding human behaviour and social process	Understanding the meaning of behaviour, awareness of group processes, lessening of moralistic point of view, sensitivity and listening attitude, intellectual understanding of behaviour, interpretation of behaviour, objective evaluation, recognition of limitation etc	Understanding of the meaning of social process, behaviour and interest, analysis of group situation and individual need, application of theory of behaviour. Use of group process, differential help, organisation and development of programme independently, application of principles and methods, imagination and creativity, use of self, acquisition of skills in the use of data etc

* Rosemary Reynolds, *Evaluating the Field Work of Students* (New York : Family Service Association of America, 1947).

APPENDIX-I : (*Contd.*)

3. Development of professional self	Appreciation of the influence of his behaviour and personality on others, self-discipline, self-evaluation, adjustment to agency's routine, discussions with professionals, planning of time and work, identification with the profession, acceptance of limitation etc	Appreciation of agency policy and programmes, integration of social philosophy, identification with profession, handling work and face frustration, self-discipline, relative self assessment, appreciation of own role, awareness of own attitudes, motives and reactions to people, sensitivity, awareness of limitation, and assumption of responsibility etc
4. Adjusting to agency setting and purpose	Familiarity with the agency's routine and differences with other agencies' functioning, constructive criticism, organization of time and work, identification with the agency and use of services of other agencies etc	Adjustment to the agency, appreciation of strengths and weaknesses of the agency, use of the service of other agencies, understanding of agency's structure and place in the community, team work, interpretation of agency's policies to others etc

5.	Fitting into the profession	Nil	Feeling related to the profession and contribution to it

Note : The above description clearly gravitates towards and reinforces traditional social work functions which are agency-based. It views social work more as a profession working towards system maintenance and social control, than an approach which initiates or supports system change through organisation of beneficiaries. In fact three areas specified by Manis, that is, important learning experiences, areas of strength, and areas needing strengthening, are more relevant for evaluation of developmental social work (See Francis Manis, p. 117).

APPENDIX-II

BLOCK PLACEMENT OF STUDENTS OF THE DELHI

	1975			1976			1977		
	M	F	T	M	F	T	M	F	T
1. Personnel Administration/ Labour Welfare	13	—	13 (36.11)	—	—	—	11	3	14 (35.00)
2. Correctional Services	—	1	1 (2.78)	3	3	6 (15)	—	1	1 (2.5)
3. Medical and Psychiatric Setting	—	12	12 (33.33)	2	9	11 (27.51)	1	8	9 (22.5)
4. Urban/Rural/Reconstruction/Organisation/ Development	5	—	5 (13.89)	2	—	2 (5)	4	—	4 (10)
5. Physically/Mentally Handicapped	—	1	1 (2.78)	—	5	5 (12.5)	—	1	1 (2.5)
6. Child Welfare	—	1	1 (2.78)	1	1	2 (5)	—	2	2 (5)
7. Social Welfare Administration	—	1	1 (2.78)	1	—	1 (2.5)	—	3	3 (7.5)
8. Research and Training	2	—	2 (5.56)	4	—	4 (10)	1	5	6 (15)
9. Adult Education	—	—	—	—	—	—	—	—	—
10. Others (Labour Welfare Centre, Commissioner for S.C./S.T., Family Planning)	—	—	—	9	—	9 (22.5)	—	—	—
Total	20	16	36	22	18	40	17	23	40

Note : 1. Generic course started from 1973-75.
2. In 1976 no placement was done in the field of personnel management.
3. The percentage of students opting personnel management shows an increase from 1975 to 1980.
4. In other types of settings only insignificant number of students opted in later years.
5. Students are required to give three options for block placement.

SCHOOL OF SOCIAL WORK, 1975-1980

1978			1979			1980			Total		
M	F	T	M	F	T	M	F	T	M	F	T
8	2	10 (28.58)	17	8	25 (46.29)	14	9	23 (62.16)	63	22	85 (35.12)
—	1	1 (2.85)	1	—	1 (1.85)	—	—	—	4	6	10 (4.13)
—	9	9 (26.71)	—	15	15 (27.78)	—	7	7 (18.9)	3	60	63 (26.03)
1	3	4 (11.42)	3	5	8 (14.8)	2	—	2 (5.4)	17	8	25 (10.33)
—	3	3 (8.57)	—	—	—	—	—	—	—	10	10 (4.13)
1	4	5 (14.29)	—	2	2	—	3	3 (8.11)	2	13	15 (6.20)
1	1	2 (5.71)	1	1	2 (3.7)	—	2	2 (5.4)	3	8	11 (4.55)
1	—	1 (2.85)	1	—	1 (1.85)	—	—	—	9	5	14 (5.79)
—	—	—	—	—	—	—	—	—	—	—	—
—	—	—	—	—	—	—	—	—	9	—	9 (3.72)
12	23	35	23	31	54	16	21	37	110	132	242

APPENDIX-II (*Contd.*)

STUDENT'S BLOCK PLACEMENT AT THE DELHI SCHOOL OF SOCIAL WORK

First and Second Preferences for Agencies of Placement, 1979

2nd preference / 1st preference	Personnel	Correctional	Medical and psychiatric	Rural/urban	Physically/mentally handicapped	Child welfare	Adult education	Social welfare administration	Research and training	Others	Only one preference	Total
Personnel	18	—	1	—	—	—	—	—	—	—	3	22
Correctional	1	1	—	—	—	—	—	—	1	—	—	3
Medical and psychiatric	1	—	4	1	1	1	2	—	—	—	—	10
Community rural/urban community	—	—	—	3	—	2	—	1	—	—	—	6
Physically/mentally handicapped	—	1	—	—	—	—	—	—	—	—	—	1
Child welfare	—	—	1	—	—	1	—	1	—	—	1	4
Adult education	—	—	—	—	—	—	1	—	—	—	—	1
Social welfare administration	—	—	—	1	—	—	—	—	1	—	—	2
Research and training	1	—	—	—	—	1	—	1	—	—	—	3
Others	—	1	—	—	—	—	—	—	—	—	—	1
Total	21	3	6	5	1	5	3	3	2	—	4	53

APPENDIX-II (*Contd.*)

Second and Third Preferences for the Agencies of Placement, 1979

3rd preference / 2nd preference	Personnel	Correctional	Medical & psychiatric	Rural/urban community	Physically/mentally handicapped	Child welfare	Adult education	Social welfare administration	Research training	Others	Only one preference	Total
Personnel	16	1	2	—	—	—	—	—	—	—	2	21
Correctional	—	—	1	—	—	—	—	—	1	—	1	3
Medical and psychiatric	1	—	5	—	—	—	—	—	—	—	—	6
Rural/urban community	—	—	1	2	—	—	—	—	—	—	2	5
Physically/mentally handicapped	—	—	—	—	1	—	—	—	—	—	—	1
Child welfare	—	—	4	—	—	—	—	1	—	—	—	5
Adult education	—	—	—	1	—	—	—	—	—	2	—	3
Social welfare administration	—	—	2	—	—	—	—	—	—	—	1	3
Research and training	—	—	—	—	—	1	—	1	—	—	—	2
Others	—	—	—	—	—	—	—	—	—	—	—	—
No 2nd preference (Not Applicable)	—	—	—	—	—	—	—	—	—	—	4	4
Total	17	1	15	3	1	1	—	2	1	2	10	53

APPENDIX-II (*Contd.*)

First and Third Preferences for Agencies of Placement, 1979

3rd preference / 1st preference	Personnel	Correctional	Medical and psychiatric	Rural/urban community	Physically/mentally handicapped	Child welfare	Adult education	Social welfare Administration	Research and training	Other	Only one preference	Total
Personnel	15	—	2	—	—	—	—	—	—	—	5	22
Correctional	1	—	1	—	—	—	—	1	—	—	—	3
Medical and psychiatric	—	1	6	—	1	—	—	—	—	2	—	10
Rural/urban community	—	—	3	1	—	—	—	—	—	2	2	6
Physically/mentally handicapped	—	—	—	—	—	—	—	—	—	—	1	1
Child welfare	—	—	3	—	—	—	—	—	—	—	1	4
Adult education	—	—	—	1	—	—	—	—	—	—	—	1
Social welfare administration	—	—	—	1	—	1	—	—	—	—	—	2
Research and training	1	—	—	—	—	—	—	1	—	—	1	3
Others	—	—	—	—	—	—	—	—	1	—	—	1
Total	17	1	15	3	1	1	—	2	1	4	10	53

APPENDIX-II (*Contd.*)

First and Second Preferences for Agencies of Placement, 1980

2nd preference / 1st preference	Personnel	Medical/ psychiatric	Rural/ urban	Child welfare	Only one preference	Total
Personnel	22	—	—	—	—	22
Medical/ psychiatric	2	5	—	1	1	9
Rural/urban	1	—	3	1	—	5
Child welfare	—	—	—	—	1	1
Total	25	5	3	2	2	37

Second and Third Preferences for the Agencies of Placement, 1980

3rd preference / 2nd preference	Personnel	Medical/ psychiatric	Rural/ urban	Social welfare administration	Only 3rd preference	Total
Personnel	22	1	1	—	1	25
Medical/psychiatric	3	—	—	1	1	5
Rural/urban	—	—	1	—	2	3
Child welfare	—	2	—	—	—	2
No second preference	—	—	—	—	2	2
Total	25	3	2	1	6	37

First and Third Preferences for the Agencies of Placement, 1980

3rd preference / 1st preference	Personnel	Medical/ psychiatric	Rural/ urban	Child welfare	Social welfare administration	No third preference	Total
Personnel	21	—	1	—	—	1	23
Medical/ psychiatric	4	1	—	—	1	2	8
Rural/urban	—	2	1	—	—	2	5
Child welfare	—	—	—	—	—	1	1
Total	25	3	2	—	1	6	37

5

FIELD WORK IN COMMUNITY SETTING
A Developmental Framework*

R. R. Singh

I

Objectives of field work (area of learning)	Level of intervention	Learning situations or tasks
I Knowledge Community—its population, need, problems, resources, power structure, response patterns to problems and agent, analysis and interpretation of problems, needs and resource, and planning suitable strategy for intervention. *II Attitudes* Rational approach to community/needs/problems, and use of resources differential approach to specific problems, imaginative, innovative and anticipatory approach. Conscious use of self, use of supervisory input, approaching the community/client groups as learner, self-discipline, tolerance, commitment and assessment	(Approaches) ↕ Remedial ↕ Rehabilitative ↕	*1st Phase* Observation, contacts and visits, preparation of the socio-economic profile with special reference to (religion, caste, class, education and occupation), pattern of land use, civic and welfare facilities, identification of problems and analysis of resources, formation of small groups, organisation of exhibition, demonstration in nutrition, symposia, debates, work with individual cases, study of functional and geographical aspects of the community, role of tradition, impediments to change, problem-solving specially the self-help efforts of the community ; social welfare institu-

* This is a revised and expanded version of a Note prepared by the Editor in 1975-76 for an off-the-campus meeting of the school supervisors of the Delhi School of Social Work, University of Delhi.

tions in and around the area, use of services, reasons for non-use, and suggestions for effective service delivery system.

III Skills

Observation and study/survey establishment of rapport, rooting the idea and evolving a consensus, determination of priorities,
Initiative in formulation, launching and undertaking a programme
Modification of programme after assessment, mobilisation of community/agency/clientele resources, and their use
Co-ordination of resources participation, public relations, meetings and conferences
Assumption of leadership roles and preparedness to accept others as leaders,
Interviewing
Referral
Recording
Budgeting
Collaboration

← Remedial Preventive →

2nd Phase

Use of agencies, leaders, individuals and groups as means to achieve stipulated objectives, use of tradition as resource for change, assistance in the provision of concrete services i.e. vaccination, health examination and education, organisation of parent-teacher association, vocational training, self-employment project, counselling service, youth clubs, women's clubs, specific study of existing services, mode of delivery, level of utilization, problems in their administration, function of councils, collaborative work, use of volunteers, ventilation of grievances through commitees, public relations, activisation of citizen's council for action projects, limitations of physical, human and service resources, their current use pattern, the workers' role as agents of, in and with the community.

IV Perspectives

Community as a sub-system of a larger system, its exploitative or exploited nature, prospect and direction of development and strategy for long-term intervention for change

← DEVELOPMENTAL →

Planning, assessment and intervention at a macro level with long-term goals and use of current action or project strategies as a means, areas of reflective-action, advocacy etc., involvement in conflict situations/confrontational practice as a *citizen* in case professional role is *too restricting*.

Note : (i) Areas of learning or learning tasks could be viewed either from a traditional or developmental perspective, or both. These perspectives differ in their *focii*. A project, for example, may be initiated by any group with or without a social worker in a community to meet a felt need and in this sense it may serve as an end in itself. Or, it may be initiated to establish a bond of intimacy, and as a means for wide-ranging interventive action involving not only the interest groups but the system as a whole. Developmental social work is evaluative, perspectival and systematic in its nature; traditional social work on the other hand may remain confined to the present needs, and projects or may be a part of the developmental approach. While traditional social work is largely remedial and rehabilitative, developmental is also preventive and promotional. For example, the latter views the underprivileged groups of a community in relation to other groups (in history) with a goal to change the perception, power structure, resource use pattern (function) of the privileged in favour of the exploited; the former however regards it as a problem of a group which can be solved by creating agencies or services to assist or rehabilitate them.

(ii) The above outline could be used in the education of social workers with community-based field work at any level selecting such areas which correspond to the stage and level of a student's learning. Phase I and II have been worked out on the assumption of a semester pattern of field work either in the first or second year of education of social work at the post-graduate level. Contents under knowledge, attitude, skills, in Col. I and Phases in Col. II could be applied to both the traditional and development approaches. The last part on perspective in Col. I however falls mainly under the developmental approach. In fact, remedial, rehabilitative and preventive aspects may be considered as interrelated phases of developmental social work in-extricably linked with its perspective.

(iii) A similar outline could be worked out for agencies also. If an agency is viewed as one of the service-giving institutions in response to a need, it will be called traditional approach. If however the same agency is regarded as a service-giving institution in relation to other need—meeting arrangements of the society with its concern for the under-privileged, and clientele participation in its policies and programmes etc., it would be called developmental. The former is largely confined to the agency and clientele systems; the latter in turn encompasses the clientele, target and institutional systems and visualizes social development through change in them. Preparation of client groups to initiate, accept or face (even resist) change i.e., relocation or resettlement, becomes a function of social worker in the developmental context. A generic programme of education may be traditional and/or developmental. It is therefore a mistake to regard such a programme as developmental only. The above framework can be helpful to organise the practice—structure of any human service profession, that is, medicine, law, education etc., with suitable modifications.

II

FIELD WORK IN DEVELOPMENTAL CONTEXT : A BREAK-UP BY SEMESTERS AND SETTINGS*

I Semester

Goals	*Tasks*
Observation of the community, its socio-economic, cultural features and process of change; Collection of information on needs, problems, priorities, resources, power structure, social and economic groups; establishment of rapport; understanding of the clientele system and target group(s) and their reactions to external agencies; skills in observation and recording of work experience; beginning experience in the practice of social work principles, methods, and initiation of action; awareness of one's perjudices and control of reactions; beginning assessment of own performance and preparedness to assume social work roles.	Profile of the community; method of need—identification, priority determination; identifying community leaders; working with 'floating' groups; problems encountered in the above mentioned areas; description of a single problem as it obtains, and as it affects the client system; self-help efforts of the community; use and non-use of services, and service delivery systems; methods of establishing rapport, understanding the dynamics of the community, and identifying leaders; initiation of interest group, or project-centred action.

II Semester

Better understanding of community service delivery system(s) and the target groups;	Narration of experiences/ learning processes; assessment of services, and of resources

* The above scheme is a revised and expanded version of the one given in the *Manual For Field Work* of the Delhi School of Social Work for guidance to students in preparing papers for group conferences. The earlier *Note* was prepared by the author for the Staff Council meeting in 1977-78 incorporating the views of those colleagues who had given their written comments on the subject.

determination of priorities in terms of problems, resources and feasible action strategies; use of indigenous, formal and informal leadership to initiate collaborative action; apprecia-tion of prosessional values and approaches; systematic collec-tion, analysis of data through observation and study, and formulation of need-based pro-grammes; built-in evaluation, reflection on theory in practi-cal work; assumption of multi-ple roles; planning of pro-grammes around the needs of groups; experience in commit-tee work, listening, observation and effective communication, participation; critical stance; conviction and commitment.

within the community; creation and improvement of services through participation and action; local leadership and its problems; supervision by the students; account of the process of change since the arrival of the worker; rationale for adopting an approach to deal with a problem; prepara-tion of an action plan; role of community leaders and social workers in implementing a programme; ways in which co-operation was sought and received; process of group for-mation and worker's facilita-tive role; records of a few group sessions to highlight the patterns of group dynamics-completing a project etc. refle-ction on action taken, effec-tiveness or otherwise of roles assumed, client groups assisted or alienated, and changes effe-cted in the structure and func-tion of the system; use of mass media; and 'oppositional' practice, if necessary.

IIIrd Semester

Understanding of the agency structure, function, plans, limi-tation, the client and the ser-vice delivery systems; apprecia-tion of integrated social work approach and also the applica-tion of a particular method; experience in committee

Report on cases/situations successfully dealt with; report on the functional aspects of organisation, place of social work/welfare unit in the hier-archy, formal and informal channels of communication; process of decision-making;

work and team work, development of professional conviction; utilisation of volunteer and other community resources to make the agency services more effective, periodic surveys and evaluation in the area of service delivery; analysis of own approach and acceptance of criticism positively; Integration of social work theory and testing of theoretical concepts; awareness of social and valuational differences; use of agency as a resource to and of the community.

system of offering services; process record of intake; summary of a client's case after social history leading to assessment and evaluation; process of a group session in a residential institution; narration of experience as a supervisee; adoption of differential approaches to specific problems; experience in the use of volunteers; interview record showing the application of social work principles, methods or skills; study of *micro* social, welfare and economic policies as implemented by the agency.

IV Semester

Understanding of the functional and dysfunctional aspects of the agency and client-systems; appreciation of the impact of agency system on the community and *vice versa*; experience in agency administration: policy-making, planning, committee work, public relations, reporting and recording, public education, co-ordination etc. exploration and raising of resources; creation of needed services and the improvement of existing ones; experience on a particular agency service project in depth; introduction of innovative and experimental approaches; reflection on

Process of institutional management and co-ordination of resources to solve problems; utilization of resources; creation of agency and community-based services; process record of collaborative work; working of different committees and the place of worker; worker's evaluation of own/agency functions; processes of policy formulation and decision-making; public relations; inter-agency co-ordination; presentation of follow-up cases; integrated use of social work methods and innovations introduced, if any; involvement with client groups in explora-

one's professional development and professional commitment, reflections on practice-theory; focus on under-privileged groups and 'catchment' areas through the extension of agency services/change in agency policy/programme.

tion-assessment-action-reflection situations; appreciation of multi-agency thrust for social development, and action in this area; use of mass media.

Note : (i) If a student in social work is placed in an agency in the two semesters of the first year, the outline of the community shall be followed in his second year of placement.

(ii) In case however a student is placed for both the years either in the same agency or community, the goals and tasks shall remain the same except that the level of involvement, review of plans and strategies in relation to other measures, and action-reflection shall be undertaken at a deeper level, with relative independence and autonomy, and with less supervisory guidance in the second year.

(iii) Students may be helped to write papers for their group conferences or seminars either on goals as they perceive and gradually appreciate them, or tasks as they begin to experience them in different situations.

III

DEVELOPMENTAL SOCIAL WORK IN COMMUNITY SETTING : ILLUSTRATIONS

I

PROCESS OF RAPPORT-BUILDING IN COMMUNITY WORK*

The beginning

The worker, when she first came to the block, was a stranger to the residents, just as they were strangers to her. Therefore to break this invisible barrier between herself and the residents,

* Edited by the author who had supervised the student. The record is based on the work done during the first 4-5 weeks (8-10 actual field work days) by Miss Neera Gautam, student of M.A. (Final) class in Trilokpuri (Block 17) during 1984.

especially women and children with whom she had chosen to work, became her foremost task.

The block consisted of two predominant groups : the Rajasthanis or Baghris (as they are called) and the scheduled castes. Unemployed youths and anti-social elements were seen roaming about. The worker was quite apprehensive when she made an 'entry' into the block of her own choice.

The entry

The worker's approach to the residents in the beginning was what really broke the ice between herself and them. She acted politely and humbly while introducing herself. She answered their queries about herself and her work very patiently, without showing any irritation even when the most personal of questions were put to her. People always responded to a warm smile and respect the worker showed towards them.

Trying to be one among the residents—from entry to progressive identification

When the worker discovered that nearly half of the population of her block was Rajasthani, she made efforts to dress in Rajasthani apparel. Her colourful Rajasthani dupattas were really appreciated by the women. On seeing the worker so dressed, women often said, "You are just like us".

The worker was genuinely fascinated by Rajasthani jewellery, especially the heavy anklets and armbands and she expressed this fascination aloud. This really pleased women, who on most occasions insisted that the worker try out their jewellery which the worker politely declined.

Since the worker's hair was short and she knew that this was not acceptable to most of the residents, she always went with her hair properly tied in a very simple way.

Role of ethnic and regional connections

The worker's maternal grandmother hailed from Rajasthan and she had spent half her lifetime there. Her family still continued to live all over Rajasthan. This fact was utilized by the worker to be accepted by the people of Rajasthani origin. In fact, women started considering the worker as a 'relative'. For instance, a woman came up to the worker with her daughter and said, "My daughter's grandmother also hailed from Rajasthan and therefore she (daughter) was worker's sister". The worker accepted this relationship without protest.

Talks about Rajasthan, and especially Jaipur, from where most people hailed and where the worker's relatives also stayed were also brought up, both by the worker and the women. This really bridged gaps that still existed between them.

Old connections with other regions

Not only her connections with Rajasthan but the fact that the worker belonged to a Pan-India family was also utilised by her. She could talk confidently about Haryana with anyone hailing from there because her late paternal grandfather belonged to Haryana. In fact a local 'Dai' from Haryana said, "something quite familiar about your language struck me".

To a person hailing from U.P., the worker's paternal grandmother from Meerut in U.P. proved an effective link. These old connections were particularly helpful in establishing a rapport with the other generation of residents in the block.

Starting with the residents

The women

The worker made conscious efforts to come to the level at which the people were. Despite place for sitting on the chair, the worker sat down wherever the women were sitting, be it the road or the door-step. This gesture of the worker was very much appreciated. For instance, once the worker was sitting on the side of a lane with a group of women when another woman came and said, "Look ! she is refusing the cot and insists on sitting where we all are sitting".

The worker tried her hand at making balls of coal.* In another instance, when the worker approached a woman, who was making brooms, she (woman) sarcastically commented : "I am making brooms, and if you also do it, it will be of help."

* Balls are made with crushed coal pieces and mud, and after drying them, they are used as fuel.

The worker without any hesitation sat down with her and offered to do the job. This gesture won a new friend.

The children

Wherever the worker sat, she picked up children in her lap, irrespective of how dirty they were. This gesture not only endeared her to the child's mother, but the entire group. The worker did not show any irritation or disgust when a small child urinated on her, a fact really appreciated by the women.

Joint celebration of festivals

On the occasion of festivals like Teej, the worker joined in 'Mehandi sessions' with women and young girls. She also enjoyed the swings with the young girls. When all the girls of the block were engaged in 'Rakhi-making' the worker too joined in this work.

On the occasion of 'Balmiki Jayanti' the worker paid her homage and prayers in the new Balmiki Temple in the area alongwith the scheduled castes residents of her block. Melas organised to mark this occasion were visited to and enjoyed with children of the block.

On the occasion of Diwali, Ramlila, performed by children of the block, was organised by the worker in a park. She helped the children make small mud temple* with idols and pictures of Gods and Godesses. She also accepted the 'Prasad' of Diwali Puja from the women with utmost respect.

Ignoring the social divide

Some of the scheduled caste families asked the worker her caste. When they came to know that she was a Brahmin, they were very surprised that the worker could sit with them and even drank their water without any inhibitions. She never hesitated to eat the food so lovingly brought for her and at times even shared it with them. All this was taken by the residents as a gesture of acceptance by the worker, and they in turn accepted her.

* On the occasion of Diwali, children make small models of temples with mud. After the mud dries they paint them. On the day of Diwali, they place idols of Gods, light 'Diyas' on the temple and offer prayers.

Encouraging trend

The worker tried to learn a little of the Rajasthani language from the residents themselves. Her efforts in this direction and the few phrases she used in her conversation were really liked. Participation in dance and singing sessions with them had also helped. When the worker sang a part of the Rajasthani song, "Pallo Latake" the women were immensely pleased.

Rationale behind such efforts

The worker felt that small efforts like these had really helped her in being able to identify herself with the people and in being accepted by them. She now shared a very informal and trusting relationship with them which was free from inhibitions. Continuation of such efforts not only endeared her to the people but also provided a whole new experience of living in a setting which was so different from her own.

On reflection, she found that the typical field situation made her think of ways of gaining an entry and situate herself in the block. This called for a change in attitude and learning and application of social skills to get a foothold in a strange surrounding. The entry was a fact now and the worker proposed to take up the challenges of her main field work assignments with self-confidence.

II

ORGANISING RELIEF WORK—LEARNING A LESSON*

The communal frenzy in Delhi and other parts of the country at the fag-end of 1984 which erupted in the wake of the assassination of the late Prime Minister created a situation which necessitated organisation of relief on a large scale. Conflicting reports about the number of dead, injured or displaced, and the extent of damage to property had appeared in different reports. Questions whether these riots were spontaneous outbursts or engineered, and what was the role of police were controversial indeed. Some blocks had been completely evacuated. All that was left

* I am grateful to Shankar Pathak for his comments on my note.

was acrid smell, stray dogs, burnt houses and goods, and smouldering fire. While there might not be any agreement on the statistics available in all the affected areas, there had been no difference of opinion about the need for relief and assistance, and also for maintaining communal harmony. Relief work for the victims was organised by the government, religious organisations, political groups, social organisations, teachers and students, and also neighbours. Co-ordination was however lacking among them. Loss of life and property has been so much that relief would need to be provided on a long-term basis. The essential pre-requisite of all relief measures would be the rebuilding of social bonds which have been strained. Some students of social work also contributed their mite in bringing succour to the needy in the relief camps. They distributed essential commodities, filled in forms for compensation claims, and also consoled the victims. This humanitarian work gave them satisfaction, and also encouragement to continue with the noble work. Since the city was under curfew, both teaching and field work had been suspended. After the situation become normal, the students placed in the communities for field work entered their areas with a deep sense of insecurity and apprehension. But the urge to do good or provide relief still prevailed.

The resettlement colonies—some of which are used by the Department of Social Work for field work—were worst affected. Students had read newspaper reports and had also heard rumours of all kinds. Some of them and their teachers had already visited these colonies with a view to assess the situation from the point of view of field work. Since mass arrests after the riots had been made or were still going on, residents of the area were tongue-tied, and volunteered very little information. Fear and suspicion gripped the people. Gulf was noted between the promises of aid and the performance. Forms for claiming compensation which were free of cost were selling at black-market rates. Victims were found guarding their plots (though their jhuggis had already been burnt) for fear that once they joined relief camps, their plots would be usurped by new encroachers. Anti social elements who had been rounded up earlier were also being released on bail and some were reportedly threatening earlier inhabitants who were returning to their places from relief camps with dire consequences.

Upon entering the community, students realised that skills required in organising camp-based and community-based relief differed a great deal. The former was easier; and the latter most difficult. They also realised that providing of relief to the victims of natural and man-made disasters was different. It was easier in the case of natural disasters where sympathises for the victims were widely shared than for the other kind where sympathises were sectionally or denominationally shared. This was an eye-opener.

When the information from their respective blocks (field work areas) started trickling, the gravity of the damage (personal, social and physical) became known to students. Some blocks had been directly affected; in other cases adjacent blocks had been affected where students found themselves strangers, and therefore more insecure in the atmosphere of suspicion and rumours which were rife. Though hesitatingly, both types of localities—known and unknown—were approached. The process of need identification, and meeting of immediate needs (food) commenced. In this process, a new realisation dawned upon students. They learnt that they had not known about the deeper social dynamics of their blocks in the past four months of field work (24 effective working days). They had not anticipated the repercussions on these social relationships of events taking place elsewhere but surreptitiously making inroads and weakening social bonds in their areas or neighbourhoods. They further realised that their work was not being viewed by the residents as purely humanitarian or neutral. Some people, without making it known, were wondering why students were helping at all ! Others who were favourably disposed towards students were found to be more reticent, or they turned their faces away from them. Some however did come forward to join them.

Students had selected their regular assignments before the riots erupted, and the above reaction of the community created a feeling among them that "too much" of relief-giving might jeopardise residents' co-operation in their projects. If relief was not given, it was inhuman, unethical, and it was bound to alienate a group still living in the affected blocks from students due to their indifference to the victims' plight. Its continuance or provision might be interpreted by another group as "over-doing" and thus erode popular support, thereby affecting adversely field work programmes which were to be executed and later evaluated. Each student was confronted with the problem of striking a balance so that its repercussions were not felt in the area of approved field work tasks. It was a kind of tight-rope walking. The release of anti-social elements had created a feeling of insecurity among students who feared that they might face threats, and their identities might be mistaken. This led to the review of old equations and approaches, and called for re-adjustment to the 'new' social set-up which was a later development.

(It reminded the new generation of social workers of the old experiences their predecessors had gained in relief work soon after Independence. Displaced persons who were living in refugee camps were helped during the day time whereas the other minority group living in the Red Fort were helped by the same group of students during nights—none of the beneficiaries being told that students were working with both the hostile groups of victims. In fact, when this fact was known, some of the students had even been threatened).

On the basis of a preliminary survey, a group of students with their supervisors identified the following tasks for relief in addition to their approved field work assignments :

1. Identification of the missing or dead.
2. Re-union of survivors.
3. Assessment of damages (loss of life and property) for compensation claims.
4. Assistance (cash, kind, long-term) to the survivors of affected families with or (now) without bread winners.
5. Social assistance to widows, and orphans (institutionalisation, pension) and so on.
6. Employment to the dependents of the deceased on compassionate grounds in those organisations where the latter worked.
7. Vocational training or retraining of dependents, education and health care.
8. Linking the families of victims to their denominational organisations for aid.
9. Free legal aid to victims, as well as to alleged culprits.

10. Rebuilding social bonds.

None of these tasks were either neutral or easy to accomplish. Each student chose what she was capable of without adding to own feelings of insecurity*. The lesson learnt was that even humanitarian acts and service required courage and entailed risks, and such convulsions changed the 'field' to such an extent as if it were to be approached anew and even re-understood (or recaptured) for any meaningful and sustained professional intervention.

Instances of helplessness or ineffectiveness of the forces of sanity, tense and uncommunicative neighbours, fractured social relationships, dazed and grieving survivors (some of them preserving available photographs, and even finger bits and bones of the dead), mutual aid and good neighbourly co-operation at great personal risks, superficial cordiality, social distance between community groups, refusal of landlords to accept back tenants who had fled for safety, re-entry of tenants through police assistance, submission of exhorbitant compensation claims, fake claims** by unscrupulous elements who were not affected at all, reported role** of slum-dwellers in riots (and future threats posed by these "vote-banks" to civic life), allegations and counter-allegations against political groups, insecure victims' unwillingness to return to their areas for fear of reprisals or of being haunted by the dead, government's decision to wind up relief camps (which warranted intervention by the High Court on a writ), shadow of the general election, individuals and organisations—sectarian, political and others – vying with one another to offer help—in order to attract attention of the new leadership in the government, sectarian politics in the adoption of orphans, peace marches, procedural delays in providing relief and inadequate solatia to victims, etc. highlighted the chain reactions

* See "Rising to the occasion" *The Statesmen* (November 18, 1984).

** Rejection rate of 14,946 applications received for relief has been reported at 44.63 per cent. For bogus and duplicate claims, see *The Statesman* (November 22, 1984).

** On the role of groups which are economically deprived, socially unintegrated, and brutalized by the pressures of a rootless urban existence, see the editorial 'Violence and Society' in *The Statesman* (November 22, and 24, 1984). The latter refers to politicization and brutalization of people.

and the complexity of the social situation. The experience was mind-boggling and the aftermath of the disaster was only to be seen to be believed. The picture that emerged was symptomat:c of a deeper and a wider socio-political and economic malaise, and presented itself as a disturbing melange. It compelled one to go deeper into the complex social dynamics of a community's existence, to realise the inadequacy of operational helping relationships to carry out welfare programmes, and to appreciate, in a broader perspective, the value of peaceful co-existence, let alone social solidarity, as a pre-condition for and a long-term goal of social development and social work. To some, it may sound like chasing an illusion or something which is not concretely formulated but it is a practical necessity for the present, and also for the future. Realisation dawned upon some workers that help may be given or withheld, misplaced or rightly placed, accepted or refused, used or misused, and it may even widen the social divide. And therefore this apparently harmless and humanitarian act required sensitivity, forethought and foresight, a social environment, an awareness of local dynamics, courage and commitment, and also a method.

III

COMMUNITY WORK IN THE FIELD OF HEALTH AND FAMILY WELFARE IN TRILOKPURI : DELHI* (AUGUST 1984—MARCH-1985)

THE ENTRY

In the community, the first task which the worker set for herself was to explore the community and its dynamics. By keeping her mind open she could observe the minute details and assimilate information about the various aspects of community life.

This was followed by choosing a block to work in. The worker chose *Block 17*. This decision was based on the following considerations : social background of the residents (half of

* Edited by the author from the report of Miss Neera Gautam, an M.A. final student who worked under him. The report shows adequately the process of guided interaction between the worker and the field.

them being scheduled castes and the other half Rajasthanis); and this block had practically not been covered by the previous students.

The worker then took upon herself to break the invisible barrier of anonymity between herself and the residents she had chosen to work with. She engineered ways of gaining an 'entry' and situating herself in the block. She made conscious efforts to identify herself with people of different backgrounds and different age-groups by making alterations in her way of dressing more suited to the background of the people) and her way of speaking (incorporating words from the local dialect in her conversation). Bringing herself to the level of the people, she shared their day to day activities as well as festivities; she used her communicative skills to build a close rapport and a trusting relationship with the people of her block. When the worker successfully accomplished the above, she became ready to take up the next challenge with confidence.

THE EXPLORATION

The stage of exploration involved meeting people and identifying the target population. Since the worker did her field work in the community during the day time, her contact was largely with women and children who became her target population. Support from menfolk was to be secured from time to time, as and when needed.

This stage further involved assessing the needs and problems of the target population in order to choose suitable areas of work to be undertaken during the year. This assessment and selection was partially based on the felt needs of the residents and partly on the need felt by the worker.

WORKER'S OBSERVATIONS

The worker, who had visited a number of blocks in the community, was struck by the large child population of block 17, particularly in a few lanes in the area inhabited by the Rajasthanis. A majority of the children were below 6 years of age and appeared very weak and malnourished. The women showed similar signs of weakness and ill-health. They complained of fatigue and several gynaecological problems. The worker found many women to be anaemic and their babies at birth were very weak and under-weight.

Also, women all over the block expressed great curiosity to know something about birth control measures and sought her advice secretly in this area. They expected the worker to reveal some 'magic formula through which they could conceive only when they wanted'. The worker discovered that they were almost completely ignorant about the concept of birth control, family planning and the small family norm.

Briefly stated, the above observations led the worker to formulate a comprehensive programme of health and family welfare including *family planning, nutrition education, growth monitoring of childern, and immunization.*

THE BEGINNING

A beginning was made by identifying the family planning and health facilities provided to the people in the area itself or adjacent to it. The worker came to know of a locally available centre of the 'Family Planning Association of India' (FPAI). In fact this centre was one of the four FPAI centres situated in Delhi. The question was whether the residents were utilizing this facility which they had been provided with. The answer was sought by the worker during her meetings with the residents of her block, individually and in groups.

The worker came to know that only a few people were aware of the very existence of this particular polyclinic and almost none out of this few knew that a centre was situated there. Having confronted the family planning workers at the centre on this issue, the worker learnt that the centre provided information to people on family planning and also took eligible women to Radhapuri centre for tubectomy, abortion/IUCD insertion, and eligible men to Raghubarpur centre for vasectomy. The worker learnt that they were short of staff and their work at present was mostly concerned with surveying the area.

This was, therefore, a case of facility being available but not being utilized effectively by those for whom it was meant. The solution that the worker foresaw was to bring the need and the resource together, that is, an effective contact point to establish a 'link' between the facility and the local people. The question which now posed itself was : *Who was to be this link* ?

THE LINK

The possibility of the worker herself emerging as the link did cross her mind, but she realized that this would not be a lasting solution since the worker's contact with the community was temporary and time-bound. Moreover, the worker wanted the project to be one of *self-help*, that is, utilization of indigenous resources of the community itself to help the community members and to ensure continuation of the project even after the worker left the scene. The worker, therefore, decided to be a link, but only temporarily, and her efforts were to be concentrated upon finding a local substitute.

Another observation in the community made by the worker provided her with the local substitute. She had learnt that 'the Dai' in the community was quite popular.

TRADITION VS MODERNITY

The traditional birth attendent, commonly called the '*Dai*', occupied an important place in the societal setting. In this community too, as in most places of the country, delivery was usually conducted at home by the *family* '*Dai*'.

The preference of the people, especially those belonging to the low income communities for the services of these traditional birth attendents over the modern services provided by the local maternity and health centres had been a well-known fact and it arose due to several easily discernable reasons. The first and foremost reason being, the convenience in getting the *Dai* at home at any time of the day; secondly, she did not charge much; payment to her could be postponed or given in cash or kind, and it was flexible i.e., depends on child's sex. Thirdly, she shared a cultural affinity with the local people, and fourthly, she performed additional job like washing the clothes, bathing the baby, disposing of the placenta and cleaning the delivery room.

A Dai was relied upon not only to conduct deliveries but also to take care of the mother and the child during the first few weeks. Some women called upon her even for abortion and treatment of sterility.

In the community, *the Dais* had their own areas of influence (shown in Appendix A). They knew the families of the area as well were as respected by the young and old alike. The *Dai* possessed vital information about the number of children a particular family had, whether or not the family wanted more children and such other details.

THE DILEMMA

Looking at all this, the worker thought that *Dais* could prove to be an effective '*link*' between the family planning centre and the people. But the major question that arose at this stage was: would the *Dais* agree to adopt this role, family planning being antagonistic to their profession, as is widely assumed ? Also would it not be against the concept of modern medicine ?

DISCUSSION WITH SUPERVISOR

Discussion with the supervisor in this respect proved to be very enlightening. He suggested to the worker reading material on this subject.

A similar experience in Karnataka* (1) where a locally trained family planning worker encouraged her kin and friends to become acceptors was brought to worker's attention. This family planning canvasser was the local midwife whose experience gave hope to the worker. She also drew inspiration from a population report (2) which supported the fact that family planning methods, especially those that require periodic resupply such as condoms were more accessible through resident community workers.

(1) **Basic needs viewed from above and below* The Karnataka experience Epstein, T.S. (Paris : Organisation for Economic Co-operation and Development, 1983).

(2) Population Report (May-June, 1984)

MEETING A DAI

A meeting was sought with a *local Dai* of block 17. While anticipating antagonism, the worker was surprised to get a positive response from her regarding the matter. The *Dai* told the worker that woman often sought information from her about family planning measures, especially sterilization. They often expressed a wish to undergo sterilization after a delivery but she never took up the matter because she did not have any idea about the subject. She added, "I know how to bring children to see the light of this world, but know nothing about how to stop them from coming, when not wanted. I would like to learn about the latter with your help".

The reason for her responding positively to the idea of family planning could be due to the "motivation money" that each case would bring to her. Also in the community setting, a family did not even think of family planning unless it had four or more children. The *Dai* then realised that she did not have much scope left in delivering so she liked to earn by motivation.

The worker utilized all this information in framing this self-help project to avail the services of *Dais* as motivators and enablers in the family planning project.

THE APPROACH

To carry out the above, a need arose to first identify the Dais of the area. The worker decided to limit her project by involving the most *popular Dais of the community* i.e. those Dais whose services were used by many families not only in their own blocks but also in other blocks. In her own block and neighbouring blocks she talked to people and asked them about the services of the Dais they used. Through this process she indentified the Dais of the community. The worker also sought the help of the 'Birth and Death' Registration Officer who gave her the names of the other Dais. So on the whole the project involved 26 Dais (for their names and addresses see Appendix 'A').

During the months of the Sept.-Oct. 1984 the worker started approaching all these 26 popular Dais who had been identified. She found that one *Dai* out of this group had spoiled 1-2 cases about 1½ years back but she did not suffer from any unpopularity in the community and people continued using her services just as before.

The worker made efforts to establish a rapport with this group of Dais. She approached each one by saying : "I have heard a great deal about you, people really praise you. After hearing all the praise, I became very anxious to meet such a popular Dai. Hearing this, *the Dais* received the worker very well and welcomed her. Her initial conversation with them revolved around general things, namely the blocks where they conducted deliveries, the time when they had started practising their profession, experience gained over this period of time they faced, whether they delivered at their own houses or at the house of the customer and so on.

It was only later when *the Dais* started trusting her that she enquired deeper into sensitive areas. These sensitive areas were: whether they were trained/untrained; whether they had a certificate of practice or not; whether they had been apprentices to other Dais before practising on their own; and also the number of cases they performed per month, charges for their services (both in case of girl and boy new borns. Information given in Appendix B).

WORKER'S ROLE

At all points of the conversation, the worker communicated her respect for *the Dai*. She did so by choosing her words carefully and by her tone of voice and expressions. She made it clear to them that she was neither from any hospital nor from any government agency and she had not come to make an enquiry on behalf of any organization. That she was a well-wisher and not someone who was attempting to discourage their practice by encouraging any hospital/clinic was conveyed to them by her.

The worker's approach varied with each *Dai*. The elderly *Dais* were given due respect and referred to as 'Amma' or as called by the community people. In fact, one *Dai* was extremely happy when the worker called her by adding 'Nani' to her name. She at once said, "I am a grandmother (Nani) to many in the community. Today, I have found a new grand-daughter (Natin) in you."

The Dais of the middle age group were referred to as 'Didi' and treated as colleagues in the service of the community people.

The worker's meaningful rapport with *the Dais* can be summed up by quoting the words of a Dai herself. She said, "Many hospitals and clinic workers have approached me for help in their projects, but I have never responded. Something in you is different and almost compels me to join hands with you".

INVOLVING THE DAIS

The idea of acting as motivators in the area of family planning and earning additional income appealed to most of *the Dais*.

Gauging a positive response from the Dai, the worker planned to initiate the project in the community. She decided to undertake intensively the project only in her own block, and in other blocks it was to be an extensive endeavour. Her plan involved the following steps :

1. Informing the Dais about the FPAI centre, its location (which was very conveniently located) and the facilities it provided. This information was to be communicated to the people through Dais.

2. Communicating to the Dais the idea of 'motivation money' for sterilization and IUCD insertion cases, thereby attracting their co-operation and involvement in this direction. Also telling them about the incentive money available to the patients themselves. This information was to be given to the people by the Dais.

3. To enable Dais to take cases of sterilization and IUCD insertion to the concerned centres, that is, Radhepuri FPAI Centre for tubectomy cases plus IUCD and abortions, and Raghubarpura FPAI centre for vasectomy cases. The workers assured this by initially accompanying the Dais with their cases to the centres herself, making them familiar with the route, and the location of the centres, introducing them to the doctors and family planning workers and showing to them the process of registration and other details.

4. Weaning the Dais off the dependence on her and enabling them to carry out the project on their own by seeking

help from the local FPAI workers. The worker tried to achieve this by encouraging regular contact between the Dais and the FPAI workers.

5. Informing the Dais of the special drive and family welfare 'Pakhwaras' during which the motivation money increased substantially in order to attract them.

6. Providing the Dais with useful information on various methods of birth control. This included telling them about the process involved in sterilization, use of contraceptives like condoms, foam, tablets, jelly, oral pills, IUCD (like copper-T) and so on. This information was to be used by the Dais in motivating people to adopt any of the above methods.

7. Informing the Dais of the availability of contraceptives at the centre free of cost.

8. Giving tips to Dais to help those people who were scared of adopting family planning methods, especially sterilization, in dispelling rumours, misconceptions and fears by emphasizing the simplicity of the operation (quickness in operation and practically no pain etc.).

CHOICE OF FACILITY UTILIZED

The worker chose to utilize the services of the Family Planning Association of India (FPAI) due to the following reasons :

(a) The existence of a local FPAI centre situated at a walking distance from Trilokpuri.

(b) The location of Radheypuri, and Raghubarpura, FPAI centres, that is, they were the closest as compared to any other hospital, where similar facilities were available.

(c) Helpful attitude and concern shown by the members to the worker. The worker was impressed by the facilities in these centres, like a fully equipped and modern operation theatre.

(d) Provision of transport facilities for women patients and the accompanying member after sterilization and IUCD and abortion. The FPAI van dropped them in front of their houses. This proved to be a big plus point compared to hospitals, some of which provided transport facilities to patients for going to the hospital but let them on their own after the sterilization, almost as if they meant nothing to them after their purpose was achieved. As a result of it a patient had to spend about Rs 50/- travelling in a taxi.

(e) Giving to the patient and the motivator, incentive/motivation money on the same day (as compared to other hospitals where this money was generally given after a week). This money could be used by the patient to supplement her/his diet at this much needed time. Necessary documents like medical certificate, leave permission certificate etc. were also made on the same day.

(f) Follow-up services performed by the staff of the local FPAI centre and the convenience in approaching them in case of any complication.

(g) Facilities for getting stitches opened were available at the local centre by a trained gynaecologist, thus saving the patient an added trip to the centre where the sterilization had been performed.

Keeping in view the above the worker incorporated the services of the FPAI in her project. The worker's role at this stage called for careful survey of many alternatives, assessment into their positives and choice on basis of what she thought was the best for the community.

A PROMISING START

The project made a promising start. Two *Dais* popular in the worker's block got intensively involved in the project. They started active work in the area and were bringing cases to the notice of the worker and the local centre. Five sterilizations (four tubectomies and one vasectomy) had already been performed and two more tubectomies were scheduled to be held in the near future.

The worker encouraged the efforts of the *Dais* and enabled them to secure the services of the FPAI for their cases. She accompanied the Dais to the centre initially. Thus making them familiar with the procedure. Introducing them to the staff concerned and at the same time preparing them to handle things on their own in future. A stage had come when these Dais had gained confidence and started functioning independently that is ceased to depend on the worker. Realizing that these Dais needed to be encouraged from time to time by praise and recognition for their noteworthy efforts, the worker sought the help of the FPAI staff in this direction.

Just introducing them to the local FPAI workers and the visiting senior members of the FPAI by saying, "This is the Dai, who had been doing such a lot of praise-worthy work" and their response, in the form of "we have heard a lot of praise about your work" acted like a catalyst with the Dais and they renewed their efforts in the field.

The successful accomplishment of the sterilizations mentioned above had led to the "demonstration effect" at two levels. Firstly, at the level of the local residents. The cases had created a favourable impression of the project, the centre and the ability of the *Dais* in assisting the potential adopters of family planning in the minds of others. Neighbours were approaching the worker and the Dai for advice and help. In fact one old woman whose daughter-in-law was successfully sterilized due to the efforts of Dai and the worker, 'adopted' the worker as her 'daughter' and as a part of her family. She told all her neighbours that the worker had looked after her *Bahu* like her own sister and that her Bahu had been very well taken care of. In response, the worker was flooded with enquiries from interested neighbours.

Secondly, at the level of the other Dais, that is, the other Dais who had seen the active Dais take cases, earning motivation money, and thereby supplementing their income, were also showing a keenness to follow suit. A few Dais who were interested enough but did not want to take the first step watched as silent spectators, the other Dais taking their cases and getting them successfully sterilized. Satisfied with results, they too started making efforts to motivate couples to adopt family planning.

ORIENTATION TO FAMILY PLANNING

Orientation sessions for the Dais at the local FPAI centre had been started in order to maintain a continued liaison between the FPAI workers and the Dais. Contraceptive education had been a feature of such sessions, as also the registration of names of the Dais. At these sessions, the worker and the FPAI workers had been giving due consideration to the opinion of the Dais in each aspect of the project. This, together with the serving of light refreshments to them, made them feel needed and important. The Dais also got a chance to meet the other Dais, their colleagues in the profession. Hearing the other Dais themselves, telling about how their cases had been sterilized successfully provided them with the much needed enthusiasm to follow suit.

Contraceptive popularization sessions

The contraceptive popularization sessions had been held by the worker in different parts of the blocks with a two-fold aim. That is not only to encourage the adoption of birth control measures but also to provide the necessary ground work for the Dais to work upon at a subsequent stage. The Dais had been encouraged to take up this role from the worker. Already four sessions demonstrating the usage of contraceptives have been held.

Problems faced and limitations felt

Problems faced in the Family Planning area of the project were as follows :

Adverse attitudes of the people towards family planning. The worker faced these at three levels :

From the husbands

Even in cases where wives were keen, husbands created problems. One major problem was the 'drinking habit' of the menfolk and their unwillingness to abstain from intercourse during the prescribed period. Secondly, the men showed great resistance to the use of contraceptives like condoms.

From the mothers-in-law

It took a lot of coaxing for the mothers-in-law to agree to the adoption of family planning, especially sterilization by the couples.

From the women themselves

Condoms were supplied to the women who showed a desire to try them, and follow-ups were made. Twelve couples had adopted the use of condoms and were using them regularly after the worker's intervention. Women were very scared of sterilization and IUCD insertion. Only a few previously spoilt cases had created so much of adverse publicity that even successful cases could not obliterate it. Moreover, the shyness of the women to talk and seek advice in this direction proved to be a hindrance.

Non-involvement of the Anganwari workers

The Anganwari workers were not involved in the project because of their loyalty with the Kalyanpuri M.C.D. Hospital. The people of the area did not think highly of this Hospital because of several spoilt cases of sterilization. Moreover, the worker herself did not find the existing services to be satisfactory and as a result preferred the services of the FPAI.

Thirdly, the preference of couples towards tubectomy as against vasectomy posed a limitation, especially in cases where the women were too weak to undergo sterilization. The men were more interested in proving their virility or felt that it would hurt their sexual functioning. Women too feared some risk to the well-being of the family's bread-winner. As a result vasectomy, even though it took a shorter time and was a much simpler method than tubectomy, did not get the necessary boost.

Problems faced as far as *Dais* were concerned included dependence of *Dais* on the worker. Some *Dais* wanted the worker to accompany them and their cases to the centres (But the weaning off process had begun and the local FPAI workers had volunteered to step in the worker's shoes). The worker also faced problems in contacting the *Dais* because of their busy schedules.

The motivation money (Rs 10) that the worker received when she directly motivated a case also posed a few problems, that is, how should the money be utilized ? The worker did not want to keep the money herself because the community people would have reacted to that adversely. (The worker gave that money to the mother-in-law of the woman who had been sterilized. This mother-in-law had created a lot of hindrance in letting her daughter-in-law be sterilized and had finally agreed due to the efforts of the worker. She had even accompanied them to the centre and helped the worker to take care of the young children of the other case throughout the day).

In fact, this problem later proved to be a premium for the worker. Her reputation as a selfless person, who did not even keep the motivation money, got a boost and this further attracted more people to the project.

Enhancing the skills of the dais

The *Dais* of Trilokpuri were unlettered and except for three Dais (Kamla of block 13, Radha of block 5 and Kesar of block 20) had not received any formal training in midwifery. They had learnt their art either from elders by acting as their apprentices or through continued experience in the profession. As a result, they lacked many of the necessary skills, were without even the basic equipment needed for conducting deliveries at home, and continued following the old and traditional practices without incorporating anything from the modern world of medicine in their profession. A number of cases had reportedly been spoilt by Dais, the latest being in block 17 itself when due to the ignorance and lack of necessary skills, the Dai (a very popular one) could neither save the twin newborns nor the young mother. Nevertheless, this incident did not stop other people from being discouraged in using her services in future.

Moreover, the Dais possessed no knowledge about the care of pregnant women, ante-natal and post-natal care, needs of the newborn and lactating mothers.

Continuing popularity

It seemed unlikely that the services of the Dais and the practice of delivery at home would be replaced in the near future by trained midwives and by Hospital/clinic delivery. Accepting this fact the best policy was to enable Dais to have the essential training to enhance their existing skills in midwifery and related fields, to improve their service delivery-system and to let them have the basic equipment.

Willingness to train

By talking to the Dais the worker cautiously enquired into the training aspect. The idea of training evoked a mixed response from them. Some of the Dais were extremely interested in the idea while others said that their practical experience made up for their lack of training. A few elderly Dais who considered themselves to be experts in the field said, "what will the clinic people teach us ? there are a few things that we could teach them". The worker impressed upon them the idea that the clinic people would benefit by knowing from their experience and the Dais from theirs and that it would be a natural "give and take process". This idea appealed to them. A few other Dais told the worker that it was only because of the worker asking them and the relationship they shared with her, which prompted them to agree to the idea of training.

There was unanimous support to the idea, the moment the Dais realized that they would be given a certificate at the end of the training. The worker utilized this fact to attract the Dais to the training which ultimately would benefit the community residents through them.

Worker's role

The worker used a flexible approach to make *Dais* feel the need for training. She modified her approach according to the attitude of the Dai towards the prospect of training. A few Dais especially the elderly ones felt that they already knew everything about their profession. Giving them the idea that other Dais and the medical staff would like to learn from their experience made them willing enough to attend the forthcoming course. The incentive of a certificate being awarded after the course was used to attract some Dais to the course. To the Dais who had some certificates which they had obtained by working as apprentices to some doctor, the need to renew their learning and getting to know the latest in their field was impressed upon, thus making them willing to attend the course which was to be arranged for them.

Identification of agencies

In the month of November 1984, the worker set about identifying agencies, preferably local, which would be willing to organize the training course for the Dais.

Two agencies were finally identified, namely, the Diocesan

Mother and Child Health Care Centre" in block 36 of Trilokpuri and the M.C.D. Hospital at Kalyanpuri.

The worker approached both agencies with her proposal. Both agencies showed a keen interest to accept the proposal and undertake the training.

Progress made

There were postponements in the schedule of training in case of both the agencies. In case of the Diocesan centre, the festival of Christmas intervened, while in case of the Kalyanpuri Hospital the staff was occupied with an 'immunization drive' in the Khichripur Complex.

The latest position was that the worker had asked both the agencies to undertake the programme, though in different ways. The Diocesan centre being a smaller organization but with very sincere and hardworking sisters as its staff showed willingness to undertake a short duration training course for the Dais. This would take the shape of an orientation course for the Dais to be held over 4 days in March 1985. The worker and the sister-in-charge were involved in drawing up a curriculum and a schedule for the training programme. Resource persons from two hospitals in Delhi were to be invited to enrich the programme with their knowledge.

In April-May 1985, the Kalyanpuri Hospital was to hold an advanced and long duration training programme for the Dais. This programme was to be conducted in two long sessions of 15 days each. The Dais were to be given certificate on the completion of training. The Dais were also to be given kits containing the basic equipmemt used to conduct a safe delivery which was to be replanished from time to time by the Hospital. Giving Dais a daily stipend to encourage them to regularly attend the sessions had also been suggested and was under consideration.

The supervisor provided support to the worker throughout this process. Discussions with him regarding the agencies to be used for training and division of the training programme between the two agencies provided a lot of insight to the worker.

Programme content

The training programme included discussions with Dais to find out their current attitudes and practices relating to care during pregnancy, at the time of birth and in the few weeks following delivery and would aim at changing their attitudes.

The training sessions focussed on essential ante-natal care, nutrition during pregnancy and lactation, high risk pregnancies, anaemia in pregnancy and lactation, clean delivery and resuscitation of the new born, breast-feeding, prevention of neo-natal tetanus, post-partum care of the normal newborn, sick newborn babies, care of low birth weight babies and the importance of maintaining records. The programme would also include topics like the need for immunization, immunization schedule and nutrition for the mother and the child under 5 years of age.

A very important aspect of the training was to emphasize to the Dais the need to maintain a liaison with the centres, and to recognize well in advance and subsequently refer high risk pregnancies to the specialized care of centres/Hospital without attempting to perform them themselves. (For details of training held refer to Appendix 'C').

An added dimension

An added dimension to this self-help "Dai Project" was to use Dais to facilitate the birth registration process in the community. Need for adding this aspect was felt because the worker observed that births usually held at home were not registered. Parents did not feel the need for registering births till the child attained the school-going age and admission to school was disallowed because there was no birth certificate.

At that stage a long procedure of acquiring affidavit from court was undertaken. But if within a month of the child's birth a birth registration form is filled and submitted to the Birth and Death Registration Officer who was available at a local clinic, the birth certificate was made without any trouble and free of cost.

Involving the dai

If birth registration forms were available with the Dai who supplied one to the family of every newborn she delivered and also informed them about the procedure involved in getting the birth certificate made, the problem would be solved. With this idea in mind, the worker involved the Dais in this task.

The worker sought the liaison of the Dais with the Birth and Death Registration Officer. Forms were distributed among the Dais involved in the project and they were motivated to collect fresh supplies from the officer. This motivation was provided by showing them that particular column in the form which required filling in the name of the Hospital/clinic/birth attendent and telling them, "Your reputation with the authorities would improve if forms with your name mentioned (in case of child being delivered by her) reach them. Also people would be very grateful to you and remember you for this service rendered. Follow-up made on the Dais showed that at least sixteen Dais were performing the task asked of them and the rest promised to start soon.

Health

The worker subsequently linked up the family planning dimension of the project with the health dimension. Work in both areas had started simultaneously that is, from the month of August 1984. In health the worker laid special emphasis on maternal and child health. The areas of *Nutrition education* to women, growth monitoring of children under 3 years of age and immunization of children were selected under the health programme. Simultaneously efforts at enabling the residents to make use of locally available medical services and, if needed, specialized services provided by hospitals and other institutions situated elsewhere, continued.

Nutrition education to women involved regular sessions during which emphasis was laid on topics like nutrition for pregnant and nursing mothers, nutrition in infancy and childhood, diet for infants and children, need to incorporate vegetables in the diet, low cost nutritious diets for the family and correcting the methods of cooking used by women. The worker also demonstrated the cooking of several low cost nutritious recipes like soya-bean, peanut brittle, palak, vegetable preparations and so on. There was a lot of response from the women. One of them said, "We have started liking the food cooked by you so much that we do not like our food". One woman actually sent some peanut brittle made by her own hands for the worker's supervisor. This was in response to as enquiry made by him as to whether she made the things which the worker had demonstrated.

GROWTH MONITORING

The project on growth monitoring was based on the promise that regular monthly weight-gain is the most important single indicator of a child's normal healthy growth. The most important objective of this project was to make the problem of malnutrition of the child visible to the mother in order to promote the healthy growth of the infants. The anganwaris of the block were involved in taking regularly the weights of children below 3 years of age and recording them on growth charts. The grade III and grade IV children in the malnourished categories needed special care and so their mothers were educated about their needs. Three phases of the project in December, January and February had been completed. The initial response of the Anganwari worker, upon seeing the large number of mothers and children who had collected in front of the Anganwari due to the worker's efforts had been in the first phase one of shock and disbelief. She said, "Where has this army come from?" But later the Anganwaris were encouraged to carry out the project on their own.

The project of *Immunization* involved motivation to families especially the mothers to get their children immunized. Two phases of the project had already been completed in the months of December 1984 and January 1985. Again the worker's personal approach to each family, constant reminders about the immunization dates and giving the message in simple and effective terms led to tremendous response from parents in both the phases. On seeing a good response from mothers the members of the immunization team were quite surprised. One of them told the Anganwari worker, "I do not think there is any need for you to continue work here because never even once have you been able to get so many children for immunization." They were even more surprised when one woman came to get her young daughter immunized. This woman had resisted all previous efforts by teams to get her children immunized but one request from the worker had brought her to the Anganwari.

DISCUSSION WITH SUPERVISOR

Discussion especially in connection with the nutrition project was very useful. The supervisor gave a lot of valuable tips on improving the nutritive content of low cost recipes.

Inter-linkages

The worker's comprehensive MCH-FP PROGRAMME (that is, Maternal and Child Health and Family Planning Programme) brought out the inter-linkage between health and family planning.

The main idea behind such integration was that when infant and child mortality was high, family planning programme was unlikely to convince unresponsive couples. The findings of the Narangwal study in Punjab in India were used here. The study concluded that integrated services were more effective than family planning by itself. The GOBI-FFF* programme of the UNICEF emphasized in the latest State of World's Children 1984 Report was also based on the integration theory.

Practical experience of the worker in the field also clearly brought out the effectiveness of the approach. *Contraceptive popularisation sessions* with the active 'nutrition education group' were very successful. Eight women and their husbands out of a group of twenty-four had already started using condoms supplied by the worker.

The integrated approach had also helped in another way making the programme successful because the worker simultaneously took up all aspects of the project and she prevented herself from being identified as a family planning worker. She started off more vigorously on fronts other than family planning and when she was accepted and trusted, she gave a fillip to the family planning dimension of the project. This led to a much wider acceptance and positive reaction towards family planning than the worker could have elicited, had she been working in an isolated manner only in the areas of family planning. People now considered her as a well-wisher and not

*GOBI-FFF : Growth Monitoring, Oral Rehydration, Breast-feeding, Immunization, Female Education, Family Spacing and Food Supplements.

someone whose main objective was to coerce them to adopt family planning.

Dais too would be provided with useful information on the subjects of health, nutrition and immunization -- during the training period so that they could also perform a multi-dimensonal role in the community.

Worker's role

The worker used all her skills to formulate, implement and develop this project. She made adequate preparation for undertaking this multi-dimensional project. She acquired knowledge in the allied fields by the use of readings both suggested by the supervisor and those she located herself.

Knowledge in the field of nutrition, and health and family planning, especially about contraceptives, their usage, advantages/disadvantages of sterilization (tubectomy/vasectomy) and of delivery and care of mother was acquired before the worker implemented the project. The process of enriching her knowledge did not stop there. In fact it continued till the end when she was at the final stages of her field work.

The worker depended heavily on her communication skills. She adapted herself according to the respondent's level of consciousness and established a close rapport with people : the Dais (young and old alike), the community women, children and the staff of the various agencies she had chosen to be involved in the project. It was on the foundation of a close relationship that the worker built up the project.

The worker played the role of a guide about the problems of the people, some felt and others unfelt. In case of the former like malnutrition and ill health, she helped the community to establish the meeting of needs as a goal and found means of achieving these goals. In case of the latter, e.g. 'Family Planning' and 'Dai Training' the worker stimulated a feeling of need in respect of this based on highlighting the advantage of action towards such a goal.

Instead of herself carrying the project on her shoulders, she encouraged local initiative. She always recognized the fact that she was there for a limited time, but the project should continue even after she left which meant finding ways to shape the project into being one of *self help*.

The worker varied her sole at different points of time. At the start of each aspect of the comprehensive project she took the initiative and put in more of herself, that is, intensively involved herself. But after the stage of 'take off' i.e. after Jan 1985, she worked on developing and giving experience to local substitutes to take up the running of the project.

Growth in the worker's professional self

More than anything else the worker was aware of the growth in herself after undertaking the project. She had gained a lot of confidence. Her ability to communicate effectively, to plan and formulate and to organize and implement had enhanced manifold. The awareness that field work was not free work (as often put by her supervisor) was never so strong before as now.

She had learnt to adopt a critical view point, to be evaluative in her approach, to anticipate problems in her way and instead of escaping from them, confronting them and finding practical solutions for each of them by herself and with people.

By practically involving herself in a project of community wide dimensions, she found herself in a better position to understand the meaning of the term 'community organization' and her own role as a professional community worker.

Future implications

This small scale self-help project mobilized by the worker in the community had diverse implications. The micro level project could be adopted on a macro level and positive results could be achieved.

It was meaningful to understand that for family planning efforts of the government to reach the grass root level i.e.. the common man, it was unreasonable to depend solely on the professionals from the Department of Health and Family Welfare. It was of importance to involve and integrate the services of para-professionals and local agents for the successful implementation of the governmental programmes. The status and acceptance that these local para-professionals enjoyed in communities made them effective links between the resources and the people.

The state should also realize that local midwives (Dais) were there to stay at least in the measureable future. Therefore efforts to make available more maternity centres and modern facilities should be accompanied by efforts to enhance their skills and their service with proper training and supply of basic equipments needed by them to conduct their work safely and beneficially to the people.

DEVELOPMENTAL SOCIAL WORK PRACTICE : A POST-SCRIPT*

In connection with community work, students are confronted by citizens with problems which they face on account of indifferent or neglectful attitudes of government officers, or those of statutory corporations. Residents of a particular block in one of the Resettlement Colonies of Delhi face the problem of unusable toilets for the past six months or more. Reports and petitions sent by them have had no effect so far, nor did have the letters sent to the Editors of newspapers make any difference to the situation. Guidelines issued by the Delhi Development Authority prescribe the mode and frequency of sanitation work but these are being observed more by their breach. The only course left before the students in field work is to organise citizens for public interest litigation. In a Department of Social Work in Delhi when preparatory work was being done in this connection, question arose whether students and/or field work supervisor concerned should only organise citizens for this cause, or also join as petitioners. Two teachers of the Department favour petitioning in this matter although the policy of the Department in such cases is yet to be formulated. They believe that when students come to know of certain problems through field work which is a supervised one, they could (and should) formally associate with citizens in moving the court. Another view does not favour such a course because a Department of Social Work is part of the University which is a statutory body and it has its own legal unit. Moreover, field work is a training programme which is *designed* to *benefit* students than offer services to clients although the Department should ensure that it does not harm the latter. Since the Department of Social Work is not a service-giving agency, the

*By the author.

question of students and field work supervisors becoming petitioners does not arise. If this role is to be assumed, it should be approved by the appropiate academic bodies of the University. In the context of social development (community work and social action) this controversy is yet to be resolved at the formal level and the only course open before students and field work supervisors at present is that they associate themselves with citizens' groups either in moving the courts or in offering "dharanas" to focus attention on a problem or seek redressal of a grievance in their individual capacities only. The verdict of the Supreme Court (known as Ratlam Judgement) is yet to be appreciated and formally accepted by the schools of social work and the professional associations for human services in the country.

APPENDIX-A

Sl. No	Name of Dai	Address	Age (yrs)	Area of influence (Block Nos.)
1.	Kesar Kaur	Block 20	60	18, 19, 20, 26
2.	Munni Bai	Block 32	40	18, 19, 20, 32, Chilla Village, Kalyanpuri Blocks 4 and 5
3.	Atri	Block 31	48	31, 32, 33, 34, 35
4.	Sona	Block 3	52	1, 2, 3, 4, 9, 10
5.	Rampyari	Block 5	65	5, 6
6.	Ladaiti	Block 5	50	3, 4, 5, 6, 9
7.	Lakhwanti	Block 24	50	22, 23, 24, 25, 26, 31
8.	Labado	Block 16	55	16, 17
9.	Sharbati	Block 16	48	15, 16, 22, 23
10.	Maina	Block 21	50	17, 21, 22, 27, 31, 32
11.	Rambai	Block 10	42	9, 10, 11, 12
12.	Dilwari	Block 27	35	26, 27, 28, 35
13.	Sharifan	Block 27	40	26, 27, 28, 35
14.	Radha	Block 4	40	3, 4, 5, 6, 7, 8, 9, 10, 11
15.	Kamlesh B.	Block 36	48	30, 31 , 33, 34, 35, 36
16.	Kamla	Block 13	50	13, 14, 17, 24
17.	Ganga Bai	Block 21	45	21, 22
18.	Naima	Block 20	35	20
19.	Kammo	Block 20	35	20, 22, 23, 24, 27
20.	Bhagwati	Block 32	35	31, 32
21.	Bismillah	Block 15	45	15
22.	Kasturi	Block 11	50	8, 9, 10, 11, 16, 17
23.	Katori	Block 17	65-70	17
24.	Shiela	Block 17	35	17
25.	Bhagwati	Block 5	50	5, 6, 7
26.	Jimmi	Block 32	40-45	31, 32, 33

APPENDIX-B

INFORMATION ON DAIS

Sl. No.	Name of Dai	Nature of services undertaken	Educational status	Trained/ untrained (level of training)	Years of practical experience	No. of cases performed per month	Charges (Rs) Boy	Girl		Remarks
1	2	3	4	5	6	7	8	9	10	11
1.	Kesar Kaur	Ante-Natal, Natal and Post-Natal care	Illiterate	Trained	15	10-12	51/- to 101-	25/- to 51/-	—	Certificate of training from Amritsar
2.	Munni Bai	,, ,,	Illiterate	Untrained	8	10-15	50-60/- or 101/-	50-60/-	—	—
3.	Atri	,, ,,	Illiterate	Untrained	7-8	7/8	51/-	51/-	—	—
4.	Sona	,, ,,	Illiterate	Untrained	10-15	4-5	51/- or less	51/- or less	—	Even performs free of charge for poor families
5.	Rampyari	,, ,,	Illiterate	Untrained	10-15	3-4	30/- to 50/-	30/- to 50/-	—	—
6.	Ladaiti	,, ,,	Illiterate	Untrained	8-10	3-6	51/- or less	51/- or less	—	Free services to poor families
7.	Lakhwanti	,, ,,	Illiterate	Untrained	10-12	10-15	80/- to 101/-	40/- to 101/-	—	—

APPENDIX-B : (*Contd.*)

1	2	3	4	5	6	7	8	9	10	11
8.	Labado	Ante-Natal, Natal and Post-Natal care	Illiterate	Untrained	14-15	4-5	51/-	51/-	—	—
9.	Sharbati	,, ,,	Illiterate	Untrained	10-12	3-4*	51/- or less	51/- or less	—	Free service to poor families *works with DDA, so can take up fewer cases
10.	Maina	,, ,,	,,	,,	10	6-7	25/- to 51/-	25/- to 51/-	—	Free for poor families
11.	Rambai	,, ,,	,,	,,	7-8	4-5	30/- to 50/-	30/- to 50/-	—	—
12.	Dilwari Begum	,, ,,	,,	,,	4-5	8-10	51/-	51/-	—	—
13.	Sharifan Begum	,, ,,	,,	,,	7-8	10-15	51/- to 101/-	51/- to 101/-	—	Apprentice to another Dai (Kanno)
14.	Radha	Ante-Natal, Natal and Post-Natal care	Literate	Trained	13	6-10	50/- to 101/-	50/- to 101/-	—	Certificate from Lady Hardinge Medical College
15.	Kamlesh Bakshi	Ante-Natal, Natal and Post-Natal care plus abortions	Literate	Untrained	15	5-8	51/- to 101/	51/- to 101	—	Apprentice to doctor previously

1	2	3	4	5	6	7	8	9	10	11
16.	Kamla	Ante-Natal, Natal and Post-Natal care plus abortions	Literate	Trained	7-8	20-30	101/-	101/-	100-200/- for abortion	Certificate from Haryana
17.	Ganga Bai	Ante-Natal, Natal and Post-Natal care	Illiterate	Untrained	10-12	4-5	25/- to 50/-	25/- to 50/-	—	Free services to poor families
18.	Naima Begum	,, ,,	,,	,,	4-5	2-3	25/- to 50/-	25/- to 50/-	—	—
19.	Kammo Begum	,, ,,	,,	,,	10	7-8	51/-	51/-	—	Apprenticeship experience.
20.	Bhagwati	,, ,,	,,	,,	7-8	3-4	51/-	51/-	—	—
21.	Kasturi	,, ,,	,,	,,	13-14	8-10	51/- to 101/-	51/-	—	Apprenticeship experience
22.	Shiela	,, ,,	,,	,,	4-5	2-3	25/- to 50/-	25/- to 50/-	—	—
23.	Katori	,, ,,	,,	,,	10-12	1-2	25/- to 30/-	25/- to 30/-	—	—
24.	Bismillah	,, ,,	,,	,,	10	5-6	51/-	51/-	—	—
25.	Bhagwati	,, ,,	,,	,,	8-10	4-5	51/-	51/-	—	—
26.	Jimmi	,, ,,	,,	,,	—		—	—	—	Left the community before worker could get complete information.

'AREA OF INFLUENCE' OF DAIS (TRILOKPURI)

Note : 1, 2, 3, 4 are numbers for blocks. →Arrows indicate influence in the same adjacent Block A, B, M, etc. are

APPENDIX-C

TRAINING THE DAIS

AIMS AND OBJECTIVES

1. To identify trained and untrained Dais operating.
2. To train untrained Dais in methods of conducting aseptic delivery which is easy to adopt and implement in the field.
3. To orient Dais and to increase their knowledge and awareness regarding primary health care.
4. To enable Dais to maintain a liaison with the local primary health centres.

TRAINING SCHEDULE

The worker's approach to the Diocesan Mother and Child Care Centre led to the organization of a five-day training programme for the Dais. The schedule and programme content is as follows :

1. **Tuesday, the 12th of March, 1985**
   Making the Dias feel at home, general group discussions about their profession and practices. Anatomy and physiology of the female reproductive system, menstruation and conception.

2. **Thursday, the 14th of March, 1985**
   Ante-natal care.
   Sepsis, asepsis and antiseptic procedure of sterilization in the field area, preparation of the place for delivery, importance of perinatal care, ante-natal check-up, ante-natal tetanus, immunization, importance and schedule danger signals in pregnancy and identification of high risk cases, their referral, diet for a pregnant woman and care during pregnancy.

3. **Friday, the 15th of March, 1985**
   Natal care.
   Management of normal labour—procedure and mechanism, aseptic delivery by using simple instruments and cord care, post-partum haemorrhage; identification and first-aid, identification of high risk cases and their referral.

4. **Tuesday, the 19th of March, 1985**
   Post-natal care.
   Care of newborn, nutrition during post-natal period, breast feeding and its advantages, weaning process, reporting births, deaths (maternal, neonatal, infant), management of diarrhoea in children, growth of child, immunization in children.

5. **Thursday, the 21st of March, 1985**
   Sharing of experiences, discussion on problems faced, dispelling superstitious beliefs, follow-up on learning experience of Dais, conduct of a verbal test for award of certificates.

Dais chosen for training

Twenty Dais were chosen for training. They were :

1. Sharbati
2. Labado
3. Ladaiti
4. Radha
5. Sona
6. Bhagwati
7. Atri
8. Rambai
9. Sheila
10. Lakhwanti
11. Kamlesh Bakshi
12. Munni Bai
13. Maina
14. Ganga Bai
15. Rampyari
16. Naima Khatoon
17. Sharifan
18. Kammo Begum
19. Dilwari Begum
20. Kesar Kaur
21. Usha

Six Dais were not included because of the following reasons :

1. Bhagwati : was not available as she had gone to her native village.
2. Katori : too old to be trained.
3. Kasturi : has scheduled delivery cases during days of training.
4. Kamla : was ill during time of training.
5. Bismillah : was out of station.
6. Jimmi : ,, ,, ,,

Results of the training programme

The training programme was held for five days. This was followed by a test for the Dais. Fifteen Dais proved themselves eligible for the award of certificates (eligibility was based not only on the score achieved by each Dai, but also on the score achieved by each Dai on a minimum attendance record of 4 out of 5 sessions held).

Details of the test are as follows:

DETAILS OF TEST HELD FOR DAIS

Sl. No.	Name of Dai	Attendance record	Questions Asked	Max. score for each	Score obtained for each question	Total score	Eligible/ ineligible for certificate
1.	Munni	5/5	(a) Objective of the course	3	3		
			(b) Preparation for delivery	3	2		
			(c) Complications during pregnancy	2	2	9/10	Eligible
			(d) Do not feed mother for 2 days after delivery : True or false ?	1	1		
			(e) Don't breast feed child for 2 days after birth : True ?	1	1		
2.	Atri	5/5	(a) Objective of the course	3	3		
			(b) Preparation for delivery	3	2		
			(c) Care of newborn	2	2		
			(d) Same as above (first Dai)	1	0	8/10	Eligible
			(e) Same as above (first Dai)	1	1		
3.	Sona	5/5	(a) What will you do if you see a hand coming out of the opening first ?	3	3		
			(b) Implications of swelling	3	3		
			(c) Objective of the course	2	1	9/10	Eligible
			(d) Breast feeding	1	1		
			(e) Care of newborn	1	1		

4.	Ladaiti	4/5	(a) Objective of course	3	3		
			(b) Preparation for delivery	3	3		
			(c) Personal hygeine of Dai	2	2	9/10	Eligible
			(d) Revival of asphixiated baby	1	1		
			(e) Breast feeding	1	0		
5.	Kamlesh	4/5	(a) Complication during delivery	3	2		
			(b) Which cases to be referred ?	3	3		
			(c) Why insist on TT for pregnant woman ?	2	2	8½/10	Eligible
			(d) Why bleeding occurs in 2-3 months ?	1	1½		
			(e) 'Bad air'—superstition or reality ?	1	1		
6.	Lakhwanti	5/5	(a) Diet for pregnant woman	3	3		
			(b) Bleeding during pregnancy	3	3		
			(c) Care of newborn	2	2		
			(d) Should Dai give injections ?	1	1		
			(e) 'Bad air'—superstition or reality ?	1	1	10/10	Eligible
7.	Maina	4/5	(a) Objective of course	3	1½		
			(b) Preparation for delivery	3	3		
			(c) Personal hygeine of Dai	3	2	7/10	Eligible
			(d) Complications during pregnancy	2	1		
			(e) Breast feeding	1	0		

8. Sharifan	5/5	(a) Objective of course	3	3		
		(b) Preparation for delivery	3	3		
		(c) Nutrition for pregnant woman	2	2	9½/10	Eligible
		(d) Nutrition for lactating mother	1	1		
		(e) Breast feeding mother	1	½		
9. Sharbati	5/5	(a) Which cases to refer to Hospital ?	3	3		
		(b) Looking after newborn in winter	3	3	9/10	Eligible
		(c) Objective of course	2	2		
		(d) Do not give mother anything to eat for 2 days after delivery	1	1		
		(e) Breest feeding	1	0		
10. Usha	4/5	(a) Objective of course	3	1		
		(b) Preparation of delivery	3	3		
		(c) Nutrition for lactating mother	2	2		
		(d) 'Bad air' : Reality or superstition	1	1	8/10	Eligible
		(e) Breast feeding	1	1		

11. Ganga	3/5	(a) Preparation for delivery	3	3		
		(b) First aid during bleeding	3	3		
		(c) How to cut the placenta	2	2	10/10	Eligible
		(d) 'Bad air' : True ?	1	1		
		(e) Breast feeding	1	1		
12. Dilwari	3/5	(a) Objective of course	3	3		
		(b) Which cases to be referred ?	3	3		
		(c) Nutrition of pregnant woman	2	2	8/10	Eligible
		(d) Care of newborn	1	0		
		(e) Breast feeding	1	0		
13. Radha	5/5	(a) Nutrition of pregnant woman	3	3		
		(b) Which cases to be referred ?	3	3		
		(c) Whether to send woman for check-up and why ?	2	2	$9\frac{1}{2}$/10	Eligible
		(d) 'Bad air' : Superstition or reality ?	1	1		
		(e) Care of newborn	1	1		

14. Shiela	3/5	(a) Objective of course	3	1		
		(b) Care of newborn	3	2		
		(c) Personal hygeine of Dai	2	2	7/10	Eligible
		(d) Preparation for delivery	1	1		
		(e) Breast feeding	1	1		
15. Rambai	4/5	(a) Objective of course	3	2		
		(b) Care of newborn	3	3		
		(c) Preparation for delivery	2	2	9/10	Eligible
		(d) 'Bad air' : superstition or reality ?	1	1		
		(e) Nutrition for newborn and immunization	1	1		

Dais found ineligible :

1. Labado : Attendance incomplete
2. Naima : Absent on 2 days due to sickness at home.
3. Kanno : Work hours clashing with training hours, and therefore absent for 3 days.
4. Bhagwati : Absence due to husband's sickness.
5. Kasar Kaur : Had to go out of station in between.

PERCEPTION OF DAIS BEFORE AND AFTER TRAINING

Sl. No.	Name of Dai	Before training			After training		
		Ante-natal care	Natal care	Post-natal care	Ante-natal care	Natal care	Post-natal care
1.	Munni	Never advised women for check-ups.	Dealing with a few types of high risk cases herself.	No information on care of new-born and immunization.	Will advise women for check-ups	Will refer all high-risk cases to hospital.	Information on post-natal care to be passed on to patients.
2.	Atri	Never advised women for check-ups.	Did not know how to deal with post-partum haemorrhage.	-do-	-do-	Confident of giving first aid in case of post-partum haemorrtage and referral to Hospital.	-do-
3.	Sona	Never advised women for immunization.	Did not know which cases to be referred ?	No information on care of lactating mothers and newborns.	Will advise women for check-ups and immunization.	Feels equipped with useful information on cases, not to be dealt by her.	-do-

4.	Kamlesh	Naver advised women for check-ups. Gave injection to anaemic women without having a certificate.	Dealt with all high-risk cases herself and never referred any case to Hospital.	No information on immunization and nutrition aspects.	Will advise women for check-ups, promised not to give injections herself	Will refer all high-risk cases to Hospital	-do-
5.	Ladaiti	Very rarely anti-natal check-ups.	No knowledge of strict personal hygeine and high risk cases.	No information on post-natal care.	Will advise women for check-ups and immunization	Will follow strict personal hygeine requirements and refer high-risk cases.	Help women and newborn in post-natal period with necessary knowledge.
6.	Lakhwanti	Giving injections to women for anaemia and weakness.	Rarely referring high-risk cases.	-do-	Promised never to give injection herself.	Will refer high-risk cases	-do-
7.	Maina	Never advised check-ups and no knowledge on immunization.	Improper methods to deliver child used plus followed lot of superstitions.	-do-	-do-	Will modify her methods and will be less superstitious in her practice.	-do-
8.	Sharifan	-do-	—	-do-	-do-	—	-do-

9.	**Sharbati**	Limited knowledge on immunization nutrition and antenatal check-up.	Limited knowledge on identification of high-risk cases.	-do-	Will use the knowledge gained in this respect.	Confident of identifying and referring such cases.	—
10.	**Usha**	Was conducting 30-40 abortions per month mostly in late stages of pregnancy ?	Giving injections to ease pain during labour.	Limited knowledge on post-natal care.	Promised never to conduct abortions especially the ones in late stages.	Promised never to give injection	Will use knowledge attained for benefit of clients.
11.	**Ganga**	Limited knowledge on antenatal care.	Limited knowledge on high-risk cases.	Limited knowledge on post-natal care.	Will provide knowledge to clients.	Will refer high cases.	Will use knowledge attained for benefit of clients.

12.	Radha	Giving injections to pregnant women.	Giving injections to ease labour pain.	—	Will learn to give injections properly from clinic.	Will abstain from giving many injections to ease pain.	—
13.	Dilwari	Never advised patients for ante-natal check-ups.	No knowledge on high-risk cases, especially haemorrhage cases.	Limited information on post-natal care.	Will advise patients to undergo check-ups and will not deliver if otherwise.	Feels confident to identify and refer high risk cases.	Will advise clients on post-natal care.
14.	Rambai	-do-	-do-	-do-	-do-	-do-	-do-
15.	Sheela	-do-	-do-	-do-	-do-	-do-	-do-

6

DOING WITHOUT KNOWING
A Note on Knowledge, Theory and Practice

Shankar Pathak

THE WORKSHOP ON FIELD WORK has been organised in order to strengthen the field work programme in schools of social work which train students who will go out as social workers. It is a widely held view that field work is concerned mainly with practice and it provides an opportunity to *apply theoretical knowledge*, which is acquired in a variety of ways but mainly through class-teaching and reading of the literature. The latest term for field work is 'professional application'. There are many assumptions behind this view of field work and its role in the preparation of social workers. These assumptions are not always clearly spelt out. They remain hidden, implicit rather than explicit. The main purpose of this note is to provoke the participants in the workshop to identify the taken-for-granted assumptions and subject them to a critical examination.

Let me briefly explain the title. It is concerned with the nature of knowledge, its constituent elements, the relationship between the elements, and the relevance of all these to social work education. There are two opposite views about the purpose of knowledge. The idealistic view is generally stated as knowledge for knowledge's sake; the instrumentalist view holds that knowledge is for use. We claim that social work is a profession (the claim is debatable) and we further claim that it has a corpus of knowledge which is scientific in character. It is obvious that we subscribe to the instrumentalist view of knowledge.

Social work had a long and passionate affair with science and it is still continuing. It has mostly been a one-sided affair. (Like all one-sided affairs it has led to considerable psychological trauma). We have always made a distinction between scientific and non-scientific knowledge. We have laid great stress on the value and status of scientific knowledge as part of our education and practice. Social work education is based on the assumption that the available scientific knowledge is transmissible through education and after education it is usable in a variety of practical situations. I do not intend to dwell on the issue whether we have, in fact, scientific knowledge. I propose to question rather what we understand by scientific knowledge. As we read more and more the literature on science, we become less certain about what is scientific knowledge. The positivist view of science is described as the 'standard view of science'. According to this view science is certified knowledge. It is also certain knowledge in the sense that it is conclusively proved and its truth-claims are established beyond doubt. A distinction is made between fact and theory, and facts are seen as value-free and independent of any theory. Scientific knowledge is governed by the principle of uniformity. The scientific ethos is characterised by autonomy, objectivity, universalism, communism and organised scepticism.

This standard view of science is under attack from different directions in recent years. Facts are no longer viewed as value-free and independent of theory, because they are collected by observation which is theory-dependent or theory-laden. Scientific knowledge is inherently inconclusive because it is incapable of being totally proved or disproved. It is only partially confirmed through empirical verification. So, some parts of scientific theory have to be taken on trust. Scientific knowledge then, is also a belief-system, though it is different from other belief-systems. Irrespective of one's ideological orientation it is generally accepted that scientific knowledge includes theory which is grounded on empirical practice—testing, confirmation, refutation —and that theory is *prior* to practice. While there are many who would consider theory and practice as related but dichotomous, there are others—mainly some Marxists, who view theory and practice as unity.

A lucid and succinct exposition of the Marxist view of knowledge is to be found in Mao Zedung speech 'On Practice'.[1]

A careful examination of it will reveal that Mao's conception of the origin and growth of knowledge in cyclical and spiral. Most others, especially the positivists, seem to believe in the linear conception of knowledge and that the growth of scientific knowledge is cumulative.

According to Mao there are two kinds of knowledge—the perceptual and the rational. These two types "are qualitatively different but are not divorced from each other; they are unified on the basis of practice".[2] Rational knowledge is superior to perceptual knowledge but it depends on perceptual knowledge. "All genuine knowledge originates in direct experience. But one cannot have direct experience of everything; as a matter of fact most of our knowledge comes from indirect experience, for example, all knowledge from past times and foreign lands .... Hence a man's knowledge consists only of two parts, that which comes from direct experience and that which comes from indirect experience. Moreover, what is indirect experience for me is direct experience for other people. Consequently, considered as a whole knowledge of any kind is inseparable from direct experience".[3] It is clear from these excerpts of the speech that Mao believes in the primacy and priority of practice over theory. Also, for him the relationship between the two is unity.

Gandhi has not spoken or written on this theme. But some of his remarks on related topics give me the impression that his view was perhaps, nearer to the Marxist conception of knowledge in the sense that it stressed the direct experience of the individual as a major source of knowledge. It is only in this perspective that we can appreciate the Sarvodaya workers' emphasis on learning by doing, initially in an apprenticeship situation of working along with a person who has considerable field experience, and later independently in one's own chosen area of field practice. And this also explains the de-emphasis on formal training by Gandhians.

Science and arts are frequently treated as mostly dissimilar in many popular discussions of science, profession, and arts. The well-known physicist and Nobel Laureate, Leon Cooper has observed that 'it is a common misconception that science is separated from the arts because science deals with fact or with information'.[4] He further observes : "The full range of possible human experience is so much, the variety of ways of looking at the same events so diverse, that it is almost impossible to recall our experience in any sensible way with no preconceptions as to what is significant, and the preconceptions often are the boldest strokes of organization".[5] Collingswood has stated that craft (the word he prefers to art) is characterised by deliberations prior to the act, and by separation of means and ends in the production of the craft. These two characteristics are also part of what we call as science. Surely there are some significant differences also between science and art or craft.

There is a good deal of aura and mystique surrounding science and scientific method. One of the popular claims of professional social work is that not only it has scientific knowledge but it also has a scientific methodology of practice what is this scientific method ? Let me quote again from Cooper :

> I have never been content with the often repeated emphasis on scientific method. Possibly there is some method in science that could be distinguished from the usual madness in every day affairs, but this seems overdone. The scientific method exists less in working laboratories than in antiquated textbooks. What science does, for all its sophistication of technique and subtlety of thinking, is quite straightforward and is duplicated in a great variety of other human activities. First, science observes. Perhaps this conjures up visions of laboratories and devoted workers in white coats. No doubt laboratories and devoted research workers in white coats exist. But their purpose—to distinguish the world in which we live from all other possibilities of our fantasy or imagination—is as necessary for the detective or the plumber as the scientist. Once the so-called facts are assembled, it is the problem of theoretical science to provide a fabric, a theory, a set of relationships—in short, an explanation—that ties together every phenomenon with every other; a task also required of the plumber if he is to locate the origin of the leak, or the detective if he is to identify the criminal.[6]

I believe I have said enough to highlight some of the features of science and also to clarify what scientific method means. You may justifiably ask what has all this got to do with field work ? So let me briefly mention some of the implications of our claims to science and scientific method in relation to practice that is field work.

1. We generally subscribe to the positivist school of knowledge (instrumentalist view) and the standard view of science. It follows from this position that theory comes before practice. It means that the students have to be given the relevant theoretical knowledge in adequate doses *before* they are sent out to *apply* the theoretical knowledge in practice. But our field work programme does not correspond to this model. Concurrent field work requires the students to begin practice even before they have acquired the theoretical knowledge. This model of field practice is nearer to the position taken by Mao and perhaps Gandhians. If we logically follow our basic position regarding the serial order of theory and practice, then we will have to organise our field work programme on a different model.

2. In my opinion, while we have borrowed a good deal of conceptual and theoretical knowledge from a variety of sources, there is very little that could be considered as scientific knowledge. This statement, I know, will be questioned and even contradicted. So let us assume for the sake of pursuing the argument that scientific knowledge exists. I would like to raise some further questions. Has this scientific knowledge been growing continuously ? Who has been adding to the existing reservoir of scientific knowledge ? How much scientific research has been done by professional social workers to create and add to the existing fund of knowledge ? Does the scientific knowledge remain static or frozen at the point of time when one completed one's education in social work ?

3. Scientific knowledge, according to Kuhn, grows as a result of research carried out within an over-arching, ruling paradigm The term paradigm is used by Kuhn in two senses :

> On the one hand, it stands for the entire constellation of beliefs, values, techniques, and so on shared by the members of a given community. On the other it denotes one sort of element in that constellation, the concrete puzzle-solutions which, employed as models or examples, can replace explicit

> rules as a basis for the solution of the remaining puzzles of normal science.[7]

At any point of time in any branch of natural science, there is one accepted paradigm as part of which theories are formulated and they are tested on the basis of scientific experiment. A paradigm attains the position of a ruling paradigm when other competing paradigms are rejected in favour of it.

In social work we do not see anything that is comparable to a ruling paradigm. Even in social sciences from which a great part of theoretical knowledge has been borrowed, it is difficult to find a ruling paradigm. What we do find is a number of competing theories out of which one may be preferred by the practitioners. Let us take for example the field of counselling and psychotherapy. During the period of 1930 to 1950 the Freudian theory became so popular in the USA that it almost attained the status of a ruling paradigm. Even during the peak of its prestige and popularity the Freudian theory of personality did not have the same status in other western countries.

During the past two or three decades, the Freudian theory has lost its position even in the United States of America and the behavioural theory of personality has been on the ascendance. Yet, we cannot say that either the behavioural theory or any other theory has become a ruling paradigm. This situation leads to many practical difficulties. What is taught as a scientific theory of personality in a particular country (and within the same country in a particular school of social work), may not reflect the universal acceptance of that theory as scientific knowledge. We have only to recall the fierce controversy and almost partisan adherence to the functional or psychoanalytical schools of case work in the United States of America a few decades ago. It was a serious problem for a graduate of school of social work who was trained on the basis of one particular theory to practice in an agency where the dominant theory was the rival theory. It will be extremely rare to find a comparable situation in any branch of natural science except for a very brief period of transition when a ruling paradigm is being challenged by a rival paradigm.

Even today, apart from the problem of transcultural applicability of Western theory of personality in non-Western cultures there is the further problem of deciding which of the several theories of personality and counselling should be considered as the scientific theory.

4. The supervision in field work is done in some schools exclusively by the field practitioners employed by the agencies and in some other schools by the faculty. There is also a variation of these two patterns in some of the schools of social work. One such variation is splitting of supervisory responsibility between the faculty and the agency staff. Another variation is that some students in the same school are supervised by the faculty and some other by the agency staff. In a comparable situation involving several students, a faculty member as supervisor may be imparting field instruction on the basis of behavioural theory of personality, and in the case of other students supervised by the agency staff the field instruction may be based on the psycho-analytical theory or *vice versa*. The more traumatic situation will be in a school which divides the supervisory responsibility and where the faculty and the agency supervisor may subscribe to competing or conflicting theory of personality.

The situation is not different in the case of students working in a community placement. One student may get field experience on the basis of the conflict model of social change and another student in a comparable situation (even within the same geographical community) under a different supervisor may be getting field experience on the basis of consensual model of social change. Neither of these two models of change can claim the status of a ruling paradigm in that particular field practice. The examples cited above indicate that neither the principles of uniformity nor the value of universalism which are said to be characteristics of science are evident in social work education and practice.

5. There appears to be a tenuous link between theory and practice in the education for social work. This is due to two reasons. As pointed out earlier, the pattern of supervision in many schools of social work is such that a major responsibility for the supervision of field work is assumed by the agency staff. The agency staff have little opportunity to update their theoretical knowledge. They are also unable to spare time for visits to libraries or for attending any short-term course which may be organized occasionally by some schools of social work. On the

other hand, the faculty of the schools are, hopefully, up-to-date in theoretical knowledge. However, this statement needs to be qualified because many schools do not have adequate reading material in their libraries, especially the journals in which normally the latest theoretical developments are published. Even when the facilities are available whether the faculty make use of them adequately to update their knowledge is a matter for speculation. Modelling is stated to be an effective means of communicating skills in practice based on scientific knowledge. The faculty supervisor is unable to provide this experience. So what happens really in supervisory meetings is a *post-mortem* of field work experience. So the students are unable to see any link between what is taught in the class and what is practised in the field. This may lead them to conclude that theoretical knowledge is irrelevant to practice. Are they wrong if they reach this conclusion ?

6. In order to contribute to the growth of scientific knowledge a scientist needs an attitude of skepticism, good deal of autonomy in his functioning, and creativity. The popular pattern of field work supervision in social work is a carryover of the earlier period of training based on apprenticeship with an experienced social worker in the agency. A sociological analysis of the supervisory process in USA by Toren some years ago revealed that supervision is antithetical to autonomy and innovation. The American educational system and the wider society of which it is a part has a good measure of democracy. Questioning and dissent are permitted. In contrast the society and the educational system in India are characterised by hierarchy, a high degree of authority of the teacher and unquestioning acceptance of what is taught. So, when the American supervisory model was transplanted in a different cultural milieu in India, it became more rigid, more authoritarian and thus left little scope for dissent and creativity.

The literature on supervision contains reference to the learning theory. The latest UGC Report on social work education also makes references to the learning theory as used in USA. Martin Hollis has recently pointed out that all theories concerning man are formulated on one of the two models of man : the Plastic Man and the Autonomous Man. He has also stated that *his* models are ideal types and no theory completely conformed to either of the models. The learning theory that is, utilized, if at all, in supervision in social work is largely based on the model of Plastic Man. "Plastic Man is not much of an individual. Within a passive conception each of us is unique only in so far as he is only instance of the intersection of a complex of laws." Plastic Man is a natural creature in a rational world of cause and effect.[8] In the Indian context theory is reinforced by the hierarchical and authoritarian sub-culture of the educational system. So we turn out students by the process of 'cloning' who go out and multiply others like them. In the absence of dissent and creativity there is little hope of developing and adding to the scientific knowledge and techniques of practice in social work.

Bertrand Russel is reported to have remarked that we are born with beliefs but we have to be trained to be sceptical. I cannot say that scepticism as a mental attitude is widespread among social work educators and that it is encouraged among students of social work. Perhaps the opposite may be true.

7. I shall say a few words about the medium of instruction in social work education in India. In most schools the students are taught through the medium of English language and they have to write the field work reports in English. However, in their field work with people the students have to make use of one or the other Indian language prevalent in that area. A few students may not know the local language at all or may not know it sufficiently in order to communicate well with people. This is especially true of foreign students admitted to Indian universities and students who join schools located in far away places where the language spoken by the people of the area is vastly different from their mother tongue. Even when the students are well-versed in the local languages, there is the problem of translating the interviews and the deliberations of the meetings in a very short period of time into English. That many of the students are not capable of performing this feat is well-known.

One of the characteristics of science is reported to be its capacity to assemble a large mass of data and to present them meaningfully in the context of theory or paradigm. Also, the reality of what is observed, the accuracy and precision in observing and in describing what has been observed is considered very essential for scientific experiment. So a special language which enables the scientist to present a large quantity of data accurately and precisely is developed by science. The students of science are able to learn and make use of this special language. An inability to develop and use competently this special linguistic framework can be a serious hurdle for the work of a scientist and the growth of science. So the medium of instruction which is different from the medium of communication in field work can pose a serious problem for the student and his learning.

Some of our own supervisory practices place a premium on presenting a mass of relevant and irrelevant observational data in a descriptive, narrative form. I am here referring to what is called as process-recording in field work. Apart from wasting considerable amount of time of the students and also of the supervisor, it is not very helpful in developing an analytical mind. It is worth-noting that neither the students of natural science nor of the biological science are required to do such detailed process-recording of their scientific observational work.

I come back to the title of this Note. Is it possible to do (that is to work with people) without knowing ? The answer is both 'yes' and 'no'. Logically speaking, with very rare exceptions it is inconceivable that there can be any human action without *prior* deliberation. In that sense doing without knowing is almost impossible. In another sense, that is, doing without acquiring theoretical knowledge through a formal course seems possible. Apart from a variety of evidences from other sources, our own concurrent field work lends ample support to this position.

NOTES

1 Cf. 'On Practice', in *Selected Works of Mao Tse-Tung*, Vol. 1, pp. 295-309.
2 *Ibid.*, p. 299.
3 *Ibid.*, p. 300.
4 *Leon* N. Cooper, p. 5.
5 *Ibid.*, p. 6.
6 *Ibid.*, p. 5.
7 Thomas S. Kuhn, p. 175.
8 Martin Hollis, p. 11.

REFERENCES

Barnes, Berry *Scientific Knowledge and Sociological Theory*, Routlege and Kegan Paul, (London ; 1974).

Collingswood, R.P., *Principles of Art*, Oxford University Press, (Oxford ; 1958).

Cooper, Leon N. 'Source and Limits of Human Intellect', *Daedlus*, (Spring 1980), pp. 1-17.

Giddens Anthony (ed.) *Positivism and Sociology*, Heineman, (London : 1974).

Hollis Martin *Models of Man*, Cambridge University Press, (Cambridge : 1977).

Kuhn, Thomas S. *The Structure of Scientific Revolutions*, Second Edition, The University of Chicago : Press, (Chicago : 1970).

Mao Zedung 'On Practice', in *Selected Works of Mao Tse-Tung*, Foreign Languages Press, Vol. 1. (Peking : 1967).

Mulkay, Michael *Science and the Sociology of Knowledge*, George Allen and Unwin, (London : 1979).

Toren Nina 'Semi-Professionalism and Social Work : A Theoretical Perspective', in Amitai Etzioni (ed.), *The Semi-Professions and Their Organization*, The Free Press, (New York : 1969).

7

FROM 'FIELD WORK' TO 'FIELD INSTRUCTION'
Need for Shift in Perspective for the Supervisory Process

Krishan Kumar

THE basic issue being raised here is that there is more of field 'work' and very little of field 'instruction' in the field work programme of social work education. Truly speaking if we look at the way in which field work process is implemented, we will have to admit that the learning goals in field work process are often lost sight of. If field work is to be recognized as a major component in professional education and practice, it is necessary that the instructional aspects of this programme are adequately stressed and properly implemented. Let us ask ourselves whether we are guided in our supervisory roles by appropriate normative standards which would ensure instructional component of field work process. My contention is that we do not interact with our students in the supervisory process backed up by instructional standards of assignments. Let me summarily reflect on the typical field work behaviour of a student and a supervisor.

A student is placed in an agency/community setting. He has approximately 20-25 days with him in which he has to complete one term's field work. About 3-4 weeks (6-8 field work days) are utilized by him in becoming familiar with the set up, establishing rapport with people, "personnel, and so on. Gradually he begins to identify, if in an agency setting, the day to day functions being handled by a social work personnel of the agency.

If it is a community setting, there is still hardly any departure from his original position (of maintaining and consolidating contacts). At best, he may start expanding his contacts, organise group games, take up coaching classes for school-going children. Having put in 3-4 weeks, the student begins to feel at ease, for his contacts have become more cordial by then. Thereafter he starts exploring problems of individuals, picks up a few cases (of school drop-outs, patients needing dispensary assistace in community setting, and conducting investigations/interviews in agency setting). All through this period, the supervisor keeps enquiring as to 'what' he has 'done' or what he has been 'doing'.

The general pattern as outlined above, leaving a few exceptions, remains the same during the rest of the field work period. There may be differences in tasks handled. (Examples : a film show, a sample survey, an excursion or trip, taking patients to hospital or observing the routine day to day functional responsibilities of a social work functionary). The first term ends at a usual note of relief for a supervisor whose evaluation report in respect of his student invariably suggests :

> The student was able to establish relationship with people. He showed interest and enthusiasm in attending to specific problems of several individuals. He showed a good understanding of the needs and problems, and so on.

Let us honestly enquire within ourselves whether we have a consciously planned 'work guide' for a student. Or is not true to admit that we have been recording or gauging progress of a student simply on the basis of what he observed, what he did, what tasks he handled and such other information as he writes in the field work reports.

It appears that in the whole process of supervision, we are generally 'listening' and 'commenting with very little *of rationally planned* and pursued instructural guidelines for students.

Some of my colleagues may react saying that they do have such guidelines. But again the question remains : "Do we all sincerely pursue and periodically check the progress of a student against such guidelines ?" My impression is that we do not. The problem seems to be rooted at two levels. Firstly, an institution may not have evolved an educational framework to guide its field work programme. The U.G.C. Review Committee has also identified this limitation when it says : 'To overcome some of these problems only one institution has tried to work out the content, and the behavioural outcomes for each year of the bachelor's and the master's programmes."* Secondly, even if attempts are made to identify the content and the behavioural outcomes of field work programme there is no guarantee that such 'contents' and behavioural outcomes are earnestly pursued by student learners and their field instructors, and that progress of a student is seen and evaluated within the context of the 'content' and the 'behavioural outcomes' of the field work programme. It is in this area where a sincere 'heart searching, is needed on our part that is, on the part of those of us who have field work supervisory responsibilities. It is not enough to suggest or even organise seminars, workshops, supervisory development programmes as a counter-measure to remedy the situation. The answer to the problem lies a great deal in heightening our sensitivity to the supervisory role followed by a genuine willingness to perform such role.

What is it which would introduce and strengthen the instructional component in the field work process ? I am inclined to suggest two propositions in this regard : (a) it is very much essential on the part of supervisors to work out an instructional guidelines highlighting objectives and their corresponding field work assignments, and (b) periodical field work workshops need to be organised at the level of respective educational institution to clearly spell out expected behavioural outcome for field work.**

**Review of Social Work Education in India, Report of the Second Review Committee*, U.G.C., New Delhi, p. 58.

**Some exercises in regard to the above have been carried out at the Delhi School of Social Work and some clarity has emerged with reference to the content of field work and the nature of field work assignment which, when pursued, would reflect the content.

CONSTRUCTING EMPIRICAL REFERRANTS FOR EVALUATION OF FIELD WORK

By 'empirical referrants' I mean such material evidence in a student's field work sequence which provide a reasonable and verifiable support to a supervisor's evaluative comments on field work performance. In other words, empirical referrants are the selective pieces of data which, when referred to, corroborate and reinforce, what would otherwise be a subjective impression.

Social work educators have always valued objective evaluation of student's performance in field work. In spite of the fact that this value commitment has been stressed time and again, we do not as yet have adequate tools to ensure this objectivity in the evaluation process. As the Second Review Committee on Social Work Education says.

> While class syllabi spell out expected content in each level of learning, there is rarely a statement of expected behavioural outcomes to provide the framework for the evaluation of the student's learning. On the other hand, most institutions utilise evaluation criteria of expected behavioural outcomes for field work but they do not spell out the content which will lead to such outcome. Because of such lack of content for guidance of the field instructor, it tends to be limited to the individual instructor's particular frame of reference as to what requires to be taught, and it is difficult to judge whether the evaluation of the student is a result of the inputs of the field instructor's teaching.

Let me cite a few typical instances of evaluative comments in order to illustrate the need of constructing empirical reference.

Illustrations

(i) "the student gained *sufficient professional maturity* in the course of his field work".

(ii) "the student established excellent relationship in the community".

Problems have often arisen and they are bound to arise in supervisory evaluation process unless we broadly identify and list down such empirical referrants which when found in the field experience of a student, would corroborate and justify comments like 'sufficient professional maturity' in illustration (i) and 'excellent relationship' in illustration (ii) In the absence of such a frame of reference our evaluative comments as supervisors are very likely to remain impressionistic. However, I do concede that impressions, after all, will have some basis somewhere either in supervisor's observations, his interaction with a student in individual and group conferences, or his visits to field work agency. Nevertheless, an attempt in this direction will surely be a very useful aid towards a realistic and objective evaluation of field work performance of student learners.

8

FIELD INSTRUCTION IN SOCIAL WORK EDUCATION

A Study of Some Field Situations in the Process of Development*

Krishan Kumar

THE CONTEXT

IT IS not out of a mere semantic preference that the term 'field instruction' is being used here in place of a popular terminology 'field work.' The preferred choice has quite consciously been made to stress that the use of the term 'field work' has unfortunately led it to be identified mainly with task or work assignment in a given field setting and not as an educational process aimed at instruction of students. To be a component of an educational system, field work needs to be essentially viewed as 'instruction' rather than 'work' or training on the job. It is concerned with the development of the learner's capacity to think and act in ways which are professionally appropriate. It sets in motion primarily a learning process with which the student begins to understand himself, acquires and develops a disciplined habit of thinking through the acquisition of both technical skills and a body of knowledge. Field work, to be an aspect of professional education therefore needs to be treated as an instructional

*In preparing this document I wish to express my feelings of indebtedness to those students of the Delhi School of Social Work, University of Delhi, who responded in their own creative way to the field work programme of the school and carried out various field assignments, the contents of some of which form the illustrative case material of this study.

process. However, for purposes of communication 'field work', 'field practice' and 'field instruction' are viewed as interchangeable. It is because of its pronounced educational emphasis that the term 'field instruction' is used in the title and scheme of the paper. However still, if there is reference to the term 'field work', it is because of our long historical association with the term. Therefore the instructional import of the term should not be under-rated.

The premise that field instruction has a unique place in the training of social workers has never been underestimated. It has been viewed as essential as a 'laboratory for natural science, the studio for painting, and the nursery school for child psychology.[1] As the United Nations puts it :

> It is primarily in the discussion of living people in their changing relationships as the students actually experience these that they can be helped to deepen their perception and refine their knowledge for direct use. It is through work in a community that they really become aware of the significance of community structure and the changing pattern of community life...
>
> It is important that students should be helped to develop the attitude of mind which leads them to make connections between study and real life...
>
> It is indeed vital that this should be done if students are to become professional practitioners in the field rather than good-natured amateurs, or technicians applying narrow skills by rule of thumb methods.[2]

In essence, therefore, what is expected of field instruction as a part of social work education is not only that it should be able to help students to acquire right understanding and appropriate attitudes but also to encourage them to '*do*' something. This latter expectation though very crucial is often misunderstood. Social work educators connected with field work of students need to unambiguously identify the components of field instruction so that the 'doing' aspect is seen by a student learner not as a random wandering in field situations, but instead, as a purposeful experience fulfilling both educational and social objectives.

Towards the task of reviewing and reconstructing the goals of social work education, an appreciable concern has undoubtedly been felt by educators during the last decade in our country.[3] Many schools of social work have, as a result, effected significant and appropriate break-through in the course curriculum. However, the field instruction aspect has not evoked as serious a concern as it deserves in spite of its being an integral part of social work education. The shift to the 'generic' content and the strengthening of the curriculum with courses on social policy, social development, social planning, social legislation, etc. have surely linked the objectives of social work education with the existing social realities. The functional role of a social worker is now seen in a new dimension. Unlike the earlier pattern where the entire social work course is centred around techniques of basic methods applicable in typical agency setting the new changes envisage an altogether new orientation for social worker. What is wanted is a multi-purpose generic social worker who is able to handle different skills wherever the situation requires.[4] In the context of this perspective, it is wondered whether social work educators have given adequate attention to the task of recognising and restructuring this aspect of social work education programme so that it could run parallel to or at least in close proximity with the new demands. Two important issues in this regard deserve serious attention and deliberation. Firstly, what should go into the students' field work activity (the doing aspect) to ensure that such activity gets linked with the objectives of social work education as they obtain today ? Secondly, how to design field introduction process whereby the basic focus is kept on the 'learner' and the 'doing' aspect does not eclipse the 'learning' aspect of professional education ?

At the Delhi School of Social Work, initial steps in the direction stated above have been taken and the present write-up is an attempt to illustrate some of the experiences in field instruction in the context of new curriculum changes. The illustrative material is spread over two sections.

In order that the case material is read and understood in its proper perspective, a brief write-up on 'Field Practice—Then and

Now' precedes it.

FIELD PRACTICE THEN AND NOW

Field practice as an essential component of social work education has been with the Delhi School of Social Work, as with other schools, for a fairly long time. In the earlier years of its functioning, the school could have access to only a limited number of welfare agencies which could provide training experience to social work students. In course of time, however, with the expansion of social welfare organisations, the school relied not only on many new agencies for field practice of its students but also gave a significant emphasis to field practice as an integral aspect of social work education.* For about two decades since 1956 the pattern of field work that obtained in the school broadly conformed to learning of social work methods—skills—case work and group work during the first year of study, and developing understanding of day-to-day functional responsibilities and tasks in relation to the following fields of special interest during the second year : (i) Community Development and Rural Welfare, (ii) Labour Welfare and Personnel Management, (iii) Medical and Psychiatric Social Work, and (iv) Institutional and After-care Services.

It was in the academic session 1973 74 when major changes in the curriculum were introduced. The changes were thought relevant to the needs of the country and they aimed at providing a generic base to the curriculum strengthened by the study of courses on Social Policy, Social Planning and Social Development. Consequent to these changes in the curriculum, the pattern of field work could not remain what it had been during the past years. A variety of questions and issues towards what should go into the field work training of students, what should be the nature of welfare tasks at service delivery levels, what contribution could the school make through its field work programme in

*In 1956 for the first time marks for field work performance were introduced in the educational curriculum. Besides, the requirements of the number of hours to be put in by a student were raised from 10 hours a week to 15 hours a week spread over to two days of work in the field setting.

the process of development and other related questions became the subject of group discussions and seminars at the School. As a result, a major change in the old field work pattern by replacing 'agency placements' with community placements as a uniform field training requirement for all the first year students. Various slum community areas and unauthorised colonies wherein the inhabitant population quite conspicuously faced adverse life situations were adopted as community placements for purposes of student's field work practice. Hardly more than a year had elapsed when the declaration of National Emergency (1975) and the concommitant zealous endeavour of the Delhi Administration led to a complete demolition of the then existing slum areas and unauthorized colonies. The uprooted families (more than 50 thousand in number) were either provided or promised with alternate one-room tenement at several resettlement colonies. These events are being purposely documented here in order to stress that they were responsible for evoking further reactions in regard to the nature and content of field practice. A legitimate and timely question was : 'Can we play any meaningful role through our field work programme in helping the uprooted families in the process of their resettlement'? 'Will the resettlement colonies not provide an ideal community setting in which the learning and the service goals linked to the problems of development could at least be modestly met'? Thus, a three-member committee constituted by the School went into the task of exploring the possibilities and potentialities of using the resettlement colonies for field practice of students. Some observations made by the Committee in their report are worth mentioning for they had a bearing in affecting not only the choice of field setting for the purposes of field practice but also in identifying 'newer' demands around which the field practice could be reorganised. The Committee stated :

> Even a cursory visit to these sites will show enormous problems which people are facing due to resettlement. Civic amenities are grossly lacking. Facilities of health and sanitation are absolutely inadequate. The acute scarcity of filtered water is glaringly conspicuous. Education of children has been disrupted because of the change of living place. . . .

> The need of the hour for most of the people is how soon to construct a house to live in. Funds. . . are lacking for the purpose, there is quite a sizeable number of families who are virtually living in shocking state for they have neither the 'Jhuggis' (which they at least had before coming over to these sites) nor a constructed house.
>
> The existing conditions of living as have been perceived by people are worse than what they were at the previously inhabited sites.[5]
>
> Immediate felt-needs of the people in these communties were identified as[6] :
>
> (i) Avenues for employment
> (ii) Easy availability of inexpensive house construction material
> (iii) Financial assistance for house construction
> (iv) Adequate provision for health and sanitation
> (v) Adequate number of public conveniences
> (vi) Transport and communication

It would be inferred that the resettlement colonies were potent with tremendous opportunities for students to locate any point of entry to the life process of people towards the ultimate goal of their economic and social development. Here was a setting in which the students could try out their creativity and skills without constraints of 'agency' policies and procedures ! The recommendations of the report and the mutual deliberations among the faculty ultimately led to adoption of Resettlement Colonies as field practice placements for students during the first year of a 2-year study programme at the school.

In the light of new demands, objectives of field practice were restated thus :

> Some of the objectives of field training in the first year are to help a student to learn and gain understanding of a particular community, to identify its needs, resources and problems and to involve the community for helping themselves in the solution of their problems. The aim is to guide

> the student to develop capacities and acquire abilities to initiate and carry out tasks in the areas of social action, social change and social development and thus prepare him for performance of preventive developmental functions in social welfare.[7]

Having stated the objectives of field work, the next important task was to prepare a broad 'reference guide' which could provide focus and direction to the nature of field assignments expected of them. It also indicated specific learning and service goals commensurate with identification of assignments.

REFERENCE GUIDE OF GOALS AND ASSIGNMENTS FOR FIELD WORK DURING THE FIRST AND SECOND TERMS[8]

First term

Goals	*Assignments*
Observation of the community, its socio-economic, cultural features. Collection of information on priorities, resources, power structure, social and economic groups; establishment of rapport; understanding of the clientele system and target group(s) and their reactions to external agencies; skills in observation and recording of work experience, beginning experience in the practice of social work principles, methods, and initiation of actions, awareness of one's prejudices and control of reactions; beginning assessment of own performance and preparedness to assume social work roles.	Profile of the community; method of need identification, priority determination, identifying community leaders; working with non-structured and floating groups; problem as it obtains, and its effects on the client system; self-help efforts of the community; use and non-use of services and service delivery systems; methods ot establishing rapport, understanding the dynamics of the community, and identifying leaders.

Second Term

Goals	*Assignments*
Better understanding of community service delivery system and the target groups; determination of priorities in terms of problems, resources and feasible action strategies; use of formal and informal leadership to initiate collaborative action; appreciation of professional values and approaches; systematic collection, analysis, and synthesis of data through observation and study for the formulation of need-based programmes; observation and evaluation; reflection of theoretical understanding in practical work; assumption of multiple roles; planning of programmes around the needs of groups; experience in committee work, listening, observation and effective communication.	Narration of experiences/processes in the assessment of service, and of resources within the community; ways of improvement; local leadership and its problems; supervision by the students; account of the process of change since the arrival of the worker; rationale for adopting an approach to deal with a problem; preparation of action plan; role of community leaders and social workers in implementing a programme; ways in which co-operation was sought and received; process of group formation and worker's facilitative role; records of a few group sessions to highlight the patterns of group dynamics—completing a project, and so on.

Observations on the reference guide

From a careful examination of the reference guide given above, it would appear that it is essentially in the nature of an instructional aid. It purports to serve two important purpose in relation to field practice. Firstly, it helps a student to become *aware* of the goals of his field training; and secondly, it suggests to him the type of field assignments he should carry out so that his effort gets *pointed* to some specific areas of work which are relevant to the goals. The same holds good for field work supervisors/instructors. As they have the responsibility to initiate and lead the supervisory process they also need a clear perspective of goals and task assignments so that they could from time to time guide, direct, ascertain and verify the progress of their supervisees in relation to stated goals and their corresponding field work assignments.

I would wish to contend that unless field work activity of a student is consciously guided with reference to accepted goals of field training and, also, unless a student is helped to undertake some well-defined assignments related to the goals, the experience of the student is very likely to turn out as one of random wandering in the field.

Illustrative case material

Having given the sequential context of field practice at the Delhi School of Social Work, that is, what it was and what it is today with reference to goals, the choice of field work setting and the field assignments expected of students, we now proceed on to the study of a few field situations in which the students were engaged very recently. The case material has been selected from out of the field records of some students who were supervised by the author during the academic session 1978-79.

An outline of several field situations

This is a summary account of a variety of field situations and the role performed by a student during two semesters of field training (August-November, 1978 and January-March, 1979, spread over to 45 days in the academic year 1978-79—working two days a week).

The purpose of documenting this 'inventory' is to demonstrate the range of a student's experience in terms of

(i) need/problem identification
(ii) involvement of people
(iii) role performed by the student worker, and
(iv) evidence of any change or improvement in the need areas identified and attended to.

Besides, it also serves the purpose of illustrating how a student field worker could be guided to make an overall review of his or her broad range of field experience by making use of the

Work at the Community level

Sl. No.	Need/problem areas	People's involvement in the helping process	Role of worker in relation to need area	Evidence of any change/improvement
1.	Insanitary conditions	Ramu (H-399) said that he had sent some letters to DDA* with regard to bad drainage system (people had complained when the drains were being constructed but were told that the engineer knew his business)	A complaint letter was lodged with the sanitary inspector written by a local resident —Conducted a survey to find out causes of insanitation and if possible to do something for an improvement in status quo. The worker interviewed a few residents, and sweepers with regard to the same	There has been slight improvement in the sense that the sweepers have become more regular than before
2.	Faulty drainage system	Local people had lodged a few complaints with the concerned authorities; got private sweepers to clean the drains	The worker met the Junior Engineer of DDA and informed him about it. He said that he was aware of it but the reconstruction of the drains would need a tremendous amount of money and so he would try to mitigate the problem, complete overhaul was out of question	The worker found that there is less of back flow and clogging of the drains than before

*Delhi Development Authority

3.	Shortage of drinking water—many hand pumps of the area do not work	The people went and complained about it at the DDA office but this did not give favourable results	The worker lodged a written complaint with the DDA office and on that basis some of the pumps were set right	Many of the hand pumps have been repaired on complaints lodged by the workers
4.	Inadequate lighting arrangement and no domestic connections	The people contacted the authorities but the reply was that they did not have enough equipments at present and that there was no order from above. A letter was written by Mr. X in the presence of the worker complaining about the electricity problems	The worker followed the matter up with authorities; he felt that the pressure exerted by him and the people might have had some indirect effect	Electric lines have been provided in the colony and whosoever wants connection for house can take it after paying a nominal charge
5.	Health problems	When viral encephalitis was detected in the area, the residents helped workers to quite an extent and even contacted some people in authority for taking necessary steps. They detected irregularities in the administration-run dispensaries and complained against the doctor. During the innoculation drive, they co-operated by bringing their children to the dispensary in large numbers	A survey was conducted by the worker to detect cases of viral encephalitis and the spraying of disinfectants was asked for from the authorities. Worker tried to organise a medical camp for the residents for which he contacted Safdarjung Hospital. This could not however be arranged due to limitations of the hospital. However M.C.D.* organized an innoculation drive for children	The spraying of disinfectants was done. M.C.D.* organised an innoculation drive for children

*Municipal Corporation of Delhi.

Sl. No.	Need/problem areas	People's involvement in the helping process	Role of worker in relation to need area	Evidence of any change/improvement
6.	Adult literacy	Quite a few people have co-operated and joined the adult literacy classes being conducted in the evening thrice a week. Some of them also helped by persuading others to join	Met* and explained to him the nature of the programme. He expressed his desire to help the worker to the best of his ability and he felt that others would also like it. The classes have been started and the people of various blocks are attending these classes and the outcome is likely to be good	The worker feels that this will improve their economic resources and also make them knowledgeable and less prone to exploitation
7.	Self employment : Match box making *project—A resident of the community (Laxmi) approached a co-worker to have self employment facility in their houses	One of the limitations of the project was the lack of moulds which was solved by the people themselves, by making a few. Mrs Y's husband agreed to take the raw materials from the hospital	The worker came to know about the match unit from a senior worker placed at the Kingsway Camp, T.B. Hospital and the matter was pursued	Persons involved in the project started earning between Rs. 10/- and Rs. 15/- per week and that too with the limited availability of raw materials

*See the chart on the following page.

8. Innoculation : Municipal Corporation of Delhi had sent their officials to innoculate children of the community	Efforts were aimed at bringing children to the dispensary in large numbers and persuading local families to make use of innoculation facilities	The worker went door to door to inform the people and ask them to bring their children to Block-I Dispensary to get the innoculation done	Quite a number of children got innoculated
9. Shortage of milk	The worker helped residents to draft an application to the Manager of Mother Dairy. Many residents signed, and it was finally submitted to the Deputy Engineer of National Dairy Development Corporation by the worker	The worker approached the distribution office of Mother Dairy and the Deputy Engineer of National Dairy Development Corporation of the booth in the colony	The worker got assurance from the authorities that it will be soon commissioned

Chart indicating the amount earned by participants in the match box making project

Name	1st week	2nd week	3rd week	4th week	5th week	6th week	7th week	Remarks
Lakshmi	2 gross	2 gross	6 gross	20 gross	15 gross	12 gross	23 gross	Quantity made
	Rs. 0.90	Re. 0.90	Rs. 2.70	Rs. 9.00	Rs. 6.00	Rs. 5.40	Rs. 10.35	Money earned
Meera	—	3 gross	6 gross	15 gross	11 gross	13 gross	20 gross	Quantity made
	—	Rs. 1.35	Rs. 2.70	Rs. 6.75	Rs. 4.95	Rs. 5.85	Rs. 9.00	Money earned
Shakuntala	—	4 gross	5 gross	16 gross	7 gross	4 gross	28 gross	Quantity made
	—	Rs. 1.80	Rs. 2.25	Rs. 2.20	Rs. 3.15	Rs. 1.80	Rs. 12.60	Money earned
Shanti	—	2 gross	7 gross	20 gross	14 gross	12 gross	35 gross	Quantity made
	—	Re. 0.90	Rs. 3.15	Rs. 9.00	Rs. 6.30	Rs. 5.40	Rs. 15.75	Money earned
Santosh	—	—	—	11 gross	14 gross	9 gross	21 gross	Quantity made
	—	—	—	Rs. 4.95	Rs. 6.30	Rs. 4.05	Rs. 9.45	Money earned

The drop in production and hence a drop in earnings was due to insufficient supply of raw materials (for the 5th and 6th weeks).

Work done with individuals

Sl. No.	Name of the person	Nature of the problem	Responsibility shared/action taken (Worker)	Present status of the person in relation to the problem
1.	Kali Devi	Patient of tuberculosis and partially blind.	Took her to Safdarjung Hospital for getting her eyes tested. Took her to T.B. Hospital, Kingsway Camp; got her X-Ray done. Got her admitted to the hospital on 23rd November and got her discharged. Applied for financial assistance to the Directorate of Social Welfare	She is almost cured now and it is expected that financial assistance will be provided to her through the Directorate of Social Welfare
2.	Ram Piari	Patient of epilepsy	Took her to Safdarjung Hospital for treatment	Not much change from the original condition
3.	Om Prakash	During the emergency, he was forcely sterilized and due to that he feels that his health has deteriorated	The worker advised him to go to any one of the major hospitals, get his treatment done. The worker did not accompany him to the hospital as he felt that he was quite capable of getting the treatment by himself	He was taking the prescribed medicines

4.	Banarsi Lal	He had met with a serious accident; lost both his legs and part of his arms. Needs artificial limbs. Was operated in Bara Hindu Rao Hospital. Applied for a grant to the Directorate of Social Welfare. He expressed his wish to sell cigarettes and sweets on a wayside shop near the bus stop if permission was granted	As per rules of the Directorate of Social Welfare the worker has tried to procure artificial limbs from the Jawahar Lal Nehru Institute of Physically Handicapped. Also the worker contacted Police Inspector and got permission for his client to open a small shop	The money shall be granted by the Directorate in due course; the plan about the shop has not been put into practice due to domestic problems of the client
5.	Durga	Was suffering from viral encephalitis; was admitted to Safdarjung Hospital and was discharged when she was slightly better but her condition deteriorated	Medicines were obtained and Dr. Acharjee was taken to her place by the worker to check up and prescribe suitable medicines	She has recovered fully and is all right now
6.	D.P. Chadda	Physically handicapped and needs a tricycle for which he wants grant from the Directorate, who in turn need quotations to grant the same	Went to various dealers and collected five quotations ranging from Rs. 829/- to Rs. 900/-	Till date, the prescribed form along with the quotations has not been submitted because he has not been able to get his medical certificate signed from the hospital

7.	Mrs. Darshana Chadda	She has three children and the youngest one is less than a year old. She was pregnant again and wanted a medical termination of pregnancy. Her husband also was in favour of it	She was wanting to contact family planning centre regarding the problem, and then decided to take the worker's opinion. The worker told them that a hospital would be a better choice since he (worker) had some contacts in Lok Nayak Jaiprakash Narain Hospital, it could be carried out there. Eventually it was carried out smoothly	She is happy about it and has not complained of any after-effects

'inventory' type of field work record on the conclusion of field training programme. Such an exercise would enable a student to look through his entire field work record to draw out various experiences and interpret them in a purposeful manner.

A reality based perspective

The purpose of documenting the foregoing case material was to illustrate how field practice could be seen as oriented to problems of development. It should, however, not be forgotten that field practice has its own basic limitation in relation to any expectation of quick and wide ranging solution strategy for problems of social development. When students work for two days a week putting in an aggregate of 15 hours inclusive of the time for recording and supervisory meetings and, also, when the educational component of field work practice is equally to be emphasized, it would be quite unrealistic to make a tall claim for field practice and its imprint on problems of change and development. Let us appreciate our genuine limitations.

> Professional rhetoric does not create change. The most effective instruments for change must come from forces outside the profession. We may help, but let us never delude ourselves that social work profession will bring about basic change.[9]

This does not mean, however, that the programme of field practice in social work education is devoid of any role in development. Field practice can always be reorganised in a manner whereby the point of emphasis in regard to 'Learning' and 'Doing' could be shifted from the traditional 'Methods' practice approach to one of the use of all available methods towards a conscious intervention in the socio-economic conditions of people as such. Educationally, the objectives of field practice will have to be located in students' understanding of human conditions, of growth, distress, of potentialities and limitations and in their attempts to help people to negotiate with a variety of problems which retard their development. The ability to verbalize, to feel, to advocate, to reflect and to conceptualize this understanding will undoubtedly be the *desired* educational goal. Along with this, if field practice could also enable a student to *interact* with problems of change and development and further, if some measure of assistance in that direction is *practically attempted through field work process*, the field practice then would be serving its purpose—a purpose which is both educationally satisfying and socially relevant. Perhaps it might have been one such experience which led a student to remark on the conclusion of his social work studies : 'Motivation for social work is not a condition precedent to join it but rather a function of field work process'.

REFERENCES

1. Helen Merrell Lynd, *Field Work in College Education*, Columbia University Press, New York, 1945.
2. *Training for Social Work : Third International Survey*, United Nations, New York, 1958, p. 251.
3. *Seminar on Thirty Years of Social Work Education*, TISS Bombay, 1967; *Review of Social Work Education in India—Retrospect and Prospect*, UGC, 1978; *Seminar on Social Work Education—Problems and Challenges*, Delhi School of Social Work, 1970 ; *South-East Asian Seminar for Social Work Education on Curriculum Development and Teaching*, Bombay, 1971.
4. Kulkarni, P.D., "Integrated Methods in Social Work and Social Work Education", *UN-ESCAP, PSSW-PWU Publication*, 1974, pp. 179-81.
5. *Committee Report on the Suitability of Resettlement Areas for Field Work* (Un-published), Delhi School of Social Work, 1976, p. 2.
6. Poonam Chowdhary, *Field Work in Community Setting—The Reactions and Opinions of Students*, M. Phil. (Un-published) thesis, 1978, Delhi School of Social Work, pp. 26-27.
7. *Manual of Field Work*, Delhi School of Social Work, University of Delhi, 1978, p. 3.
8. Also reproduced and cited in 'Training of Trainers' United Nations Social Welfare and Development Centre for Asia and the Pacific, Manila, January 1980, pp. 242-244.
9. Felice Davidson, *A Design of Social Work Practice*, Columbia University Press, 1974, p. 239.

9

PROCESS OF LEARNING AND TEACHING THROUGH FIELD WORK

Mrs. Sunanda Koushik

THREE distinctive areas can be identified in the learning and teaching process in social work :

(1) The student himself e.g. intelligence, his previous exposure to varied experiences in life, his attitude, interests etc., in learning.

(2) The external environment, i.e. the agency—its personnel, programmes, procedures etc., and the classroom.

(3) The supervisory relationship and processes. Ideal learning is possible as an outcome of the integration of all the three areas.

Learners may be grouped into two categories : the intellectual learner and the emotional learner.

The following are some of the patterns of learning :

(1) The *Little Jack Horner*—puts up his best behaviour before the supervisor but relates poorly to others. A *Glib* learner, tries to get away with minimum work and yet pretends to be a *Good Boy*.

(2) The *awkward learner*—shy of the supervisor, he is painfully conscious of a *cultural gap* between himself and the supervisor. (Occasionally a male student from rural area facing an urban female supervisor finds himself in this situation.)

(3) The *arrogant superior*—is conscious of his ability and gets sceptic about his tasks as he feels they are "too simple" and meets them with a reaction : "Do you take me to be such a fool ?" He tends to neglect smaller details of his work. Unless loaded with work he gets "bored".

(4) The *argumentative incompetent*—spends time expressing doubts, makes his supervisor explain repeatedly. He spends much of his time arguing and is a poor learner. He generally projects his own frustration and is difficult to be "professionalised". He creates a lot of disturbance around and even poses a danger to the total learning environment.

(5) The *pure intellectual.* He soon begins to hate social work, gets disturbed and wants to leave. Such a student is often a merit scholar in his early career.

Remedial supervision

(1) The "Jack Horner" must have enough workload to keep him occupied. He is likely to affect his peer group adversely and hence the supervisor's impartial bearing is very significant. He deserves the supervisor's mute support and a steady assurance of justice being done. Every student gets this support from his supervisor during individual conferences. "Horner" himself needs to be reminded of small jobs which he tends to ignore.

(2) The "awkward learner" is unduly conscious of an imaginary cultural gap between himself, his peers and his supervisor. He imagines his home environment to be inferior. Such a "feeling" could displace him from his learning situation.

His supervisor should draw him at once into the professional fold : assigning tasks, making the student feel responsible, working with the supervisor, help the student identify with the agency and the profession. The "agency culture" is a good path to the "professional culture". Individual and group conferences reduce this "cultural gap". Soon the student appreciates the professional and academic content of conferences and the cultural gap disappears.

Awkwardness due to sex difference is a situation beyond the supervisor's control. Transfer to a same sex supervisor seems to be the only answer.

(3) The "arrogant superior" usually confronts the supervisor individually but does relatively less harm to the group. The supervisor has to consciously exercise his patience. In case this student is arrogant to his supervisor before others, the peer group controls the situation indirectly by withdrawing from such a student or by direct criticism. Lack of appreciation of his qualities and

performance does disturb the arrogant superior. The supervisor will some time get a chance to point out to this student that his friends are moving away.

(4) The "argumentative incompetent" should best be ignored. The supervisor-student transaction needs to be strictly restricted to prove business. Once again a great deal of patience from the supervisor is indicated.

(5) The "pure intellectual" requires more counselling than supervision.

CASE ILLUSTRATIONS

Case I :

Fluctuations in performance in different semesters

This student from Vidarbha, opting for labour welfare was placed in a school for the deaf mute. His task was to apply integrated social work methods to the identified problems. The student comprehended the task and the situation extremely well and brought out a masterpiece of field work assignment. In the mid-second semester both the supervisor and student felt that the agency could no longer provide further experiences for the student's growth. By mutual agreement he was placed in another agency of his choice.

The timings of the agency were 6 p.m. to 10 p.m. (a Trade Union Office) but obviously the student could not make meaningful use of his agency experience. He appeared baffled by the labour welfare set-up.

In the third semester he was placed under professional supervision in a factory. He now started looking very nervous but performed his routine task well. At the time of the semester evaluation he admitted to the faculty supervisor that he was being paid by his field work agency for clearing some clerical backlogs at the personnel department (viz. completing personal files of workers). He was accredited for his honesty and was made to appreciate that he had acquired skills of interviewing workers in the process.

In the fourth semester his performance improved.

Case II :

Supervisor-supervisee relationship

"Miss Y.K."

"In the first two semesters I learned much about systematic work, recording and reporting but my supervisor was too paternalistic and I hated his concern in my personal affairs.

In the third semester I was placed at the Mental Hospital. The supervisor made me aware that I was a "grumbler".

In fact I was shocked that I had this placement before completing my course in psychiatric information. I learned my psychiatry from a co-student who had done her Abnormal Psychology at the graduate level and had gained my confidence.

In my fourth semester I had the most wonderful supervisor who was very professional in approach. I was thrilled at my evaluation conference with her. I know much more about myself and am glad the Institute accepted my request for continuing at the same agency for block field work.

This student learned mainly out of identification with the supervisor.

10

TASK-ORIENTED LEARNING THROUGH AGENCY PLACEMENT

Miss Sheila Tudu

THE calender of activities presented is for a Remand Home for girls. This calender was prepared keeping in mind the Jr. MSW students who are for the first time being exposed to social work. This exercise was undertaken after having identified the following learning areas for a student in this agency :

1. The development stages of childhood and adolescence.
2. Communication with children.
3. The therapeutic skills of workers and difference in the case of residential and non-residential workers.
4. Group dynamics, group interaction, its use as a therapeutic experience in the case of specially organized groups.
5. The nature of institutions, its impact on the clientele system and the role of residential staff.

The specific tasks given in the calender are under three major areas :

I. Description of agency
II. Office procedures and formalities
III. Working with inmates

An attempt has been made here to correlate tasks with the learning areas. The calender of activities is, therefore, a suggested scheme for the utilisation of field work hours on weekly basis. It needs an experiment to find out as to what calender is most practical. It covers two terms of field work programme.

Calender of activities—Remand home for girls

Field work week	Description of agency-I	Office procedures and formalities-II	Working with inmates-III	Remarks and learning areas
1st and 2nd week	1. Physical lay out of the agency	1. Objectives and activities of the agency	1. Meeting the inmates	Observation and rapport —building
3rd to 6th week	2. Campus map —accommodation, open space, facilities etc.	2. Facts about the set-up of the agency 3. Policies for admission, discharge 4. Expansion of service 5. Educational and vocational training	2. Adjustment of inmates among themselves 3. Adjustment with authorities concerned. 4. Teaching the inmates—home work 5. Adjustment with social work students	1. The development stages of childhood and adolescence 2. Communication with children
7th and 8th week	3. Inmates' profile	2, 3, and 5 as above	6. Problems of engagement of inmates 2, 3 and 4 as above	1 and 2 as above Formation of groups of inmates according to age and interests
9th and 10th week	4. Organizational structure. 3 as above	2, 3, and 5 as above	3 as above 7. Organising groups of inmates 8. Physical growth activities —games, sports, scouting 9. Social activities, that is, get-together, cultural programmes, trips, visits	1 and 2 as above 4. Group dynamics, interaction etc. 5. Nature of institution and role of staff

11th to 13th week	3 and 4 as above 5. Staff profile	3, 4 and 5 as above	8 and 9 as above 10. Creative activities—craft, art, scrap book, music and dance	1, 2, 4 and 5 as above
			11. Mental growth activities i.e. educational, games, discussions, debates	3. Therapeutic skills of workers
14th till the end of the placement	4 organizational structure	3, 4 and 5 as above	8, 9, 10 and 11 as above 12. Manual work—gardening 13. Counselling of parents and inmates	1, 2, 3, 4 and 5 as above
			2, 3 and 4 as above	Students' preparation for withdrawal from the agency

11

SUPERVISOR-SUPERVISEE INTERACTION : Some Illustrations*

R. R. Singh

I

YOUR digging into the "Reaction in Retrospect" on supervision has led me into a tough exercise. No wonder it is difficult—although helpful—for clients to split up global feeling into concrete examples. I have tried to visualise the process of supervision as a judicious blend of 'pushing', 'being with' and 'pulling' the supervisee in a desired direction. It is understood that the pace, distance covered, the starting point etc. would vary (though a clear cut distinction among the three may be lacking) leading to a growth in both the supervisor and the supervisee and satisfaction to both. I will enumerate some examples.

(a) *Pushing* : The creation of healthy anxiety when needed, by playing up the lapses and direct/indirect demonstration of expectations, for example :

(i) discussions on workload (how it falls short of expectations).

(ii) When one record was submitted late, the first line of the "fortnightly" read : "one record submitted one day late".

(iii) When I asked a patient his age twice and faithfully recorded his 'annoyance' at it—your comment was :

* Edited from written responses received from three students. These students had been supervised by the editor during 1978-81 and had completed their course or field work when they wrote their reactions.

"How did it happen ? full concentration needed".

(iv) I cannot forget the linear diagram drawn which by hand showed how there was no improvement in the recording in the last week then.

(b) *Being with* : Always being available whenever help was needed. At times you have referred to certain 'readings' while walking on the campus. Meaningful conferences with discussions, suggestions, interpretations etc. supplemented by direct teaching and the use of records of earlier students were a great help. Your visits to the agency did not appear to be *threats* and there too, the 'on-the-spot' teaching and comments were very relevant and helpful e.g. the distinction between 'needs' and 'wants' of a client in the case of a person who could not speak initially.

(c) *Pulling* : Making the insignificant look significant with creative thinking e.g. 'can we visualise a new role for a social worker as a family member or friend'. Providing insight like the effects of colour ; how one could get useful information by observing patients watch a cricket match on TV—which was then going on etc.

The acceptance of some new idea through or from the student, say for example, the "optimist-pessimist approach".

Allowing the student to gradually develop independence in work, e.g. making plans for and carrying out the outdoor programme for the patients.

And the most important of all yourself—investment in your work, the regularity, the meticulous going through records (the spelling corrections; your pointing out where the recorded interviews appeared "not in flow" or contrived; it was through these corrections that I learnt the careful use of the word 'should', etc.), the concern, the use of the social work principles and philosophy in daily life (how you stressed on 'role' is just one small example) was the most important reason why I respected you and felt a sense of pleasure and obligation to work.

It was all this and much more (the etcs. above are meaningful). When I was going through readings on supervision to guide my own students—which I had never done earlier, I was "stunned at how I was handled" or "stunned at how you handle your supervisees".

As far as my comments about the previous year's supervision as a comparison are concerned, I am sorry to say that it was supervision for the sake of it. The first few (2-4) months were moments of great anxiety and no attempt was made to make the student come to grips with it. Expectations were not clearly shown and one was at a loss regarding the *what* and *how* of things. May be this happens initially—I cannot say. One advantage of working under *A* was his goading us to action—achievement or programme orientation. We really worked hard, but integration of theory was not really optimum. With *B* it was more theory and conceptualisation and the learning by doing suffered. But all the same I felt I had been constantly learning under the supervision of both. It was certainly much better than no supervision or a mockery of supervision as it happens in some cases. I feel that it is the supervisor who makes all the difference.

II

SUPERVISION : REACTIONS OF A STUDENT IN RETROSPECT

Anticipation of "supervision" is both a relief and a source of anxiety for students commencing their MSW. Relief, because supervision is synonymous with help and guidance, and a source of anxiety because one is beset by fears of whether one will come up to the expectations of the supervisor, whose placement on a strict—lax scale has already been revealed to new students by those who have interacted with the supervisor for a year.

In the best of my knowledge, I had the strictest and most demanding of supervisors who expected us to work with consistency, to learn from our failures, because failures were to be a means and not an end, to be perceptive and analytical, to write systematic and detailed reports and to hand in our work on time. We were expected to read a lot of things, apply it in practice; learn from our practice and relate it back to theory. We were expected to relate to the people and learn about them and from them.

At times I felt that the supervisor's expectations were much too high and it was a strain to constantly live up to what was expected. It was almost as if the supervisor thought better of us, than we thought of ourselves. These high demands were disadvantageous and advantageous for us. Disadvantageous for us at that moment, because we felt the work too much of an uphill task at times and grumbled about it too when we thought we could never cope. But in the long run, it proved advantageous because we discovered some of our latent potential and in a way were made to develop.

Had the supervision not been "close", and strict, we would have enjoyed ourselves *then*, our work load being lighter but would have remained dissatisfied today.

At times, it was also felt that the supervisor did not tell us how to do a thing, but questioned us and left us short of the answer which we had to provide ourselves. At these times we felt helpless. In retrospect, I realize that this was a way of making us think and reason for ourselves, but at that time when an answer was needed immediately and we were a bit frustrated and at a dead-end, what we wanted was a ready solution.

The frequent supervisory visits, the conferences according to schedule, the closely read and remarked upon reports, the feed-back in the conferences and in the evaluation reports that helped us to know ourselves and to grow, and the constant contact between supervisor and students, were all what we regarded as signs of an interested supervisor. This was the source of envy from the other students and it kept us working at our best. Had the supervisor been lax and disinterested, our input and output would have been less than half of what it actually was.

The conferences were stimulating in the sense we could question and not just accept the supervisor's statements and we gained more insight into, not only our work but ourselves as workers and became more self-analytical. However I felt at times, that had the supervisor been less strict, he would have been more approachable and had he been more approachable and had we been less anticipatory of the reactions to our mistakes, we would have opened up more with questions, difficulties and failures and doubts. The times when we did, we did so hesitantly and as we felt, "at our own risk".

What was common impression was that the supervisor was on a different plane and would make no mistakes and hence expected us to do the same. We did make many mistakes however, which were accepted by the supervisor, but yet the feeling that we have to live up to an ideal and be perfect, prevailed

All in all, while we were being supervised we did resent to a certain extent, the high expectations and heavy work load as compared to other students, but now we realize that without the very same two factors we resented, we would never have had a satisfying, enriching year of field work—which gave us a firm foundation of ideal social work principles and practices which we will carry over to the new year. When one reaches for the "ideal", it is bound to be difficult, but rewarding. This is what I will tell the new students who are under the same supervisor and who are already weighed down by their pre-formed impressions of the year ahead for them.

III

SUPERVISION IN RETROSPECT—REACTIONS OF A STUDENT

First I'ld like to say that I was genuinely surprised at the final evaluation you gave me. I was surprised because I felt it was a proper evaluation of me and my field work. By 'surprise', I mean, I did not expect such a fair evaluation. Then I was doubly surprised when you asked me to write and tell you of how I thought you could have been a better supervisor to me.

All through the year, I had built up the impression that you were unable to understand me, that you were at a different wave length. Throughout, there was a distance between us. A distance brought about by little incidences, minor incidences, but which made me feel that you were not my supervisor, but that I was your *supervisee*—that you were the overseeing and all-seeing eye.

What I want to state clearly is that when I look back, in retrospect of your supervising, I see you were, in comparative terms, a good supervisor. A supervisor who was *correct* in everything he did, who discharged his duties to the smallest detail. A very correct person. Also, I wish to state that I do not feel you are 'lacking' in anything, but I feel that you would have been an effective supervisor to me if you would have taken into account my peculiar 'bent of mind' as an individual, and supervised *me* and not supervised a *student*, with me fitting the student role.

Observing me (and you are known for your power of observation), you would have known that I don't particularly take institutional authority easily. I'll elucidate. I mean the type of authority used in instances like when I went to another community in the morning of a field work day. Another teacher of the school met me there and told me that what I was doing was contrary to 'regulations'. The matter was reported to you, and you put in a sentence into my fortnightly evaluation saying that the student went to a different field work placement on a field work day, and had not taken permission from the supervisor, and neither he was informed by him about it. To me, that was like punishing me for it by putting it in like a black mark on my evaluation—"Rule flouted by student". That sort of thing brings up resentment in me. It puts a distance between us, a barrier. I would expect you to ask me why I went. I would like to feel that you are on my side. To me, you then seemed like the 'coloured-circuit camera' that is placed at the I.T.O. crossing, to check that no one disobeyed the traffic signal lights. I would have liked to have been *asked* for an explanation for why I went. So when I read the fortnightly evaluation, I just signed it quietly, like I would sign a statement that said that I wholeheartedly endorse the accusation of your being a close-minded man, who was keeping his supervisee on a leash. This instance, and one or two others, (which I cannot recall lucidly) brought about this gap between us. They are small instances in which of course your action was the *right* course of action. It could be wholly justified, but it inevitably brought about in me a feeling that you had closed your mind too much, and made yourself incapable of understanding me.

That is why, when I read your final evaluation, I was genuinely surprised—more than surprised—confused. It was diametrically opposed to the opinion I held about you so far. The evaluation showed you to be an open minded man, who could see my point of view, and who was at my wave-length of communication—I then wished that I had read the evaluation

5 months earlier. I needed you to talk to me like you did in the evaluation, and help me in my orientation (in what you called—"intellectualizing"). When I had fallen flat on my face, as far as field work was concerned. What I did not need then, and what I got, was evaluation reports that stated that my work and effort was declining. It was true that my work output as well as interest was lagging, but at that time I needed the help mentioned above. I do recall instances when you made attempts to be informal, but it just made me smile—the distance remained.

So I look back with regret at the past year at having misunderstood you. I might have been a little harsh in this note, and it seems to show that much of the "fault" lies with you. No, it doesn't. It's just that I, in my times of insufficiency (and misunderstanding) needed this extra effort from you.

12

REFLECTIONS ON FIELD WORK PRACTICE AND SUPERVISION IN SCHOOL SOCIAL WORK

Kiran Mehta

(I) A BREAKAWAY from the traditional lines, it may be in any field, brings about a temporary imbalancing of the existing theories, methods and norms of that field. At this juncture, the existing theories are put to a critical examination and the previous learnings are put to a test. It is however interesting to note the way in which one adapts to the new area, approach, and thrust and maintains one's professional dignity and does not let the 'agency' distort the profession.

According to my knowledge of social work education, this fear, that my agency was trying to distort the existing role of a school social worker, was deeply felt by me at the beginning of my work. As I had just passed my MSW, I had to take up my work and new responsibilities with a challenge. Under the comprehensive schemes of 10+2 education pattern, the government was stressing for the need to bring the student community nearer to the general community and its problems by introducing SUPW* in the schools.

This is how Community-service was taken up by our school, not as a mere activity, as was the practice in the past, but as a subject, which would be assessed. It was for the first time in the history of schools, that such a subject was being introduced.

* Socially Useful Productive Work: Every student is engaged in SUPW for a fixed amount of time.

Naturally there were many doubts, apprehensions and misconceptions regarding this in the minds of students, teachers, parents and educators. The teachers with their already heavy teaching load had no time to spare, either to understand or help in the programme.

In this way an entirely new programme was launched with all the good intentions of the Principal, some educators and the social workers. Nevertheless it was a programme which was thrust upon the school community and the entire responsibility of planning, educating, and organising was left to the social worker. For the fresh graduate in the profession it was a difficult task. Firstly the role that she was being asked to perform was completely different from the one that she expected. She would have to be more of a 'community-service teacher' than a students' counsellor. She would no longer be a mere patient and experienced listener to students' problems but an active teacher and guide who would have to use element of 'authority' far more than her counsellor 'self' would like. With the uphill task of placing 150 students in the community-service projects, educating them, sustaining their interest, supervising them and assessing them required a differential use and combination of knowledge of social work on my part.

In other words we had begun the work of 'conscientization' among the students. We hoped to expose them to the community at large and its problems and thereby bring some change in their attitudes, learning and consciousness of the reality around them. Their naive understanding of the community outside the school had to be changed to a critical one. To assess now, after working for two years, as to whether we achieved it or not, would require deeper thinking.

However, working against many odds, namely the reluctant teachers; doubtful parents were scared of exposing their children to the open community, and the naive students, I planned out various projects to be taken up by students in the nearby community.* These projects would involve concrete helping of the

* Various projects were—Non-formal education in slums; Hospital service; Blind welfare services; Road-safety; Chattarpur farm project; school services; remedial classes; preparing cultural programmes and puppet shows for the slums etc.

community by the students. However there were certain projects like working at the school farm, survey of the village for literacy and the running of non-formal education centres in slum areas, which gave rise to questioning in the young minds, which was a significant outcome of introducing this subject.

With my limited experience of handling so many students, planning out the curriculum and educating them, I had to make use of all my knowledge that I had acquired so far. Discussions, lectures on the subject, visiting welfare institutions, skill exercises through personal demonstrations by communicating with the community in front of the students, through written work by making the students write reports, simulation games at inter-school workshops*, suggesting guided readings to a selected few, and through periodic recapitulation in classroom, were some of the education methods/techniques followed by me.

There is no doubt that during the first year of my tenure I faced a lot of opposition from the school community, as the programme was so much different from the regular class-room setting, in which the teachers were asked to devote extra time and the students were supposed to give more than take. The main opposition was from teachers who had still to accept the role of a counsellor and who were now asked to accept this new role of social worker and at the same time regard community-service as a subject with equal status. They regarded it as a big joke or source of entertainment for students which would distract them from the serious learning of the class-room.

Working in such conditions was certainly not very pleasant or satisfying all the time but it definitely led to a greater professional self-dependence in me. It would be quite appropriate to quote Charlotte Towle's words :

The social work student has a supervisor at hand to help him think what to do and why, or even tell him 'the whats and the whys'. But overnight she cannot help him ingrain the 'hows'.

(II) As I had largely to depend on my knowledge and experiences at the School of Social Work, while initiating the new dimension of school social work, in addition to physical incom-

* A training-cum-orientation workshop for non-formal education was held jointly by Springdales and Abner Memorial Schools.

patibility of coping with 150 students in the first year*, supervision of the trainees from Delhi School of Social Work was also a difficult and tricky affair in the beginning. As my own concepts and convictions regarding the feasibility of the programme were yet to form, it was hard to guide my supervisees. Hence my job as a supervisor was that of a teacher and guide who was still learning herself. I would not deny that at some time the students had to work out their own solutions, as either I was too busy in administrative or organizational work, or that I had no ready-made, tailor-cut answers.

Initially they were not asked to take on a very definite role in the programme, but merely to observe and report back, in addition to just 'being' with the students. For some supervisees, it was tough to handle school students as they were not used to it and moreover as they were also still in their student life. Some of them were disappointed as they had to do a lot of community work, which they had not normally expected in their second year field work training. Their ideas of school social work were traditional and had now to be subjected to a change.

Now that I look back in retrospect, I feel that all these negative aspects of handling were in fact a boon for both myself and supervisees in many ways. In their first term they proved to be an excellent medium of feedback from the field for me. In other words I learnt and became more confident as I had two representatives from my profession to assist me.

The trainees were given the job of relating with students in the field and helping them in various projects. In this way they were learning not only to perceive and understand the minds and behaviour of the youth but also how to tackle them. In other words the supervisees were doing the work of supervising—an experience that I had not enjoyed when I was a student. This fact gave them a definite feeling of confidence and scope for applying their social work knowledge under my guidance. As the supervisees were young themselves, they could easily identify with the needs and problems of students and I was, thus able to

* In the second year of my tenure, the number was reduced. Then senior teachers were also directly involved in the programmes.

exploit their capacity and zeal to the fullest.

They definitely got an advantage by being directly involved with the students, as they could identify the problem-children without apparent interference in the lives of students. As they got accepted by the student community as 'friends' they could offer fruitful counselling services to a few, whom they identified and discussed with me before starting the treatment process.

By and large I gave them enough independence in their work, after the initial phase of one to two months was over, which led to a smooth and frank flow of ideas from me to them and vice-versa. Although I stressed on punctuality and systematic functioning, I did not push them too hard, which led to a more creative and enjoyable experience on their part.

I would like to end by quoting R.W. Revans : "We may one day discover that nobody ever taught anyone anything : we may find our powers are limited to providing the student with the best conditions in which he may learn for himself. In short, the teacher in social work education is probably a figment of our imagination. In reality there are only learners who happen to be at different stages and with different responsibilities and who are expressing their learning in different ways. But in the meantime there is plenty for us all to learn, and we must be perennial learners if we would gladly teach."

13

RECORDING AS A TOOL IN EFFECTIVE SUPERVISION

Miss Cecilia Thangarajan

RECORDING and supervision have always been important elements in social work education and practice. However supervision may very often be mistaken by the supervisee for just informing the supervisor of the number of clients she interviewed, the regular agency work she attended to, the programme she was planning for the agency and so forth. In short field work becomes more target oriented and supervision restricted to directing students to achieve tangible targets.

In order to make supervision more effective the student should not only be guided in her work, but should also be helped to relate theory to practice and in the process experience personal growth. Recording could be used as a means to achieve this dynamic end. In this creative effort the student besides her regular casework and group work recording can pick out items from her day's work and reflect on them. The guidelines for such reflection are given below :

1. Activity done refers to any activity carried out in field work ranging from an interview, a home visit or a programme conducted or even a supervisory conference, mentioning the objective of such an activity.

2. Learning content refers to what the student learnt from the activity. It may be at a mere observation level, knowledge or factual level, or it can be at an interpretation, analysis or synthesis level.

3. The process learnt is in other words how he learnt it.

This could be conveyed by focussing on the way in which he acquired such learning.

4. Assistance refers to what or who assisted the student to arrive at this learning. It could be a theory explained in class, a book which the student read or guidance given at a supervisory conference.

5. Blocks to the learning content would help the student to reflect on himself to see if there are any factors like prejudices, m sconception, etc. which hinder learning process.

6. Feeling component again is an attempt to help the student to be in touch with her feeling.

7. Clarification sought offers a scope for the student to bring at an individual level anything that she is not able to comprehend, limitations she has in the field and clarification with regard to how theory is related to practice.

An illustration on next page will explain the use of this pattern of recording. A first year student placed in the institute for T.B. and chest disease accompanied a group of doctors to a nearby slum area to observe an immunisation programme. This was how she reported the experience.

When the student reported for supervisory conference the supervisor helped her to focus on the learning content by first of all helping her to identify the objective of the visit. The objective as identified by the student was to observe how the immunisation programme was carried out in a community. With this objective in mind she began to recall her observations reflecting and analysing what she had learnt from it which was quite considerable. She also observed that the block to her learning was the fact that she had quite forgotten the purpose of her visit. The learning content as she expressed at the supervisory conference was as follows :

Thus recording here was a tool for more effective supervision wherein emphasis is on the growth of the student in learning and improving her knowledge in human behaviour, developing her skills in handling situations, and developing proper attitudes required for social work practice.

Activity done	Learning content	Process of learning	Assistance received	Block	Feeling component	Clarification
Visited N. Madras areas where SWALLOUS a voluntary organization is working	Learnt the organization structure, functioning of SWALLOUS. The various programmes conducted by the organisation	By visiting and discussion with organization members	Supervisory guidance to observe and analyse, all that went on during programme	The fascination to these organizations may have been a block to learn more about community	Felt very happy to know many organizations are working with the people	Of what use is the observation ?

Activity done	Learning content	Learning process	Assistance received	Block	Feeling component	Points for clarification
Visit to North Madras Slum : Objective was to observe the immunisation programme in progress	1. Community requires prior education regarding TB, measures of prevention before accepting immunisation	Observed how this was undertaken by Caritas organization	Supervisory guidance to reflect on activity with objectives in mind	—	Happy to have learnt how a programme should be conducted	
	2. Any Community Health Programme undertaken by a hospital or agency will be successful if an area where an organization is already working is chosen	Since it was an input by the hospital staff who are not full time workers in a community the preparation was done by an organisation and the hospital needed only to step in				
	3. Application of inter-agency approach to a programme	Organization and functioning of Swallous—An organization working in the community. Caritas—organisation engaged in health education. Hospital—involved in immunisation programme				

14

TRAINING OF SOCIAL WORK STUDENTS IN THE FIELD OF MENTAL HEALTH

R.K. Upadhyay

BACKGROUND

THE Central Institute of Psychiatry, Ranchi has been conducting a course of two years duration in Psychiatric Social Work (DPSW) for those with M.A. in Sociology, Psychology and Anthropology. Those with M.A. (Social Work) are admitted directly to the 2nd year of DPSW course thereby getting an exemption of one year. The department has the services of one Assistant Professor assisted by two PSWs. Student's number has varied from three to eight in the last ten years.

The Assistant Professor and Head of the Department has to work as field work supervisor and co-ordinator and also as teacher for social case work, group work, and community organisation etc. Selection of students is done on the basis of interviews and marks of M.A. examination.

Field work

Students are posted to work only with psychiatric patients served by the Central Institute of Psychiatry. However, they do visit some agencies in correctional and medical field.

There are no field work days. Everyday classes are held in such a way that they can get enough time to work with patients attending out-patient department, child guidance clinic, and with patients admitted as in-patients. Case work and group work are the two main methods practised by the trainees at different stages of hospitalisation throughout their stay of two years. The second year has more intensive field work than the 1st year.

Supervision is done through visit to the wards/clinical rooms, individual conferences and group conferences. Case conferences are held wherein the trainees have to present cases with other trainees in psychology and psychiatry from social work angle. This angle has been under evaluation. Initially DPSW trainees used to supplement history presented by the students of psychiatry and discuss rehabilitation and casework approach. Today, the trainee PSWs present history of the patient in family, school and in community which includes data on his sexual, recreational and personal life as well. Psychiatrists present only symptoms, development of symptom, and diagnostic formulations. Psychologists present diagnostic formulations only. Treatment and rehabilitation part is usually presented by PSW or sometimes by psychiatrist also. The likely approach to emerge for case conferences is that the PSW will present social diagnosis with full focus on treatment and rehabilitation.

Reading assignment relevant to help the patient is a common feature of field work practice. Psychiatrist/ward doctor supervise the students alongwith other trainees from psychiatric angle. The field work reports of DPSW mainly consist of (i) case history, (ii) casework including counselling with patients, (iii) group work, (iv) work with the relatives of patients from different angles—diagnostic, therapeutic, or rehabilitative. Allotment of cases to them for case work/group work is done usually by the ward doctor/psychiatrist or supervisor. Sometimes the student himself in consultation with the ward doctor and/or supervisor chooses cases for help through group work or case work.

Though evaluation is a continuous process, it is done formally only at the end of the second year. No separate marks are assigned for it. There is only one thing which is perhaps unique. Trainees at the end of the second year have, *as part of examination*, to work on a case from psycho-social diagnostic angle within 1½ hours and the examiners (including external one) judge the reports of students and hold viva-voce on the case and on case work theory etc. This is conducted on the pattern of the clinical examinations held for M.B.B.S. courses. Marks allotted for this clinical examination in social casework are 100 only. There is no block placement. Recently trainees are being put on emergency duty alongwith psychiatrists and psychologists at night.

Observation and comments

The difference in the nature of field work at C.I.P. with that of any other school of social work emanates from at least four sources which are specific to C.I.P., Ranchi.

1. D.P.S.W. course admits students with two different backgrounds—one with M.S.W. and another with M.A. (Sociology, Psychology and Cultural Anthropology).
2. D.P.S.W. course is run alongwith courses for psychiatrists (DPM) and clinical psychologists (D.M. & S.P). Students from all the courses sit together for common classes on psychology, anthropology, psychiatry, and so on.
3. There is only one agency where students have to work with patients/clients.
4. The head of CIP is a psychiatrist who has the overall responsibility to run the course and thus exercises a lot of control over the course content.

When confronted with students in the 2nd year with social work (MSW) and non-social work background (M.As), the supervisor finds difficulty in allotment of cases. MSWs are usually good at the social work methods whereas M.As after one year of training become good at psychiatric information. Cases for MSWs are selected in such a way that their inadequate psychiatric orientation and information does not become a handicap. They are asked to work with families of the patients or recovered patients with problems at home. (See the chart). It takes about 4 months when MSWs are able to acquire and assimilate adequate psychiatric information to work with these patients. For example, an MSW is not aware of what happens to a person when he becomes a schizophrenic (in terms of loss in the capacity of reasoning, thinking, memory, relating etc.).

The second year students of DPSW (with M.As) need more help in writing the record as compared to MSWs who have learnt and practised recording in social work setting. The recording of DPSW with M.As (final year) is more in tune with psychologists/ psychiatrists than with social workers. Psychiatrists etc. with their emphasis on history, record their work with patients in a summary form, and this form of recording is not encouraged and permitted in DPSW course as it does not, for obvious reasons, serve the purpose of field work in social casework and group work. There is little emphasis on psychotherapy for DPMs etc. on account of which they do not undertake process recording as expected of DPSWs.

The DPSWs create problems for supervisor when they compare (which they usually do) their work etc. with DPMs. They invariably compete with them in psychiatric information so much so that one DPSW batch was declared superior to DPM, DM & SPs in psychiatric knowledge by the Director of the Institute after viva-voce.

CHART

Difference between field work requirements of MSWs and DPSWs with M.As.

	1st Semester	2nd Semester
MSWs	1. Observe how the clinical work is being carried out	1. Case work/group work with patients in need of therapeutic help
	2. Observe patients on the ward	2. Participation in group therapy programmes
	3. Take up cases for social history	3. Pre-discharge counselling
	4. Take up patients for history or social case work who have problems in family	4. Presentation of cases in case conferences
DPSWs with MAs	1. Take up cases for history	
	2. Take up any case for social case work and/or group work	
	3. Pre-discharge counselling either individually or in group	Same as done by MSWs
	4. Present cases in case conference	

Notes : DPSWs with M.As in Psychology show better grasp of theoretical knowledge than those with Anthropology and Sociology. MSWs usually neglect social work contents and pay attention to psychiatric information and understanding.

The DPSW with M.As (in the final year) demand more demonstration of group work or casework sessions than MSWs. The DPSW with M.As are poor in the practice of these methods for the following reasons :

(a) too much of emphasis on psychiatric information given by the total set-up.
(b) lack of social work staff.
(c) poor social work information of the Director of the Institute.
(d) lack of support to social work staff to strengthen social work content.

When MSWs feel themselves superior to other M.As in the University, the DPSWs at CIP are constantly under stress because of the lower status they are ascribed to by their co-trainees. This frustration, sometimes prompts them to leave the course or at least results in poor motivation to undertake field work which requires hard work. The arguments put forth by the PSWs is that the DPM with less lectures, and less clinical work enjoy better paid jobs and status than DPSWs. To maintain themselves in C.I.P. setting DPSWs have to assimilate a lot of psychiatric knowledge along with social work practice. Sometimes, they learn more of psychiatry than of social work.

The DPSWs with M.As (2nd year) are fully aware of scope of their practice in DIP setting but the MSWs take about four months to know and work with patients at different stages of hospitalisation. Their orientation being more general, they take time to pick up skills necessary to work with the clients served by C.I.P.

Field work required of DPSW suffers because CIP Director is not a social work man; he does not lend full support to the DPSW staff, and also because students have to work in only one agency. If agencies are more, learning through field work can increase significantly.

Block placements

Though CIP does not have any provision for block placement for DPSWs, it does work as block placement agency for MSWs from different schools of social work.

The MSWs on block placement exhibit poor psychiatric information and therefore they remain isolated in the Institute as well as in the hostel for trainees. This is more because of the nature of set-up which emphasizes only psychiatric knowledge and capacity to work therapeutically with psychiatric patients. These students find it quite difficult to work with patients and try to avoid/resist assignments. Many times, this resistance is more because of the fact that they think of Block Placement as "pleasure placement". The trainees with this conception try to manipulate the supervisor through various means.

In nutshell, one will be justified in saying that social work content has remained by and large a neglected aspect in the training of psychiatric social workers who are social workers first and psychiatric social workers later. Emphasis, then, should be on identifying and delineating the exclusive (along with over-lapping) areas of social work practice in psychiatric setting, and field work programme for psychiatric social workers must reflect the adequate place of social work practice in psychiatric setting.

15

EMPLOYMENT PROBLEM OF TAMIL WEAVERS IN A RESETTLEMENT COLONY
A Developmental Approach

Shankar Pathak

I

BACKGROUND

APPROXIMATELY 300 to 400 Tamil speaking families who were originally residing in Karol Bagh, Moti Bagh and R. K. Puram localities were shifted to Kalyanpuri, Trilokpuri, resettlement colonies in 1976 during the period of Emergency. Most of these families, however, reside in Block No. 22 in Trilokpuri. The women of these families were working as domestic maids in the South Indian families in Karol Bagh, Moti Bagh and R. K. Puram. The men were doing a variety of jobs in these localities. Their forcible shifting to the new resettlement colonies seriously disrupted their previous employment arrangements. In the initial stages due to lack of adequate transport facilities, these families remained unemployed and hence on the point of starvation. Subsequently, however, most of the women were able to resume the work in the South Indian families in the three localities mentioned earlier. Also some of the men were able to find a variety of employment opportunities such as hawkers, cleaners, bearers in tea shops, etc.

As part of their efforts to provide employment to some of the skilled weavers who were unemployed during the early stage of their transfer to the resettlement colonies, the students of the

Delhi School of Social Work in co-operation with the DSIDC* officials and with the assistance of the State Bank of India worked out a scheme of self-employment for 66 skilled weavers. These weavers originally belonged to Chinalpatti area in Tamil Nadu and for generations were weavers by occupation. They left their native places due to acute poverty during a period of 5 to 10 years before the Emergency and came to Delhi in search of employment and settled down in Karol Bagh, Moti Bagh and R. K. Puram localities. So it was thought that their traditional occupational skills could be harnessed in order to provide employment opportunities for them. As part of the self-employment scheme for which loans were made available by the State Bank of India, the 66 weavers were advanced on an average of Rs. 2,500/- per person for purchasing a loom and for using part of the money as working capital for purchasing raw material. The DSIDC officials at that time gave several assurances to assist the weavers in the purchase of raw materials and the marketing of their product.

The scheme became a reality through the strenuous efforts of one of the students of Delhi School of Social Work and 66 weavers. Half of these weavers have their looms in Kalyanpuri and the other half in Trilokpuri. The weavers purchased the looms for weaving the handloom cloth and installed them in one of the sheds made available by the DSIDC at Kalyanpuri and also at Trilokpuri. Each of the weavers was to pay rent of approximately Rs. 22/- per month to the DSIDC as his contribution towards the hire of the shed. The looms started functioning by December 1976. The weavers were able to produce and sell the cloth and thus find self-employment for themselves for a period of about six months. After six months, however, the looms had to be closed down and the weavers were once again thrown out of employment, because of the non-payment of bills amounting to nearly Rs. 36,000/- by three private traders who had purchased their cloth. It may be mentioned that these parties were introduced by the local DSIDC officials to the weavers. Repeated efforts by the students of Delhi School of Social Work, the weavers and stray attempts by some of the DSIDC officials were

* Delhi State Industrial Development Corporation.

not effective in securing payment of the bills. Some of these traders went to the extent of issuing bad cheques which were dishonoured by the banks. The weavers being too poor and without any resources at their command to initiate legal action had to be silent victims to the intrigues of the private traders and the apathy of the DSIDC officials.

A variety of alternative plans were thought of by the students of Delhi School of Social Work and the weavers to enable the latter to earn their livelihood by restarting their weaving work. The main problem, however, was lack of working capital, mounting arrears by way of rental to DSIDC and interest on loan taken by the State Bank of India and the inability to find safe marketing facilities.

One such alternative was worked out during a field visit of the officials to these colonies arranged at the initiative of the Delhi School of Social Work in February, 1978. The team included the Director of Industries, Delhi Administration, Resident Representative of KVIC in Delhi and the Chief Projects Officer, DSIDC. It was proposed that the Delhi KVIC should open a Khadi spinning and weaving centre at Trilokpuri which might initially provide employment for about ten weavers and gradually to others as well. There were several practical and technical hurdles in this scheme such as the feasibility of adapting the looms for Khadi weaving, and training of the weavers for this work. The weavers expressed their willingness to join the scheme, despite some difficulties they had to face. The only progress so far has been the acquisition of a shed in Trilokpuri which is lying vacant since July 1978. It may be mentioned that Mr. V. Ramachandran, Member-Secretary of KVIC was kind enough to visit Trilokpuri in April 1978, and talk to some of the weavers. He also prepared and submitted a long Note on the possible rehabilitation of the weavers to the KVIC Board.

Recently, Janab Barkatullah Khan Chauhan, Chairman, All-India Handloom Board also visited Trilokpuri and held a discussion with the weavers. His advice to them was that they should form a co-operative and subsequently help would be secured for supply of yarn and marketing of cloth. This proposal of forming a co-operative has been made by others before. But, the weavers' reaction was not favourable. Recently they have begun to think along these lines as a result of various developments including the visit of Mr. Chauhan. The indications are that they will decide to form a co-operative and most, if not all, the weavers, will join it.

Instead of helping the weavers in securing repayment of the cloth sold by them to the private parties or by any other alternative way of enabling the weavers to work on the looms, the DSIDC have been issuing notices to the State Bank of India and also to the weavers to vacate the sheds for non-payment of rent. As a result, the State Bank officials were compelled to issue notices to the weavers for payment of the loans along with interest and failing which they would auction the looms. It may be mentioned that the Bank officials are sympathetic to the weavers problems, but were compelled to act in view of the pressures from the DSIDC on them. In the meanwhile, as a result of the efforts of the student of the Delhi School of Social Work and his teacher a local voluntary organisation was located which is interested in working out a scheme whereby the weavers in these two localities can find employment by restarting the work on the looms. The organisation concerned is Bhartiya Krishak Aur Udyog Sudhar Kendra. However, this organisation was unable to take any concrete action for lack of space for purposes of storage of raw materials and finished product, and opening of a bleeching and dyeing unit in the Kalyanpuri—Trilokpuri areas. If land or other facilities like shed could be made available at concessional charges, this organisation is ready to provide employment to 66 weavers.

At present 33 weavers at Kalyanpuri owe approximately Rs. 89,000 to the State Bank of India and Rs. 14,000 to the DSIDC. The other 33 weavers of Trilokpuri owe a total amount of Rs. 67,000 to the State Bank of India and Rs. 12,000 approximately to the DSIDC as a rental. The weavers have not been working on the looms since April 1977. Most of them are unemployed.

For the welfare of the weavers, following actions are necessary :

1. Recovery of the amount due from the three traders.
2. To restrain the DSIDC from issuing further notices to

the State Bank of India for the removal of the looms which are hypothecated to the Bank.

3. The State Bank has been issuing notices to the weavers for the repayment of the loan and interest and failing this they have threatened to auction the looms. The Bank may be persuaded not to issue any more notices and not to auction the looms.
4. If possible, the State Bank may be requested to write off or waive the interest due on the loan for the period they have remained unemployed.
5. To ask the DSIDC also to waive the rent for the same period as above, and/or to prevail upon them to take action for the recovery of the amount due to the weavers from the three traders.
6. To assist the weavers in restarting the looms by providing work and safe facilities for marketing of their product.

EDITOR'S NOTE

A court case has been filed against the weavers for the recovery of loans.

In connection with self-employment project for women in another block of the same community, after the lapse of two years, another student of the M.A. (Previous) class happened to contact the Bank, the DSIDC, and other officials. She was enquiring as to how this project to assit weavers was conceived ? What was the original proposal ? On what conditions loans were given ? etc. She wanted to establish whether the court case filed against them was proper ? These documents were not made available and on the basis of whatever little she could see through the files she suspected foul play all along. Irregularities noted were serious. The matter was discussed with the supervisor. The student is contacting the Legal Aid Society, and other advocates to fight on behalf of the weavers, and call for all the original documents connected with the scheme in the court so that it could be determined how the weavers were in the wrong. Officials concerned are trying to hush up the matter and are not co-operating with the worker nor allowing her to see the files.

The matter is *subjudice* at present. The field work has assumed altogether a different dimension and the student wishes to pursue the matter even after the current field work term is over. If the lower court decides against the weavers, stay proceedings may be initiated at the High Court. The weavers however are hoping for a day when political intervention in the matter will rid them of their present predicament.

16

SELF-EMPLOYMENT PROJECT
An Exploration in Developmental Social Work

R.R. Singh

THE COMMUNITY

TRILOKPURI, a trans-Yamuna ressettlement colony, is part of the Kichiripur complex. It consists of 36 blocks with five hundred houses in each block. The population is approximately 2 lakhs. During the emergency Delhi was cleared of its slums and the people were shifted to re-settlement colonies around Delhi. Though the people here come from different States and backgrounds they share the same indigent and improper housing and unhygeinic living conditions. Of the many problems, the main ones are of education and unemployment.

THE SITUATION

The workers in this community came across in Block 15 a group of muslim women proficient in the art of stitching and embroidery. Most of the women possessed sewing machines but due to restrictions imposed on them by their religious tradition, they were unable to go out and earn their livelihood by using their talent. These illiterate, but skilled women and girls felt desperate need to supplement their family earning as they all

Field Work Placement : Trilokpuri Resettlement Area
Supervisees : Miss Mala Dodeja and and Miss Rosita Ratnam M.A. (Previous) students.

came from the low income group with earnings below Rs. 400 per month. The women were thus in search of ways which could provide them work at home. Therefore the need to identify a leader arose, who could shoulder the responsibility of managing a group for collective production and distribution, and a person who could perform the function of a middleman between suppliers and workers in the community.

IDENTIFICATION OF A LEADER

On getting to know the women better we found that almost all the women in Block 15 seemed to know Saira. Looking deeper into the matter, we discovered that a man had been bringing embroidery work from some export house to be worked on by the women. In this situation Saira had emerged as leader as she had organized a group of women, and saw to it that the work was done well and on time. Thus her house became a centre from where the women took work. Saira herself approached us and asked us to help her in setting up a project where she would be incharge and would work on a commission basis. She was also prepared to go to the town to collect materials and return the finished product, if it could not be delivered to her at home.

SAIRA'S BACKGROUND

Saira's husband was a carpenter by profession, but due to a prolonged spell of illness (heart condition) he was forced to quit and was therefore unemployed. Saira, a mother of seven children, of whom two daughters are earning and two sons are apprentices, felt the need to support her large family. In a project of this kind there was a possibility that her unemployed husband could be able to help her out, thus making it a family project.

MEETING WITH WOMEN OF THE BLOCK

A meeting was held in Block 15 to discuss the starting of such a project. All the women appeared very enthusiastic and said that they would be grateful, if we could find them work. We said that just our efforts were not enough. They would have to get together and work for it, not just people from Block 15, but from other blocks as well. One of the women, who we had spoken to earlier, explained that we would not be giving them work personally, and that we were only trying to negotiate a direct contact between them and the agencies that provided work. We explained that they would have to choose a leader to take charge as we were there only for a short spell of time—one woman Fareeda, agreed to take up with Saira the responsibility of getting and distributing work. In this meeting we also discussed the type of work the women could do. Only few women knew knitting and crochet, but most of them knew stitching and embroidery.

SEARCH FOR WORK

Khadi village industries commission
Here most of the work was given on contract annually. At that time, the only work they could offer was mirror embroidery, and our women did not know how to do it. Since the KVIC did not work with the aim of making profit, they were not good pay masters.

Delhi social welfare advisory board
Here they asked us for a list of women who needed work, and said that it would be their responsibility to provide them with work. They also informed us about the four centres working in Trilokpuri under the Gandhi Smarak Harijan Suraksha Samiti. On investigation we discovered that these four centres existed only on paper. We submitted a list of women, but nothing was done about it.

Meeting with a voluntary worker in a school
This worker worked in collaboration with Khadi Gram Udyog, who gave her bulk orders for stitching Kurtas, Pyjamas, Blouses etc. She said that each woman would have to take a test before she could be given work. All the women were to personally give the test, and if they qualified, one of them was to take charge.

Two batches of women were taken for the test in groups of five. The women tried out their hand but their work was later rejected as they found it to be unprofitable. The women were paid only Re. 1 per blouse and they were expected to provide materials like thread and hooks themselves. Nothing could be done to raise this amount for Khadi Gram Udyog worked on a non-profit basis.

Various export houses

We contacted export houses all over Delhi, but unfortunately we were not able to strike a compromise with them for the reasons stated below : (1) The distance between the export house and Trilokpuri was great; (2) some export houses did not provide the materials and the women were not keen on buying materials, as it was risky, and waste only lessened their profits; and (3) some did not have regular flow of embroidery work.

Export house A

This was the only agency that met all our condition and proved to be profitable. This was a family that handled all the hand embroidery work for the company. They were the sole distributor and the first middleman. This family was responsible for getting the work done and handling back the finished work on time. They are the distributors for many large export houses. They further distributed this work to people in and around Delhi. They thus became the second middlemen who further distributed it to workers.

Here a controversy arose around the fact that Saira could take the advantage of workers, as she fixed her own commission. If the work came through other middlemen who delivered it in the community, the commission was usually fixed by the agent himself and it varied between 10-25 paisa per piece. Usually in this case the margin of profit was limited. We found that if the work was collected directly from the agency, the commission taken was more, but the women were to be paid a higher amount. For example, if a work worth Rs. 6 came through other middlemen, the commission was fixed for 50 paisa, but if the women collected it directly from the organisation, they managed to make Re. 1 per piece. Further the work was collected from other centres in Trilokpuri. For a piece of Rs. 1.25 the commission was 25 p., and for work worth Rs. 4, the commission was 35 p. and if the work was worth Rs. 6 the commission was 50 p. per piece. Taking an average of these rates, and also taking into consideration that the bigger pieces of work take two days to do, if 75 pieces get done per day, the middlewoman makes about Rs. 26.50 per day, which is ten times more than the earning of an ordinary worker.

Discussion with the supervisor

We therefore had a discussion with our supervisor as we realized that the distribution was not fair. The middlemen were exploiting workers. But we concluded that there was no other solution at hand. The advantages outweighed the disadvantages. These were : (1) one person makes more money than others, but many women get work in the bargain; (2) secondly from Saira's point of view it would become a family business with her unemployed son and husband; and (3) as Saira was a resident of the community itself, she would ensure regular flow of work. The strategy decided upon was to involve more women as middlewomen and in the process minimize exploitation through keen competition. It was also decided that later a co-operative of workers could be formed or a non-profit making agency may be pursuaded to take up this responsibility. One such agency had already refused to come forward.

We found that most export houses paid nearly the same amount, the only difference being some export houses gave out all their work to sole distributors, and others handled the workers directly. The rates also depended on whether the materials were provided by the company or not. The women preferred the materials to be supplied as it made their burden much lighter.

THE TWO COMMUNITY CENTRES FUNCTIONING IN TRILOKPURI

Here, two women in partnership, got work directly from export houses and distributed it in the community. Most women, unless they were really desperate did not go to them because they were paid a meagre amount and they knew that most of the money was pocketed by them. These two women had a very elaborate network of contacts in the community and were flourishing in business.

THE GROUP DYNAMICS

Twenty women who attended the meeting decided on having Saira and Fareeda as their leaders. In the meantime, Fareeda started taking work from one of the centres in the community. The lady used to deposit and collect the work from her house so she did not see the need to go out in search of work. Therefore as it developed, all the responsibility was that of Saira's alone. Saira was accompanying us to the various export houses. During this time a couple from an unrecognized agency dealing in hand embroidery came to Trilokpuri with work and in search of labour. Saira made a very hasty contract with this couple that she would take up distribution work on the basis of a commission. This was done without our knowledge and without finding out the background of the organisation concerned. The work continued for a month and soon Saira realized that there was no mention of payment and the women began to ask her for the same. Everytime the topic of money came up she was assured that it would be given in due course. Tension was building up in the community and one day when the couple came to the community to give work, Razia, Saira's neighbour, who had also been taking work from Saira—saw them coming and at once organized a group of over 50 women for a show down, with all the women demanding payment. The visiting lady started crying and assured them that they would be paid in due course. Saira was helpless because she had to maintain relations with the lady and also keep the workers happy. After this incident another woman Razia started getting work to distribute from Block 24 and a man also brought the work to her house. She started insinuating that Saira would not be able to pay them and very cleverly drew the women to her side.

THE COMPETITION GREW

Now Saira and Razia sit in the same lane, some 10 feet apart on their charpais with their group of women surrounding them.

The two main leaders were openly competing with each other, as regards the number of women each employed and the payment they gave. According to Razia, she has about 50-60 workers from all over the community. Saira has about 40-50. Many of the workers take work from wherever it is available. Only Saira does not like her workers going elsewhere, but when she runs short of work, she has no control over them.

Inspired by the success of these two women Rehana and Ameena decided to try their hand at the same business and they have now started taking work on a larger scale after seeing Saira's success. Rehana has about twenty workers, but they are not strictly her workers.

Ameena had been taking work earlier from Saira, till she decided to branch off on her own. She made her beginning with about ten workers. The dynamics of the group has been illustrated in the diagram in three phases.

GROUP EFFECTIVENESS

The group came into being, developed and underwent change in response to a need. The effectiveness of the group can be measured in our case by its productivity.

The productivity of this group is determined by the nature of interaction among the members, leadership style, and incentive in the form of learning. The productivity on the other hand depends on the skill. Some women being more skilled than others complete work faster and thus earn more. The average earning of a woman is approximately between Rs. 2.50—Rs. 3.00, per day after putting in about 4-5 hours a day. Thus when there is a steady flow of work, one woman earns about Rs. 17 per week. The total money earned by doing this work depends on the number of working members which varies between 1-4. For example : if in a family there are 3 women/children working they earn about Rs. 50 per week.*

* Since the project has been in existence only for 6-8 weeks, it is premature to find out how the additional income is used by the families concerned. This aspect will be pursued by the next batch of students as part of field work on the basis of which action strategies will be devised in the following areas : (a) distribution of work ; (b) increase in earnings without exploitation; (c) family budgeting and counselling; and (d) the establishment of a non-formal co-operative organisation.

There is however no certainty of a regular flow of work. For example, there is no work in the community, the day the leader has to collect finished product and return the same. At the organizational level there are certain periods when most of the consignments are dispatched and it takes time before the next consignment arrives.

The flow of work is to be assessed on an annual basis in terms of lean and busy months, discontinuties in work during the monsoon season and so on. Only then a total picture of annual income per month would emerge.

CRITICAL EVALUATION

Advantages of the project :

1. Women's employment at home
2. Supplementation of family income
3. Opportunity of work for young girls who do not go to school or are not sent to school, and
4. Prospects of the emergence of new leaders

Disadvantages

1. Disproportionate earning of middlemen ;
2. Uncertainty about the flow of work and payment ;
3. Possibility of cheating ;
4. Younger girls may not be sent to school and be made to work to increase family income.
5. Continuing section of the weaker sections by the exploitative pattern of capitalist development in the urban informal sector.

FUTURE PLANS

1. To introduce leaders to as many agencies and export houses as possible, so that if the work stops coming from one, there will always be other alternatives.

2. Initiate and motivate more women to learn ;

3. Try for healthy competition in required skills between leaders, and for the emergence of more leaders ; and

PHASE I

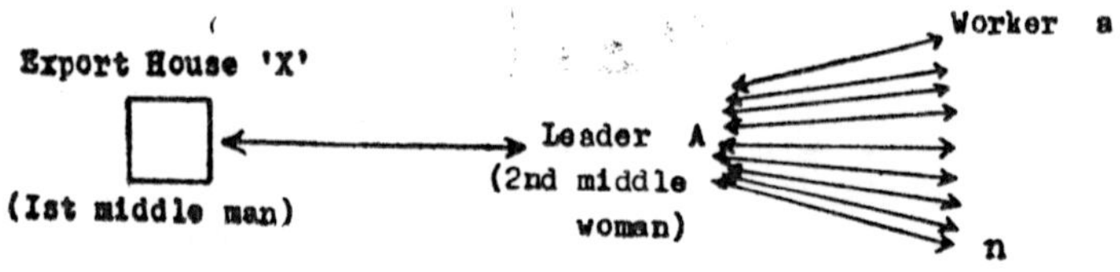

No of workers vairies from a→h (n represents the total No. of workers.)

PHASE - II

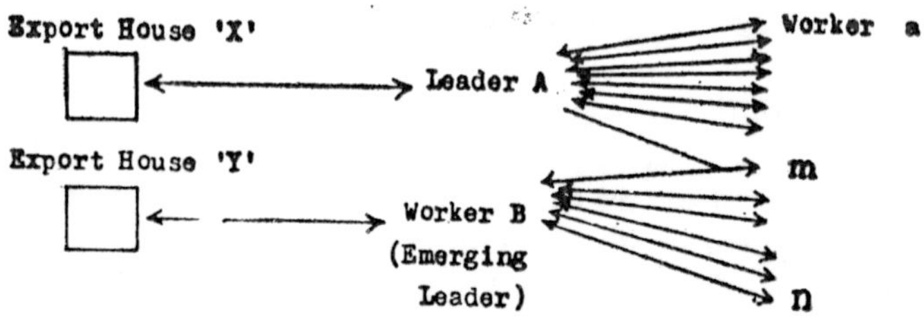

No. of workers left with A=a→m

No. of workers left with B (gone from)=m→n.

X Leader 'B' emerged due to the frastration among workers because of exploitation by middle man.

PHASE - III

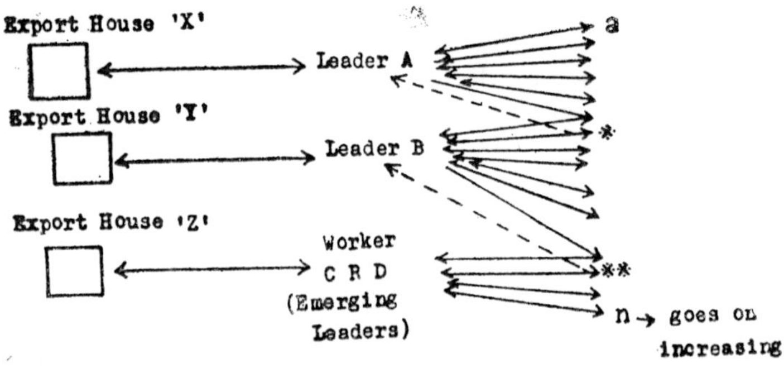

Leader A→The arrow is only unidirectional in a few cases, it indicates that
Leader B→workers are no more inclined to taking work from their former leader owing to the frustration and exploitation by her.

* The worker goes to Leader A only when she is left with no alternative.

** The worker goes to Leader B (Ex-leader) only when she cannot procure work from leaders C & D.

4. Try and introduce other kinds of work like knitting, stitching and crochet so that the workmanship can be put to test and best use.

For those who are unable to take part in the project, efforts may be made to introduce other projects. For the semi-skilled workers sewing classes are being held in the block itself by an agency to help acquire skill.

5. Assist group leaders to establish direct contacts with organisations so that the number of middlemen is reduced ;

6. Follow-up by new workers.

REFLECTIONS ON THE PROJECT EXPERIENCE

Block 15 being a Muslim block, we had great difficulty initially in communicating with people. It took nearly two months for them to have confidence. Assistance in individual cases of need helped establish better rapport. Once the barrier was broken, the women themselves approached us with various problems, the major one being their skill in sewing and embroidery going waste. We therefore decided to concentrate our efforts in this particular area. It took seven months of work before we were able to organize a group, identify their leaders and see some results.

This group can be classified as need-based, growth oriented, an informal group. The focal point of it is income supplementation.

FUTURE PROSPECTS

Over a period of six months, and on an average eight hours work per week, the project has developed gradually and now it has reached a stage where the women have gained confidence and have made enough contacts to carry on the project. Women have become motivated and a number of leaders have emerged which to an extent helped eliminate severe exploitation of women in several ways.

Though in the beginning our efforts were concentrated only in block 15 (with 30 women from block 15 itself), now there are about 25 women coming from other blocks. We need to identify leaders from other blocks as well to expand the project.

Changing Phases of the work Distribution System and the Elimination of Brokerage

PHASE - I

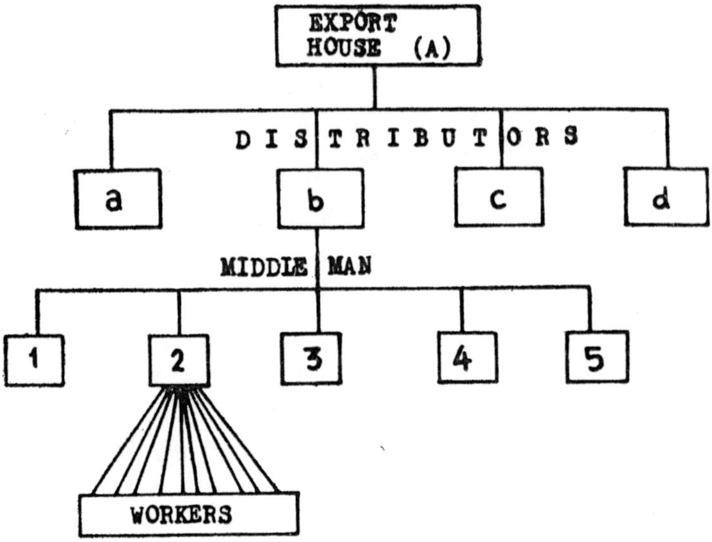

Including Distributors two or More Middleman were involved in Phase I. Between the export-house and workers there were four tiers.

PHASE - II

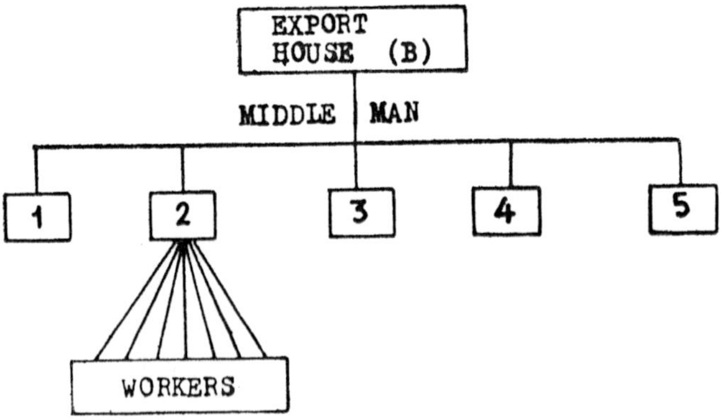

Four tier system of Phase I was reduced to three tiers in Phase II.

COMMENT

The concern initially in the above record was remedial. Students identified the need to help women and they thought that regular productive work would help them to supplement their income. Efforts in this direction continued until the question of exploitation by middlemen was brought up. Developmental component in the task—centered approach was thus gradually introduced in this way by the supervisor without calling it so. This focus sharpened at the stage when the students were asked to prepare summary. Such a review offered them a 'useful experience' as they put it. Developmental perspective thus emerged in this case through piece-meal efforts. In the earlier phase emphasis was more on exploration, organization, resource use, women's education and local group dynamics. Later such aspects as anticipation of problems, supply of raw material, seasonal flow of work, possibility of children not going to school or increase in the number of drop-outs on account of the remunerative nature of project, in-equitable distribution of earnings between the leader and workers, idea of an informal co-operative, use of additional income by women, and need for counselling in this area emerged which showed their interrelatedness. Need for different types of work was also discovered. The record therefore presents an approach which was piece-meal, programme-centred and intuitive (a stage of "doing something" to help the poor women) and it progressed into a developmental concern. This experience occurred through an additive process when the field was being explored to work on. The other approach could have been to impart this perspective right from the beginning and see that the same was guided and sustained throughout, although regression or reversion to the traditonal approach was also a possibility. Neither the field nor workers however were ready for this alternative in the beginning, and emphasis on other aspects by the supervisor would have proved far too demanding on students who were untiring in their efforts to achieve 'something'. Students were helped however to appreciate that although the number of middlemen had been brought down by their efforts, this should on y be regarded as a means to an end—the latter being the organisation of workers in the informal sector to challenge the pattern broader exploitative process of dependent development and thereby make the field work more functional to the developmental needs of the society.

APPENDICES

APPENDIX-I

A BIBLIOGRAPHY

BOOKS

Brown, S. Clement and Cloyne, E.R. *The Field Training of Social Workers*. London; George Allen & Unwin, 1966.

Buford, H. Junker, *Field Work : An Introduction to the Social Sciences*, Chicago : University of Chicago Press, 1960.

Carr, E.H. , *What is History* ? London: Pelican Book, 1961.

Clifford Manshardt, *Pioneering on Social Frontiers in India*, Tata Institute of Social Sciences, Bombay, 1967.

Delhi School of Social Work, *Field-work Supervision*, Delhi: Delhi of School Social Work, 1957; *Field Work Practices in Schools of Social Work in India*.

Guzzetta Charles *et al* (ed.) *Education for Social Work Practice : Selected International models*, Vienna and New York : International Association of Schools of Social Work and Council on Social Work Education, 1984.

Kent, Bessie, *Social Work Supervision in Practice*, Oxford: Pergamon Press, 1969.

Kulkarni, P.D. *Social Policy and Social Development in India*, Association of Schools of Social Work in India, 1979, Part II.

Manis, Francis, *Field Practice in Social-work Education*, California: Sultana Press, 1972.

Moorthy M.V. & Rao S. Narayana, *Field Work and Social Work*, Waltare, Department of Sociology and Social Work, 1970.

P.S.G School of Social Work, *Field Work Teaching in Social Work : A Report of the Seminar*, 1961.

Pathak, Shankar, 'Social Work Education: Basic Issues and Problems', in his book *Social Welfare, Health and Family Planning in India*, Marwah Publications, New Delhi, 1978.

Pathak, Shankar, *Social Welfare,: An Evolutionary and Developmental Perspective*, Delhi, Macmillan, 1961.

Petes, Dorothy E., *Supervision in Social Work*, London: George

Allen and Unwin, 1967.

Reynolds, Rosemary, *Evaluating the Field Work of Students*, New York: Family Service Association of America, 1947.

Reynolds, B.C. *Learning and Teaching in the Practice of Social Work*, New York: Rinehart and Company, 1942.

Robinson, Virgina P., *Supervision in Social Casework*, Chapil Hill; University of North Canolina Press, 1936.

Srinivas, M.N., *The Field Worker and the Field*, Delhi: Oxford University Press, 1979.

Taylor, Charles, *Social Theory As Practice*, Delhi: Oxford University Press, 1983.

Towle, Charlotte, *The Learner in Education for Professions*, Chicago: University of Chicago, 1954.

United Nations, Training for Social Work: *Fifth International Survey*, New York, 1970.

University Grants Commission, *Review of Social Work Education in India, Retrospect and Prospect,* University grants Commission, New Delhi, 1978.

Williamson, Margaret, *Supervision: Principles and Method*, New York: Woman's Press, 1950.

JOURNALS

Amachan, Kloh-Ann. 'Explorations into dynamics of learning in field-work', *Smith College Studies in Social Work*, (46(3) Jan· 1976) pp. 163-217.

Baker, Ron, field work teaching in social work, some concepts, Strategies and Issues' *Australian Social Work*, 30(2) Jan. 1977 11-27 p.

Banerjee G.R. 'Professional self and supervision in social work' *Indian Journal of Social Work*, (35:4, Jan. 1975), p. 309-16 p.

Baraclough Joan, 'Code of ethics for social work', *Social Work Today*. (6:12, Sep . 1975) p. 379-81

Barbaro, Fred, 'The Field instruction component in the administration concentration, some problems and suggested remedies', *Journal of Education for Social Work*. (15(1) Wint. 1979) p. 5-11

Bisno, Herbert, 'Theoretical framework for teaching social work methods and skills with particular reference to undergraduate social welfare education', *Journal of Education for*

Social Work (5:1, Fall 1969)

Blanck, Rubin, 'Practice theory, then and now', *Smith College Studies in Social Work* (47(2) Mar. 1977) p. 95-103

Blavo, E.Q. 'Field work management and supervision', *Journal for Social-Work Education in Africa* 182, Dec. 1974)p. 0-12

Bromley, Geoffrey, 'Interaction between fields and residential social workers', *British Journal of Social Work*, (7(3) Aug. 1977) p. 285-299

Brown, Allan G. 'Worker style in social work', *Social Work Today* (8(29) April 26, 1977), p. 13-15

Corroll, Nancy K. 'Three dimensional model of social work practice., *Social Work* (22(5) Sept 1977), p. 428-433

Chein, J.M.N. 'Does trainee meet the needs of the profession? *International Social Work*, (19(5) 1976)p. 6-11

Cooper, Terry, 'Growth in the process of helping', *Social Work Today*, (11(6) Oct. 1979) p. 5-22

Confidence in, 'Principle in Practice', *Social Work Today*(6:8, July 1975)P. 253-54

Currams, Robert, 'What community development presupposes', *Social Work Today*, (2:16' Nov. 1971) p. 3-7

Cowen, E. 'Well trained as helpers?' *New Society*, 25:570, Sept. 1973)p. 578-9

Davis, Hilary and Taylor Paul 'two agency placements in social work training', *Social Work Today*, (4:8, July 1973) p. 245-50

Davis, Leorand F. Oil and water? The importance of quality of residential placement in field work training' *Social Work Today*; (7(2) April 1976) p. 38-39

Donnison, David, 'Training for social work ', *Social Work Today*, (10(24) Feb. 1979), p. 17-20

Doran, P J. 'Great-Britain: Role and functions of volunteers in community work', *Community Work Abstracts*. (No. 5, September 1975) p. 11-16

Drowning, Ruppret A. 'Bridging the gap between education and practice', *social casework* (55.6, July 1974) p. 352-9

Fanshel, David, 'Status differentials: men and women in Social-work , '*Social Work*, (21(6) Nov, 1976), p. 441-454

Fiorendo, Soleded, A., 'Social work in social development' *Social Work Education and Development newsletter*(18, April 1977) p. 6-9

First year students in social work education', *Australian Social Work*, (32(3), Sept, 1979) p. 11-17

Gangrade, K.D. 'Student recording in field work supervision', *Indian Journal of Social Work*, (35:4, Jan. 1975) p. 353-57

Garzino, Salvatope J. 'Multidimensional student evaluation: An integrated approach to a social work research course' *Journal of Education for Social Work*, (15:1, Wint 1979) p. 36-43

Georgiou, Nick, 'Students view-point' *Social Work Today*, (8:23, March 1977) p. 20-21

Getzel, G.S. *et al.* 'Supervising in groups as a model for today', *social casework*, (52:3, March 1971) p. 154-163

Gill, Owen, 'The making of professional client' *Social Work Today* 8:8, No. 1976) p. 19

Gilterman, Alex and Germain, L.B. 'social work practice: A life model', *Social Service Review* (50:4, Dec. 1976) p. 600-610

Gutridge, Penny, 'Student Supervision, The step before reflection', *Social Work Today* , (8:22, March 1977) p. 12-13

Hawker, Maurice, 'Co-operation/Co-ordination: professional disaster *Social Work Today*, (8:17, Feb. 1977) P. 18

Henry, C. George, 'An examination field work models at Adelphi University School of Social of Work, *Journal of Education for Social Work*, (11:3, Fall 1975) p. 62-68

Herberg, Dorothy Chave, Study of work participation by graduate female social workers: some implications for professional social work training, *Journal of Education for Social Work* (9:3, 1973) p. 16-23

Hutchinson, Eric. 'Social work education: A view from the field; *Social Work Today*. (8:20, Feb. 1977) p. 10-12

Irvine, Elizabeth E. 'Organization of social work training', *International Social Work* (13:1, 1970) p. 18-20

Kadushin, Alfred. 'Supervisor—Supervisee, A Survey. '*Social Work*. (19:3, May 1974) p. 288-97

Kent, B. 'Totally integrated syllabus: An experiment in social work education'. *International Social Work*, (17:4, 1974), p. 11-23

Keung, Ho. Men. 'Implications of teacher-student relationship in social work education'. *Journal of Education for social work* (11:1, Wint 1975) p. 74-82

Kolevzon Michael S. Evaluating the supervisory relationship in field-placements' *Social Work.* (24:3, May 1979) p. 241-43

Knott, Ben. H. 'Symbolic interaction and social work education,' *Journal of Education for Social Work.* (9:3, 1973) p. 24-31

Lee, William. E. 'conflict of model'. *New Society* (25:568, Aug. 1973) p. 457-8

Lichtenberg, Philip. 'Introduction of radical theory and practice in social work education: personality theory' *Journal of Education for Social Work.* (12:2, 1976) p. 10-16

Leighniger, R.D., 'Systems, theory and social work : A re-exiamination.' *Journal of Education for Social Work.* (13 : 3, Fall 1977) p. 44-49.

Mackey R.A. 'Generic aspects of clinical social work practice. *Social Case Work.* (57 : 10, Dec. 1976) p. 619-624.

Manager, George W. 'Trends : social work practice in mental health'. *Abstracts for social workers.* (6 : 3, Fall 1970) p. 9-14.

Mathew, Grace. 'Educational and helping aspects of field work supervision'. *Indian Journal of Social Work.* (35 : 4, Jan. 1975) p. 325-31.

Mayer, John and Rosenblatt. A. 'Sources of stress among student practitioners in social work : A sociological view'. *Journal for Education for Social Work.* (10 : 3, fall 1974) p. 56-66.

Manis, Francis. Education for social work : Field work in developing nations. *International Social Work.* (14 : 2, 1921) p. 17-20.

Mcculloch J.W. and Brown, M. 'Methods of assessing field work students', *Probation.* (16 : 3, Nov. 1970). p. 79-83.

Mc Daniel, Clyde, O. and Hunt, D.L.G. 'Towards a revision of curriculum for masters level education in urban schools of social work', *Indian Journal of Soical Work.* (34 : 3, Oct. 1973) p. 259-74.

Mcnew, Emily, 'Field interaction at Merywood ; its micro, macro and modular', *Journal of Education for Social Work.* (6 : 1, Spring 1970) p. 29-40.

Miller, R.R. 'Student Research Perspective on race in case work practice.' *Smith College Studies in Social Work.* (41 : 1, Nov. 1970)

Millard, D.W. 'Examination of students' field work'. *Social Work Today.* (3 : 14, Oct. 1972). p. 13-16.

Minahan, Anee and Pincus, Allen. 'Conceptual framework for

social work practice'. *Social Work*. (22 : 5, Sep. 1977) p. 347-352.

Moffat, Jean. The student-supervisor relationship in social work education'. *Australian Journal of Social Work*. (22 : 3, Sept. 1969). p. 27-33.

Morales, A. 'Beyond traditional conceptual frameworks'. *Social Work*. (22 : 5, Sept. 1977) p. 387-393.

Munson, C.E. 'Professional autonomy and social work supervision'. *Journal of Education for Social Work*. (12 : 3, fall 1976) p. 95-102.

Pavlin, F. and Channon. G. 'Professional Socialization'. *Australian Social Work*. (26 : 4, Dec. 1973) p. 7-27.

Pathak, S.H. 'Supervision in social work : historical development and current trends.' *Indian Journal of Social Work*. (35 : 4, Jan. 1975) p. 317-23.

Pins, Arnulf M. 'Changes in social work education and their implication for practice'. *Social Work*. (16 : 2, April 1971)

Povlin, Frank. 'Student Unit : The advantages and disadvantages of group placement'. *Australian Journal of Social Work*. (22 : 4, Dec. 1969) p. 10-13.

Rankin, G. 'Supervision and assessments. Science—art—theory on Mumbo-Jumbo'. *Social Work Today*. (5 : 8, 1974) p. 246.

Riches, G. 'Community work placement in social work training'. *Social Work Today*. (2 : 9, July 1971) p. 9-11.

Shapiro, Ben, Lion. 'Mutual helping—A neglected theme in social work practice theory'. *Canadian Journal of Social Work Education*. (3 : 1, April 1977). p. 33-44.

Schwartz, E.E. 'Macro social work : A practice in search of some theory'. *Social Service Review*. (51 : 2, Jan. 1977) p. 208-227.

Social work education and Development Newsletter. (Nov. 1974) p. 11-16.

Souflee, F. and Schmitt, G., 'Educating for practice in Chicago Community', *Journal of Education for Social Work* (10 : 3, fall 1974). p. 75-84.

Stein, Herman D., Social Work's Developmental and change functions : Their roots in practice. *Social Service Review*. Vol. 50, 1976.

Stickland, G. 'Student community work'. *Community Development*

Journal. (12 : 2, April 1977) p. 122-126.

'Student-supervision'. *Social Work Today*. (5 : 11, Sept. 1974). p. 350-51.

Thangavelu, R. 'Field work supervision : Its place in social work education'. *Indian Journal of Social Work*. (35 : 4, Jan. 1975) p. 15.

Tropman, E.J. 'Agency constraints affecting links between practice and education'. *Journal of Education for Social Work*. (13 : 1, Wint. 1977). p. 8-14.

Valentine, Vera, R. 'Who's for field work' *Social Work Today*. (6 : 17, Nov. 1975). p. 552-54.

Vreugdenhil, E. 'Field education and the shy student'. *Australian Social Work*. (29 : 3, Sep. 1976). p. 5-14.

Wilson, Doreen. 'Supervision and assessment'. *Social Work Today*. (6 : 7, Jan. 1975) p. 206-207.

Wijnberg, M.H. Schwartz, M.C. 'Models of student supervision. apprentice growth and role—system models'. *Journal of Education for Social Work*. (13 : 3, Fall 1977). p. 107-113.

REPORTS

Association of Schools of Social Work in India, *Report of the Seminar on Field Work in Social Work Education*. Waltare 1964 ; Workshop on Field Work, Madurai, 1978.

Drucker, David. *Exploration of curricula of social work in some countries of Asia with special reference to the relevance of social work education to social development goals*. Bangkok, United Nations Children's Fund, 1972.

M.S. University of Baroda, faculty of social work. A seminar on supervision, 1958.

United Nations. ECAFE/UNICEF *Seminar on Developmental Aspects of Social Work Training Curricula* Bangkok, 1972. p. 135

DISSERTATIONS

Chowdhary, Poonam, *Field Work in Community Setting : The Reactions and Opinions of Students*. M.Phil dissertation in Social Work submitted to the University of Delhi, 1978.

D'Souza Philomena, *Field Instruction in Social Work Education* Ph.D. thesis submitted to the Tata Institute of Social Sciences, Bombay, 1978.

For an advanced level treatment of field work process in a holistic and critical perspective, the following references should be consulted.

1. Capra Fritjof. *The Tao of Physics* : (Fontana/Collins, 1982).
2. Capra Fritjof. *The Turning Point : Science, Society and the Rising Culture*. Flamingo, 1982.
3. Popper Karl R. *Conjectures and Refutations : The Growth of Scientific Knowledge*. London : Routledge and Kegan Paul, 1963.

APPENDIX-II

LEARNING PATTERNS OF STUDENT WITH SPECIAL REFERENCE TO FIELD INSTRUCTION LEARNING*

The objectives of identifying learning patterns are :

1. To individualize learner and his particular manner of coping with learning and the pace at which he learns.
2. To identify problems he might encounter in the process of learning. Broadly the initial approach to learning is characterised by the following modes :

THE INTELLECTUAL LEARNING MODE

His approach is through the intellect. He is able to identify the problem more clearly by analysis. He needs to identify the whole and then examine its parts. He has to particularise from the general. He has a feeling of security if he can fall back on his reading, analyse and develop a frame of reference which he can utilise for his work. He makes easy connections with theory. He is easily able to assess behaviour of a person, dynamics in a group and social factors. . . . His recordings show ability to be precise about his attempts to portray the client-worker relationship. Because his thinking ability is way beyond his "doing", he feels a sense of frustration and inability to achieve recording to his high expectations of self. Because he achieves well in the class-room and he is somewhat apt to be conscious of his self-image and grade achievement, he feels the frustration of not meeting his own self-expectations.

Intellectual learners tend to be more introspective and self-conscious. They also tend to be more fearful in risking themselves emotionally or eliciting emotional material from their clients. They tend to want more structuring, and therefore, react

**Courtsey* : College of Social Work, Silver Jubilee Year, *Workshop for Social Work Educators*, November 11th-28th, 1980, Bombay.

with frustration when flexibility is required in their response to the field situation. Such a learner is slower to learn in the initial stages. However, as he masters the knowledge area, he becomes more comfortable and begins to risk himself. In the end he may go ahead of the other types of learners when greater integration can take place between the thinking, on the one hand and the feeling and the doing, on the other. Hence, the intellectual learner will initially take much longer in the field than the intuitive worker, but be far ahead of others in the classroom. He requires much help in structuring his learning and he should not be forced beyond the pace he sets for himself. He makes many intellectual demands on the teacher in the field because he wants to clarify the totality of the situation with which he grapples in the field.

The intellectual learner also shows many doubts and raises many queries about practice. While some of these are valid, quite a few result from his own insecurities and inadequacies and his discomfort in facing and working through the presenting problem.

The intellectual learner needs a variety of situations to stimulate his responses and to engage his learning. While he approaches each task with a measure of anxiety, he learns best when faced with situations that provoke his interest and curiosity.

Such a student is very critical of the professional role models with which he is presented in professional practice. While he may admire a good professional model, he will be frustrated if the instructor does not challenge his thinking and stimulate him towards activity. He needs more frequent affirmation from his instructor but at the same time expects critical comments as a way of arousing his challenge and stimulating activity for improving his learning.

He is more preoccupied with the "why" rather than what and how and he needs greater structuring and assistance with the what to do and how to do it.

The intellectual learner, as a practitioner, makes the greatest contribution to social work knowledge. If he remains in the practice situation, he is apt to move into supervisory and administrative positions which give him greater scope for his conceptual abilities. He is also likely to gravitate into teaching.

THE INTUITIVE LEARNING MODE

The intuitive learner's approach in learning is by his natural capacity to work with people and absorb them as through his very pores. He responds immediately to the practical aspects of problem-solving, the responses are usually appropriate, establishes excellent working relationships and appears highly invested in the work. He is less apt to see the situation as a whole, generalises to a limited degree, is less apt to establish cause-effect relationships and to utilise or apply theory at a conscious level. When theory is discussed, it appears as a revelation, or he appears to become bored and disinterested. If he is expected to respond to the theory, he becomes confused and self-conscious, and reports that when he tries to do this consciously in the field, he cannot easily respond to the client, or he claims that it does not work. He uses "self" as a method of work to a larger extent than the intellectual learner who clings to the theory for practice.

Because the intuitive learner works at the feeling level, he is very responsive to clients and evokes their emotions and feeling. He does not necessarily show conscious understanding of this transaction, and so his recordings may not do adequate justice to the quality of his work. Much is learnt through conferences, rather than recordings of student's abilities and achievements.

The instructor must help him to conceptualise so that he begins to appropriate the "why", in his responses. While the intellectual learner is preoccupied by "why" the intuitive learner emphasizes "what needs to be done and does it emphatically. He needs to develop skills to organise his diagnostic thinking, to analyse and to generalise, because such a person uses self as major investment in practice. He is administratively less organized which demands again a more conceptual approach.

He can work in almost any situation and with any type of client. He makes the least emotional demand on the instructor and is often a joy to teach because he does not raise instructor's anxiety about his ability to handle a situation. Such a student also requires very little structure in the setting and can put up with a number of physical limitations in the setting without affecting his work. His responses are apt to be flexible and easily meet the need of a situation.

To enable such a student to conceptualise, he needs to be helped to write diagnostic assessments, summary of several interviews, show session or community related activities, and relate his own role in the process recording. He is apt to make very specific future plans for the client and concretises them. He has to be helped to see the overall goals for the client, the group, the members of the group, or the community. He is much more programme than process oriented as the specificity they provide are more apparent to him than the process. He is less apt to understand the reason behind the programme but perceives mainly the immediate impact of it on the beneficiaries. Because he has less anxiety in initiating relationships and activities, he is apt to get fully involved and do too many things unless the instructor limits the student.

He is apt to respond to instructor in the same feeling way and is likely to get very much involved with him as a model if he finds instructor responding with appreciation to his work. He becomes stilted, anxious and immobilised if instructor makes more intellectual demands to analyse his activity and may deteriorate in the learning.

In the class-room, he applies whatever he is doing to the theory he is learning. He gets stimulated to find theory which applies but gets easily bored when he cannot relate it to his personal experience. Theory for its own sake has less meaning. Such a learner is very active in class when the learning touches these experiences otherwise he is silent and withdrawn (unlike the intellectual learner who has to be fully involved in the class-room to be able to catch hold of something he can begin to use). The intuitive learner is, therefore, less apt to contribute to the discussion and when he does, it is more by way of illustrations and concretising the same situation. Instructors are often puzzled why such students, who are such "naturals" in the field do not take leadership in the class-room. The reason is attributable to the above considerations.

Such persons make an excellent and very effective contribution at the field level but do not add to the knowledge base of the profession, because of their more limited ability to conceptualise. This is very unfortunate because they are apt to be very creative, and if they could translate their actions into thoughts, they could be the major contributors of knowledge.

THE EXPERIENTIAL LEARNING MODE

This student approaches all learning tasks by mastering them through doing. He is the trial and error learner. He has to break down activity into minute manageable parts. He is the slowest of all three learners because of his learning pattern. He is also the least creative. He makes emotional demands on the instructor, who has to almost carry him through the initial experience, and he is therefore, apt to be less rewarding than the other two types of learners. He is apt to be very diffident, needs considerable structure and support, and must be helped to organize his thinking, feeling and doing. He usually has very little self-confidence and appears to lack a positive self-image or defends himself by an unrealistic self-image. If he has had a previous protected experience, especially in the case of Indian women students, it increases the anxiety of approaching tasks and new situations. The student requires considerable support and assurance for the instructor and can learn best from one who is warmly empathic, puts less stress on minutes of activity but helps student, instead, grasp broad essentials in learning. Such student does get threatened at the success of other students in the placement and this further acts to lower the self-image.

Recordings of these students are apt to focus mainly on the "doing". They are less apt to show either feeling or thinking. In fact, such a learner is less apt to risk feeling till he is more comfortable in the doing. He shows little intellectual perception of process or interaction, has few comments on assessment, and plans for further work tend to be mainly in the tangible areas of activity. Such a learner is less creative than the intuitive learner, and his activities tend to have a stereotyped quality as he creates and recreates a familiar situation for mastery of the task.

The experiential learner only learns "after the facts". After a disastrous situation, he is more apt to be clear of what he could have done. He has difficulty in handling clients who show personality problems such as those who are hostile or aggressive. He may respond more easily to clients who are dependent, and, therefore, he can focus on the doing aspects with them. They please his self-image by giving him a measure of success in accomplishing some action.

The instructor has to focus on the "why" and the "what" as this student is, otherwise, only preoccupied with the "how". He wants, like the intellectual learner, assistance with skills—how shall I do it—but unlike the intellectual learner, who can pose all the alternatives, and needs help with selecting the appropriate strategy, he needs to be stimulated first to think of all the possible strategies. This learner requires several similar rather than dissimilar situations (unlike the intellectual learner) to learn from, and a great deal of reinforcement in learning. Such a learner requires a non-threatening, less critical but more supportive relationship from the supervisor in order to be able to act constructively or else he will quickly withdraw from the learning situation by isolating a few activities, and finding protection through repetitive doing. He is a very constricted learner, and freedom to grow can be nurtured only with tremendous support and investment of the instructor. Since what the student accomplishes in relation to instructor's investment is very limited, such a student tends to be the least gratifying to the instructor. Therefore, the instructor must be alert to her own feelings, and handle these in the interest of the student as a learner.

This student makes least contribution to knowledge or practice. He safeguards himself by finding a niche where activity is routinised, and the agency is also such which feels comfortable with such a person, who is least likely to threaten its status quo and does activities which no one in that organisation particularly w shes to do on a day-to-day basis.

APPENDIX-III

STUDENT YOUTH IN ADULT EDUCATION : AN INTERFACE BETWEEN PROFESSIONALS AND VOLUNTEER GROUPS*

RAJSHREE MAHTANI
&
HUTOKSHI PATEL

This case record attempts to present an example of social work intervention in an unstructured setting in terms of placement of students, where the interventional process is viewed in a developmental perspective, and where the various principles and methods of social work are brought into play in an integrated manner depending on the objective conditions of the field work setting.

INITIAL PLAN FOR WORK

Two women MSW Part II students (one of whom had a Bachelors degree in Social Work) in a 'floating placement', where in collaboration with the NSS Unit of the University of Bombay, they would be involved in initiating the National Adult Education Programme (NAEP) in slum communities. The specific role(s) that the student social workers would play evolved out of a series of discussions held with the Programme Officer of the NSS unit, who collaborated as a co-worker. The field instructor who is also a faculty member of the College of Social Work, was at this stage, as well as later, more of a consultant.

The student social workers were to undertake multifarious tasks : to identify, recruit and guide the NSS students in the process of implementing the NAEP. In addition, the students

* Edited in consultation with the students by Dominic D' Souza, Field Instructor, College of Social Work, Nirmala Niketan, Bombay. (1977-1978).

decided that they would need to work with the administrative set-up of the NSS Unit and with the slum communities, where the NAEP was to be implemented.

There were several reasons for the choice of the field work placement. Firstly, student youth were recognised as being potential change agents. Secondly, the NAEP was viewed as a possibility of a novel entry point into a slum community where social work practice might contribute to development.

The specific objectives drawn up for working in the field work placement were :

1. To widen the knowledge and awareness of NSS students with regard to the living conditions of the lower economic groups - especially of slum-dwellers.
2. To develop sensitivity among NSS students towards the poor and deprived sections of society.
3. To enable NSS students to initiate, support and participate with the slum dwellers in the process of reflective discussions while conducting NAEP classes.
4. To plan and implement NAEP classes in the slum communities so that these classes benefit both the learners as well as NSS students.

CONTACT WITH VARIOUS COLLEGES

It was felt that since NAEP would require instructors who were hard working and dedicated, important consideration needed to be given to the recruiting of NSS students. Accordingly, various colleges were contacted, and the student social workers had formal as well as informal discussions with NSS students. Eventually, 14 NSS students were chosen from one college to conduct a survey of the slum communities to obtain the number of illiterates.

"When we started contacting students, we learnt how to deal with different types of student volunteers and professors-in-charge. We had to interpret our role to the professors-in-charge as well as to student volunteers, and build working relationships with them. We dealt with volunteers as a group and utilising group work skills we made attempts to facilitate volunteers to share their ideas and feelings in the group. Also as the students came from two different colleges, they were helped to accept and work with each other. We tried to accept their limitations in working with poverty groups and emphathised with their fear of entering a slum community for the first time."

Thus, the specific tasks, carried out were, firstly, preparing NSS students for conducting the survey, and simultaneously, in developing their understanding of slums, and inclulcating appropriate attitudes towards slum dwellers. The student social workers also had to work with the college professors-in-charge of NSS.

CONDUCTING THE SURVEY

The objective of the survey was two-fold. Firstly, it was to obtain the number of illiterates in two slums, who wished to become literate. Secondly, it was felt that NSS students should carry out the survey, as it would immediately bring them into contact with slum dwellers and their living conditions. Most of the NSS students, especially the first year students, had never been in a slum before. The questionnaire for the survey was prepared by the student social workers. The survey took about 4-5 weeks, after which the data were tabulated and analysed with the help of NSS students. On the basis of data, tentative groups for attending classes were formed. Thus, the NSS students were exposed to some basic research skills as well as oriented to function as instructors through a number of practical sessions.

"We had to deal with individual NSS students, which called for sharpened casework skills. For example, during the orientation sessions, we had to discuss the difficulties of each student. By professing support, and using reflective discussion we helped them to overcome some of the difficulties and anticipate some of the situations that they were likely to encounter in the slum communities. Besides, we discussed the problems of slum itself - the origin of slums etc. This was done so that students could visualise their activity in a larger context."

SETTING UP NAEP CLASSES

The actual classes were set-up in November. The long gap was due to NSS students terminal examinations and then, a rural camp. While organising classes, it was discovered that the slum dwellers were not enthusiastic to attend classes. This response was contrary to the survey, which revealed that they were reasonably eager to attend classes. Therefore, the emphasis of the student social workers now shifted to the community, and their major tasks centred around finding out reasons behind slum dwellers' reluctance and attempting to overcome it. Various individual and group contacts were made, and the skills of community work were utilised. Conscious attempt was made to involve leaders of the slum communities. This process was beneficial and by the first week of December, two of the classes had started. By the first week of January there were a total of 5 classes, with about 15 learners in each.

CONDUCTING THE NAEP CLASSES

Two NSS students were responsible for one class of 15 learners. The dynamics of each class was unique, and contributed to learning experience of NSS students as instructors. They learnt to deal with drop-outs, slow learners etc. Additionally, regular meetings were held of all (14) NSS students, where they could share their varied experiences, and contribute to each others' learning. A major problem faced here was that the learners were more comfortable while using the conventional method of teaching-learning than the method for NAEP classes. Therefore, the classes were conducted according to the method the learners found easy.

TERMINAL STAGE

Termination of work occurred by the end of February. Here the tasks of the student social workers were two fold : firstly, to terminate the social work activity with NSS students, and secondly to guide NSS students in terminating their activity with slum dwellers.

The social workers terminated their activities with the two slum communities in the second week of March. Prior to this, the NSS students were involved in planning the follow-up programme for learners. Some persons from the communities who had undergone formal education, and were willing to be instructors were identified and oriented to conduct the NAEP classes. It was decided that these instructors would continue till July, after which a new batch of NSS students would take over as instructors of the NAEP classes.

AN EVALUATION

"The activities of this academic year have brought into focus two major points. Firstly, these have emphasised the need to work with NSS students on a much more extended level than just programme implementation. Secondly, and perhaps more important, these have brought to light that while literacy is not the primary perceived need of an average slum dweller, there has to be great in-puts in developing motivation to see the utility of literacy in their daily life in a city."

"These activities have also brought to focus that there is a great deal of scope in utilising the knowledge, skills and attitudes of social work profession."

"Social workers are increasingly placing reliance on developmental approach to social work. This placement gave an excellent opportunity to practise this approach. We related with college students, who essentially had healthy personalities. Our discussion with them made them view the reality situation, especially the poverty conditions and social problems that exist in India with special reference to slum communities. Based on this analysis, we helped them to draw up a plan of work : what and how they would teach learners in the slum communities. Hence, we attempted to create self-awareness as well as made them more aware of the reality outside them. It is our hope that the learners from the slum communities, with the help of the NAEP classes, will be able to understand better the why of what is happening around them and hence, may be able to think and work out ways of handling the problems that they face."

"This placement demanded not only skills for creating self-awareness but also the knowledge and skills required to work in a community. This being the first experience in community work, we benefitted very much. We were able to apply a good deal of theory especially from community work lectures to the field situation. We had to study the community in terms of its geographical, political and socio-economic background. We also realised that we had to be careful not to antagonise any of the leaders and not to take sides with local political parties especially in the initial stage of contacting people in the slum communities. Community dynamics is now better understood by us."

"Hence, this placement has given us very varied experience and has contributed very much to our learning as compared to our earlier experiences, when we were placed in a higly structured setting."

APPENDIX-IV

SEQUENTIAL ARRANGEMENT OF FIELD WORK EXPERIENCES

(Continuity, Sequence and Integration)

BSW Part-I	BSW Part-II	BSW Part-III	MSW Part-I	BMSW Part-I MSW Part-II	BMSW Part-II
(1)	(2)	(3)	(4)	(5)	(6)
		I. ORIENTATION VISITS			
I. Visits related to developmental programmes, that is, projects in communities, in schools and community health programmes.	I. Visits related to social welfare porammes (e.g. correctional, institutional, rehabilitaton programmes).	I. Visits related to area of problem analysis selected (child, health, communities) and to understand the tasks and functions of social workers and policy and programmes in the area of problem selected.	I. Visits related to programmes of social development/ welfare and to develop understanding of the tasks and functions of professional social workers.	Not required.	Not required.

Courtesy : College of Social Work (Affiliated to the University of Bombay). Nirmala Niketan, 38, New Marine Lines Bombay-400 020.

APPENDIX-IV : (*Contd.*)

(1)	(2)	(3)	(4)	(5)	(6)
		II. PLACEMENT			
II. Placed in an agency with a group of 3 to 6 students (all BSW) to carry out tasks jointly through mutual support.	II. Placee in an agency to undertake individual assignments requiring use of rudimentary social work process/skills as well as shared tasks in the social work team at various levels (BSW I, II, III, MSW I, II).	II. Placed in an agency related to problem area selected (child, health, community) by the students, and where tasks in the team can offer opportunity to use all methods of practice integratively and to provide leadership role.	II. Placed in an agency to undertake individual assignments requiring use of rudimentary social work process/skills as well as to work in shared tasks in the social work team. (Combine elements of BSW II and III).	II. Placed in an agency to undertake individual assignments requiring use of more advanced social work process/skills and where possible, undertake leadership functions.	II. Placed in an agency or to work around a problem area. The latter may involve work in a specific area with several agencies, or work without agency auspices e.g. youth from different communities.
		III. AGENCY, CLIENT SYSTEM AND TASKS			
III. Provide understanding of the nature of the client system and the relationship of services to identified needs. How	III. Provide understanding of the client system and the relationship of social work services to needs. Study working of a	III. Provide understanding of the client system and the relationship of the selective use of methods of social work intervention	III. Provide understanding of the client system and the relationship of social work services to needs.	III. Provide understanding of the client system and the relationship of selective use of methods of social work intervention	III. While instructor initiates discussion the student undertakes self-responsibility in the exploration

agency is perceived by the client system and relationships with it.	project. Make suggestions.	in solving identified problems in, and the client system.		in solving identified problems in, and of the client system.	and understanding of the client system of the agency, and identifying the agency tasks in relation to client system.

IV. ASSIGNMENT OF TASKS

IV. Assign projects which utilise the students' past experience and the application of beginning new knowledge related to programmes e.g. organisation of sports or picnics for low income, socially deprived children, survey for organising an	IV. Assign tasks to develop rudimentary skills in social work, emphasis on process of work with people-individuals/families, groups, projects/ tasks in communities which involve organisation of people/people's involvement in problem-solving.	IV. Identify problem (s) of client system with which the student will be specifically engaged, and work out tasks around it (them) which gives students the opportunity to utilise the various modes of intervention in social work and begin to	IV. Assign tasks to develop rudimentary skills in social work, emphasis on process of work with people-individuals/families, groups projects/ tasks in communities which involve organisation of people/people's involvement in problem-solving.	IV. Identify problem (s) of client system with which the student will be specifically engaged, and work out tasks around it (them) which gives students the opportunity to utilise the various modes of intervention in social work and demons-	IV. In the process of developing understanding of agency tasks, student locates specific assignments for self and works out plan of work with instructor. Alternatively, the student may begin exploration to set up a new

APPENDIX-IV : (*Contd.*)

(1)	(2)	(3)	(4)	(5)	(6)
immunisation or nutrition programme.	Tasks must be problem/need focussed. The persons must be victims of their circumstances but otherwise show normal ego development.	demonstrate through practice the need for an integrated practice approach to problem—solving. Enable client system in identifying, utilising and developing resources.	Tasks must be problem/necd focussed. The persons must be victims of their circumstances but otherwise show normal ego development.	trate through practice the need for an integrated approach to problem—solving.	project/further develop a project in the agency or one which is outside agency auspices or one involving several agencies. Assignment should have a component of a special contribution to the agency.
V. NATURE OF SOCIAL WORK PROCESS					
V. Begin the development of social work process : making contacts, initiating activity, planning, programming, team work, utilising resources, interviewing,	V. Work should be specifically related to learning to initiate and carry out a task with the client system, study the facts around problem/needs, assess from facts, identify focus of	V. Work should be specifically related to learning to carry out a task with the client system, study the facts around the problem/need, assess from facts, identify focus of	V. Work should be specifically related to learning to carry out a task with the client system, study the facts around the problem/need, assess from facts, identify focus of work, develop a	V. The focus of work is on action in interpersonal, inter-group processes requiring considerable knowledge and skills to initiate and achieve change at individual/family/	V. Increase skills in process (clinical/developmental) in working with people beyond those expected at the level of MSWII. Student should show utilisation

short term task-oriented group (e.g. preparing for sports), use of simple programme media, home visit . . . . (e.g. for a survey or to obtain client/clients participation) : exposure to community from which client system served, use of resources, fund raising, evaluation of activity. In the 2nd term, movement towards undertaking some individual tasks should be faciliat-ed. Tasks to be assigned around programme skill early childhood development programmes (creche, balwadi, first and second	work, develop a contact for work, utilise simple problem—solving skills (exploration, ventilation, logical discussion, programme media organisation around a specified task), evaluation of programmes.	work, develop a contract for work, utilise simple problem—solving skills (exploration, ventilation, logical discussion, programme media organisation around a specific task), evaluation of programme. Utilise task to show integrated approach to problem—solving in the agency.	contract for work, utilising simple problem—solving skills (exploration, logical discussion, programme media, organisation around a specific task), evaluation of programme, Utilise task to show integrated approach to problem—solving in the agency.	group/community orgnisational level. Student may begin to use theories such as those related to behaviour, communication, society, organisations, to explain observed phenomena in assigned tasks and to plan the course of action. Tasks assigned should provide opportunity to relate to micro-level, and view self as a change agent.	of knowledge from the areas of social and behavioural sciences and social work praetice to analyse tasks and related action plan to the analysis. Provide opportunity to relate practice from micro to macro level, and push experiences of work in the wider context. Problem—solving should be viewed in a holistic framework.

APPENDIX-IV : (*Contd.*)

(1)	(2)	(3)	(4)	(5)	(6)
year or primary school). —nutrition (education and development of an applied nutriton programme). —non-formal education (school drop-outs, adolescents, youth, women, men). —recreation. In the above tasks, teach work with a family around simple tasks identified e.g. health of a balwadi child requiring medical referral ; about the group through the dynamics around task-					

oriented groups or recreational groups ; about community related tasks.					

VI. TEAM WORK

VI. Learn to work in a social work team at the level of a paraprofessional.	VI. Work in a social team and initiate beginning contacts with other professions to elicit information or give information (e.g. doctors, teachers).	VI. Work in an inter-disciplinary team using consultation giving information/consultation,) and playing the advocacy role for the client system or interpreting the system to improve service delivery.	VI. Work in an inter-disciplinary team to elicit information or give information (e.g. doctors, teachers) and work in team of social workers.	VI. Provide leadership in the professional team and play consultative role to other disciplines as well as utilise other disciplines for own development.	VI. Provide leadership in the professional team, play consultative role, initiate use of consultation from (within) agency and from outside resources, for the members of the team, play advocacy role on behalf of the client system to improve the service.

APPENDIX-IV : (*Contd.*)

(1)	(2)	(3)	(4)	(5)	(6)
		VII. ADMINISTRATIVE ASSIGNMENTS			
VII. Around tasks learn to keep reports, statistics.	VII. Learn to maintain simple service statistics of agency, plan and programme with others.	VII. Provide opportunity to undertake administrative tasks such as planning, programming, development of simple policies around tasks undertaken, maintenance of service statistics, ledgers, accounts, correspondence and report especially some opportunity to survey/evaluate a specific scheme in the agency utilising a simple tool such as a questionnaire, or a form, and write a simple report. Provide opportunity to supervise	VII. Learn to plan and programme in a team with others, maintain service statistics, ledgers, accounts, correspondence, simple reports.	VII. Administrative tasks should be in relation to the needs of the client system, the strategies, goals, policies, writing agenda and minutes, writing reports. Undertake evaluative studies on projects, analyse agency data prepare reviews, work out proposals for funding specific projets. Provide opportunity to plan and conduct meeting.	VII. Undertakes tasks related to policy planning, organisation, administration. These tasks should involve considerable analysis and cognitive thinking, the development of appropriate strategies/programmes, and administration of the activity initiated. The responsibilities undertaken should include the work of others and not only own tasks.

		staff at para-professional level, or such workers as balsevikas or support staff. Provide leadership to the team. Provide opportunity to plan and conduct meetings.			(Accountability for those placed under him/her). Provide opport-unity for super-vision e.g. BSW I/II students, NSS volunteers, other groups of youth, women, etc. Exercise skills related to supervision.

VIII. RECORDING

VIII. Simple reporting of facts especially in the first term. In the second term, the student should also begin to identify his cwn role and give some impressions of his observations in the light of class-room	VIII. Process of activity should emerge rather than only reporting of facts. Student should be also eliciting facts around a problem and hence show some ability to organise these facts in relation to assessment and	VIII. Process of work and dynamics of interaction within a system/sub-system should be evident. Worker/client system res-ponses, and activity of workers in enhancing objectives of work with the system	VIII. In the beginning there will be simple reporting of facts. By the end of the fist term, some process should emerge.	VIII. Analytical in style, selective in facts, brief.	VIII. Analytical selective administrative record, teaching record.

APPENDIX-IV : (*Contd.*)

(1)	(2)	(3)	(4)	(5)	(6)
learning.	the identification of problem for work.	should be evident.			
		IX. FIELD INSTRUCTION			
IX. Instruction is intially in groups though recording is individual and corrected weekly. In the Second term, individual conferences, around student tasks, should be planned, along with group conferences.	IX. Instruction should be a combination of both individual and group. As responabilities are increasingly individual, it is necessary to provide instruction around such individual tasks.	IX. Instruction should be a combination of both individual and group, preferably, alternate weeks of individual/group instruction	IX. Combination of individual and group but there may be greater need for individual in the beginning weeks of placement due to assignment of individual tasks before much theory learning has taken place in the class.	IX. Instruction : Combination of individual and group alternately.	Ix. Instruction : Group related, where appropriate, and use of field instructor as consultant.

APPENDIX-V

DEVELOPMENT OF A PROFESSION: FIELD-INSTRUTION CORRELATES*.

JACK ROTHMAN

This article discusses field instruction in social work with reference to the development and maturation of professions. The premise is that professions go through phases as they develop starting with heavy reliance on the field for practice skills acquisition, proceeding to an equal sharing between the field and the University, and culminating in the assumption of major responsibility by the University. It is suggested that social work is in the middle phase. Professional maturation will require increased responsibility by schools of social work for the transmission of the skills of practice to students.

I would hypothesize that social work may be located in the middle stage because of a heavy and even disproportionate weighting of time and energy given to application considerations. Professional maturation would lie in shifting the balance of class and field to new balance that would also include class and field but with a heavier weighting on the academic knowledge side.

I believe further that increased responsibility by our professional schools for teaching professional application skills and strengthening and concretizing the academic or theoretical aspect of such training will contribute to the projection of the profession into a more advanced stage of development.

ROLE STRAIN IN AGENCY FIELD INSTRUCTORS

Berelson points out that a tension exists between a professional

An extract from Social Service Review (June 1977)

outlook or conception and an academic conception[30]. The distinction between the two he outlines thus:

Professional Conceptions		Academic Conception's
Training	as against	Education
Development of skills	as against	Development of wisdom
Development of depth	as against	Development of breadth
Specialist	as against	Cultivated man
Techical expert	as against	Scholar-Teacher

Teachers in professional schools face these divergent pulls all the time, but the interplay must be strongest in the operating field situation. Berelson's findings imply that teachers in the professional schools resolve the dilemma by coming down the academic side. Other professions that provide practice experiences for students find this tension existing in quite the same way social work does.

The commonly held assumption is that field work provides an opportunity to apply the theory learned in the classroom to actual situations and real problems. Logically, there are four possible relationships between class and field:

1. Class and field integrate: The students has an opportunity to try out theory in practice in a direct and systematic way.

2. Class and field supplement each other: The two are different but they reinforce each other in providing what the student needs to engage in the practice of the profession. The classroom, for its domain, provides general theory, and the field, in its sphere, offers specific skills and develops professional self-discipline.

3 Class and field are unrelated: The two give different things to the student. One may concentrate on preparing the the student to be a practitioner, while the other may be irrelevant to that task. Thus the classroom may be providing theory that is so broad and general or so out of touch with the realities of the world of practice that it serves no purpose in educating students. Or the field situation may be so limited and restricted by the immediate problems, methods, or goals of specific agencies that it does not provide the grounding for emerging problems or methods that the student will encounter

as he progresses in his professional career.

4. Class and field are in conflict: In this circumstance, not only does the student learn different things in the class and field, but these things are at odds with one another. Thus he might learn in the classroom that behaviour modification is the most efficacious treatment method and in the field that only ego therapy is acceptable practice. The student is given discrepant information and antagonistic orientations.

"Application training" implies a broader teaching technology than has been typically associated with "field instruction" in social work.

GREATER DIRECTION AND CONTROL BY THE SCHOOL OF THE EDUCATIONAL EXPERIENCE FOR TEACHING APPLICATION SKILLS :

This implies increased faculty involvement in teaching skills and relating such skills to conceptual and theoretical constructs. Class-room faculty during part of the application training programme should structure tasks and exercises, monitor them, conduct seminars and other educational experiences, and in other ways become more closely indentified with the process of teaching application skills. Through greater faculty participation, integration may more readily be achieved and new knowledge relative to practice conveyed to students in a more direct way. In this way, faculty are also kept current with new developments in practice. Further, the essential responsibility of the school for the total education of the student, including practice skills, is made manifest in this proposition.

APPENDIX-VI

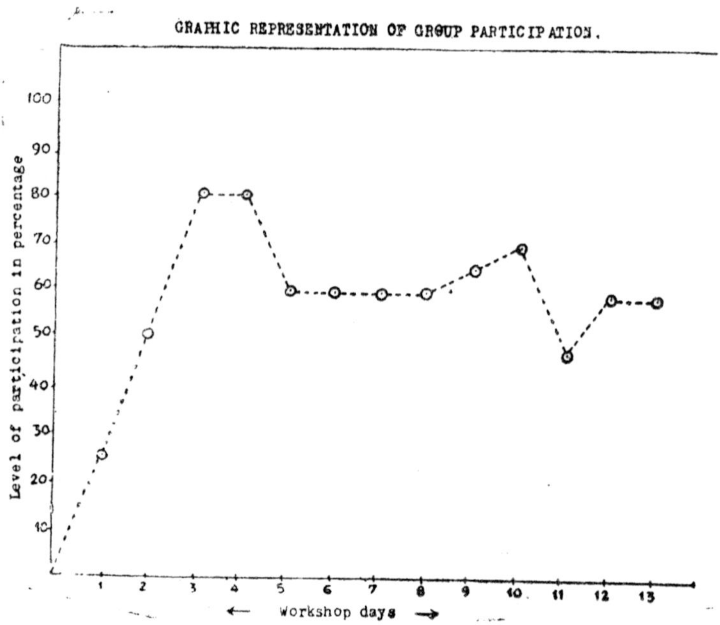

Note : The sublects discussed :

1st day : Review of field work at different levels.

2st day : Plenary session on organisation and administration of field work.

3rd day : Plenary and sub-group discussion on content of field work.

4th day : Plenary and sub-group discussion on selection of agencies and placement of students.

5th day : Plenary and sub-group discussion on supervision.

6th day : Plenary and sub-group discussion on evaluation.

7th day : Sub-group discussion on evaluation and review session.

8th day : Plenary and sub-group discussion on field work record.

9th day : Plenary session on block placement.

10th day : Plenary session on New Areas of Field Work.

11th day : Observation visit and fim show-sub-group discussion on evaluation.

12th day : Plenary session on measures to strengthen field work and sub-group discussion on evaluation.

13th day : Reports on evaluation, BSW and concluding session.

Approximate reallocation of time for different areas of field work at the faculty development workshop, March 16, 1981-March 29, 1981.

Sl. No.	Areas	Allotted time (Hrs.)		Revised allotment of time (Hrs.)
1.	Review of field work	3.00		3.00
2.	Review of field work at different levels and proeedure of the workshop	3.00		3.00
3.	Organisation and administration	3.30		5.15
4.	Content of field work	6.30		7.15
5.	Selection of agencies	2.45	5.15	7.05
6.	Placement of students	3.30		
7.	Supervision	6.15		9.30
8.	Evaluation	6.15		9.30
9.	Review session	6.30		2.00
10.	Field work record	6.15		9.30
11.	Block placement	3.30		2.00
12.	Staff development	2.45		2.00
13.	New areas of field work practice	3.30		4.00
14.	Developmental field work	2.45		2.45
15.	Evaluation of workshop by groups	—		3.15
16.	Agency visit	6.30		3.00
17.	Measure to strengthen field work	3.30		3.00
18.	Review session	2.45		2.00
19.	Presentation of reports/recommendations and paper on developmental perspective	3.30		4.00
	Total	73.35		81.25

Note : (i) Drafting of Plenary/Sub-group reports etc. was done by the participants before or after working hours.

(ii) March 21, 1981 was a holiday.

(iii) Total time spent on registration, inaugural and concluding sessions was 3 hours and 30 minutes.

(iv) Average work hours for thirteen days comes to six hours per day according to the old schedule, and 6 hours and 30 minutes per day according to the revised schedule.

(v) Areas of field work, that is, supervision. evaluation, field work records. content and organisation and administration consumed maximum time (nearly fifty per cent) in that order of priority.

APPENDIX-VIII

PROFILE OF PARTICIPANTS

Total number of schools/faculty of social work participating in the workshop 27

Total number of participants from the schools/faculty of social work 35

TABLE 1 : **Distributions of participants by sex and level of field work responsibilities shouldered by them**

Sex	Undergraduates	Nature of supervision postgraduates	Both	N.R./N.A.	Total
Male	1	16	3	2	21 (60%) (61.11%)
Female	3	9	2	—	14 (40.00%)
Total	3 (8.57%)	25 (71.43%)	5 (14.28%)	2 (5.71%)	35

TABLE 2 : **Distribution of participants by sex and teaching experience**

Sex	Teaching Experience					
	Upto 5 yrs.	5-10 yrs.	10-15 yrs.	15-20 yrs.	N.R.	Total
Male	13	3	3	2	1	21 (60%)
Female	5	4	2	1	2	14 (40%)
Total	18 (51.43%)	7 (20.00%)	5 (14.28%)	3 (8.57%)	3 (5.71%)	35

TABLE 3 : **Distribution of participants by their age and sex**

Sex	Age Upto 25 yrs.	25+—35 yrs.	35+—45 yrs.	45+—55 yrs.	Total
Male	2	14	3	2	21 (60%)
Female	2	5	4	3	14 (40%)
Total	4 (11.43%)	20 (54.28%)	7 (20.00%)	5 (14.28%)	35

TABLE 4 : **Distribution of participants by sex and educational qualification**

Sex	Educational Qualification M.A. (S.W.)/ Sociology	M. Phil	Dip. S.S.A.	M.A.+Dip. S.S.A.	Ph. D.	Total
Male	14	2		2	3	21 (60%)
Female	8	1	1	4		14 (40%)
Total	22 (62.86%)	3 (8.57%)	21 (2.86%)	6 (17 14%)	3 (8.57%)	35

TABLE 5 : **Distribution of participants supervising undergraduate students by area of practice**

Duration of supervising undergraduates	Area of practice						
	Labour welfare	Correctional administration	Social work education	Adult education/school social work	Case work/group work	Family and child welfare	Total
2+—4 years	1	—	1	—	—	—	2
4+—6 years	—	—	—	1	—	1	2
6+—8 years	—	1	1	—	—	—	2
8+—Above	—	—	1	—	—	—	1
No response	—	—		—	1	—	2
Total	1	1	3	1	1	1	9

TABLE 6 : **Details of participants supervising post-graduate students by area of practice**

Duration of supervising post-graduate	Area of practice: Community organisation community development	Labour welfare industrial relations	Personnel/ administration/ community development	Correctional administration	Medical/ psychiatric social work	Tribal welfare	Family and child welfare	Unspecified	Total
Upto 3 yrs.	5	2	1	—	3	1	—	1	13
3+—6 yrs.	1	1	—	—	—	1	1	—	4
6+—9 yrs.	—	1	—	2	—	—	—	—	3
9+—12 yrs.	2	—	—	—	—	—	—	—	2
12+—Above	1	—	—	—	—	—	—	—	1
No Response	—	—	1	—	2	—	—	4	7
Total	9	4	2	2	5	2	1	5	30

APPENDIX-IX

SUPERVISION : GUIDELINES FOR DISCUSSION

I Concept of Supervision and the role of the supervisor in relation to :

Phases in field work

(a) Orientation	Role of the supervisor in relation to
(b) Induction	
(c) Implementation	each of these
(d) Evaluation	

2 *Specific educational experiences* :

	Specific objectives of each
(a) Camps	
	activity and mutual expectation of student
(b) Field work	
	and supervisors
(c) Evaluation	
	Behavioural outcome specification

II Objectives of supervision

General objectives

Objectives in relation to field work curriculum specified at each year and each level of learning, eg., BSW I, II, and III; MSW I and II

Specific objectives

a. Specific objectives in relation to field/agency
b. Objectives in relation to the student-emphasising more the learner than the work done by him.

Areas of supervision

2. (a) Core skills, e.g. observation, interviewing, relationship, recording, administrative, procedurs. etc.

(b) Specific skills, work with individuals, groups and communities.

(c) *Development of professional attitudes*
Use of field supervision

III Methods of supervision

Making an educational contract with students.

Individual conferences. Its objectives and methodology preparation for conference. Use of recording. Discussion on issues emerging from recording. Dealing with the feeling aspect of students.

Group conferences :
Objective and methodology. Preparation for group conferences. Use of group dynamics. Encouraging peer group learning.

Observation of student at work
Explaining and discussing the process with the student. observation vs spying.

Through role modelling and demonstration
Behaviour of the supervisor in the agency-relationship with agency personnel, communication skills etc. teaching by doing.

Field work seminars
Objectives,methodology. Role of the supervisor. Guidelines for discussion.

A. **Problems in supervision**

1. *Agency constraints* :
Lack of physical amenities, attitude of agency towards supervision, interference of agency

2. *Different types of learners* :
Differential background and experiences of students and types of learners. Impact of these factors on

learning

3. *Relationship-psychological process*
   Importance of relationship-how to build it. Positive relationship. How to utilise such a relationship for learning?
   Negative relationship. How to diagnose it and reduce it or eliminate it altogether? Possibility of transferring student to another supervisor; the process involved in this.

B. *The supervisory process*
   The three phases and the role of the supervisor in relation to each phase.

C. *Preparation in relation to Traditional Field Work and Developmental Field Work.*
D. Development of teaching records-conducting research.
C. Use of authority by the supervisor
D. i. Supervision in the context of three methods of social work
   ii. Different settings
   iii. Integrated methods

APPENDIX-X

FACULTY DEVELOPMENT WORKSHOP ON FIELD WORK GUIDELINES FOR DISCUSSION

Review of field work at different levels

Field work in social work education with special reference to traditional and developmental perspectives; Field work programme at the under-graduate, post-graduate levels—the rationale; organisation and practice; objectives of social work education and field work, field work in different semesters : whether concurrent or block? why? ; duration per week—basis? ; problems in field work and how they are being met?

(Plenary session I ; Group sessions; participants to meet in two groups: one for under-graduate level ; the other for post-graduate level.)

Organisation and administration

How is field work co-ordinated? Is it left to individual supervisors/Field Work Co-ordinator/Director/Head of the Department? ; How is co-ordination achieved? : Field work department as administrative sub-unit/considerations in the organisation of field work programme ; co-ordination of programmes of similar agencies in a particular area (medical, correctional etc.) for equalising field work opportunities to the extent possible; establishment of own agencies by schools.

(Plenary session II ; Group session II : two groups—one for under-graduate and the other for post-graduate levels.)

Content of field work

Present emphasis at the under-graduate, and post-graduate levels ; traditional and developmental approaches - content of field work in different agencies/areas and in different semesters - the rarionale, identification of objectives and tasks ; linkage between under-graduate and post-graduate levels;

(Plenary Session III : Group Session III.)

Selection of agencies

Existing practice; problems in the selection of agencies; development of criteria for the selection of agencies to strengthen field work; ways to establish closer agency - school contacts; Concept of agency as limitation for social work practice.
(Plenary session IV Group session IV).

Placement of students

Rationale for concurrent placement ; Rationale for placing students in different agencies/criteria of placement; term-wise placement change? ; Desirability or otherwise of 'one year - one-agency' placement ; placement of students in unserviced areas for community work - why? : problems - the educable/non-educable students, admission policy etc.
(Plenary Session V; Group Session V).

Supervision

Existing practice : weekly time devoted for reports, individual and group conferences ; considerations governing these ; supervision as teaching, helping and administrative process ; what is looked for in the learner in assessing progression/regression in field work? ; school-agency supervisor relationship ; focus of conferences ; agency visits- periodicity with reasons ; field work connected teaching/assignments including seminars/surveys ; impact on field work of teacher's orientation ; mode of determining field work tasks in community setting/agency setting ; learning theory ; learning process - motivation of students ; supervisor-supervisee relationship - positive/negative ; participant role of the supervisor ; Co-ordination of resources for effective student performance ; preparedness of the supervisor ; problems in supervision - social accountability, fostering attitudes, field work environment in the school ; the problem trainee; differential expectations, supervisory role model ; dependency ; need for variety in field work experiences; progression in learning - How? ; Supervisee as substitute staff; innovations in supervision.
(Plenary Session VI ; Group Session VI).

Evaluation

Content of evaluation - learning centred/target or task centred, or both and how? ; evaluation in structured and unstructured setting ; pros and cons of existing practices ; difficulties of supervisors ; complaints of students ; differences between supervisor - supervisee expectations; evaluation versus appeasement.

(Plenary Session VII; Group Session VI)

Review Session: Plenary Session VIII

Field work record

Expectations in recording - semester-wise; different types of recording ; casework, group work, community work recording - content, format etc ; recording in integrated social work practice; structured/unstructured settings and records ; problems in recording.

(Plenary Sessions IX; Group Session VIII)

Block placement

Objectives; expectations; arrangements; type of guidance; ways to make block placement more meaningful.

(Plenary session X)

Staff development

Existing programmes ; orientation ; actual placement and documentation (reflective) of experience; effective ways for staff development; interlinkage between theory and practice.

(Plenary session XI).

New areas of field work practice/placement:

Review of experiences in unconventional areas - Chipko movement; dairy development corporation, school-community relations.

(Plenary Session XII).

Developmental field work

Meaning of integrated approach to field situation ; client organisations; "oppositional" practice; political component of field work and social work roles: selection of target groups (weaker sections) ; examination of policies, programmes and their impact;

application of social work skills and acquisition of new skills; influence of agency orientation and structure on field work practice-based on a case of child guidance centre; problem of status quo vs. change through the auspicies of the school ; etc. research component of field work ; interlinkage between theory and practice—how?

(Plenary session XIII ; Group session - X).

Preparation of reports by rapporteurs.

Measures to strengthen field work

Problems in different areas and ways to meet them; Periodic review of supervision, programme content, opportunity offered by the agency and its inclusion or otherwise for field work placement; need for collective thinking by staff.

(Plenary Session : XIV).

Review session : Plenary XV.

Concluding session

Presentation of reports of the plenary group sessions, and valedictory function.

APPENDIX-XI

SCHEDULE OF WORKSHOP

PROGRAMME-SCHEDULE

Monday, 16th March, 1981	Introduction to the workshop and presentation of background paper discussion Review of field work at different levels
Tuesday, 17th March, 1981	Organisation and administration
Wednesday, 18th March, 1981	Content of field work Selection of agencies and placement of students
Thursday, 19th March, 1981	Selection of field (agencies) & placement of students
Friday, 20th March, 1981	Supervision Coffee-break
Sunday, 22nd March, 1981	Evaluation
Monday, 23rd March, 1981	Evaluation
Tuesday, 24th March, 1981	Field work record
Wednesday, 25th March, 1981	Field Records Planning) Block Placement Staff Development
Thursday, 26th March, 1981	New areas of field work practice/ Placement Developmental field work Group evaluation
Friday, 27th March, 1981	Presentation of report/discussion on Visit

Friday, 27th March, 1981	Film show: Urban Community Development Evaluation in sub-groups Visit to Jahangirpuri resettlement area
Saturday, 28th March, 1981	Visit to Library Field work in the department of social work, University of Delhi Measures to strengthen field work Evaluation and review session
Sunday, 29th March, 1981	Drafting and presentation of reports of the plenary and group sessions recommendations and evaluation paper on perspectives on Field work

APPENDIX - XII

Faculty Development Workshop On Field Work
From 16th March to 29th March 1981

LIST OF PARTICIPANTS

Ms. Saraswati Shastri College of Social Work, ICSW Andhra Pradesh Branch, Red Hills, Hyderabad-500004.

Mrs. Sanober Shekar, Tata Institute of Social Sciences, Deonar, Bombay-400088.

Dr. Bajrangi Lal, Faculty of Social Work, Kashi Vidyapith, Varanasi. (U.P.)

Mrs. Sandhya Joshi, Faculty of Social Work, M.S. University of Baroda, Fatehgunj. Baroda.

Mrs. Kanan verma, Madras School of Social Work, 32 Casa Major Road, Egmore, Madras-600008.

Mr. Sebastian Rupert Mamilly, Rajagiri College of Social Sciences, P.O. Rajagiri, Kalamassery-683104. (Kerala)

Miss Kunda G. Babtiwale, Tirpude College of Social Work, Civil Lines, Nagpur.

Mrs. Anjali Sen Choudhury, Department of Social Work, Indian Institute of Social Welfare & Business Management. College Square West, Calcutta-700073.

Mrs. Sunanda Koushik, Karve Institute of Social Service, Hillsid, Karvenagar, Pune-411029.

Mrs. Sumati M. Godbole, Karve Institute of Social Service, Hill-side, Karvenagar, Pune-411029.

Miss Cecilia Thangarajan, Department of Social Work, Stella Maris College, Cathedral Road, Madras-600086.

Miss Meena Cholkar, Shri V.T. Krishnamachari Institute of Rural Development, At & Post : Samiala, Baroda-391410.

Miss Sheila Tudu, Faculty of Social Work, M.S. University of Baroda, Fatehgunj, Baroda.

Mrs. K.C. Mandloi, Indore School of Social Work, 14 Old Sehore Road, Indore.

Mrs. G. Pramod Kumar, Department of Social Work, Andhra University, Waltair. (A.P.)

Prof. T.N. Rajarathnam, Department of Social Work, Sri Ramakrishna Mission Vidyalaya Arts College, Coimbatore-641020. (Tamil Nadu)

Prof. I.S.F. Irudayaraj S.J. Loyola College, Madras-600034.

Prof. John D., Department of Social Work, Sacred Heart College, Tirupattur-635601. (Tamil Nadu)

Mr. S.A. Deshpande, C.H. Chaudhari Arts & S.G. Patil Commerce Bollege, Taloda, District : Dhulia (Maharashtra)

Mr. P. Narasimharao, Department of Social Work, A.M.A.L. College, Anakapalle-531001, District : Viskha. (A.P.)

Mr. Mahendu Datta, Department of Social Work, Visva-Bharati, P.C. Sriniketan P.O., (West Bengal)

Mr. K. Shanmugavelayutham, Tirpude College of Social Work, Civil Lines, Sadar, Nagpur-440001.

Prof. P.M. Vasave, Department of Social Work, Centre for Studies in Rural Development, Ahmednagar. (Maharashtra)

Mr. Dominic Mathew, Loyola College of Social Work, Sreekariyam P.O., Trivandrum-695017.

Mr. S. Rangaswamy, Madurai Institute of Social Work, Alagarkoli Road, Madurai-625002.

Mr. P.K. Cherian, MSS Institute of Social Work, West High Court Road, Bajaj Nagar, Nagpur.

Mr. N.A. Ganihar, Department of Social Work, Karnatak University, Dharwar-580003.

Mr. N. Venkataswamy Reddy, Department of Social Work, Bangalore University, Palace Road, Banglore-560009.

Mr. M.S. Chandrashekarappa, Department of Sociology and Social Work, Mysore University, Manasagangotri, Mysore.

Mr. Arun Kumar, MSS Institute of Social Work, West High Court Road, Bajaj Nagar, Nagpur.

Dr. Fakhrul. Islam, Department of Social Work, Lucknow University, Luckdow-226007.

Mr. Shelat Indubhai, Faculty of Social Work, M.S. University of Baroda, BARODA-390002.

Local participants

Mrs. Aruna Bhardwaj, Department of Social Work, 3, University

Road, Delhi-110007.

Mrs. A. Bhandari, Department of Social Work, 3, University Road, Delhi-110007.

Mrs. Savitri Devi, Department of Social Work, 3, University Road, Delhi-110007.

APPENDIX-XIII

LIST OF RESOURCE PERSONS

Dr. R.R. Singh, Department of Social Work, University of Delhi. Delhi-110007.

Mr. Krishan Kumar, Department of Social Work, University of Delhi, Delhi 110007.

Dr. K.V. Sridharan, Director, Vishwa Yuvak Kendra, Circular Road, Chanakyapuri, New Delhi.

Dr. R.K. Upadhyaya, Faculty of Social Work, Kashi Vidyapith, Varanasi, U.P.

Prof. R.K. Bhattacharya, Institute of Business Management and Social Welfare, Calcutta, West Bengal.

Mr. K M. Sharma, Faculty of Social Work, M.S. University of Baroda, Baroda, Gujarat.

Mrs. Kalindi Mazumdar, College of Social Work, Nirmala Niketan, Bombay.

Miss Lalitha Ignatius, Madras School of Social Work, Casa Major Road, Madras.

Mrs. Kiran Mehta, NSS Unit, Department of Social Work, Delhi University, Delhi-7

Mrs. Poonam Dhavan, Co-ordinator, National Adult Education Programme, University of Jammu, Jammu (J & K).

Mr. V.G. Panwalkar, Tata Institute of Social Sciences Bombay.

INDEX